First Children's Dictionary

REVISED EDITION
Senior editor Marie Greenwood
Project editor Suneha Dutta
Editors Jolyon Goddard, Olivia Stanford
Art editors Shipra Jain, Kartik Gera
Assistant editors Anwesha Dutta, Debangana Banerjee, Sayantani Chakrabarti
Assistant art editors Jaileen Kaur, Seepiya Sahni
DTP designer Bimlesh Tiwary
Managing editors Laura Gilbert, Alka Thakur Hazarika
Managing art editors Diane Peyton Jones, Romi Chakraborty
CTS manager Balwant Singh
Senior producer, pre-production Nadine King
Producer Srijana Gurung
Publisher Sarah Larter
Publishing director Sophie Mitchell
Jacket editor Ishani Nandi
Jacket designer Dheeraj Arora
Art director Martin Wilson
Lexicographer and consultant Sheila Dignen

ORIGINAL EDITION
Lexicographer Sheila Dignen
Senior editor Elinor Greenwood
Senior art editor Janet Allis
Designers Mo Choy, Gill Shaw
Managing editors Mary Ling, Sue Leonard
Managing art editors Rachael Foster, Cathy Chesson
DTP designer Almudena Díaz
Picture research Sean Hunter
Production Jenny Jacoby

First published in Great Britain in 2002 by
Dorling Kindersley Limited
80 Strand, London WC2R 0RL

17 18 10 9 8 7 6 5 4 3 2
003-285397-Nov/2016

fresh

A CIP catalogue record for this book is available from the British Library.
ISBN: 978-0-2412-2827-2

Printed and bound in China

A WORLD OF IDEAS:
SEE ALL THERE IS TO KNOW
www.dk.com

Introduction

First Children's Dictionary is a stunning and entertaining new word finder for young children.

An interactive dictionary

First Children's Dictionary provides a valuable and fascinating insight into the world of words. The striking design and interactive features stimulate children's natural curiosity and appetite for words.

Dictionary skills

The clear design and layout help children to learn important dictionary skills. *First Children's Dictionary* helps to widen vocabulary and improve spelling and grammar as well as develop children's awareness of words.

More than 4,000 entries

Each word is clearly defined with simple, age-related vocabulary. The definitions are written in full sentences, making them easy to understand and help children learn how to write correctly in sentences, using capital letters and full stops. Example sentences illustrate use and meaning.

Over 800 illustrations

The eye-catching colour graphics and photographs bring the definitions to life.

More than just a dictionary

While *First Children's Dictionary* acts as a tool to look up spellings and meanings of words, there is more to it than that:

☛ **Opposites** – words with opposite meanings that are formed by adding common prefixes, such as *unhappy* or *dishonest*, help children learn how to use these prefixes correctly.

☛ **Spelling notes** – warning notes are included for words that sound the same but are spelled differently, e.g. *pale/pail*.

☛ **Word collections** – fun-filled pages of words under one theme are valuable aids to creative writing.

hissssss

Contents

Alphabetical order 4
All about words 6
More words 8
Using the dictionary 10

The dictionary 12–245

Word collections

Animal 17
At the beach 27
In the city 44
Costume 50
Dinosaur 60
Entertainment 71
Food 83
Ghosts and fantasy 89
Growth 94
Horse 102
Insect 108
Night life 137
At the park 145
To the rescue 168
Robots 171
Shape up! 180
Space 195
Sport 196
Time 216
Transport 221
Weather 238

Spelling tips 246
Writing 248
Facts and figures 250
Animal families 252
Map of the world 254
Acknowledgements 256

Alphabetical order

To look up a word, you need to find where it belongs among all the other words in the English language. This is why a dictionary arranges words in alphabetical order.

Get in order!

Here is the alphabet in the correct order. Remember this, and using a dictionary will be easy!

a b c d e f g h i j k l m n o p q r s t u v w x y z

Putting words in order

To put words into alphabetical order, you compare their first letters, then their second letters, then their third, and so on. For example, look at this list of animals.

1	**A**nt	**A** is before **C**
2	**Ca**t	**Ca** is before **Cr**
3	**Cra**b	**Cra** is before **Cre**
4	**Cre**ature	**Cre** is before **Cro**
5	**Cro**codile	**Cr** is before **Cu**
6	**Cu**b	

Animal mixer

See if you can arrange these animals in alphabetical order. Look at the box on the right to help you. (*Answers on page 256*)

It's nonsense!

Make sense of nonsense by putting the letters of these mixed-up words into alphabetical order. Here's a clue, they are all things you can eat! Follow this example. (*Answers on page 256*)

Silly sentence

Sort this nonsense sentence by putting the words into the correct alphabetical order. (*Answer on page 256*)

All about words

To make a sentence we use different types of words. Each word in a sentence has its own name and its own job to do.

Nouns

A **noun** is a word that names a thing, a person, or a place. **Cat**, **teacher**, **spoon**, and **city** are all nouns.

A **common noun** names things, people, or places in general. **Carrot**, **bird**, **friend**, and **school** are all common nouns.

A **proper noun** names one particular person or place. Proper nouns begin with a capital letter. **Tom**, **New York**, and **France** are all proper nouns.

The days and months are also proper nouns, so they begin with capital letters, for example **Monday**, **Tuesday**, **January**, and **February**.

One or two?

We use a **singular** noun if there is only one of something. We use a **plural** noun if there is more than one. We usually add *-s* or *-es* to make plural nouns. For nouns that end in *-y*, we change the *-y* to *-ies*.

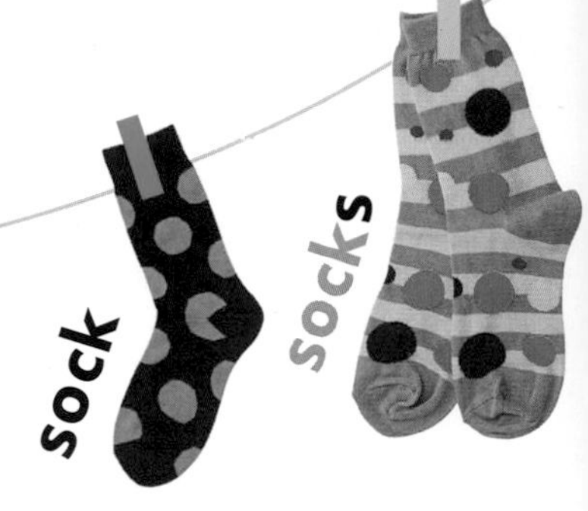

Singular	Plural
sock	socks
dog	dogs
box	boxes
princess	princesses
baby	babies
family	families

Curious plurals

A few nouns stay the same in the singular and the plural.
For example:
One **sheep**; three **sheep**

Some nouns change completely in the plural.
For example:
One **mouse**; two **mice**
One **man**; three **men**

Adjectives

An **adjective** is a word that is used to describe a noun. **Big**, **yellow**, **sticky**, and **dark** are all adjectives.

An adjective can come before a noun. *Look at the **big, yellow** Sun.*

Or it can come after the verb *be*. *The Sun is **big** and **yellow**.*

This piglet is...

small

hairy

pink

Comparing things

To compare people or things, some adjectives can change. For example, **tall** becomes **taller** or **the tallest**.

Some adjectives do not change. Instead, we use **more** and **the most** before the adjective to compare people or things.

tall

*This flower is **beautiful**.*

Verbs

A **verb** is sometimes called an **action word** because it is a word that describes what a person or thing is doing. **Sit, think, sleep, sing**, and **climb** are all verbs. A sentence must contain a verb to make sense. "**Be**" is also a verb. The parts of "be" are: I **am**, you **are**, he **is**, she **is**, we **are**, they **are**. For example: *I **am** very tall.*

Now and then

The **tense** of a verb shows when something happens. Notice how the verb changes according to which tense it is in.

If an action happens now, the verb is in the **present tense.**
*The boy **kicks** the ball.*

If the action is happening now and continues to happen, the verb is in the **present progressive tense.**
*The boy **is kicking** the ball.*

If the action happened in the past, the verb is in the **past tense.**
*The boy **kicked** the ball.*

If the action will happen in the future, we can use **will** or "be" **going to.**
*The boy **will kick** the ball.*
*The boy **is going to kick** the ball.*

taller

the tallest

*This flower is **more beautiful.***

*This flower is **the most beautiful.***

Some tricky past tenses

We usually make a past tense by adding *-ed* to the verb.
*We work**ed** hard yesterday.*

Some verbs have different past tenses.

Present	Past
catch	caught
do	did
eat	ate
make	made
see	saw

a b c d e f g h i j k l m n o p q r s t u v w x y z

More words

Here are some more examples of types of words and how they are used in sentences.

Adverbs

An **adverb** is a word that gives more information about a verb. *She opened the present* ***quickly***.

A lot of adverbs end with the letters *-ly*. **Quickly, slowly, sadly,** and **noisily** are all adverbs.

Adverbs can also tell us when something happens.
I ***always*** *do my homework.*
We'll get home ***soon***.

Prepositions

A **preposition** usually comes before a noun. It often shows where something is. *The cat is* ***on*** *a branch* ***in*** *the tree.*

Here are some common prepositions:

in
on
into
above
below
under
between
through
near
beside
behind
in front of

Follow the adverbs...

Follow the arrows linking the verbs to the adverbs.

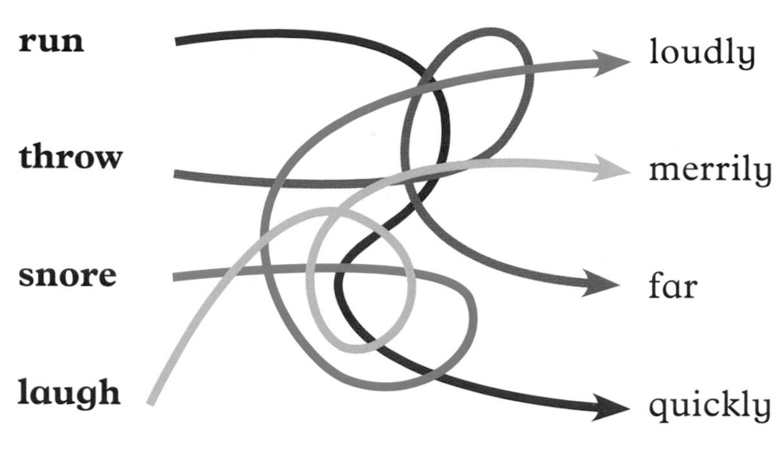

cat **under** the basket

cat **between** the chair legs

cat **in** the basket

Pronouns

A **pronoun** is used instead of a noun.
The girl picked up the apple and ***she*** *ate* ***it***.

She replaces *the girl* and *it* replaces *the apple*. We often use pronouns so that we don't repeat the same word too many times.

Cheetahs are big **and** they're fast.

Conjunctions

Conjunctions are used to join together different parts of a sentence. **And**, **but**, **or**, and **because** are conjunctions.
The teacher was angry ***because*** *I was late.*

You can have an apple **or** an orange.

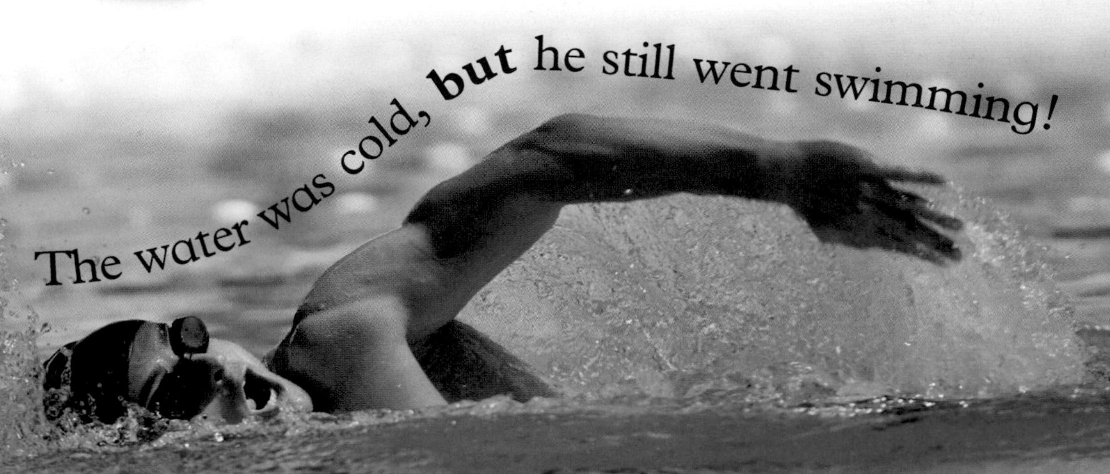

The water was cold, **but** he still went swimming!

Using the dictionary

Read the information on these pages to get the most out of your dictionary. Most pages in the book look like this double page from the letter **R** section (below).

Getting directions

When you travel somewhere, there are usually signs to help point you in the right direction. It's the same when you are looking up words in this dictionary. Look at this double-page example.

Top left

This is the first headword on this page.

A new letter

This big "R" shows that you are starting the section of words that all begin with "R".

Top right

This is the last headword on this page.

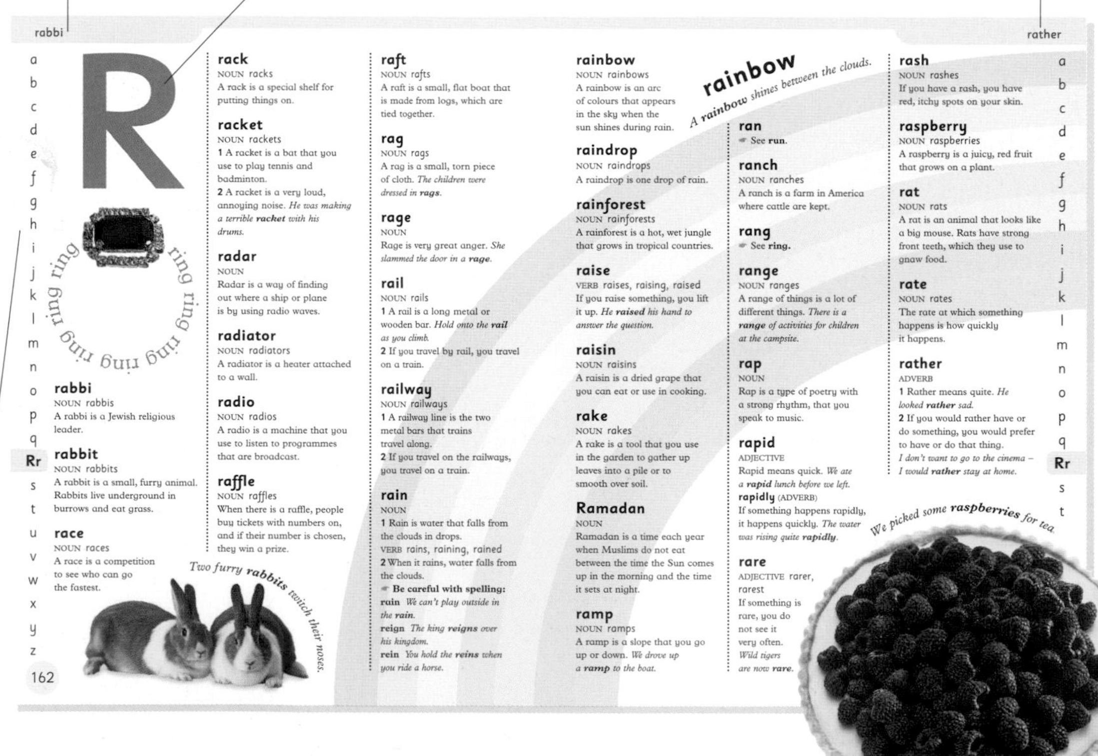

rabbi

R

ring ring ring ring ring ring

rabbi
NOUN rabbis
A rabbi is a Jewish religious leader.

rabbit
NOUN rabbits
A rabbit is a small, furry animal. Rabbits live underground in burrows and eat grass.

race
NOUN races
A race is a competition to see who can go the fastest.

*Two furry **rabbits** twitch their noses.*

rack
NOUN racks
A rack is a special shelf for putting things on.

racket
NOUN rackets
1 A racket is a bat that you use to play tennis and badminton.
2 A racket is a very loud, annoying noise. *He was making a terrible **racket** with his drums.*

radar
NOUN
Radar is a way of finding out where a ship or plane is by using radio waves.

radiator
NOUN radiators
A radiator is a heater attached to a wall.

radio
NOUN radios
A radio is a machine that you use to listen to programmes that are broadcast.

raffle
NOUN raffles
When there is a raffle, people buy tickets with numbers on, and if their number is chosen, they win a prize.

raft
NOUN rafts
A raft is a small, flat boat that is made from logs, which are tied together.

rag
NOUN rags
A rag is a small, torn piece of cloth. *The children were dressed in **rags**.*

rage
NOUN
Rage is very great anger. *She slammed the door in a **rage**.*

rail
NOUN rails
1 A rail is a long metal or wooden bar. *Hold onto the **rail** as you climb.*
2 If you travel by rail, you travel on a train.

railway
NOUN railways
1 A railway line is the two metal bars that trains travel along.
2 If you travel on the railways, you travel on a train.

rain
NOUN
1 Rain is water that falls from the clouds in drops.
VERB rains, raining, rained
2 When it rains, water falls from the clouds.
Be careful with spelling:
rain *We can't play outside in the **rain**.*
reign *The king **reigns** over his kingdom.*
rein *You hold the **reins** when you ride a horse.*

rainbow
NOUN rainbows
A rainbow is an arc of colours that appears in the sky when the sun shines during rain.

rainbow
*A **rainbow** shines between the clouds.*

raindrop
NOUN raindrops
A raindrop is one drop of rain.

rainforest
NOUN rainforests
A rainforest is a hot, wet jungle that grows in tropical countries.

raise
VERB raises, raising, raised
If you raise something, you lift it up. *He **raised** his hand to answer the question.*

raisin
NOUN raisins
A raisin is a dried grape that you can eat or use in cooking.

rake
NOUN rakes
A rake is a tool that you use in the garden to gather up leaves into a pile or to smooth over soil.

Ramadan
NOUN
Ramadan is a time each year when Muslims do not eat between the time the Sun comes up in the morning and the time it sets at night.

ramp
NOUN ramps
A ramp is a slope that you go up or down. *We drove up a **ramp** to the boat.*

ran
See **run**.

ranch
NOUN ranches
A ranch is a farm in America where cattle are kept.

rang
See **ring**.

range
NOUN ranges
A range of things is a lot of different things. *There is a **range** of activities for children at the campsite.*

rap
NOUN
Rap is a type of poetry with a strong rhythm, that you speak to music.

rapid
ADJECTIVE
Rapid means quick. *We ate a **rapid** lunch before we left.*
rapidly (ADVERB)
If something happens rapidly, it happens quickly. *The water was rising quite **rapidly**.*

rare
ADJECTIVE rarer, rarest
If something is rare, you do not see it very often. *Wild tigers are now **rare**.*

rash
NOUN rashes
If you have a rash, you have red, itchy spots on your skin.

raspberry
NOUN raspberries
A raspberry is a juicy, red fruit that grows on a plant.

rat
NOUN rats
A rat is an animal that looks like a big mouse. Rats have strong front teeth, which they use to gnaw food.

rate
NOUN rates
The rate at which something happens is how quickly it happens.

rather
ADVERB
1 Rather means quite. *He looked **rather** sad.*
2 If you would rather have or do something, you would prefer to have or do that thing. *I don't want to go to the cinema – I would **rather** stay at home.*

*We picked some **raspberries** for tea.*

rather

a b c d e f g h i j k l m n o p q Rr s t u v w x y z

162

Check your alphabet

The alphabet running down the edge of each page helps you to sort words into alphabetical order. The highlighted letter tells you which letter section you are in.

Picture it

There are pictures illustrating some of the words.

Looking at a word

This dictionary tells you lots of things about words and how to use them.

Part of speech

This tells you whether the headword is a **noun**, **verb**, **adjective**, or **adverb**. *(See pages 6-9)*

What does it mean?

The meaning of the word is given for each entry. If a word has more than one meaning or part of speech, it is listed below the headword.

Extra information

Extra information is given about spellings and opposites.

hear
VERB hears, hearing, heard
If you can hear a sound, you notice it. *Did you **hear** that bird?*
☛ **Be careful with spelling:**
hear *I can **hear** music.*
here *Come **here**!*

held
☛ See **hold**.

happy
ADJECTIVE happier, happiest
If you are happy, you feel pleased.
☛ **Opposite:** unhappy

Headword

The big, bold word at the head of each entry is the word you are looking up.

Example sentence

Example sentences use the headword as it might be used in everyday life. The headword is in heavy black type.

Irregular forms

Some words do not follow the usual rules for their past tense or plural form. Follow the hand symbol ☛ to take you to the main entry for this word.

Word collections

Full-page and half-page word collections provide extra vocabulary on a variety of subjects.

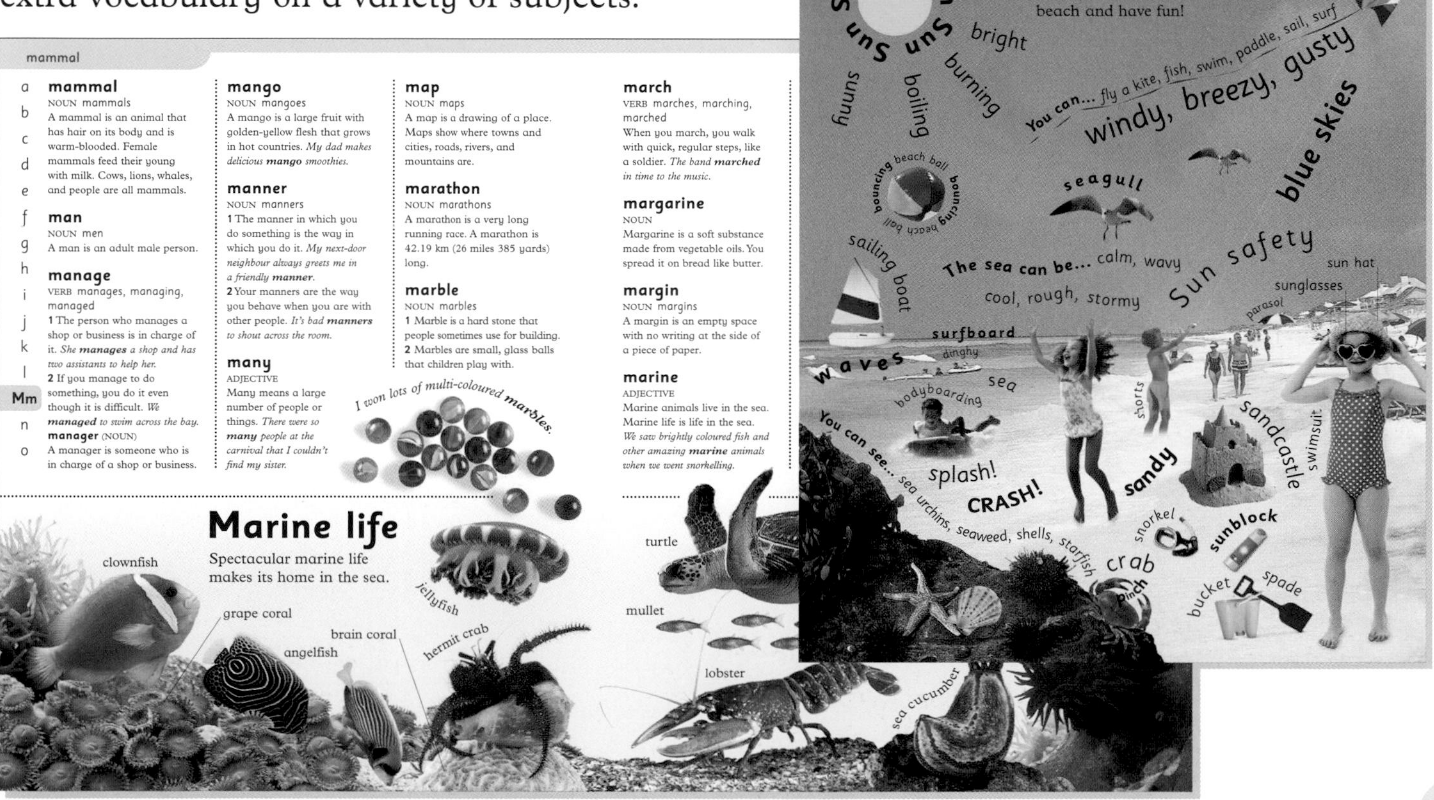
mammal

a b c d e f g h i j k l Mm n o

mammal
NOUN mammals
A mammal is an animal that has hair on its body and is warm-blooded. Female mammals feed their young with milk. Cows, lions, whales, and people are all mammals.

man
NOUN men
A man is an adult male person.

manage
VERB manages, managing, managed
1 The person who manages a shop or business is in charge of it. *She **manages** a shop and has two assistants to help her.*
2 If you manage to do something, you do it even though it is difficult. *We **managed** to swim across the bay.*
manager (NOUN)
A manager is someone who is in charge of a shop or business.

mango
NOUN mangoes
A mango is a large fruit with golden-yellow flesh that grows in hot countries. *My dad makes delicious **mango** smoothies.*

manner
NOUN manners
1 The manner in which you do something is the way in which you do it. *My next-door neighbour always greets me in a friendly **manner**.*
2 Your manners are the way you behave when you are with other people. *It's bad **manners** to shout across the room.*

many
ADJECTIVE
Many means a large number of people or things. *There were so **many** people at the carnival that I couldn't find my sister.*

map
NOUN maps
A map is a drawing of a place. Maps show where towns and cities, roads, rivers, and mountains are.

marathon
NOUN marathons
A marathon is a very long running race. A marathon is 42.19 km (26 miles 385 yards) long.

marble
NOUN marbles
1 Marble is a hard stone that people sometimes use for building.
2 Marbles are small, glass balls that children play with.

march
VERB marches, marching, marched
When you march, you walk with quick, regular steps, like a soldier. *The band **marched** in time to the music.*

margarine
NOUN
Margarine is a soft substance made from vegetable oils. You spread it on bread like butter.

margin
NOUN margins
A margin is an empty space with no writing at the side of a piece of paper.

marine
ADJECTIVE
Marine animals live in the sea. Marine life is life in the sea. *We saw brightly coloured fish and other amazing **marine** animals when we went snorkelling.*

a b c d e f g h i j k l m n o p q r s t u v w x y z

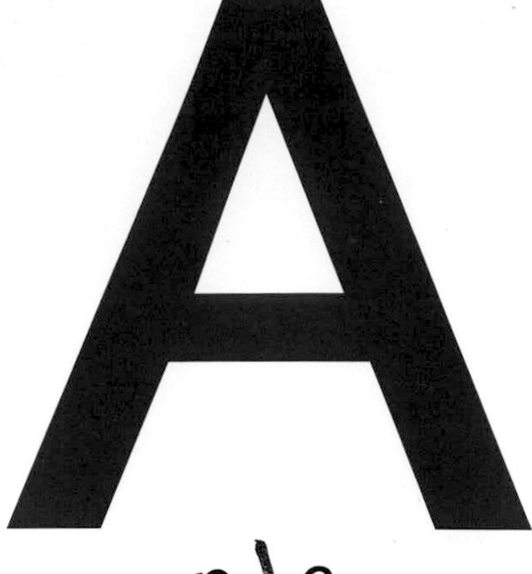

abbreviation
NOUN abbreviations
An abbreviation is a short way of writing a word. For example, "TV" is an abbreviation for "television".

able
ADJECTIVE
If you are able to do something, you can do it. *I am **able** to ice skate!*
ability (NOUN)
If you have the ability to do something, you can do it. *Chameleons have the **ability** to change colour.*

abroad
ADVERB
If you go abroad, you go to another country. *We sometimes go **abroad** for our summer holidays.*

absent
ADJECTIVE
If you are absent, you are not in the place you would normally be in. *My sister was **absent** from school yesterday because she was ill.*

absolutely
ADVERB
Absolutely means the same as completely. *The water's **absolutely** freezing!*

absorb
VERB absorbs, absorbing, absorbed
If something absorbs water, it soaks it up. *The tissue paper quickly **absorbed** all the water.*
absorbent (ADJECTIVE)
If something is absorbent, it absorbs water easily.

abuse
VERB abuses, abusing, abused
To abuse someone means to hurt a person or treat a person very badly.

accent
NOUN accents
Your accent is the way you say words when you speak. People from different places speak with different accents.

accept
VERB accepts, accepting, accepted
If you accept something, you take it when someone offers it to you. *She went up onto the stage to **accept** her prize.*

access
VERB accesses, accessing, accessed
When you access a program or document on a computer, you open it and use it. *Anyone can **access** these files.*

accident
NOUN accidents
1 If there is an accident, something bad happens and someone is hurt. *There was an **accident** on the motorway.*
2 If something was an accident, it happened by chance and no one did it deliberately. *I didn't mean to drop your phone – it was an **accident**.*
accidentally (ADVERB)
If you do something accidentally, it is an accident. *I **accidentally** spilled my drink.*

accurate
ADJECTIVE
Something that is accurate is exactly right. *Can you make an **accurate** copy of the picture hanging on the wall?*
☛ **Opposite:** inaccurate
accurately (ADVERB)
If you do something accurately, you do it so that it is exactly right. *Make sure you measure the line **accurately**.*

accuse
VERB accuses, accusing, accused
If you accuse someone of doing something, you say that the person did it. *She **accused** him of stealing her money.*

ache
VERB aches, aching, ached
If a part of your body aches, it hurts. *I was tired, and my head **ached**.*

achieve
VERB achieves, achieving, achieved
If you achieve something, you manage to do it. *I had finally **achieved** my dream of singing on stage!*
achievement (NOUN)
An achievement is something good that you achieve. *Winning the cup was a great **achievement** for our team.*

acid
NOUN acids
An acid is a chemical. Lemon and vinegar both contain acids.

acorn
NOUN acorns
An acorn is the seed of an oak tree.

acrobat
NOUN acrobats
An acrobat is a person who performs difficult gymnastic tricks on stage or in a circus.

act
VERB acts, acting, acted
1 The way that you act is the way you behave. *My friend was **acting** very strangely.*
2 When you act, you pretend to be a character in a play or film. *If you enjoy **acting**, you might want to join a drama group and **act** in a play.*

action
NOUN actions
1 An action is something that you do. *Do you know the **actions** to this song?*
2 An action film is one with a lot of exciting events.

active
ADJECTIVE
If you are active, you are moving about rather than sitting still.

activity
NOUN activities
An activity is something that you can do for fun. *There are lots of after-school **activities**.*

acrobat

actor
NOUN actors
An actor is someone who acts in plays, films, or television programmes. A woman who is an actor is sometimes called an **actress**.

add
VERB adds, adding, added
1 If you add something, you put it with other things. *I **added** some more water to my drink.*
2 When you add up numbers, you count them together to find a total.
addition (NOUN)
When you do addition, you add numbers together.

address
NOUN addresses
1 Your address is the number of the house and the name of the street where you live.
2 Your email address is the set of words that someone uses to send emails to you.

adjective
NOUN adjectives
An adjective is a word such as "big" or "funny" that describes what someone or something is like. *There are two adjectives in the sentence: He showed us his **new** bike, which we all thought was **amazing**.*

admire
VERB admires, admiring, admired
1 If you admire someone, you like and respect the person very much. *Which famous sports stars do you **admire** the most?*
2 If you admire something, you enjoy looking at it. *She stood back and **admired** her painting of the view from her bedroom window.*

Aa b c d e f g h i j k l m n o p q r s t u v w x y z

admit

VERB admits, admitting, admitted

If you admit that you did something wrong, you tell the truth and say that you did it. *He **admitted** that he had told a lie.*

adopt

VERB adopts, adopting, adopted

When people adopt a child, they take the child into their home and become his or her parents.

adult

NOUN adults

An adult is a grown-up.

advantage

NOUN advantages

If you have an advantage, you have something good that will help you. *Being tall gives you an **advantage** when you play basketball.*

☛ **Opposite:** disadvantage

adventure

NOUN adventures

An adventure is something new and exciting that you do.

adventurous (ADJECTIVE)

Someone who is adventurous enjoys doing new and exciting things.

adverb

NOUN adverbs

An adverb is a word such as "quickly", "slowly", or "cheerfully" that describes how you do something. Adverbs describe verbs. *There are two adverbs in the sentence: I opened the present **slowly**, then smiled **happily**.*

advertise

VERB advertises, advertising, advertised

To advertise something means to tell people about it so they will want to buy it. *A lot of companies **advertise** things on TV.*

advertisement

NOUN advertisements

An advertisement is a picture or short film that shows you how good something is and tries to persuade you to buy it. You can shorten this word to **advert**.

advice

NOUN

If you give someone advice, you suggest to them what they should do.

advise

VERB advises, advising, advised

If you advise someone to do something, you tell them that they should do it. *I **advise** you to wear a cycle helmet when you ride your bike.*

aeroplane

NOUN aeroplanes

An aeroplane is a vehicle that can travel through the air and carry passengers or goods. This word is often shortened to **plane**.

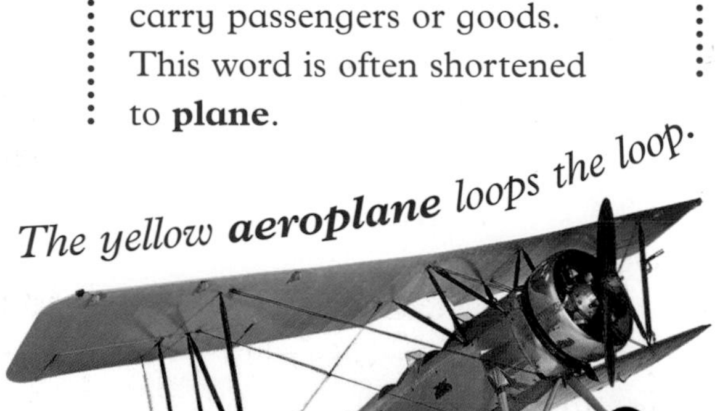

*The yellow **aeroplane** loops the loop.*

affectionate

ADJECTIVE

If you are affectionate, you show someone that you like or love them. *My cat is very **affectionate**.*

afford

VERB affords, affording, afforded

If you can afford something, you have enough money to buy it. *I can't **afford** that computer game.*

afraid

ADJECTIVE

If you are afraid, you are scared. *My sister is **afraid** of spiders.*

afternoon

NOUN afternoons

The afternoon is the time between midday and the evening.

again

ADVERB

If you do something again, you do it one more time.

age

NOUN ages

Your age is how old you are. *Write your name and **age** on the list.*

aggressive

ADJECTIVE

Someone who is aggressive often argues and fights. An animal that is aggressive is likely to attack another animal.

ago

Ago means in the past. *I started school two years **ago**.*

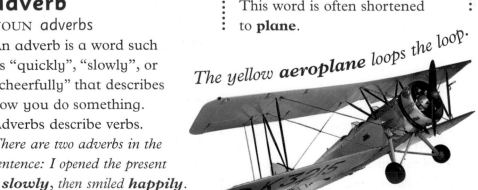

agree

VERB agrees, agreeing, agreed
If you agree with someone, you think the same as they do. *I **agree** with you that it's a really good film.*
☛ **Opposite:** disagree

ahead

ADVERB
Something that is ahead of you is in front of you.

aid

NOUN
Aid is food and clothes that are given to people who need them. *Charities often send emergency **aid** to people after a natural disaster.*

aim

VERB aims, aiming, aimed
If you aim at something, you point something at it and try to hit it. *It's best to **aim** at the centre of the target.*

air

NOUN
Air is the mixture of gases around us that we breathe. *Let's open the window to get some fresh **air**.*

aircraft

NOUN
An aircraft is any vehicle that can fly.

air force

NOUN
The air force is the part of the army that fights from the air.

airport

NOUN airports
An airport is a place where people go to travel by plane.

alarm

NOUN alarms
An alarm is a loud noise that warns you of something. *Quick – that's the fire **alarm**. Let's get out!*

album

NOUN albums
An album is a book that you put photos or stamps in so that you can look at them.

alien

NOUN aliens
An alien is a creature from another planet.

alike

ADVERB
Things that are alike are similar or the same. *The two brothers look very **alike**.*

alive

ADJECTIVE
People, animals, and plants that are alive are living.

alkali

NOUN alkalis
An alkali is a chemical that is the opposite of an acid.

all

ADJECTIVE
1 All of something is every part of it. *I can't believe he ate **all** the cake!*
2 All means everyone. *Are you **all** ready to leave?*

Allah

NOUN
Allah is the Muslim name for God.

allergy

NOUN allergies
If you have an allergy to something, it makes you ill. *I've got a peanut **allergy**.*
allergic (ADJECTIVE)
If you are allergic to something, you have an allergy to it. *My sister's **allergic** to cats.*

alligator

NOUN alligators
An alligator is a large reptile that lives in swamps and rivers.

alligator

allow

VERB allows, allowing, allowed
If you allow someone to do something, you let them do it. *I wish my parents would **allow** me to stay up later.*

almost

ADVERB
Almost means nearly. *The film is **almost** finished.*

alone

ADJECTIVE
If you are alone, you are by yourself and no one is with you.

aloud
ADVERB
If you say something aloud, you say it so that other people can hear it.

alphabet
NOUN alphabets
The alphabet is all the letters that are used in writing.
alphabetical (ADJECTIVE)
The letters of the alphabet are usually written in an order called "alphabetical order".

already
ADVERB
If you have already done something, you did it earlier. *I've **already** finished my homework.*

also
ADVERB
Also means as well. *My dad can play the piano and he can **also** sing.*

alter
VERB alters, altering, altered
If you alter something, you change it. *You can use a computer program to **alter** photographs.*

altogether
ADVERB
Altogether means including everyone or everything. *The journey took five days **altogether**.*

always
ADVERB
If you always do something, you do it all the time or every time. *I **always** walk to school.*

amazing
ADJECTIVE
Something that is amazing is very good or very surprising. *She's an **amazing** dancer!*
amazed (ADJECTIVE)
If you are amazed, you are very surprised. *I was **amazed** when I saw all the presents!*

ambulance
NOUN ambulances
An ambulance is a vehicle for taking sick or injured people to hospital.

anchor
NOUN anchors
An anchor is a large, heavy metal hook that digs into the seabed to stop a boat from drifting away.

ancient
ADJECTIVE
Something that is ancient is very old. *We found some **ancient** coins in the ground.*

angel
NOUN angels
An angel is a messenger from a god.

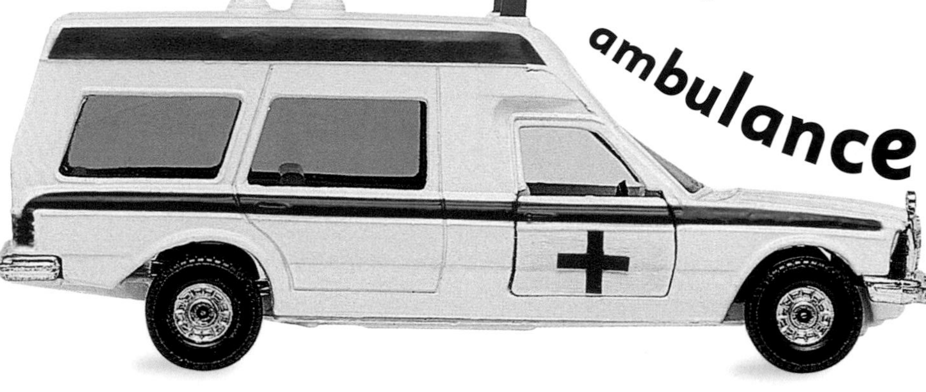
ambulance

amount
NOUN amounts
The amount of something is how much there is of it. *I'd never seen such a huge **amount** of food before.*

amphibian
NOUN amphibians
An amphibian is an animal that can live in water and on land.

amuse
VERB amuses, amusing, amused
If something amuses you, it makes you laugh. *His jokes really **amused** us.*
amusing (ADJECTIVE)
Something that is amusing makes you laugh.

angle
NOUN angles
An angle is a corner where two lines meet. A square has four angles, and a triangle has three.

angry
ADJECTIVE
If you are angry, you feel cross and upset about something. *My mum was **angry** when I kicked the ball through the window.*
anger (NOUN)
Anger is the feeling of being angry.

animal
NOUN animals
An animal is any living thing that breathes and moves around. Insects, fish, birds, mammals, and reptiles are all types of animal.

Animal

Animals fall into these main groups.

Birds

Birds have wings and feathers.

Mammals

Mammals feed their young with milk.

Amphibians and reptiles

Amphibians live on land and in water. Reptiles have scaly skin and lay eggs.

Insects and arachnids

Insects are small animals with six legs. Arachnids have eight legs.

Fish

Fish live underwater and breathe through gills.

Aa b c d e f g h i

animated
ADJECTIVE
An animated film is made using drawings, models, or pictures made on computers.

ankle
NOUN ankles
Your ankle is the joint between your leg and your foot.

anniversary
NOUN anniversaries
An anniversary is a date that you remember because something important happened then.

annual
ADJECTIVE
An annual event happens once a year.

another
ADJECTIVE
1 Another means one more. *Would you like* ***another*** *biscuit?*
2 Another means a different one. *Have you got* ***another*** *pen? This one doesn't work.*

answer
VERB answers, answering, answered
If you answer, you say something when someone has spoken to you. *I asked how old he was, but he didn't* ***answer.***

anticlockwise
ADVERB
If something moves anticlockwise, it moves in a circle, the opposite way to the hands of a clock.

antiseptic
NOUN antiseptics
An antiseptic is a chemical that kills germs.

anxious
ADJECTIVE
If you feel anxious, you feel worried or nervous. *Most people feel* ***anxious*** *before they go on stage.*

announce

It's time to ***announce*** *the winner.*

announce
VERB announces, announcing, announced
If you announce something, you say it aloud so that everyone can hear.
announcement (NOUN)
When you make an announcement, you announce something.

annoy
VERB annoys, annoying, annoyed
If something annoys you, it makes you feel cross. *Sometimes my little brother really* ***annoys*** *me!*
annoying (ADJECTIVE)
Something that is annoying makes you feel cross. *This game is really* ***annoying!***

ant
NOUN ants
An ant is a type of small insect that lives in very large groups.

antelope
NOUN antelopes
An antelope is an animal like a large deer that lives on the plains in Africa and Asia.

antenna
NOUN antennae
An antenna on an insect or snail is one of the two long, thin parts on its head that it uses for feeling and touching things.

antibiotic
NOUN antibiotics
An antibiotic is a medicine that cures an infection.

any
ADJECTIVE
1 Any means some. *Have you got* ***any*** *sweets?*
2 Any means whichever one you want. *You can choose* ***any*** *toy in the shop!*

anybody
Anybody or anyone means any person at all. *It's a secret, so don't tell* ***anybody.***

anything
Anything means a thing of any kind. *There isn't* ***anything*** *to do!*

apart
ADVERB
If things are apart, they are away from each other. *I don't like being* ***apart*** *from my family.*

q r s t u v w x y z

apartment
NOUN apartments
An apartment is a home that is on one floor of a large building.

ape
NOUN apes
An ape is an animal like a monkey that lives in forests in warm countries, and feeds on insects and fruit.

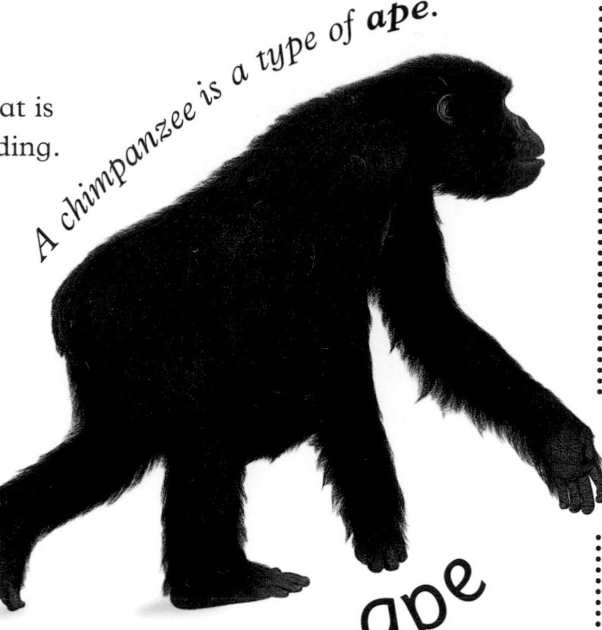

*A chimpanzee is a type of **ape**.*

apologize
VERB apologizes, apologizing, apologized
If you apologize, you say that you are sorry. *I **apologized** for being late.*
apology (NOUN)
An apology is something you say to show that you are sorry.

apostrophe
NOUN apostrophes
An apostrophe is the mark (') that you use in writing, for example in the sentence: *That's my sister's coat.*

app
NOUN apps
An app is a small program or game that you can download onto your phone, tablet, or computer. App is short for **application**.

appeal
NOUN appeals
If there is an appeal, it is often an emergency and people ask for money, food, or other help. *Please support the earthquake **appeal**.*

appear
VERB appears, appearing, appeared
If something appears, you can suddenly see it. *The Sun **appeared** from behind the clouds.*
☛ **Opposite:** disappear

appearance
NOUN
Your appearance is what you look like. *You shouldn't worry so much about your **appearance**.*

appetite
NOUN appetites
Your appetite is the feeling you have when you want to eat food. *He has a huge **appetite**!*

applause
NOUN
Applause is clapping and cheering. *The audience gave a round of **applause** when the play finished.*

apple
NOUN apples
An apple is a round fruit with a smooth skin and crisp flesh.

appointment
NOUN appointments
If you have an appointment with someone, you have arranged to meet them at a certain time.

appreciate
VERB appreciates, appreciating, appreciated
If you appreciate something, you are glad to have it and feel grateful for it. *Thank you. I really **appreciate** your help.*

apprentice
NOUN apprentices
An apprentice is someone who learns to do a job by working with a person who does that job.

approach
VERB approaches, approaching, approached
When you approach a place, you come near to it. *The train slowed down as it **approached** the station.*

approximately
ADVERB
Approximately means more or less, but not exactly. *There are **approximately** 30 children in each class.*

apricot
NOUN apricots
An apricot is a small, orange fruit with soft flesh.

aquarium
NOUN aquariums
An aquarium is a glass tank that you keep fish in.

Aa b c d e f g h i j k l m n o p q r s t u v w x y z

aquatic
ADJECTIVE
Aquatic animals or plants live in water.

arch
NOUN arches
An arch is a curved part of a building or bridge that you can sometimes walk under. *The cathedral had a central* ***arch****.*

architect
NOUN architects
An architect is a person who designs buildings.

area
NOUN areas
An area is a piece of land or ground. *There's a play* ***area*** *behind our school.*

argue
VERB argues, arguing, argued
When people argue, they talk or shout at each other in an angry way because they do not agree about something. *My two brothers are always* ***arguing****!*
argument (NOUN)
When people argue, you can say that they are having an argument.

arithmetic
NOUN
Arithmetic is adding, subtracting, multiplying, and dividing numbers.

arm
NOUN arms
Your arm is the part of your body between your shoulder and your hand.

armour
NOUN
Armour is metal clothing that knights used to wear to protect themselves in battle.

Knights wore suits of shining ***armour*** *in battle.*

army
NOUN armies
An army is a large group of soldiers who fight on land.

arrange
VERB arranges, arranging, arranged
1 If you arrange to do something, you plan to do it. *I* ***arranged*** *to meet my friend in the park.*
2 When you arrange things, you put them neatly in a special order. *We* ***arranged*** *the food on the table so that it looked nice.*

arrest
VERB arrests, arresting, arrested
When the police arrest someone, they catch them and officially accuse them of a crime.

arrive
VERB arrives, arriving, arrived
When you arrive at a place, you get there. *We* ***arrived*** *at the stadium just before the start of the game.*

arrow
NOUN arrows
1 An arrow is a pointed stick that you shoot from a bow.
2 An arrow is a pointed shape that shows you which way to go.

arrow

art
NOUN
Art is drawing, painting, and sculpture.

article
NOUN articles
1 An article is an object. *There are some interesting* ***articles*** *in the museum.*
2 An article is a piece of writing in a newspaper or magazine.
3 The words "a", "an", and "the" are articles.

artificial
ADJECTIVE
Something that is artificial is not real. ***Artificial*** *flowers are made of plastic, so you don't have to water them.*

artist
NOUN artists
An artist is someone who draws or paints pictures, or makes sculptures.

ashamed
ADJECTIVE
If you feel ashamed, you feel bad about something you have done. *I was **ashamed** of myself for telling a lie.*

ask
VERB asks, asking, asked
1 If you ask a question, you say it to someone because you want to know the answer. *"Are you OK?" the teacher **asked** me.*
2 If you ask for something, you say that you would like it. *He **asked** me for a pen.*

asleep
ADJECTIVE
If you are asleep, you are resting and your eyes are closed.

assembly
NOUN assemblies
An assembly is a meeting of all the teachers and children in a school.

assistant
NOUN assistants
An assistant is someone who helps another person.

asthma
NOUN
Asthma is an illness that makes it difficult for you to breathe.
asthmatic (ADJECTIVE)
Someone who is asthmatic suffers from asthma.

astonished
ADJECTIVE
If you are astonished, you are very surprised. *I was **astonished** when they told me what had happened.*

astronaut
NOUN astronauts
An astronaut is a person who is trained to travel into space.

astronomy
NOUN
Astronomy is the scientific study of stars and planets.
astronomer (NOUN)
An astronomer is someone who studies astronomy.

asylum
NOUN
If someone asks for asylum, they ask to stay in a country so that they can escape from danger in their own country.

ate
☛ See **eat**.

athlete
NOUN athletes
An athlete is a person who runs in races or takes part in sports competitions.
athletics (NOUN)
The competitions in which people run and jump are called athletics.

atlas
NOUN atlases
An atlas is a book of maps.

atmosphere
NOUN
The atmosphere is the air around the Earth.

atom
NOUN atoms
Atoms are the tiny parts that everything is made of.

attach
VERB attaches, attaching, attached
1 When you attach something, you fix it to something else. *First, **attach** the string to your kite.*
2 When you attach a document to an email, you send it with the email.
attachment (NOUN)
An attachment is a document that you attach to an email.

attack
VERB attacks, attacking, attached
To attack someone means to hit them or try to hurt them in some way. *We were worried that wild animals might **attack** us.*

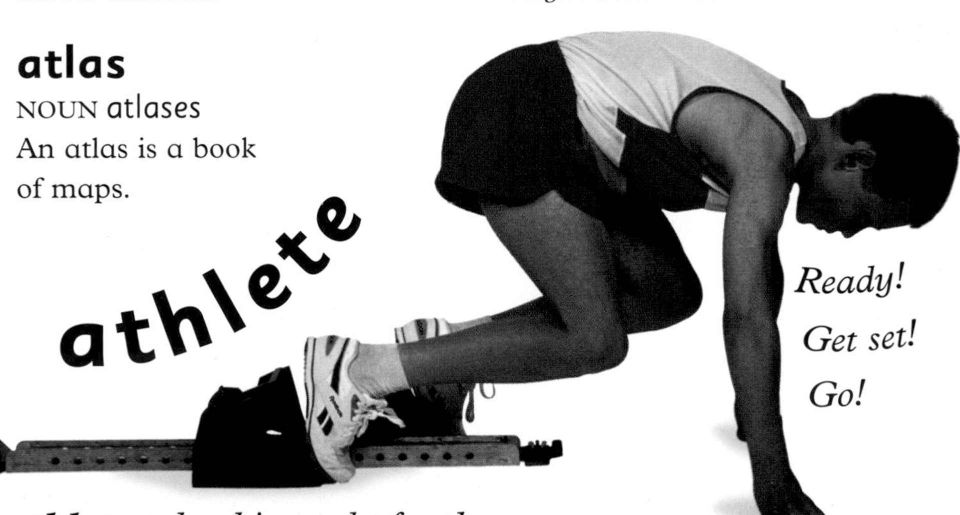
athlete
Ready!
Get set!
Go!
*The **athlete** takes his marks for the race.*

Aa b c d e f g h i j k l m n o p q r s t u v w x y z

attempt
VERB attempts, attempting, attempted
If you attempt to do something, you try to do it.

attention
NOUN
If you pay attention, you listen or watch carefully.

attitude
NOUN attitudes
Your attitude toward something is what you think of it and how you behave.
*He had a good **attitude** toward his work.*

attract
VERB attracts, attracting, attracted
If something attracts an object, it makes it come nearer.

attractive
ADJECTIVE
Someone who is attractive looks nice or behaves in a kind, friendly way, so that other people feel they want to be with them.

*Magnets **attract** metal pins.*

audience
NOUN audiences
The people who come to watch a show or concert are called the audience.

aunt
NOUN aunts
Your aunt is the sister of one of your parents, or the wife or partner of your uncle. You often call your aunt **aunty** or **auntie**.

author
NOUN authors
An author is a person who writes books, poems, or plays.

autistic
ADJECTIVE
Someone who is autistic has a condition that sometimes makes it difficult for them to communicate with other people.
autism (NOUN)
You can say that someone who is autistic has autism.

autograph
NOUN autographs
A famous person's autograph is their signature. Some people collect autographs as a hobby.

automatic
ADJECTIVE
Something that is automatic works by itself, without anyone touching it or controlling it.

autumn
NOUN
Autumn is the time of the year before winter, when the weather starts to get colder and the leaves on some trees fall off.

avalanche
NOUN avalanches
An avalanche is a large amount of snow, rocks, and ice that suddenly slides down a mountain.

average
ADJECTIVE
An average amount is normal and usual.

avocado
NOUN avocados
An avocado is a pear-shaped fruit that has a tough green skin and smooth, creamy flesh.

avoid
VERB avoids, avoiding, avoided
If you avoid something, you keep away from it.

awake
ADJECTIVE
If you are awake, you are not asleep.

aware
ADJECTIVE
If you are aware of something, you know about it.
☛ **Opposite:** unaware

awful
ADJECTIVE
Something that is awful is very bad.

awkward
ADJECTIVE
If something is awkward, it is slightly difficult to do.

axe
NOUN axes
An axe is a tool for chopping wood.

B

baby
NOUN babies
A baby is a very young child.

back
NOUN backs
1 Your back is the part of your body that is between your neck and your bottom.
2 The back part of something is the part opposite the front. *We sat at the **back** of the hall.*
ADVERB
3 If you go back to a place, you go there again.

background
NOUN backgrounds
The background is the part of a picture that is behind the main things or people.

backpack
NOUN backpacks
A backpack is a bag that you carry on your back.

backward
ADVERB
If you move backward, you move in the direction that is behind you. *He fell **backward** into the water.*

bacteria
NOUN
Bacteria are very small organisms that live inside you and all around you. Some cause disease, while others help your body.

bad
ADJECTIVE
1 Something that is bad is nasty and not very nice. *The weather was really **bad**.*
2 Someone who is bad does things that are wrong or against the law.
3 Food that is bad is rotten. *Meat will go **bad** if you don't keep it in the fridge.*
badly (ADVERB)
If you do something badly, you don't do it very well. *Some of the children behaved very **badly**.*

badge
NOUN badges
A badge is a small picture or sign that you pin onto your clothes. *We all had to wear **badges** with our names on.*

badminton
NOUN
Badminton is a game in which you use a racket to hit a shuttlecock over a high net.

bag
NOUN bags
A bag is a container that you can carry things in.

baggy
ADJECTIVE
Baggy clothes fit loosely around your body. *These trousers are too big for me – they're really **baggy**.*

a shuttlecock

badminton

a badminton racket

Baisakhi
NOUN
Baisakhi is a Sikh festival that takes place in April.

bake
VERB bakes, baking, baked
When you bake something, you cook it in an oven. *Shall we **bake** a cake?*
baker (NOUN)
A baker is someone who bakes and sells bread and cakes.

a
Bb
c
d
e
f
g
h
i
j
k
l
m
n
o
p
q
r
s
t
u

balance

VERB balances, balancing, balanced

1 When you balance, you keep your body steady and don't fall over. *Can you **balance** on one leg?*

NOUN

2 If you have good balance, you can keep your body steady and not fall.

balcony

NOUN balconies

A balcony is a small platform outside an upstairs window of a building, where you can sit.

bald

ADJECTIVE

Someone who is bald has no hair.

ball

NOUN balls

1 A ball is a round object that you use to play games and sports.

2 A ball is a big, grand party where there is dancing.

ballet

NOUN

Ballet is a type of dancing in which you dance on the ends of your toes and move very gracefully.

barbecue

balloon

NOUN balloons

A balloon is a bag of very thin rubber that you can fill with air or other gases.

ban

VERB bans, banning, banned

If people ban something, they say that you are not allowed to do it. *The teachers have **banned** football in the playground.*

banana

NOUN bananas

A banana is a long, thin fruit with a yellow skin that you peel off.

band

NOUN bands

1 A band is a group of people who play music together.

2 A band is a narrow strip or circle of something. *The team captain usually wears a special arm **band**.*

bandage

NOUN bandages

A bandage is a strip of material that you wrap around a wound to keep it clean.

bang

NOUN bangs

1 A bang is a sudden loud noise. *The firework went off with a loud **bang**.*

VERB bangs, banging, banged

2 When something bangs, it makes a loud noise.

3 When you bang on something, you hit it hard. *We **banged** on the door.*

bank

NOUN banks

1 The bank of a river is the ground along the edge of it.

2 A bank is a place where people can put their money to keep it safe. People can also borrow money from a bank.

bar

NOUN bars

1 A bar is a long, narrow piece of metal. *There were **bars** on all the windows.*

2 A large, usually rectangular piece of chocolate is called a bar of chocolate. *I ate half a **bar** of chocolate on Saturday.*

3 A bar is a place where people can buy drinks.

barbecue

NOUN barbecues

1 A barbecue is a grill that you use to cook food outside.

2 A meal that you cook outside in this way is also called a barbecue. *We're having a **barbecue** tonight.*

bar chart

NOUN bar charts

A bar chart is a graph on which bars of different lengths show the different amounts of things. *The **bar chart** shows the favourite colours chosen by the pupils in my class.*

barcode

NOUN barcodes

A barcode is a pattern of thick and thin lines that is printed on things you buy in shops. The barcode contains information about the things.

bare
ADJECTIVE
1 If a part of your body is bare, it is not covered by clothes.
2 If something is bare, it is empty. *The room was completely **bare**.*
☛ **Be careful with spelling:**
bare *We walked on the beach in **bare** feet.*
bear *Are there **bears** in this forest?*

bargain
NOUN bargains
A bargain is something that you buy for less money than it is really worth. *You can find lots of **bargains** if you shop in the sales.*

barge
NOUN barges
1 A barge is a long boat with a flat bottom that is used on canals.
VERB barges, barging, barged
2 If you barge into someone, you bump into them roughly.

bark
NOUN
1 Bark is the rough wood on the outside of a tree trunk.
VERB barks, barking, barked
2 When a dog barks, it makes a rough, loud noise.

Bar Mitzvah
NOUN Bar Mitzvahs
A Bar Mitzvah is a celebration that takes place for a Jewish boy on his 13th birthday.

barn
NOUN barns
A barn is a large building on a farm where animals are kept or things are stored.

barrel
NOUN barrels
A barrel is a large, cylindrical container that people keep liquids or food in.

base
NOUN bases
The base of something is the bottom part of it.

baseball
NOUN
In baseball, teams have to hit a ball with a long, narrow bat and then run around four points called **bases** to score runs.

basic
ADJECTIVE
Basic things are simple and easy to learn. *My uncle taught me some **basic** magic tricks.*

basket
NOUN baskets
A basket is a container that you use for carrying things. It is made of strips of cane or straw.

basketball
NOUN
In basketball, teams of players bounce a ball and throw it to each other. They throw it through a high **basket** to score.

bat
NOUN bats
1 A bat is a special stick that you use to hit a ball in sports.
2 A bat is an animal that flies around at night and lives in caves and dark places. Bats eat insects or fruit, and rest hanging upside down.

*A **basketball** player jumps to put the ball in the **basket**.*

bath
NOUN baths
A bath is a large container that you sit in to wash your body.

bathroom
NOUN bathrooms
A bathroom is a room in a house with a bath in it.

Bat Mitzvah
NOUN Bat Mitzvahs
A Bat Mitzvah is the occasion of a Jewish girl reaching the age of twelve. *At my **Bat Mitzvah**, I gave a speech and then we had a big party in the garden.*

battery
NOUN batteries
A battery is a small, metal object that stores a small amount of electricity. You put batteries into things like torches to make them work.

battle
NOUN battles
A battle is a fight between two armies that are at war.

bay
NOUN bays
A bay is a place on the coast where the land curves inward.

beach
NOUN beaches
A beach is an area of sand or pebbles next to water.

bead
NOUN beads
Beads are small pieces of wood or glass that you thread on a string to make a necklace.

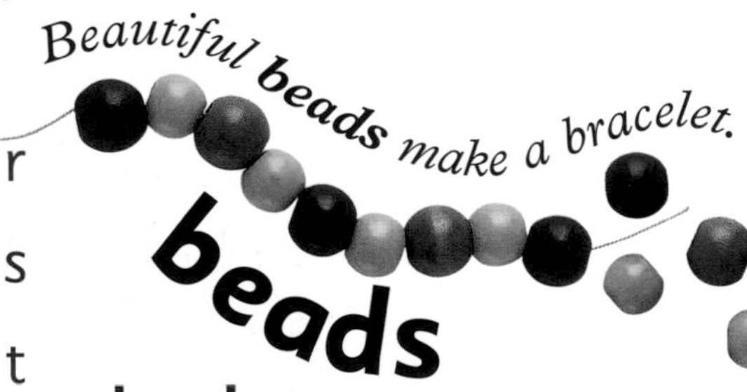
Beautiful beads make a bracelet.
beads

beak
NOUN beaks
A bird's beak is its hard, pointed mouth.

beam
NOUN beams
1 A long, narrow ray of light is called a beam of light. *I could see the **beam** of light from her torch.*
2 A beam is a long, thick piece of wood.

bean
NOUN beans
A bean is a seed or pod that you can eat as a vegetable. *We had sausages and baked **beans** for lunch.*
☞ **Be careful with spelling:**
bean *I love baked **beans**!*
been *Where have you **been**?*

bear
NOUN bears
1 A bear is a large animal with thick fur that lives in forests and mountain areas. Most bears eat meat, but some also eat honey, berries, and fruit.
VERB bears, bearing, bore, borne
2 If something will bear your weight, it will support it.
3 If you cannot bear something, you hate it. *I can't **bear** this programme!*
☞ **Be careful with spelling:**
bear *Are there **bears** in this forest?*
bare *We walked on the beach in **bare** feet.*

beard
NOUN beards
A man's beard is hair that grows on his face if he does not shave.

beast
NOUN beasts
A beast is a large, fierce animal.

beat
VERB beats, beating, beat, beaten
1 If you beat someone in a game, you win and they lose. *My brother always **beats** me at chess.*
2 If you beat something, you hit it many times. *She **beat** the drum in time to the music.*

beautiful
ADJECTIVE
Someone or something that is beautiful is lovely to look at or hear. *The garden was full of **beautiful** flowers.*
beautifully (ADVERB)
If you do something beautifully, you do it in a lovely way.

beaver
NOUN beavers
A beaver is an animal with very strong teeth. Beavers cut down trees with their teeth to build dams in rivers.

become
VERB becomes, becoming, became, become
To become something means to change into it. *A tadpole **becomes** a frog after four months.*

bed
NOUN beds
1 A bed is a piece of furniture that you sleep on.
2 A flower or vegetable bed is a piece of ground where you grow flowers or vegetables.

bedroom
NOUN bedrooms
A bedroom is a room with a bed in it.

bee
NOUN bees
A bee is a flying insect that makes honey. Bees live together in large groups and feed on nectar from flowers.

beef
NOUN
Beef is the meat from a cow or bull.

At the beach

Let's go down to the beach and have fun!

a
Bb
c
d
e
f
g
h
i
j
k
l
m
n
o
p
q
r
s
t
u
v
w
x
y
z

beefburger
NOUN beefburgers
A beefburger is a round, flat piece of minced beef that is cooked and often eaten in a bread roll.

beehive
NOUN beehives
A beehive is a house for bees where a beekeeper collects honey.

beetle
NOUN beetles
A beetle is an insect with hard, shiny wing cases.

beg
VERB begs, begging, begged
1 When a dog begs, it sits up on its back legs to ask for something.
2 If you beg for something, you ask for it very strongly. *I* ***begged*** *Dad to take me to the fair.*

begin
VERB begins, beginning, began, begun
When something begins, it starts. *The story* ***begins*** *in a castle.*
beginning (NOUN)
The beginning of something is where it starts. *The* ***beginning*** *of the film is a bit boring.*

behave
VERB behaves, behaving, behaved
The way you behave is how you speak and act in front of other people. *All the children* ***behaved*** *well today.*
behaviour (NOUN)
Your behaviour is how you behave. *The teacher was pleased with our* ***behaviour*** *today.*

believe
VERB believes, believing, believed
If you believe something, you think that it is true. *Do you* ***believe*** *his story?*
belief (NOUN)
A belief is something that you believe. *Different people have different* ***beliefs****.*

bell
NOUN bells
A bell is a piece of metal that makes a ringing sound when you hit it or shake it.

belong
VERB belongs, belonging, belonged
If something belongs to you, it is yours. *That book* ***belongs*** *to me.*
belongings (NOUN)
Your belongings are the things that belong to you. *Remember to take all your* ***belongings*** *home with you.*

belt
NOUN belts
A belt is a narrow strip of leather or material that you wear around your waist.

bench
NOUN benches
A bench is a long, wooden seat.

bend
NOUN bends
1 A bend in the road is a place where it goes round a corner.
VERB bends, bending, bent
2 If you bend something, you press it or curve it so that it is not straight.
3 If you bend over, you lean forward so that your head goes toward the ground. *Can you* ***bend*** *over and touch your toes?*
bent (ADJECTIVE)
Something that is bent is not straight. *Keep your knees* ***bent*** *when you land.*

berry
NOUN berries
A berry is a small, round, juicy fruit with seeds inside. *Some wild* ***berries*** *are poisonous.*

best
ADJECTIVE
The best person or thing is the one that is better than all the others. *This is the* ***best*** *cake I've ever tasted!*

bet
VERB bets, betting, bet
1 If you bet that something is true, you believe that it is true or will happen. *I* ***bet*** *you she gets full marks in the test.*
2 If you bet money, you risk it in a game. If you win, you win more money, but if you lose, you lose your money.

better
ADJECTIVE
1 A person or thing that is better than others is quicker, cleverer, or nicer.
2 If you are better, you are well again. *I feel **better** today.*

beware
VERB
If you tell someone to beware, you are telling them to be careful.

Bible
NOUN Bibles
The Bible is the holy book of the Christian religion.

bicycle
NOUN bicycles
A bicycle is a vehicle with two wheels that you ride by turning the pedals with your feet. You can shorten the word bicycle to **bike**.

big
ADJECTIVE bigger, biggest
Something that is big is large.

bikini
NOUN bikinis
A bikini is a swimming costume in two pieces that women and girls wear.

bill
NOUN bills
1 A bird's bill is its beak.
2 A bill is a piece of paper that shows you how much you have to pay for something.

billion
NOUN billions
A billion is a thousand million (1,000,000,000).

bin
NOUN bins
A bin is a container where you put things that you want to throw away.

biodegradable
ADJECTIVE
Things that are biodegradable rot away naturally when thrown away.

biography
NOUN biographies
A biography is a book that tells the story of someone's life.

biology
NOUN
Biology is the study of animals and plants.

bird
NOUN birds
A bird is an animal that has wings and feathers on its body.

birthday
NOUN birthdays
Your birthday is the day you were born on, which you celebrate each year.

biscuit
NOUN biscuits
A biscuit is a small, crisp cake.

bit
NOUN bits
A bit is a small piece of something. *Would you like a **bit** of chocolate?*

bite
VERB bites, biting, bit, bitten
If you bite food, you cut it with your teeth. *She **bit** into the cake.*

*Toucans have big, colourful **bills.***

bitter
ADJECTIVE
Something that is bitter tastes sour and not sweet. *Lemons taste very **bitter**.*

black
ADJECTIVE
Something that is black is the colour of night.

blackbird
NOUN blackbirds
A blackbird is a bird that lives in gardens and fields. The male has black feathers and a yellow beak, and the female has brown feathers.

blackboard
NOUN blackboards
A blackboard is a dark board that you write on with chalk.

blade
NOUN blades
1 The blade of a knife or sword is the long, sharp part.
2 One stem of grass is called a blade of grass.

blame
VERB blames, blaming, blamed
If you blame someone for something, you say that they did it or it is their fault. *She **blamed** me for spilling the water.*

blank
ADJECTIVE
A blank piece of paper has nothing written on it.

blanket
NOUN blankets
A blanket is a thick, soft cover that you put on a bed to keep you warm through the night.

blast
NOUN blasts
1 A blast is a powerful explosion.
VERB blasts, blasting, blasted
2 When a rocket blasts off, it leaves the ground and goes up into the air.

bleed
VERB bleeds, bleeding, bled
When you bleed, blood comes out of your body. *My finger's **bleeding**!*

blew
Blew is the past tense of the verb **blow**.
☛ **Be careful with spelling:**
blew *I **blew** the candles out.*
blue *I've got **blue** eyes.*

blind
ADJECTIVE
1 Someone who is blind cannot see.
NOUN blinds
2 A blind is a piece of material that you pull down to cover a window.

blindfold
NOUN blindfolds
A blindfold is a piece of cloth that you put over someone's eyes during a game, so that they cannot see.

blink
VERB blinks, blinking, blinked
When you blink, you shut your eyes and then open them quickly.

blister
NOUN blisters
A blister is a sore lump that forms on your skin when something has rubbed against it. *I had **blisters** on my feet after the long walk.*

blizzard
NOUN blizzards
A blizzard is a very heavy snowstorm.

blob
NOUN blobs
A blob is a small lump of something with no shape.

*Five, four, three, two, one... **blast** off!*

block
NOUN blocks
1 A block of something is a solid piece of it.
2 A block is a very big building. *We live in a **block** of flats.*
VERB blocks, blocking, blocked
3 If something is blocking a road or path, it is in the way. *A fallen tree **blocked** the road.*

blog
NOUN blogs
A blog is a website where someone writes about their own life or ideas.

blond / blonde
ADJECTIVE
Someone who is blond has light-coloured hair. We use **blond** for boys and men, and **blonde** for girls and women.

blood
NOUN
Blood is the red liquid that flows around inside your body.

blossom
NOUN blossoms
The blossom is the flower or flowers on a fruit tree that appear on it before the fruit.

blouse
NOUN blouses
A blouse is a shirt that a girl or woman wears.

blow
VERB blows, blowing, blew, blown
1 When you blow, you push air out of your mouth.
2 When the wind blows, it moves.
3 When something blows about in the air, the air moves it about. *It was so windy my hat **blew** off!*

blue
ADJECTIVE
Something that is blue is the colour of the sky on a sunny day.
☛ **Be careful with spelling:**
blue *I've got **blue** eyes.*
blew *I **blew** the candles out.*

Bluetooth
NOUN
Bluetooth is a kind of technology that makes it possible to connect things like phones and computers without any wires.

blunt
ADJECTIVE
Something that is blunt has a round end and is not sharp. *These scissors are no good – they're **blunt**!*

blurb
NOUN blurbs
A blurb is a short piece of writing that tells you what a book or film is about.

blurred
ADJECTIVE
If something is blurred, you cannot see it clearly.

blush
VERB blushes, blushing, blushed
When you blush, your face turns red because you are embarrassed or shy.

board
NOUN boards
A board is a flat piece of wood or very stiff paper.

boast
VERB boasts, boasting, boasted
If you boast, you tell people about something in a proud and annoying way. *My sister's always **boasting** about how good she is at dancing!*
boastful (ADJECTIVE)
Someone who is boastful boasts a lot.

boat
NOUN boats
A boat is a vehicle that can travel on water and carry people or goods.

body
NOUN bodies
1 Your body is all the physical parts that you are made of.
2 A body is a dead person.

boil
VERB boils, boiling, boiled
When a liquid boils, it becomes very hot and starts to bubble.

bold
ADJECTIVE bolder, boldest
1 Someone who is bold is very brave.
2 Bold writing is darker than normal.
boldly (ADVERB)
If you do something boldly, you do it in a bold way. *She walked **boldly** to the front of the hall.*

bolt
NOUN bolts
1 A bolt is a piece of metal that you slide across to lock a door.
VERB bolts, bolting, bolted
2 If you bolt a door, you lock it with a bolt.

bomb
NOUN bombs
A bomb is a weapon that explodes and damages buildings and other things around it.

bone
NOUN bones
Your bones are the hard, white parts of your body that make up your skeleton.

bonfire
NOUN bonfires
A bonfire is a large, outdoor fire.

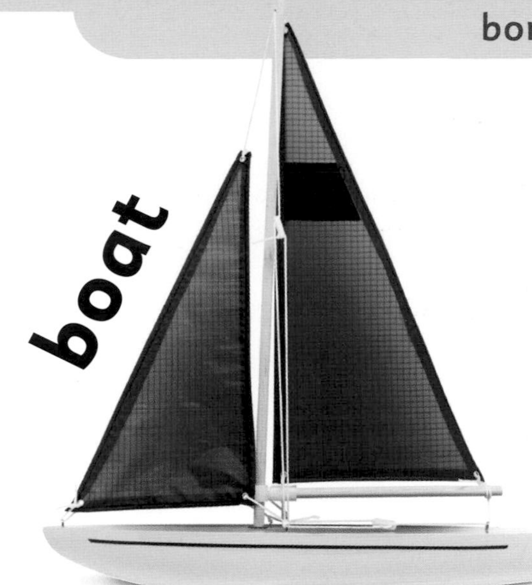

book
NOUN books
1 A book is a set of pages filled with words or pictures that are joined together inside a cover.
VERB books, booking, booked
2 When you book something, you arrange for it to be kept for you. *You can **book** tickets online.*

boom
VERB booms, booming, boomed
If something booms, it makes a deep, loud sound.

boomerang
NOUN boomerangs
A boomerang is a curved piece of wood that comes back to you when you throw it through the air.

boot
NOUN boots
A boot is a type of shoe that covers your foot and part of your leg.

border
NOUN borders
The border between two countries is the line that divides them from each other.

a Bb c d e f g h i j k l m n o p q r s t u v w x y z

bored
ADJECTIVE
If you are bored, you feel tired and annoyed because you have nothing interesting to do.
boring (ADJECTIVE)
If something is boring, it is not exciting or interesting.

born
VERB
When a person or animal is born, they come into the world as a baby.

borrow
VERB borrows, borrowing, borrowed
If you borrow something, you take it for a while and then give it back. *Please may I **borrow** your pen?*

boss
NOUN bosses
The boss is the person who is in charge of a job.

both
ADJECTIVE
Both means not just one thing, but two. ***Both** teams played well.*

bother
VERB bothers, bothering, bothered
1 If you do not bother to do something, you do not do it because it seems like too much effort.
2 If something bothers you, it makes you feel worried.

bottle
NOUN bottles
A bottle is a tall container for liquids.

bottom
NOUN bottoms
1 The bottom of something is the lowest part of it. *The boat sank to the **bottom** of the sea.*
2 Your bottom is the part of your body that you sit on.

bought
☛ See **buy**.

bounce
VERB bounces, bouncing, bounced
If something bounces, it springs back when it hits something. Something that is **bouncy** bounces easily.

bow
NOUN bows
1 When you tie a bow, you tie a piece of string or ribbon so that it has two loops and two loose ends.
2 A bow is a curved piece of bendy wood with a string called a bowstring attached to each end. The bow is used for shooting arrows.

bow
VERB bows, bowing, bowed
When you bow, you bend forward from the waist as a sign of respect.

bowl
NOUN bowls
1 A bowl is a round, deep container that can be used for food.
VERB bowls, bowling, bowled
2 When you bowl in a game, you throw a ball.

bowling
NOUN
Bowling is a game in which you roll a heavy ball at wooden pins called skittles, and try to knock them over.

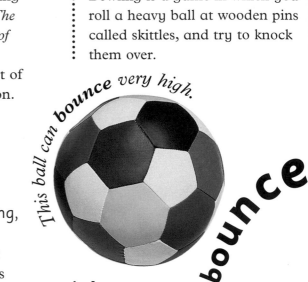

This ball can bounce very high.

box
NOUN boxes
A box is a container.

boy
NOUN boys
A boy is a child who will become a man when he grows up.

brace
NOUN braces
A brace is a piece of wire that you wear over your teeth to help straighten them.

bracelet
NOUN bracelets
A bracelet is a piece of jewellery that you wear around your arm or wrist.

bracket
NOUN brackets
1 Brackets are punctuation marks ( ) that you put around extra words or ideas in a piece of writing.
2 Brackets are supports fixed to a wall.

Braille
NOUN
Braille is a kind of writing with raised dots instead of letters. People who are blind read the dots by feeling them with their fingertips.

brain
NOUN brains
Your brain is the part of your body inside your head that controls how you think and move.
brainy (ADJECTIVE)
Someone who is brainy is clever.

brake
NOUN brakes
1 The brake is the part on a vehicle that slows it down and stops it.
VERB brakes, braking, braked
2 When you brake, you slow down and stop a vehicle by using the brakes.
☛ **Be careful with spelling:**
brake *We had to* ***brake*** *when we saw a dog in the road.*
break *Be careful you don't* ***break*** *the window.*

branch
NOUN branches
The branches on a tree are the parts that grow out of the trunk.

brave
ADJECTIVE braver, bravest
Someone who is brave does not show that they are afraid even when they have to do dangerous things. *It was very* ***brave*** *of you to go back to rescue the others.*
bravely (ADVERB)
If you do something bravely, you do it in a brave way. *The people fought* ***bravely*** *to protect their town.*

bread
NOUN
Bread is a food that is made from flour, yeast, and water and baked in an oven.

break
NOUN breaks
1 A break is a short time when you stop working and rest or relax.
VERB break, breaking, broke, broken
2 If you break something, you damage it so that it is in lots of pieces or does not work any more.
☛ **Be careful with spelling:**
break *Be careful you don't* ***break*** *the window.*
brake *We had to* ***brake*** *when we saw a dog in the road.*

breakfast
NOUN breakfasts
Breakfast is the meal that you eat in the morning.

breath
NOUN breaths
When you take a breath, you take air into your lungs through your nose and mouth. *I took a deep* ***breath*** *and dived into the water.*

breathe
VERB breathes, breathing, breathed
When you breathe, you take air into your lungs through your nose or mouth, and then push it out again.

breed
NOUN breeds
A breed of an animal is one particular kind. For example, an Alsatian is a breed of dog.

breeze
NOUN breezes
A breeze is a gentle wind.

bribe
VERB bribes, bribing, bribed
To bribe someone means to offer them something so that they will do what you want them to do.

brick
NOUN bricks
Bricks are blocks of baked clay that are used for building houses.

bride
NOUN brides
A bride is a woman on the day she gets married.

bridegroom
NOUN bridegrooms
A bridegroom is a man on the day he gets married.

bridesmaid
NOUN bridesmaids
A bridesmaid is a woman or a girl who helps a bride on her wedding day.

bridge
NOUN bridges
A bridge is a structure built over a river, road, or railway line so that you can cross it easily.

How did you ***break*** *my beautiful plate?*

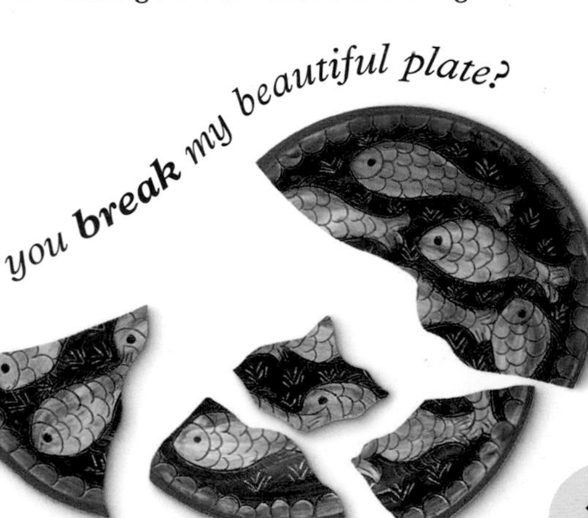

a
Bb
c
d
e
f
g
h
i
j
k
l
m
n
o
p
q
r
s
t
u
v
w
x
y
z

brief

ADJECTIVE
Something that is brief only lasts for a short time.

bright

ADJECTIVE brighter, brightest
1 Something that is bright shines strongly and gives off a lot of light.
2 A bright colour is strong and clear. *She was wearing a **bright** blue scarf.*
3 Someone who is bright is clever.
brightly (ADVERB)
If a light shines brightly, it is bright. *The moon was shining **brightly**.*

brilliant

ADJECTIVE
1 Something that is brilliant is very good. *It's a **brilliant** film!*
2 Someone who is brilliant is very clever.
brilliantly (ADVERB)
If you do something brilliantly, you do it very well. *Everyone played **brilliantly**, and we won the game.*

brim

NOUN brims
1 The brim of a hat is the part that sticks out around the edge.
2 The brim of a cup is the top edge of it. *The cup was full to the **brim**.*

brim
Ribbons decorate the brim of her hat.

bring

VERB brings, bringing, brought
If you bring something with you, you take it with you when you go somewhere. *Don't forget to **bring** your new computer game when you come to my house.*

broad

ADJECTIVE broader, broadest
Something that is broad is very wide. *The river is too **broad** to swim across.*

broadband

NOUN
Broadband is a way of passing electronic signals backward and forward to connect computers to the internet.

broadcast

VERB broadcasts, broadcasting, broadcast
To broadcast a programme means to show it on television or send it out on the radio.

broccoli

NOUN
Broccoli is a dark green vegetable.

broke

☛ See **break**.

bronze

NOUN
Bronze is a shiny, brown-coloured metal.

brooch

NOUN brooches
A brooch is a piece of jewellery that you pin onto your clothes.

broom

NOUN brooms
A broom is a stiff brush with a long handle that you use for sweeping. *In stories, witches ride through the air on **broomsticks**.*

brother

NOUN brothers
Your brother is a boy who has the same mother and father as you do.

brought

☛ See **bring**.

brown

ADJECTIVE
Something that is brown is the colour of mud.

brownie

NOUN brownies
A brownie is a small, sticky chocolate cake. *My mum makes the best **brownies** in the world!*

browse

ADJECTIVE browses, browsing, browsed
1 When you browse in a shop, you look around but do not buy anything.
2 When you browse on a computer, you look for information.

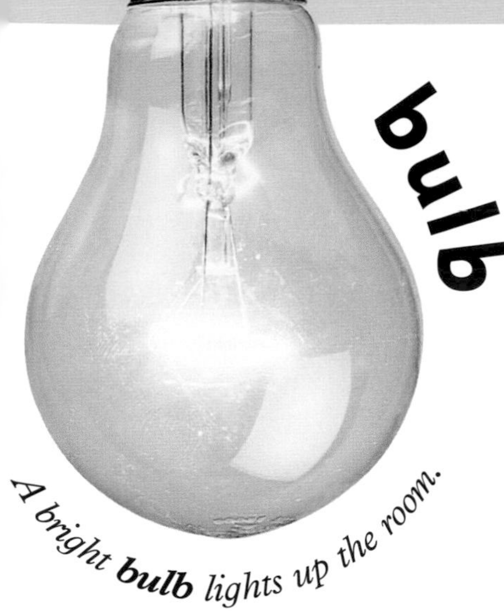

A bright ***bulb*** *lights up the room.*

browser
NOUN browsers
A browser is a program that allows you to use the internet on a computer or your phone.

bruise
NOUN bruises
A bruise is a dark, painful mark that you get on your skin when you hit or bump it.

brush
NOUN brushes
1 A brush is a tool that has a handle and a back with stiff hairs set in it. You use a brush to clean things or for painting.
VERB brushes, brushing, brushed
2 When you brush something, you clean it using a brush. ***Brush*** *your teeth every day.*

bubble
NOUN bubbles
A bubble is a very light ball of air with a thin layer of liquid around it.

bucket
NOUN buckets
A bucket is a container with a handle that you use for carrying water or soil.

bud
NOUN buds
A bud is a new flower or leaf on a plant, before it has opened.

Buddhist
NOUN Buddhists
A Buddhist is someone who follows the teachings of the Buddha and believes in personal spiritual development.

buffalo
NOUN buffaloes
A buffalo is a member of the cattle family. The buffalo has curved horns.

bug
NOUN bugs
1 A bug is an insect.
2 If there is a bug in a computer program, there is a problem and it does not work properly.

buggy
NOUN buggies
A buggy is a seat on wheels for pushing a young child in.

build
VERB builds, building, built
When you build something, you make it by putting things together. *These birds use leaves and small twigs to* ***build*** *their nest.*

building
NOUN buildings
A building is a structure such as a house, factory, or school.

built
☛ See **build**.

bulb
NOUN bulbs
1 A bulb is the round glass part of an electric light.
2 A bulb is the part of some plants that grows underground. You can plant bulbs in the soil to produce new plants. *We planted some daffodil* ***bulbs*** *in the garden.*

bulge
VERB bulges, bulging, bulged
If something is bulging, it is so full that it looks round and fat. *His bag was* ***bulging*** *with presents.*

bull
NOUN bulls
A bull is a male cow. A male elephant or whale is also called a bull.

bulldozer
NOUN bulldozers
A bulldozer is a machine with a large, metal blade at the front that moves earth and rocks.

A ***bulldozer*** *clears land for building.*

a
Bb
c
d
e
f
g
h
i
j
k
l
m
n
o
p
q
r
s
t
u
v
w
x
y
z

bullet
NOUN bullets
A bullet is a small piece of metal that you fire out of a gun.

bully
NOUN bullies
1 A bully is a mean person who hurts or frightens other people.
VERB bullies, bullying, bullied
2 If someone bullies you, they are mean to you or hurt you.

bump
NOUN bumps
1 A bump on the road is a part that sticks up. *It was difficult to ride my bike over the* ***bumps****.*
2 A bump on your body is a sore part where you have hit it.
VERB bumps, bumping, bumped
3 If you bump into something, you knock into it. *Don't run – you might* ***bump*** *into someone.*

bun
NOUN buns
1 A bun is a bread roll that you eat a burger in.
2 A bun is a small cake.

bunch
NOUN bunches
A bunch is a group of things that are fastened together. *We bought a* ***bunch*** *of flowers for the teacher.*

bundle
NOUN bundles
A bundle is a group of things that are loosely joined together.

bungalow
NOUN bungalows
A bungalow is a house that has no upstairs, but has all its rooms on one level.

bunk beds
NOUN
Bunk beds are two beds, one above the other.

burglar
NOUN burglars
A burglar is a person who steals things from people's homes.

burn
VERB burns, burning, burned or burnt
1 If you burn something, you damage it or destroy it using fire. *We* ***burned*** *all the old wood on a bonfire.*
2 If you burn yourself, you hurt a part of your body on a fire. You may burn if you hurt your skin by staying in the sun too long.

burrow
NOUN burrows
A burrow is a hole under the ground where a small animal lives.

burst
VERB bursts, bursting, burst
If something bursts, it splits open. *My balloon has* ***burst****!*

bury
VERB buries, burying, buried
If you bury something, you put it in the ground and cover it over.

bus
NOUN buses
A bus is a vehicle that carries passengers on the road.

bush
NOUN bushes
A bush is a large plant that looks like a small tree.

business
NOUN businesses
A business is an organization that makes and sells things.

busy
ADJECTIVE busier, busiest
If you are busy, you are doing lots of things.
busily (ADVERB)
If you do something busily, you do it in a busy way. *He was* ***busily*** *cleaning his football boots.*

butcher
NOUN butchers
A butcher is a person who cuts up and sells meat.

butter
NOUN
Butter is a soft, yellow food that is made from milk. You can spread butter on bread.

buttercup
NOUN buttercups
A buttercup is a small, yellow, wild flower.

butterfly
NOUN butterflies
A butterfly is an insect with large, colourful wings.

button
NOUN buttons
Buttons are the small, round objects on your clothes that you fasten when you put your clothes on.

buy
VERB buys, buying, bought
When you buy something, you pay money for it and it becomes yours.

cabbage
NOUN cabbages
A cabbage is a vegetable with large, green leaves.

cabin
NOUN cabins
1 A cabin is a small wooden hut.
2 A cabin is a room for passengers or crew on a plane or ship.

cable
NOUN cables
A cable is a bundle of wires that carry electrical power or signals.

cactus
NOUN cacti
A cactus is a plant with a thick, green stem and prickly spines. Cacti grow in hot, dry deserts.

cage
NOUN cages
A cage is a small room or box with bars, where you can keep an animal or bird.

calculate
VERB calculates, calculating, calculated
When you calculate the answer to a sum, you work it out.
calculation (NOUN)
A calculation is an answer to a sum that you have worked out.

calculator
NOUN calculators
A calculator is a small electronic machine that you use for doing maths.

calendar
NOUN calendars
A calendar is a chart that lists all the days, weeks, and months of the year.

calf
NOUN calves
A calf is a young cow or bull. A young elephant or whale is also called a calf.

call
VERB calls, calling, called
1 If you call to someone, you shout to them. *We **called** for help.*
2 What you call someone is the name that you give them. *We **call** our dog Max.*
3 If you call someone, you phone them. *I'll **call** you later.*
4 If you call on someone, you visit them.

calm
ADJECTIVE calmer, calmest
1 If something is calm, it is still and quiet. *The sea was **calm** after the storm had passed.*
2 If you feel calm, you feel peaceful and relaxed.
calmly (ADVERB)
If you do something calmly, you do it in a quiet, relaxed way. *I **calmly** picked up my bag and walked out.*

camel
NOUN camels
A camel is an animal with one or two humps on its back. Camels live in hot deserts and store fat in their humps to help them go without water or food for a long time.

camera
NOUN cameras
A camera is a machine that you use for taking photographs or for making videos or films. In the past, film was used to make the pictures, now photographs are usually taken with digital cameras.

A cow with her calf

a b Cc d e f g h i j k l m n o p q r s t u

camouflage
NOUN
Camouflage is when an animal has a pattern or colour on their body that helps them look like the things around them so that they are hard to see and can hide.

camp
VERB camps, camping, camped
When you camp, you sleep in a tent outdoors. *We went **camping** in the forest.*

can
NOUN cans
1 A can is a metal container for food or drink.
VERB can, could
2 If you can do something, you are able to do it.

canal
NOUN canals
A canal is a river made by people that boats can travel along.

cancel
VERB cancels, cancelling, cancelled
If you cancel an event, you decide that it will not happen. *The game was **cancelled** due to the bad weather.*

cancer
NOUN cancers
Cancer is a serious disease that can develop in your body.

candle
NOUN candles
A candle is a stick of wax with a piece of string called a wick running through the middle. You can burn candles to give light.

cannon
NOUN cannons
A cannon is a very large gun that fires heavy metal balls.

canoe
NOUN canoes
A canoe is a light, narrow boat that you move along using a paddle.

cap
NOUN caps
A cap is a hat with a stiff part sticking out at the front, over your eyes.

capable
ADJECTIVE
If you are capable of doing something, you can do it.

capacity
NOUN
The capacity of a container is the amount that it can hold.

capital
NOUN capitals
The capital of a country is the city where it has its government offices and its parliament. *Paris is the **capital** of France.*

capital letter
NOUN capital letters
Capital letters are big letters such as A, B, or C that you use at the beginning of sentences or at the beginning of names.

cap

captain
NOUN captains
1 The captain of a ship or plane is the person who is in charge of it.
2 The captain of a team is the leader of the team.

capture
VERB captures, capturing, captured
To capture someone means to catch them. *A lion escaped from the zoo, but it was soon **captured** again.*

car
NOUN cars
A car is a vehicle with an engine that people can drive and travel in.

caravan
NOUN caravans
A caravan is a home on wheels in which people live or have holidays.

card
NOUN cards
1 A card is a piece of stiff paper with a picture or words on it. You send people cards for their birthday.
2 Playing cards are pieces of stiff paper, often with pictures on them, that you use for playing games.
3 Card is stiff paper. Very strong card that is used to make boxes is called **cardboard**.

cardigan
NOUN cardigans
A cardigan is a knitted jumper that fastens down the front.

care
VERB cares, caring, cared
1 If you care about something, it is important to you. *Most people **care** about how they look.*
2 If you care for someone, you look after them. *I helped **care** for my sister when she was ill.*
NOUN
3 If you take care to do something well, you will not make any mistakes.

careful
ADJECTIVE
If you are careful, you do something well. *Be **careful** you don't spill your drink.*
carefully (ADVERB)
If you do something carefully, you do it in a careful way. *She picked up the small bird **carefully**.*

careless
ADJECTIVE
If you are careless, you do not think about what you are doing and so you make a mistake or do something silly. *It was very **careless** of you to drop your phone in the bath.*

carnival
NOUN carnivals
A carnival is a special event with a street procession, music, and dancing.

carnivore
NOUN carnivores
A carnivore is an animal that eats meat.

carol
NOUN carols
A carol is a special song that people sing at Christmas.

carpenter
NOUN carpenters
A carpenter is someone who works with wood and makes things out of wood.

carpet
NOUN carpets
A carpet is a soft covering for a floor.

carrot
NOUN carrots
A carrot is a long, thin, orange vegetable.

carry
VERB carries, carrying, carried
When you carry something, you hold it and take it somewhere.

carton
NOUN cartons
A carton is a cardboard or plastic box that milk or drinks are sold in.

cartoon
NOUN cartoons
1 A cartoon is a film in which the characters are drawn, rather than being real people.
2 A cartoon is a funny drawing in a newspaper, magazine, or book.

carve
VERB carves, carving, carved
When you carve something, you cut it into a shape. *The statue is **carved** out of stone.*

case
NOUN cases
A case is a container that you keep or carry things in.

carrot

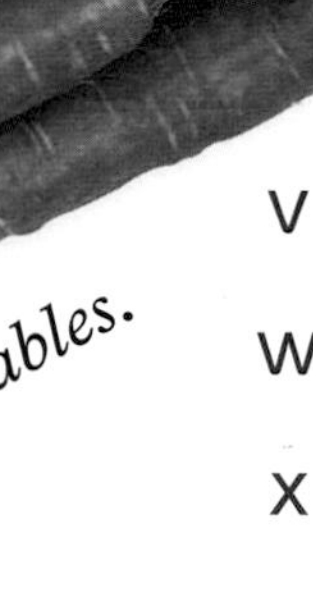

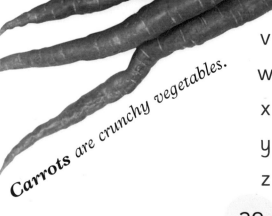

Carrots are crunchy vegetables.

a b Cc d e f g h i j k l m n o p q r s t u v w x y z

castle
NOUN castles
A castle is a large house with high stone walls and strong defences to protect it against attacking armies.

cat
NOUN cats
A cat is an animal with soft fur that people often keep as a pet. Animals such as lions and tigers are large wild cats.

catalogue
NOUN catalogues
A catalogue is a book that has information about all the things you can buy from a place.

catch
VERB catches, catching, caught
1 If you catch something, you get hold of it while it is moving. ***Catch** the ball!*
2 To catch someone means to take them prisoner. *The police have **caught** the two thieves.*
3 When you catch a bus, train, or plane, you get on it.
4 If you catch an illness, you get it. *I **caught** chickenpox from my brother.*

caterpillar
NOUN caterpillars
A caterpillar is the young form of a butterfly or moth. Caterpillars look like small, fat worms, and some are furry or hairy.

caterpillar

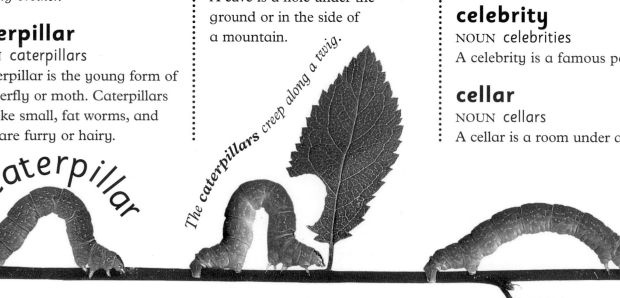

*The **caterpillars** creep along a twig.*

cathedral
NOUN cathedrals
A cathedral is a very large church.

cattle
NOUN
Cattle are cows and bulls.

caught
☛ See **catch**.

cause
NOUN causes
The cause of something is what makes it happen. *What was the **cause** of the fire?*

cautious
ADJECTIVE
If you are cautious, you are careful because you are afraid that there may be danger.
*I was quite **cautious** the first time I went ice-skating, but I soon got used to it.*
cautiously (ADVERB)
If you do something cautiously, you do it in a cautious way. *She **cautiously** opened the door.*

cave
NOUN caves
A cave is a hole under the ground or in the side of a mountain.

CCTV
NOUN
CCTV is a system of cameras that show things that are happening in public places. CCTV is short for **closed-circuit television**.

CD
NOUN CDs
A CD is a small plastic disk on which music or computer information can be stored. CD is short for **compact disk**.

ceiling
NOUN ceilings
The ceiling is the part of a room that is above your head.

celebrate
VERB celebrates, celebrating, celebrated
When you celebrate, you do something enjoyable for a special reason. *How are you going to **celebrate** your birthday?*
celebration (NOUN)
A celebration is an event where people celebrate something. *There will be a big **celebration** if we win the World Cup.*

celebrity
NOUN celebrities
A celebrity is a famous person.

cellar
NOUN cellars
A cellar is a room under a house.

centimetre

NOUN centimetres

We use centimetres to measure how long something is. There are 100 centimetres in a **metre**.

centre

NOUN centres

1 The centre of something is the middle part of it. *There's a volcano in the **centre** of the island.*
2 A centre is a building where particular events take place. *There's a gym at the sports **centre**.*

century

NOUN centuries

A century is a period of 100 years.

cereal

NOUN cereals

1 Cereal crops are crops such as wheat and oats that are grown on farms.
2 A breakfast cereal is often made from wheat or oats.

ceremony

NOUN ceremonies

A ceremony is a formal event to mark a special occasion such as a wedding.

certain

ADJECTIVE

If you are certain about something, you are sure about it. *Are you **certain** this is the right bus?*

certainly (ADVERB)
If something is certainly true, you are sure it is true. *I **certainly** know how to play this game!*

certificate

NOUN certificates

A certificate is an official piece of paper that shows that something has happened.

chain

NOUN chains

A chain is a line of metal loops that are joined together and used like a rope. *The anchor has a long **chain**.*

chair

NOUN chairs

A chair is a piece of furniture that you sit on.

chalk

NOUN

Chalk is a type of soft, white rock. You can use pieces of chalk to write on a blackboard.

challenge

NOUN challenges

A challenge is something difficult that you try to do. *Getting to the top of the mountain will be a real **challenge**.*

champion

NOUN champions

A champion is someone who has won a competition or shown that they are the best at a sport.

chance

NOUN chances

1 If you have the chance to do something, it is possible for you to do it. *I hope I get the **chance** to go to Disneyland one day!*
2 If something happens by chance, it just happens but it was not planned in advance.

change

VERB changes, changing, changed

1 If something changes, it becomes different. *Tadpoles **change** into frogs.*
2 If you change your clothes, you put on different clothes. *I **changed** into my pyjamas.*

NOUN

3 Change is money that you get back when you give too much to pay for something. *I gave the man 50p and he gave me 5p **change**.*

channel

NOUN channels

1 A channel is a long, narrow stretch of water.
2 A channel is a television or radio station.

chapter

NOUN chapters

A chapter is part of a book.

character

NOUN characters

A character is a person in a book or film.

charge
VERB charges, charging, charged
1 When people charge an amount of money, they ask you to pay that amount. *They don't **charge** very much for ice creams.*
2 When you charge a machine such as a phone, you put electricity into it.
3 To charge at someone means to run at them to attack them.

charity
NOUN charities
A charity is an organization that collects money to help people.

chart
NOUN charts
A chart is a map or diagram that shows information.

chase
VERB chases, chasing, chased
To chase someone means to run after them. *It was amazing to watch a cheetah **chasing** a gazelle.*

chat
VERB chats, chatting, chatted
If you chat to someone, you talk to them in a friendly way.

chatroom
NOUN chatrooms
A chatroom is a website where people can write messages to each other.

cheap
ADJECTIVE cheaper, cheapest
Something that is cheap does not cost much money. *This game is really **cheap**!*

cheat
VERB cheats, cheating, cheated
If you cheat, you do something that is against the rules in a game because you want to win.

check
VERB checks, checking, checked
If you check something, you look at it to make sure it is all right. *Remember to **check** your spelling.*

cheek
NOUN cheeks
Your cheeks are the sides of your face.

cheeky
ADJECTIVE cheekier, cheekiest
If you are cheeky, you speak rudely to someone.

cheer
VERB cheers, cheering, cheered
When people cheer, they shout to someone to encourage them or show that they like them. *Everyone **cheered** when he crossed the line and won the race.*

cheerful
ADJECTIVE
If you are cheerful, you are happy.
cheerfully (ADVERB)
If you do something cheerfully, you do it in a cheerful way. *She was singing **cheerfully** as she walked along.*

cheese
NOUN cheeses
Cheese is a solid, salty food that is made from milk.

cheetah
NOUN cheetahs
A cheetah is a spotted animal that belongs to the cat family. Cheetahs live in Africa and hunt other animals. They are extremely fast runners.

*The **cheetah** is the fastest land animal.*

cheetah

chef
NOUN chefs
A chef is someone who cooks food in a restaurant.

chemical
NOUN chemicals
A chemical is a substance that is made or used in a science laboratory.

chemist
NOUN chemists
A chemist is a shop where you can buy medicines or toiletries.

cherry
NOUN cherries
A cherry is a sweet, red fruit with a small stone in the middle.

chess
NOUN
Chess is a board game for two people that you play on a board with black and white squares. The winner is the person who traps the other player's king.

chest
NOUN chests
1 Your chest is the front of your body below your shoulders and above your stomach.
2 A chest is a wooden box. *We found a map in an old **chest**.*

chew
VERB chews, chewing, chewed
When you chew food, you move your teeth up and down on it to break it up. *The meat was tough and difficult to **chew**.*

chicken
NOUN chickens
A chicken is a bird that is kept on farms for its eggs and meat.

chickenpox
NOUN
Chickenpox is an illness that gives you itchy spots on your body.

chief
NOUN chiefs
A chief is a leader of a group of people.

child
NOUN children
A child is a boy or girl.
childhood (NOUN)
Your childhood is the time when you are a boy or girl. *My dad had a very happy **childhood**.*
childish (ADJECTIVE)
Someone who is childish behaves like a young child.

childminder
NOUN childminders
A childminder is someone who looks after children while their parents are at work.

chimney
NOUN chimneys
A chimney is a pipe above a fire. It takes smoke out of a building.

chimpanzee
NOUN chimpanzees
A chimpanzee is a kind of ape that lives in forests in central Africa. Chimpanzees eat fruit and nuts, and sometimes small animals.

chin
NOUN chins
Your chin is the part at the bottom of your face.

chip
NOUN chips
1 Chips are long, thin pieces of fried potato.
2 A computer chip is the part inside a computer that stores information and makes the computer work.
3 If there is a chip in something, a small piece has broken off it.

chocolate
NOUN chocolates
Chocolate is a sweet, brown food made from crushed and roasted cocoa beans, milk, and sugar.

choice
NOUN choices
If there is a choice, there is more than one thing that you can choose.

choir
NOUN choirs
A choir is a group of people who sing together.

choke
VERB chokes, choking, choked
If you choke, you cannot breathe because something is stuck in your throat. *Be careful you don't **choke** on that sweet.*

choose
VERB chooses, choosing, chose, chosen
If you choose something, you decide that it is the thing you want. *I **chose** chocolate ice cream for pudding.*

chop
VERB chops, chopping, chopped
If you chop something, you cut it with a knife or axe.

chore
NOUN chores
A chore is a small, boring job that you have to do at home.

chorus
NOUN choruses
A chorus is the part of a song that you repeat after each verse.

In the city

There is a lot to see and do in the city.

City life is...
active, crowded, exciting, fast
vibrant
noisy
lively
buzzing
busy
rushing
dynamic
multicultural
market
SKYSCRAPERS
high, tall, majestic
apartments
modern
office blocks
cinema, restaurant, family outings
building
billboard
SHOPPING CENTRE
traffic lights
park
greenery
hotel
BEEP!
street food
street vendor
traffic
honks, roars, jams
street musician
strumming
theatre
sports stadium
road signs
library
art gallery
cyclist
vehicles
zebra crossing

Christian
NOUN Christians
A Christian is a person who follows the teachings of Jesus Christ and believes that Jesus is the son of God.

Christmas
NOUN
Christmas is the Christian celebration of the birth of Jesus Christ.

church
NOUN churches
A church is a building where Christians go to pray.

cinema
NOUN cinemas
A cinema is a building where people can go to watch films.

circle
NOUN circles
A circle is a shape that is flat and round.

circumference
NOUN
The circumference of a circle is the measurement around the edge of it.

circus
NOUN circuses
A circus is a show with clowns, jugglers, acrobats, and sometimes animals. It travels around the country and is performed in a very big tent.

citizen
NOUN citizens
A citizen is someone who lives in a country, city, or town.

city
NOUN cities
A city is a very large town.

clap
VERB claps, clapping, clapped
When people clap, they hit their hands together to make a loud sound. It can show that they like someone's acting or singing.

class
NOUN classes
A class is a group of people who learn something together. *There are 32 people in my* ***class****.*

classroom
NOUN classrooms
A classroom is a room in which you have lessons.

clause
NOUN clauses
A clause is a group of words that contains a verb and is one part of a sentence. *For example, there are two clauses in the sentence: We were happy because we won the game.*

claw
NOUN claws
An animal's claws are its long, curved, pointed nails.

clay
NOUN
Clay is a type of earth that is used to make pots and bricks. It is made into the right shape by a potter when it is wet, then it is baked in a hot oven called a kiln until it is hard.

clean
VERB cleans, cleaning, cleaned
1 If you clean something, you remove dirt from it. *Your shoes are dirty – you need to* ***clean*** *them.*
ADJECTIVE cleaner, cleanest
2 Something that is clean has no dirt on it.

clear
ADJECTIVE clearer, clearest
1 Something that is clear is easy to see through. *The water was so* ***clear*** *that I could see the fish.*
2 If something is clear, it is easy to see, hear, or understand. *You must all get on with your work now. Is that* ***clear****?*
3 If a place is clear, you can move through it easily. *The road is* ***clear*** *now.*
VERB clears, clearing, cleared
4 If you clear something, you remove everything from it. *Will you help me* ***clear*** *the table?*

clever
ADJECTIVE cleverer, cleverest
Someone who is clever can learn and understand things quickly.

click
VERB clicks, clicking, clicked
When you click on something on a computer, you choose it by pressing the mouse once or twice.

cliff
NOUN cliffs
A cliff is a high, steep side of a mountain.

climate
NOUN climates
The climate in a place is the type of weather that it usually has.

a b Cc d e f g h i j k l m n o p q r s t u v w x y z

climb
VERB climbs, climbing, climbed
When you climb, you move upward, using your hands and feet. *He managed to **climb** over the wall.*

cling
VERB clings, clinging, clung
If you cling onto something, you hold onto it very tightly. *We **clung** on tight as the roller coaster set off.*

clip
NOUN clips
1 A clip is a fastener that you use for holding something in place.
2 A clip is a small part of a film.

cloak
NOUN cloaks
A cloak is a piece of outer clothing that you wrap around you and fasten around your neck.

clock
NOUN clocks
A clock is an instrument that shows the time.

clockwise
ADVERB
If something moves clockwise, it moves in a circle in the same direction as the hands on a clock.
☛ **Opposite:** anticlockwise

close
VERB closes, closing, closed
1 When you close something, you shut it.
ADJECTIVE
2 Something that is close to a place is near to it. *My house is **close** to the river.*

cloth
NOUN cloths
1 Cloth is material that is used to make clothes and other things.
2 A cloth is a piece of material that you use for cleaning things.

clothes
NOUN
Clothes are the things that you wear on your body.

cloud
NOUN clouds
1 A cloud is a mass of tiny drops of water, or pieces of ice, floating high in the air.
2 The cloud is a part of the internet where you can store your documents and photographs.
cloudy (ADJECTIVE)
When it is cloudy, there are a lot of clouds in the sky.

clown
NOUN clowns
A clown performs in a circus. Clowns make people laugh.

The clock's hands move in a *clockwise* direction.

club
NOUN clubs
A club is a group of people who meet because they are interested in the same thing. *We have a drama **club** at our school.*

clue
NOUN clues
A clue is a piece of information that helps to solve a mystery.

clumsy
ADJECTIVE clumsier, clumsiest
If you are clumsy, you move in a rough, careless way, so you are likely to knock things over or damage them.

clung
☛ See **cling**.

coach
NOUN coaches
1 A coach is a bus that takes people on long journeys.
2 A coach is a person who teaches people how to play a sport.

coal
NOUN
Coal is a hard, black rock that is burned as a fuel. Coal is made from fossilized plants that died millions of years ago.

coast
NOUN coasts
The coast is the part of the land where it meets the sea.

coat
NOUN coats
1 A coat is a piece of clothing you wear over your other clothes to keep you warm when you are outside.
2 An animal's coat is its fur. *Polar bears have a very thick **coat**.*
3 A coat of paint on the wall or doors is a layer of paint. Sometimes, a few coats of paint are needed to paint something well.

cobweb
NOUN cobwebs
A cobweb is a very fine, sticky net that is made by spiders to trap flies and other small insects.

cocoa
NOUN
Cocoa is a brown powder that is made from the seeds of the cacao tree and is used to make chocolate cakes and biscuits, and hot chocolate.

code
NOUN codes
1 A code is a set of signs, symbols, or letters for sending secret messages.
2 Code is the instructions for computer programs.
VERB codes, coding, coded
When you code, you write instructions for computer programs.

coffee
NOUN coffees
Coffee is a hot drink that you make by adding hot water to powder made from roasted coffee beans.

coin
NOUN coins
A coin is a piece of money made of metal.

cold
NOUN colds
1 A cold is an illness that makes you sneeze and cough. *I've had this horrible **cold** for five days now!*
ADJECTIVE colder, coldest
2 Something that is cold is not warm or hot. *It's too **cold** to play outside.*

collage
NOUN collages
A collage is a picture that you make by sticking pieces of paper or cloth onto paper or card.

collar
NOUN collars
1 The collar of a shirt or jacket is the part that goes around your neck.
2 A collar is a thin strip of leather that you put around the neck of a dog or cat.

collect
VERB collects, collecting, collected
1 If you collect things, you get as many of them as you can and put them together.
2 If you collect something, you go and fetch it.
collection (NOUN)
A collection is a group of things you have collected together. *The museum has got an amazing **collection** of fossils.*

colour
NOUN colours
Red, yellow, and blue are the names of some colours.
colourful (ADJECTIVE)
Something that is colourful is decorated with bright colours. *I like wearing **colourful** clothes.*

column
NOUN columns
1 A column is a tall, round post that supports a building.
2 A column is a list of words or numbers that are written underneath each other.

comb
NOUN combs
A comb is a piece of plastic or metal with teeth, that you use to make your hair look neat.

combine
VERB combines, combining, combined
When you combine things, you mix or join them together.
combination (NOUN)
A combination is a set of things that have been mixed or joined together.

come
VERB comes, coming, come, came
1 When you come to a place, you arrive there. *Hurry up! The train is **coming**.*
2 If you ask someone to come with you, you are asking them to go with you to a place. *Do you want to **come** to the cinema?*

comedy
NOUN comedies
A comedy is a film, play, or television show that makes you laugh.
comedian (NOUN)
A comedian is someone who says or does funny things.

comet
NOUN comets
A comet is a huge ball of dust, ice, and gases that travels around the sun and looks like a bright star with a long tail behind it.

comet

a b Cc d e f g h i j k l m n o p q r s t u v w x y z

comfortable
ADJECTIVE
Something that is comfortable is pleasant to sit in, lie on, or wear. *What a lovely **comfortable** bed!*
☛ **Opposite:** uncomfortable

comma
NOUN commas
A comma is the punctuation mark (,) that you use to divide different parts of the same sentence.

command
VERB commands, commanding, commanded
1 If you command someone to do something, you tell them to do it. *"Stay away!" he **commanded**.*
NOUN commands
2 A command is a sentence in which you tell someone to do something.

comment
NOUN comments
A comment is something that you say about a person or thing.

common
ADJECTIVE
If something is common, you see it quite often.

communicate
VERB communicates, communicating, communicated
When people or animals communicate, they talk to each other to exchange ideas. Or, they give information to each other in another way, such as by moving their hands or writing.

company
NOUN companies
1 A company is a group of people who work together to make or sell something. *My aunt works for a computer **company**.*
2 If you enjoy someone's company, you enjoy being with them.

compare
VERB compares, comparing, compared
If you compare two things, you look at them to see how they are similar and how they are different.
comparison (NOUN)
If you make a comparison between two things, you compare them.

compass
NOUN compasses
1 A compass is an instrument that shows the direction you are facing. The magnetic needle on a compass always points north.
2 A compass is a tool that you use for drawing circles.

compatible
ADJECTIVE
1 If people are compatible, they get on well together.
2 If machines are compatible, they can be used together.

competition
NOUN competitions
A competition is an event where people race against each other or play games to see who is the best. *Our team came second in the swimming **competition**.*

complain
VERB complains, complaining, complained
If you complain, you say that you are not happy about something. *Everyone **complained** because the bus was late.*
complaint (NOUN)
If you make a complaint, you complain about something.

complete
VERB completes, completing, completed
1 If you complete something, you finish it.
ADJECTIVE
2 Something that is complete is finished and contains all the parts.

*Have you **completed** the jigsaw?*

complicated
ADJECTIVE
Something that is complicated has a lot of different parts and is very difficult to do or understand. *The story in the film is very **complicated**.*

compose
VERB composes, composing, composed
If you compose music, you write it.
composer (NOUN)
A composer is someone who writes music.

computer
NOUN computers
A computer is an electronic machine that can receive and store information. Computers can do calculations, and you can also play games on them.

concentrate
VERB concentrates, concentrating, concentrated
When you concentrate, you think carefully about what you are doing.
concentration (NOUN)
Concentration is when you concentrate. *You need a lot of* ***concentration*** *to do maths.*

concert
NOUN concerts
A concert is an event where people sing or play music for an audience to listen to.

concrete
NOUN
Concrete is a mixture of cement, stones, and water. It is hard like rock and used for building.

condition
NOUN
The condition that something is in is the state it is in. *My bike is quite old, but it's still in good* ***condition****.*

conduct
VERB conducts, conducting, conducted
1 When you conduct music or singing, you stand in front of musicians or singers and control the way that they play or sing.
2 If something conducts heat or electricity, it allows heat or electricity to pass through it. *The metal copper* ***conducts*** *electricity well.*

confess
VERB confesses, confessing, confessed
If you confess, you admit that you have done something wrong.

confident
ADJECTIVE
If you are confident, you believe that you can do something well. *Be* ***confident*** *– I'm sure you can win!*
confidence (NOUN)
Confidence is the feeling you have when you are confident. *You need a lot of* ***confidence*** *to go up on stage and sing.*

confused
ADJECTIVE
If you are confused, you do not understand what is going on. *I was a bit* ***confused*** *by the story in the film.*

conjunction
NOUN conjunctions
A conjunction is a word that joins different parts of a sentence together. Conjunctions are also called **connectives**. Examples of conjunctions are "and", "but", "so", and "because".

connect
VERB connects, connecting, connected
If you connect things, you join them together.

conscious
ADJECTIVE
If you are conscious, you are awake and aware of what is happening around you.
☛ **Opposite:** unconscious

consequence
NOUN consequences
A consequence is something that happens as a result of something else.

conservation
NOUN
Conservation is protecting animals, plants, and the environment.

consider
VERB considers, considering, considered
If you consider something, you think about it carefully. *I'm* ***considering*** *applying to be on a television show.*

considerate
ADJECTIVE
Someone who is considerate thinks about other people and does not do things that will annoy or upset other people.
☛ **Opposite:** inconsiderate

consonant
NOUN consonants
A consonant is any letter of the alphabet that is not a vowel. Examples of consonants are b, f, m, s, and w.

a b Cc d e f g h i j k l m n o p q r s t u v w x y z

constellation
NOUN constellations
A constellation is a group of stars.

construct
VERB constructs, constructing, constructed
If you construct something, you build it.
construction (NOUN)
A construction is something that someone has built.

consume
VERB consumes, consuming, consumed
If you consume something, you eat or drink it, or use it. *Big car engines **consumes** a lot of fuel.*

contain
VERB contains, containing, contained
If a box or bag contains things, it has those things inside it. *The box **contained** some amazing-looking sweets.*

container
NOUN containers
A container is anything that you can put or keep things in.

content
ADJECTIVE
If you are content, you feel happy and satisfied. You can also say that you are **contented**.

contents
NOUN
The contents of a box, bag, or other container are the things that are inside it.

continent
NOUN continents
A continent is one of seven very large areas of land that make up the world. Most continents include several different countries. *Africa and Europe are **continents**.*

continue
VERB continues, continuing, continued
If you continue to do something, you keep on doing it. *We **continued** to play even when it started raining.*

construct

*A crane lifts blocks to **construct** a building.*

control
VERB controls, controlling, controlled
1 When you control something, you make it go where you want it to go or do what you want it to do.
NOUN controls
2 Controls are the buttons and knobs that make a machine work. *Pass me the **controls** – it's my turn to play the game!*

conversation
NOUN conversations
A conversation is a talk between two or more people.

convince
VERB convinces, convincing, convinced
If you convince someone, you persuade them to believe something. *He **convinced** me that it was real gold.*

cook
VERB cooks, cooking, cooked
1 When you cook food, you prepare it and heat it so that you can eat it.
NOUN cooks
2 A cook is someone who prepares and cooks food.

cool
ADJECTIVE cooler, coolest
1 Something that is cool is slightly cold. *Put the drinks in the fridge to keep them **cool**.*
2 Something that is cool is good or nice.

copper
NOUN
Copper is a shiny reddish brown metal.

copy
NOUN copies
1 A copy is something that has been made to look exactly like something else.
VERB copies, copying, copied
2 If you copy something, you make another one that is the same. *Can you **copy** this drawing?*
3 If you copy someone, you do the same as them.

coral
NOUN corals
Coral is a hard substance that is made of the skeletons of small sea animals. Coral is mainly found in warm seas.

core
NOUN cores
The core of something is the middle part of it.

cork
NOUN
A cork is a small object that is used to fill the top of a wine bottle.

corn
NOUN
Corn is a general name for the seeds of plants such as wheat, oats, or sweetcorn.

corner
NOUN corners
A corner is a point where two lines or edges meet, or the point where two roads meet.

correct
VERB corrects, correcting, corrected
1 If you correct your work, you find the mistakes and put them right. *I **corrected** all the spelling mistakes in my homework.*
2 Something that is correct is right and has no mistakes.
☛ **Opposite:** incorrect
correction (NOUN)
A correction is a change that you make to something so that it is correct.
correctly (ADVERB)
If you do something correctly, you do it right, without mistakes.

corridor
NOUN corridors
A corridor is a passage inside a building that leads to other rooms.

cost
NOUN
1 The cost of something is the amount you have to pay for it.
VERB costs, costing, cost
2 The amount that something costs is the amount that you have to pay for it. *This game **costs** a lot of money.*

costume
NOUN costumes
1 A costume is a set of clothes that you wear when you are dressing up in a play.
2 The costume of a time in history is the type of clothes that people wore then.

cosy
ADJECTIVE cosier, cosiest
A place that is cosy is warm and comfortable.

cot
NOUN cots
A cot is a bed with high sides that a baby sleeps in.

cottage
NOUN cottages
A cottage is a small house in the country.

cotton
NOUN
1 Cotton is a type of cloth that is used for making clothes. *My shirt is made of **cotton**.*
2 Cotton is thread that you use for sewing.

cough
VERB coughs, coughing, coughed
When you cough, you push air out of your lungs with a sharp noise.

could
☛ See **can**.

count
VERB counts, counting, counted
1 When you count, you say numbers in the right order. *Can you **count** to 100?*
2 When you count things, you say how many there are. *I **counted** five horses in the field.*

*A clown wears a **costume** and make-up.*
costume

a b Cc d e f g h i j k l m n o p q r s t u v w x y z

counter
NOUN counters
1 A shop counter is the table where you pay for things.
2 A counter is a small, round object that you move around on a board when you are playing a game.

country
NOUN countries
1 A country is an area of land with its own borders, people, and laws.
2 The country is the land outside towns and cities. This is also called the **countryside**.

couple
NOUN couples
1 A couple of things or people means two of them. *I hope you are better in a **couple** of days.*
2 A couple is two people who are married or going out with each other.

courage
NOUN
Courage is being brave when you are in danger. *You need a lot of **courage** to stand up to bullies.*
courageous (ADJECTIVE)
Someone who is courageous is brave.

course
NOUN courses
1 A course is a set of lessons. *I did a drama **course** last summer.*
2 One course of a meal is one part of it. *We had chicken for the main **course**.*
3 A course is an area on which some sports or games are played. *We played on the golf **course**.*

court
NOUN courts
1 A court is a place where judges and other people decide whether someone has done something wrong, and how they should be punished.
2 A court is a piece of ground with lines marked on it where some games are played. *We play tennis on the tennis **court**.*

cousin
NOUN cousins
Your cousin is related to you because their mother or father is the sister or brother of one of your parents.

cover
NOUN covers
1 A cover is a piece of material that you put over something to protect it.
VERB covers, covering, covered
2 When you cover something, you put something over it. *I **covered** the cake with a thick layer of icing.*
☛ **Opposite:** uncover

cow
NOUN cows
A cow is a female animal that eats grass and is kept on a farm to produce milk and beef. A female elephant or whale is also called a cow.

coward
NOUN cowards
A coward is a person who is scared easily.
cowardly (ADJECTIVE)
Someone who is cowardly behaves like a coward.

cowboy
NOUN cowboys
A cowboy is a man who looks after cattle (cows and bulls) on farms in the USA.

crab
NOUN crabs
A crab is a shellfish with a hard covering over its body. Crabs have ten legs, and the front pair of legs end in claws, which the crab uses to catch its prey. *We saw a big **crab** in the rockpool.*

crack
NOUN cracks
1 A crack is a line or split on the surface of something where it has broken.
2 A crack is a sudden loud noise. *We heard a **crack** of thunder.*
VERB cracks, cracking, cracked
3 If you crack something, you break it so that the surface is split but it does not fall to pieces. *I **dropped** my glasses and cracked them.*

cracker
NOUN crackers
1 A cracker is a thin, dry biscuit that you eat with cheese.
2 A cracker is a paper tube that contains a small present. Two people pull the tube until it comes apart, and one of them wins the present.

cradle
NOUN cradle
A cradle is a baby's bed that can swing from side to side.

Crabs live by the seashore.

craft
NOUN crafts
1 A craft is an activity in which you make something. *They enjoyed seeing all the arts and* ***crafts*** *at the show.*
2 A craft is a boat, aeroplane, or spaceship.

cramp
NOUN
When you get cramp, your muscles hurt because you have done too much exercise.

crane
NOUN cranes
A crane is a large machine that lifts heavy objects.

crash
NOUN crashes
1 A crash is an accident in which cars or other vehicles bang into each other.
2 A crash is a loud noise.
VERB crashes, crashing, crashed
3 When cars crash, they bang into each other.
4 When a computer crashes, it stops working.

crawl
VERB crawls, crawling, crawled
When you crawl, you move along on your hands and knees. *I* ***crawled*** *under the table to look for my pen.*

crayon
NOUN crayons
A crayon is a coloured pencil or stick of wax that you use for drawing.

crazy
ADJECTIVE crazier, craziest
Someone who is crazy is very silly or strange. *He's so* ***crazy*** *– he's the funniest person I know!*

creak
VERB creaks, creaking, creaked
If something creaks, it makes a low, squeaking sound. *The barn door* ***creaked*** *as I opened it.*

cream
NOUN
1 Cream is a thick, white liquid that you often eat with sweet foods. Cream is the part of milk that contains a lot of fat and rises to the top of the milk.
2 Cream is a substance that you put on your skin. It keeps your skin feeling soft and comfortable.

create
VERB creates, creating, created
When you create something new, you design it and make it. *How do people* ***create*** *new computer games?*

creature
NOUN creatures
A creature is any animal, bird, fish, or insect.

creep
VERB creeps, creeping, crept
When you creep along, you walk very slowly and quietly. *I* ***crept*** *downstairs while everyone was asleep.*

creepy
ADJECTIVE creepier, creepiest
Something that is creepy is slightly frightening.

crew
NOUN crews
A crew is a team of people who work together.

cricket
NOUN crickets
1 A cricket is an insect with long legs that can jump high.
2 Cricket is a game in which teams have to hit a ball with a bat and then run between two sets of sticks called wickets to score runs.

crime
NOUN crimes
A crime in a bad act that is against the law. *Stealing is a* ***crime****.*
criminal (NOUN)
A criminal is someone who has broken the law.

a b Cc d e f g h i j k l m n o p q r s t u v w x y z

crisp

NOUN crisps

1 Crisps are thin, crunchy pieces of fried potato.

ADJECTIVE crisper, crispest

2 Food that is crisp is firm. *Bake the biscuits until they are nice and* ***crisp****.*

criticize

VERB criticizes, criticizing, criticized

If you criticize someone, you tell them that they have done something wrong.

crocodile

NOUN crocodiles

A crocodile is a reptile that lives on land and in water. Crocodiles are fierce and hunt at night for fish and small animals.

crooked

ADJECTIVE

Something that is crooked is not straight.

cross

VERB crosses, crossing, crossed

1 If you cross a road or river, you go across to the other side.

2 If you cross your legs or fingers, you put one over the other.

NOUN crosses

3 A cross is a mark or an object like "+" or "x".

ADJECTIVE

4 If you are cross, you are angry.

crossing

NOUN crossings

A crossing is a place where you can cross the road safely.

crossroads

NOUN

A crossroads is a place where two roads cross each other.

crossword

NOUN crosswords

A crossword is a word puzzle with clues. The words cross over each other on a square grid.

crowd

NOUN crowds

A crowd is a large number of people all together in one place.

crown

NOUN crowns

A crown is a circle of gold or silver with jewels. Kings and queens wear crowns on their heads on special occasions.

cruel

ADJECTIVE

Someone who is cruel is unkind and often hurts other people or animals.

cruise

NOUN cruises

A cruise is a holiday on a ship that sails to several places.

crocodile

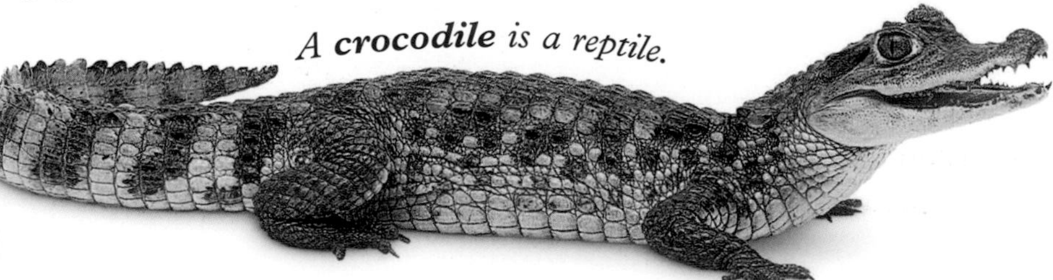

A ***crocodile*** *is a reptile.*

crumb

NOUN crumbs

A crumb is a very small piece of bread, cake, or biscuit.

crunch

VERB crunches, crunching, crunched

When you crunch food, you bite it or chew it noisily.

crush

VERB crushes, crushing, crushed

If you crush something, you squeeze it very hard. *Don't walk on the flowers – you'll* ***crush*** *them!*

crust

NOUN crusts

1 The crust is the hard part on the outside of bread.

2 The Earth's crust is its outer layer of hard rock.

cry

VERB cries, crying, cried

1 If you are upset, you cry, and tears come out of your eyes.

2 When you cry, you shout loudly. *"Help me!" he* ***cried****.*

cub

NOUN cubs

A cub is a young animal, such as a fox, lion, or bear.

cube

NOUN cubes

A cube is a solid shape with six square sides.

cuddle

VERB cuddles, cuddling, cuddled

When you cuddle someone, you hold them in a loving way.

culture
NOUN cultures
People's culture is all their traditions and customs.

cunning
ADJECTIVE
Someone who is cunning is clever at tricking people.

cup
NOUN cups
A cup is a container with a handle that you use for drinking from.

cupboard
NOUN cupboards
A cupboard is a piece of furniture with a door at the front that you use for keeping things in.

cure
VERB cures, curing, cured
1 If doctors cure someone, they make them better again after they have been ill.
NOUN cures
2 A cure is a medicine or treatment that makes someone better after they have been ill.

curious
ADJECTIVE
1 If you are curious, you want to find out about something. *I was **curious** to see what was behind the door.*
2 Something that is curious is strange but interesting. *We saw some very **curious** fish at the aquarium.*
curiosity (NOUN)
Curiosity is the feeling that you want to find out about something. *My **curiosity** got the better of me, and I looked inside the box.*

curly
ADJECTIVE
Curly hair is curved, not straight.

curry
NOUN curries
A curry is made from meat or vegetables cooked in a hot, spicy sauce.

cursor
NOUN cursors
The cursor on a computer screen is the small mark that shows your position when you click with your mouse.

curtain
NOUN curtains
A curtain is one or two pieces of cloth that you can pull across a window to keep out the light or to cut out draughts.

curve
NOUN curves
A curve is a line that bends smoothly round.
curved (ADJECTIVE)
Something that is curved is in the shape of a curve.

cushion
NOUN cushions
A cushion is a type of pillow that you put on a chair to lean against.

custom
NOUN customs
A custom is something that people have done in the same way for a long time.

customer
NOUN customers
A customer is someone who buys something from a shop.

cut
NOUN cuts
1 A cut is a wound on your body that was made by something sharp.
VERB cuts, cutting, cut
2 When you cut something, you divide it into pieces, using scissors or a knife. *Shall I **cut** a slice of cake for you?*
3 When you cut something on the computer, you delete it.

cute
ADJECTIVE cuter, cutest
Something that is cute is pretty and nice. *What a **cute** kitten!*

cutlery
NOUN
Cutlery is the knives, forks, and spoons that you use for eating.

cycle
VERB cycles, cycling, cycled
When you cycle, you ride a bicycle.
cyclist (NOUN)
A cyclist is someone who rides a bicycle.

cyclone
NOUN cyclones
A cyclone is a tropical storm with very strong winds.

cylinder
NOUN cylinders
A cylinder is a solid or hollow object that looks like a tube, with circular ends and straight sides.

cymbal
NOUN cymbals
Cymbals are round pieces of metal that you bang together as a musical instrument.

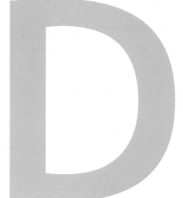

daffodil
NOUN daffodils
A daffodil is a yellow, trumpet-shaped flower that you see in the spring.

dagger
NOUN daggers
A dagger is a short knife that people use as a weapon.

daily
ADVERB
Something that happens daily happens every day.

dairy
NOUN dairies
A dairy is a place where milk is stored and butter, cheese, and yoghurt are made. **Dairy products** are foods containing milk, such as butter and yoghurt.

daisy
NOUN daisies
A daisy is a small white or pink flower with a yellow centre.

dam
NOUN dams
A dam is a wall that is built across a river to hold it back.

damage
VERB damages, damaging, damaged
If you damage something, you harm it. *Carry the painting carefully so you don't **damage** it.*

damp
ADJECTIVE damper, dampest
Something that is damp is slightly wet. *Don't sit on the grass – it's **damp**.*

dance
VERB dances, dancing, danced
When you dance, you move around to music.

dandelion
NOUN dandelions
A dandelion is a common, yellow wild flower that produces seeds in a fluffy ball.

dandelion flower

danger
NOUN dangers
If there is danger, there is something that might hurt you. ***Danger** – deep water!*
dangerous (ADJECTIVE)
If something is dangerous, it could hurt you. *Rock climbing is a **dangerous** sport.*

dare
VERB dares, daring, dared
1 If you dare someone to do something frightening, you tell them that they should do it to show they are not afraid. *I **dare** you to jump off that wall.*
2 If you dare to do something frightening, you are brave enough to do it. *I wouldn't **dare** to be cheeky to a teacher!*
daring (ADJECTIVE)
Someone who is daring is brave enough to do frightening or dangerous things.

dark
ADJECTIVE darker, darkest
1 When it is dark, there is no light.
2 A dark colour has a lot of black in it. *He was wearing a **dark** blue jumper.*
darkness (NOUN)
Darkness is when there is no light. *She looked out into the **darkness** outside.*

dandelion seeds

dart
NOUN darts
A dart is a small arrow that you throw at a board in the game of darts.

dash
VERB dashes, dashing, dashed
If you dash somewhere, you run there quickly. *He **dashed** upstairs.*

data
NOUN
Information and facts about something are called data.

database
NOUN databases
A database is a collection of information that is stored on a computer.

date
NOUN dates
1 The date is a particular day of the year. *The **date** today is 3rd May.*
2 A date is a sweet, sticky fruit with a stone in the middle.

daughter
NOUN daughters
Someone's daughter is their female child.

seeds blowing

dawn
NOUN
Dawn is the early part of the day when it starts to become light. *We set off at **dawn**.*

day
NOUN days
1 Day is the time when it is light.
2 A day is a period of 24 hours. *It's my birthday in five **days**!*

dazed
ADJECTIVE
If you are dazed, you feel shocked and you cannot think clearly.

dazzle
VERB dazzles, dazzling, dazzled
If a bright light dazzles you, it shines into your eyes so that you cannot see.

dead
ADJECTIVE
Someone who is dead is no longer living.

deadly
ADJECTIVE
Something that is deadly can kill you.

deaf
ADJECTIVE
Someone who is deaf cannot hear.

deal
VERB deals, dealing, dealt
1 When you deal cards, you give some to each person in a game.
2 When you deal with something, you do the things that need to be done to sort it out. *Who is going to **deal** with all this mess?*

dear
ADJECTIVE dearer, dearest
1 You write "Dear ..." at the beginning of a letter.
2 A dear person is someone you love very much. *She has been a very **dear** friend to me.*
3 Something that is dear costs a lot of money.
☛ **Be careful with spelling:**
dear *__Dear__ Grandma, I hope you are well.*
deer *Lots of **deer** live in the forest.*

death
NOUN deaths
Death is when someone dies.

debt
NOUN debts
A debt is an amount of money that you owe to someone.

decade
NOUN decades
A decade is a period of ten years.

deceive
VERB deceives, deceiving, deceived
If you deceive someone, you make them believe something that is not true.

dawn

***Dawn** is the start of a new day.*

a b c Dd e f g h i j k l m n o p q r s t u v w x y z

decide
VERB decides, deciding, decided
If you decide to do something, you make up your mind to do it. *We **decided** to go to the beach for the day.*

decimal
NOUN decimals
1 A decimal system is one that counts in tens.
2 A decimal is a number written with a dot, for example 1.5. *How can you write ½ as a **decimal**?*

decision
NOUN decisions
A decision is something that you decide to do. *Have you made a **decision** yet?*

deck
NOUN decks
The deck on a ship is one of the floors.

declare
VERB declares, declaring, declared
If you declare something, you say it out loud for everyone to hear. *I **declare** you are the winner!*

decorate
VERB decorates, decorating, decorated
If you decorate something, you paint it or put things on it to make it look nice. *We **decorated** the school hall for the party.*
decoration (NOUN)
Decorations are things you put up in a place to make it look nice.

decorate

*People like to **decorate** their houses.*

decrease
VERB decreases, decreasing, decreased
When something decreases, it becomes less. *The temperature usually **decreases** at night.*
☛ **Opposite:** increase

deep
ADJECTIVE deeper, deepest
Something that is deep goes down a long way. *The river is too **deep** to wade across.*

deer
NOUN
A deer is an animal with hooves that eats grass and leaves. A male deer is called a stag and has large, branching horns called antlers. A female deer is called a doe.
☛ **Be careful with spelling:**
deer *Lots of **deer** live in the forest.*
dear ***Dear** Grandma, I hope you are well.*

defeat
VERB defeats, defeating, defeated
If you defeat someone, you win a game or a battle against them.

defend
VERB defends, defending, defended
If you defend something, you protect it or guard it. *They sent soldiers to **defend** the city.*

definitely
ADVERB
If something is definitely true, it is certain that it is true. *I can **definitely** come to your party on Saturday.*

definition
NOUN definitions
A definition is a sentence that explains what a word means.

degree
NOUN degrees
We measure the temperature in degrees. We use the symbol ° to show degrees, for example 29°.

delay
VERB delays, delaying, delayed
If something is delayed, it happens or arrives later than you expected. *The bus was **delayed** because of the snow.*

delete
VERB deletes, deleting, deleted
If you delete writing, you remove it.

deliberate
ADJECTIVE
If something is deliberate, someone does it on purpose.
deliberately (ADVERB)
If you do something deliberately, you do it on purpose. *I didn't break the window **deliberately** – it was an accident!*

delicate
ADJECTIVE
If something is delicate, it is not very strong and will break easily.

delicious
ADJECTIVE
Food that is delicious tastes very nice. *There were lots of* ***delicious*** *cakes to choose from.*

delighted
ADJECTIVE
If you are delighted, you are very pleased. *We were* ***delighted*** *when we beat the other team and won the trophy.*

deliver
VERB delivers, delivering, delivered
If you deliver something to someone, you take it to them.

demand
VERB demands, demanding, demanded
If you demand something, you ask for it very firmly. *He* ***demanded*** *his phone back.*

democracy
NOUN democracies
A democracy is a country in which everyone votes to choose the government.
democratic (ADJECTIVE)
A democratic country is one in which everyone votes to choose the government.

den
NOUN dens
1 A den is a secret place where you can play or hide.
2 An animal's den is its home.

denim
NOUN
Denim is a type of strong cloth that is used for making jeans and other clothes.

dense
ADJECTIVE
Something that is dense is very thick and difficult to see through. *We couldn't see because of the* ***dense*** *fog.*

density
NOUN
The density of an object is how heavy it is in relation to its size.

dent
NOUN dents
A dent is a hollow place in the surface of something after someone has hit it or pressed it.

dentist
NOUN dentists
A dentist is a person who examines and makes repairs to your teeth.

deny
VERB denies, denying, denied
If you deny something, you say that you did not do it. *She* ***denied*** *breaking the window.*

depend
VERB depends, depending, depended
If you depend on someone, you need them to help you or look after you.

depressed
ADJECTIVE
If you feel depressed, you feel very unhappy.

depth
NOUN
The depth of something is how deep it is.

describe
VERB describes, describing, described
When you describe something, you say what it is like. *Can you* ***describe*** *the man that you saw?*
description (NOUN)
If you give a description of something, you describe it.

desert
NOUN deserts
A desert is a large area of dry, sandy, or stony land where there are very few plants.
☛ **Be careful with spelling:**
desert *Africa's largest* ***desert*** *is the Sahara.*
dessert *We had ice cream for* ***dessert****.*

deserve
VERB deserves, deserving, deserved
If you deserve something, it is fair that you should have it because of something that you have done. *I think you* ***deserve*** *a prize for trying so hard.*

design
VERB designs, designing, designed
When you design something, you draw it and plan what it will be like. *We're trying to* ***design*** *a new play area.*
designer (NOUN)
A designer is someone who designs things.

design

a b c **Dd** e f g h i j k l m n o p q r s t u v w

desk
NOUN desks
A desk is a table that you use for working on.

dessert
NOUN desserts
A dessert is a sweet dish that you eat at the end of a meal.
☛ **Be careful with spelling:**
dessert *We had ice cream for **dessert**.*
desert *Africa's largest **desert** is the Sahara.*

destroy
VERB destroys, destroying, destroyed
To destroy something means to damage it so badly that it cannot be used again. *The fire completely **destroyed** the shed.*

detail
NOUN details
A detail is one small part of something. *I can't remember all the **details** of the story that I read last week.*

detective
NOUN detectives
A detective is someone who tries to find out who committed a crime by looking at all the clues.

determined
ADJECTIVE
If you are determined to do something, you feel very strongly that you want to do it and nothing will stop you. *We're **determined** to win this match!*

detest
VERB detests, detesting, detested
If you detest something, you hate it.

develop
VERB develops, developing, developed
When something develops, it grows and changes. *Tadpoles gradually **develop** into frogs.*

device
NOUN devices
A device is a small machine or tool.

dew
NOUN
Dew is small drops of water that form on the ground at night.

diagonal
ADJECTIVE
A diagonal line goes across something from one corner to the opposite corner.

diagram
NOUN diagrams
A diagram is a drawing that shows what something looks like or how it works.

dial
NOUN dials
A dial is a circle with numbers round it.

diameter
NOUN diameters
The diameter of a circle is a straight line connecting the centre of a circle with two points on its perimeter.

diamond
NOUN diamonds
A diamond is a jewel that looks like shiny glass.

diary
NOUN diaries
A diary is a book in which you write down the things that you do and how you feel each day.
A **video diary** is a film in which you record your diary.

*He rolled the **dice**.*

dice
NOUN
A dice is a small cube that has a different number of spots on each side. You roll a dice in some games to see how far forward you should move.

dictionary
NOUN dictionaries
A dictionary is a book that explains what words mean and shows how they are spelt.

die
VERB dies, dying, died
When a living thing dies, it is no longer alive. *The plant **died** because we kept forgetting to water it.*

diesel
NOUN
Diesel is a kind of fuel that is used in lorries and some cars.

diet
NOUN diets
1 Your diet is all the different kinds of food that you eat. *You should try to eat a healthy **diet**.*
2 If you are on a diet, you eat less food because you want to lose weight.

different
ADJECTIVE
Things that are different are not the same.
difference (NOUN)
A difference between two things is a way in which they are different. *What's the **difference** between an alligator and a crocodile?*

difficult
ADJECTIVE
Something that is difficult is hard to do. *That test was really **difficult**!*
difficulty (NOUN)
A difficulty is something that is difficult. *I had a few **difficulties** with my maths homework.*

dig
VERB digs, digging, dug
When you dig, you make a hole in the ground.

digest
VERB digests, digesting, digested
When you digest food, your stomach breaks it down so that your body can use it to give you energy.

digit
NOUN digits
A digit is a number from 0 to 9. Bigger numbers are made up of more than one digit. For example, 275 is a three-digit number.

digital
ADJECTIVE
1 A digital device uses a special kind of technology to work. *This is the latest kind of **digital** TV.*
2 A digital watch or clock shows the time as numbers such as 8:30, rather than on a dial.

dilute
VERB dilutes, diluting, diluted
If you dilute a liquid, you add water to make it weaker. *The orange juice was too strong, so she **diluted** it with water.*

dim
ADJECTIVE dimmer, dimmest
A dim light is not very bright. *A single **dim** light bulb lit the room.*

dinghy
NOUN dinghies
A dinghy is a small sailing boat.

dining room
NOUN dining rooms
A dining room is a room in which you eat meals.

dinner
NOUN dinners
Dinner is the main meal of the day.

dinosaur
NOUN dinosaurs
Dinosaurs were reptiles that lived on Earth for more than 150 million years. The last dinosaurs died out 65 million years ago.

dinosaur

Tyrannosaurus rex
Say: tie-ran-oh-saw-rus reks

Triceratops
Say: try-ser-a-tops

Euoplocephalus
Say: yoo-oh-plo-sef-al-us

Deinonychus
Say: die-no-nike-us

Corythosaurus
Say: kor-ith-oh-saw-rus

a b c Dd e f g h i j k l m n o p q r s t u v w x y z

dip
VERB dips, dipping, dipped
If you dip something into a liquid, you put it in and then take it out again. *I **dipped** the strawberry into the chocolate sauce and then ate it.*

direct
VERB directs, directing, directed
1 If you direct someone to a place, you tell them how to get there. *Can you **direct** me to the sports centre, please?*
2 The person who directs a film or play is in charge of it and tells other people what they should do and how they should act.
ADJECTIVE
3 A direct way to a place is short and quick. *We got a **direct** flight to New York.*
director (NOUN)
A director is someone who directs a film.

direction
NOUN directions
The direction you are moving in is the way you are going or the place you are travelling toward. *We set off in the **direction** of the beach.*

dirty
ADJECTIVE dirtier, dirtiest
Something that is dirty is not clean. *Can you please take off your **dirty** football boots?*

disabled
ADJECTIVE
Someone who is disabled cannot use a part of their body very well because it is weak or injured.
disability (NOUN)
Someone who has a disability is disabled.

disagree
VERB disagrees, disagreeing, disagreed
If you disagree with someone, you have different ideas to them and you think they are wrong.
☛ **Opposite:** agree

disappear
VERB disappears, disappearing, disappeared
If something disappears, it goes out of sight. *The Sun **disappeared** behind a cloud.*
☛ **Opposite:** appear

disappointed
ADJECTIVE
If you are disappointed, you are sad or upset because something did not happen the way you wanted it to happen. *We were **disappointed** with the weather.*

disaster
NOUN disasters
A disaster is a terrible event in which people are injured or killed and things are damaged.

discover
VERB discovers, discovering, discovered
If you discover something, you find it or learn about it. *We **discovered** an old map in the attic.*

discuss
VERB discusses, discussing, discussed
If you discuss something, you talk about it with someone else. *We **discussed** what we should do with the money we had found.*
discussion (NOUN)
If you have a discussion, you discuss something.

disease
NOUN diseases
A disease is an illness.

disguise

disguise
NOUN disguises
A disguise is a set of clothes or a mask that you wear to hide who you really are.

disgusting
ADJECTIVE
Something that is disgusting is very unpleasant and makes you feel a bit sick. *Yuck! This food is **disgusting**!*

dish
NOUN dishes
1 A dish is a plate or bowl that you serve food in.
2 A dish is a kind of food that has been cooked or prepared in a particular way. *My aunt cooked a delicious vegetarian **dish**.*

dishonest
ADJECTIVE
Someone who is dishonest tells lies or steals things.
☛ **Opposite:** honest

dishwasher
NOUN dishwashers
A dishwasher is a machine that washes plates, cups, and other things you use for eating.

disk (or disc)
NOUN disks (or discs)
A disk is a flat, circular object that has computer information on it.

dislike
VERB dislikes, disliking, disliked
If you dislike something, you don't like it.
☛ **Opposite:** like

display
VERB displays, displaying, displayed
A display is an arrangement of things that you put somewhere for people to look at. *There's a **display** of all our art in the hall.*

disposable
ADJECTIVE
If something is disposable, you throw it away after you have used it.

disposable

disqualify
NOUN disqualifies, disqualifying, disqualified
If you are disqualified from a competition, you are not allowed to continue in the competition because you have broken the rules.

dissolve
VERB dissolves, dissolving, dissolved
If something dissolves in water, it mixes with the water so that you can no longer see it. *Salt and sugar will **dissolve** in water.*

distance
NOUN distances
The distance between two places is how far apart they are.

distract
VERB distracts, distracting, distracted
If you distract someone, you take their attention away from what they are doing. *I was trying to watch a film, but my little sister was **distracting** me.*

distribute
VERB distributes, distributing, distributed
If you distribute things, you give them out to a lot of people. *The teacher **distributed** the books around the class.*

district
NOUN districts
A district is one area in a town, city, or country.

disturb
VERB disturbs, disturbing, disturbed
If you disturb someone, you interrupt them and stop them from doing what they are trying to do. *I'm going to sleep, so please don't **disturb** me.*

ditch
NOUN ditches
A ditch is a long, thin hole by the side of a road or field.

dive
VERB dives, diving, dived
When you dive, you jump headfirst into water.
diver (NOUN)
A diver is someone who dives into water, or someone who swims under the water with a tank of air on their back.

divide
VERB divides, dividing, divided
1 If you divide something, you split it into parts so that you can share it out. *I **divided** the cake into ten pieces.*
2 When you divide numbers, you find out how many times one number goes into another. For example, ten divided by five is two. You can write this sum as $10 \div 5 = 2$.
division (NOUN)
When you do division, you divide numbers.

*He **dived** into the swimming pool.*

dive

divorce
VERB divorces, divorcing, divorced
When people get divorced, they end their marriage.

Diwali
NOUN
Diwali is the Hindu festival of light.

a b c **Dd** e f g h l m n o p q r s t u v w x y z

doll

dizzy
ADJECTIVE
When you feel dizzy, your head spins and you feel as if you are going to fall over.

do
VERB does, doing, did, done
When you do something, you carry it out and finish it. *Have you **done** your homework yet?*

doctor
NOUN doctors
A doctor is a person who looks after people who are sick or injured.

document
NOUN documents
1 A document is a piece of paper with important information on it.
2 A document is a piece of writing that you store on a computer.

documentary
NOUN documentaries
A documentary is a film or television programme about real people or the real world. *We watched a **documentary** about lions.*

dog
NOUN dogs
A dog is an animal that people often keep as a pet. You can train dogs to do some kinds of work, such as herding sheep.

doll
NOUN dolls
A doll is a toy that looks like a baby or person.

dollar
NOUN dollars
A dollar is a unit of money that is used in the United States of America and some other countries.

dolphin
NOUN dolphins
A dolphin is a large sea animal. Dolphins swim to the surface to breathe air, and they are known for being friendly and intelligent.

donate
VERB donates, donating, donated
If you donate something, you give it to another person in order to help them. *You can **donate** your old toys to charity.*
donation (NOUN)
A donation is an amount of money that you donate. *He kindly made a **donation** to our school fund.*

donkey
NOUN donkeys
A donkey is an animal like a small horse. Donkeys have long ears and soft coats.

door
NOUN doors
A door is a piece of wood or metal that you go through to get into a room or car.

dot
NOUN dots
A dot is a very small, round spot.

double
VERB doubles, doubling, doubled
If you double an amount, you make it twice as big.

doubt
NOUN doubts
If you have doubts about something, you are not sure about it.

dough
NOUN
Dough is a mixture of flour and water that you use to make bread.

doughnut
NOUN doughnuts
A doughnut is a small, round cake that is fried in oil and covered in sugar.

dove
NOUN doves
A dove is a pale-coloured bird that looks like a pigeon. Doves are often used as a symbol of peace.

download
VERB downloads, downloading, downloaded
When you download information, you copy it from the internet onto your computer.

downstairs
ADVERB
If you go downstairs, you go to a lower floor in a building.

doze
VERB dozes, dozing, dozed
When you doze, you sleep lightly for a short time. *My grandad was **dozing** in the chair.*

draft
NOUN drafts
A draft is a rough copy, or plan, of a drawing or piece of writing.

drag
VERB drags, dragging, dragged
If you drag something along, you pull it along the ground. *We **dragged** the heavy box into the kitchen.*

dragon
NOUN dragons
A dragon is a fierce, imaginary animal in myths and fairy tales. Dragons can fly and usually breathe fire.

dragonfly

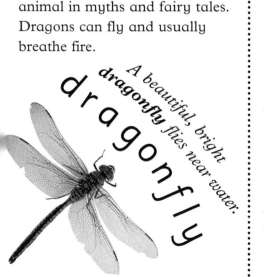

*A beautiful, bright **dragonfly** flies near water.*

dragonfly
NOUN dragonflies
A dragonfly is an insect with large, shimmering wings that you often see flying near water.

drain
NOUN drains
1 A drain is a pipe or ditch that takes away waste water.
VERB drains, draining, drained
2 If water drains away, it flows away slowly.

drama
NOUN dramas
A drama is a work performed on stage, radio, TV, or film. *Have you seen the latest TV **drama**?*

drank
☛ See **drink**.

draw
VERB draws, drawing, drew, drawn
1 When you draw something, you make a picture of it with a pencil, pen, or crayon.
2 When you draw curtains, you move them across a window.
NOUN draws
3 When a game ends in a draw, both people or teams have the same number of points.
drawing (NOUN)
A drawing is a picture that someone has drawn.

drawer
NOUN drawers
A drawer is a part of a piece of furniture that you can slide in and out and keep things in.

dreadful
ADJECTIVE
Something that is dreadful is very bad or unpleasant.

dream
VERB dreams, dreaming, dreamed or dreamt
1 When you dream, you have thoughts and pictures in your mind while you are asleep.
2 If you dream of doing something, you hope that you will be able to do it one day. *She has always **dreamed** of becoming a famous singer.*
NOUN dreams
3 A dream is something that you dream about.

dress
NOUN dresses
1 A dress is a piece of clothing that has a top and a skirt joined together.
VERB dresses, dressing, dressed
2 When you get dressed, you put on clothes.
☛ **Opposite:** undress

drew
☛ See **draw**.

dried
☛ See **dry**.

dream

*She **dreamed** about eating **doughnuts**.*

a b c Dd e f g h i j m n o p q r s t u v w x y z

drift
VERB drifts, drifting, drifted
If something drifts along, water or air carries it along slowly. *The little boat **drifted** down the river.*

drill
NOUN drills
A drill is a tool that makes holes in wood or metal.

*Water **dripped** from the tap.*

d r i p

d r i n k

drink
NOUN drinks
1 A drink is a liquid that you take into your mouth and swallow. *I'm really thirsty – I need a **drink**!*
VERB drinks, drinking, drank, drunk
2 When you drink, you take liquid into your mouth and swallow it.

drip
VERB drips, dripping, dripped
When water drips, it falls slowly, drop by drop. *I was so wet that water was **dripping** off my clothes.*

drive
VERB drives, driving, drove, driven
When you drive a car or train, you make it move along.
driver (NOUN)
A driver is someone who drives a car or train.

drone
NOUN drones
A drone is an aircraft that does not have a pilot but is controlled by someone on the ground.

droop
VERB droops, drooping, drooped
If something droops, it hangs down in a weak or tired way. *The flowers were all **drooping** because they needed water.*

drop
NOUN drops
1 A drop is a small amount of liquid. *We only had a few **drops** of water left.*
VERB drops, dropping, dropped
2 If you drop something, you let it fall out of your hands. *Catch the ball – don't **drop** it!*

drought
NOUN droughts
A drought is a long period of time when there is not enough rain. *A lot of crops died during the **drought**.*

drove
☛ See **drive**.

drown
VERB drowns, drowning, drowned
If someone drowns, they die because they have gone under water and have not been able to breathe.

drug
NOUN drugs
1 A drug is a medicine that doctors use to treat people who are ill or in pain.
2 A drug is an illegal substance that some people take to make them feel differently. Taking this kind of drug is dangerous.

drum
NOUN drums
A drum is a musical instrument that you hit to make a banging sound.

dry
ADJECTIVE drier, driest
Something that is dry is not wet. *We came in from the rain and changed into **dry** clothes.*

duck
Ducks go QUACK QUACK!
drake

duck
NOUN ducks
A duck is a waterbird that has oily, waterproof feathers and webbed feet for swimming.
A male duck is called a drake, and baby ducks are called **ducklings**.

due
ADJECTIVE
If something is due at a particular time, it should arrive or happen at that time. *The bus is **due** at 10:30.*

duet
NOUN duets
A duet is a piece of music that is played or sung by two people.

dug
☛ See **dig**.

dull
ADJECTIVE duller, dullest
1 Something that is dull is not bright or shiny. *It was a **dull**, grey day.*
2 Something that is dull is boring.

dump
VERB dumps, dumping, dumped
If you dump something, you put it down or throw it away carelessly. *They **dumped** the shopping bags on the floor.*

dune
NOUN dunes
Dunes are hills of sand near the sea or in a desert.

dungeon
NOUN dungeons
A dungeon is an underground prison in a castle.

during
PREPOSITION
During means while something is happening. *I fell asleep **during** the film.*

dusk
NOUN
Dusk is the time of evening when it starts to get dark. *The park closes at **dusk**.*

dust
NOUN
Dust is made of tiny pieces of dirt that float in the air and settle on surfaces.

dustbin
NOUN dustbins
A dustbin is a large container that you put rubbish in.

duty
NOUN duties
If something is your duty, it is your job and you must do it. *It is the guard's **duty** to make sure the doors are locked.*

duvet
NOUN duvets
A duvet is a warm cover for a bed that is filled with feathers or other light material.

DVDs

DVD
NOUN DVDs
A DVD is a disk with music, pictures, or a film stored on it.

dye
VERB dyes, dyeing, dyed
If you dye something, you change its colour by soaking it in a coloured liquid.

dynamite
NOUN
Dynamite is a powerful substance that explodes when it touches fire.

dyslexic
ADJECTIVE
Someone who is dyslexic finds it difficult to learn reading, writing, and spelling because their brain muddles up letters and words.

a b c Dd e f g h i j k l m n o p q r s t u v w x y z

a b c d Ee f g h i j k l m n o p q r s t u v w x y z

E

each
ADJECTIVE
Each means every single one. ***Each*** *player needs their own controller.*

eager
ADJECTIVE
If you are eager to do something, you want to do it very much. *Both teams were* ***eager*** *to start the game.*

eagle
NOUN eagles
An eagle is a large bird of prey. Eagles have very good eyesight for spotting prey a long way off.

ear
NOUN ears
Your ears are the parts of your body that you hear with.

early
ADVERB earlier, earliest
1 If you are early, you arrive before the time you are expected.
2 Early means near the beginning of the day.
I hate getting up ***early****!*

earn
VERB earns, earning, earned
When you earn money, you get it by working for it.
I sometimes ***earn*** *some pocket money by cleaning my mum's car.*

earring
NOUN earrings
Earrings are pieces of jewellery that you wear on your ears.

Earth / earth
NOUN
1 Earth is the planet that we live on.
2 Soil is also known as earth.

The planet we live on is called ***Earth****.*

earthquake
NOUN earthquakes
An earthquake is a violent shaking of the ground, caused by movement deep inside the Earth's crust. Earthquakes often cause damage to buildings.

east
NOUN
East is one of the four main compass directions. The Sun rises in the east in the morning.

Easter
NOUN
Easter is the festival when Christians celebrate Jesus Christ rising from the dead.

easy
ADJECTIVE easier, easiest
Something that is easy is simple and not difficult to do. *These sums are* ***easy****!*
easily (ADVERB)
If you do something easily, it is simple and not difficult for you. *We managed to find our way home quite* ***easily****.*

eat
VERB eats, eating, ate, eaten
When you eat, you take food into your mouth and swallow it.

echo
NOUN echoes
An echo is a sound that you hear when you speak in a cave or an empty room, and your voice bounces back off the walls.

eclipse
NOUN eclipses
An eclipse of the Sun happens when the Moon comes between the Earth and the Sun, so the Sun is hidden for a short time. An eclipse of the Moon happens when the Earth comes between the Sun and the Moon, so the Moon is hidden for a short time.

eczema
NOUN
Eczema is a dry, itchy skin condition.

edge
NOUN edges
The edge of something is the part that is not in the middle. *There were trees around the **edge** of the lake.*

edit
VERB edits, editing, edited
When you edit something you have written, you read it and change some parts of it to make it better.

educate
VERB educates, educating, educated
To educate someone means to teach them important things such as reading and writing.
education (NOUN)
Education is the teaching that you get when you are at school.

eel
NOUN eels
An eel is a long, thin fish that looks like a snake and lives in rivers and the sea.

effect
NOUN effects
An effect is a change that something causes. *Too much sun can have a harmful **effect** on your skin.*

effort
NOUN
If you make an effort, you try hard.

egg
NOUN eggs
Some animals such as birds, fish, and reptiles lay eggs as a way of having babies. The babies grow inside the egg and then hatch out when they are ready to be born. We often cook and eat hen's eggs.

Eid-ul-Fitr
NOUN
Eid-ul-Fitr is the Muslim festival to celebrate the end of Ramadan.

either
ADJECTIVE
Either means one or the other. *I've got two pens. You can borrow **either** one.*

elastic
NOUN
Elastic is a stretchy material.

elbow
NOUN elbows
Your elbow is the part in the middle of your arm, where you can bend your arm.

elect
VERB elects, electing, elected
When people elect someone, they choose them by voting for them.
election (NOUN)
An election is a time when people vote to choose someone for public office, such as when a country votes to choose or change a government.

electricity
NOUN
Electricity is a form of energy that we use for cooking and lighting, and to make machines work. Electricity is produced at a power station and carried to people's homes along cables and wires.
electric (ADJECTIVE)
Something that is electric uses electricity to work.

electronic
ADJECTIVE
An electronic machine has special small parts inside it that control how it works using electrical energy. Computers and televisions are electronic machines.

elephant
NOUN elephants
An elephant is a very large animal that lives in Asia and Africa. Elephants have long trunks, which they use to pick up their food. Many elephants have long, white tusks made of ivory.

Elephants have long trunks.

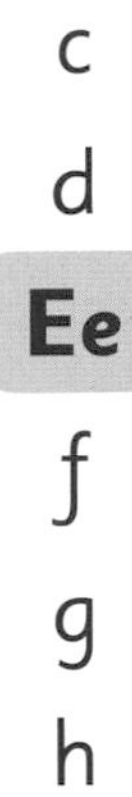

email
NOUN emails
1 An email is a message that you send to someone from your computer to their computer.
VERB emails, emailing, emailed
2 When you email someone, you send them a message from your computer to their computer.

embarrass
VERB embarrasses, embarrassing, embarrassed
If something embarrasses you, it makes you feel shy or slightly ashamed. *My dad is always **embarrassing** me!*

emergency
NOUN emergencies
An emergency is an unexpected situation. If there is an emergency, something bad suddenly happens, and people are in danger. They will need help immediately. *You can call 999 if there's an **emergency**.*

empty
ADJECTIVE
1 Something that is empty has nothing inside it.
VERB empties, emptying, emptied
2 If you empty something, you take everything out of it.

enchanted
ADJECTIVE
In stories, if something is enchanted, someone has put a spell on it.

encourage
VERB encourages, encouraging, encouraged
If you encourage someone, you tell them that they are doing well and make them feel that they want to continue trying. *We cheered to **encourage** our team.*

encyclopedia
NOUN encyclopedias
An encyclopedia is a book with information about a lot of different things. An online encyclopedia is an encyclopedia that you can use on the internet.

end
NOUN ends
1 The end of something is the place where it stops or finishes.
VERB ends, ending, ended
2 When something ends, it stops or finishes. *I thought that lesson would never **end**!*

endangered
ADJECTIVE
An endangered animal or plant is one that is very rare and might soon become extinct.

enemy
NOUN enemies
An enemy is someone who hates you and fights against you.

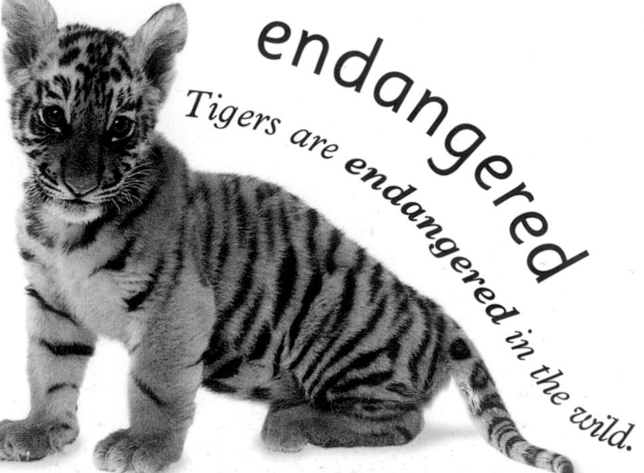

*Tigers are **endangered** in the wild.*

energy
NOUN
1 If you have a lot of energy, you feel strong and lively.
2 Energy is power that we use to make machines work. *Electricity is a form of **energy**.*

engine
NOUN engines
An engine is a machine that uses fuel to make something move.

enjoy
VERB enjoys, enjoying, enjoyed
If you enjoy something, you like doing it.

enormous
ADJECTIVE
Something that is enormous is very large.

enough
ADJECTIVE
Enough means as much as you need. *There's **enough** for everyone.*

enter
VERB enters, entering, entered
When you enter a place you go into it. *No one must **enter** this room!*

entertain
VERB entertains, entertaining, entertained
If you entertain people, you amuse them by doing things that they can watch. *Some jugglers **entertained** the crowd.*

entertainment
NOUN
Entertainment is things people enjoy watching or listening to, such as films or shows.

Entertainment

Here are some words about entertainment – from fireworks to films!

fascinating, amazing
beautiful, spectacular
colourful, **dazzling**,
interesting, magical

pop!
bang!
blast, flash, sparkle
explode!
Z-o-o-m...
whistle!...
boom!
fireworks...

theme park
fun ride
exciting
scary
whoosh!
scream machine
thrilling
amusement park

science fiction
theatre
documentary
fantasy
actor
cinema
drama
animation
comedy, musical
screen
action, adventure
film
show
movie

computer gaming

gadgets

steering simulator

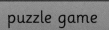

racing game

controller

puzzle game

matching game

enthusiastic
ADJECTIVE
If you are enthusiastic about something, you like it a lot and are very interested in it.
☛ **Opposite:** unenthusiastic

entrance
NOUN entrances
The entrance is the way into a place. *There was a secret **entrance** to the castle.*

entry
NOUN
If you are allowed entry to a place, you can go in. *The sign said, "No **entry**!"*

envelope
NOUN envelopes
An envelope is a paper container that you put a letter or card in when you send it to someone.

environment
NOUN
The environment is the land, water, and air around us. *Recycling is good for the **environment**.*

episode
NOUN episodes
An episode is one programme in a TV or radio series.

equal
ADJECTIVE
Things that are equal are the same size, number, or amount. *Choose two pieces of string that are **equal** in length.*
equally (ADVERB)
If you divide something equally, you give each person the same amount.

Equator
NOUN
The Equator is an imaginary line around the middle of the Earth that divides the northern half of the world from the southern half. The Equator is drawn onto maps and globes.

equipment
NOUN
Equipment is a group term for the things that you need for a job or a sport.

error
NOUN errors
An error is a mistake.

erupt
VERB erupts, erupting, erupted
If a volcano erupts, it explodes suddenly and ash and hot, liquid rock come out of it.

escalator
NOUN escalators
An escalator is a moving staircase that carries people between different floors in a building.

escape
VERB escapes, escaping, escaped
If you escape, you get away from a person or place. *They **escaped** from the castle at night.*

especially
ADVERB
Especially means more than anything else. *I love animals, **especially** cats.*

estimate
VERB estimates, estimating, estimated
If you estimate an amount, you guess how much it is. *I **estimate** that we have five minutes before the bus leaves.*

even
ADJECTIVE
1 An even surface is flat and level.
☛ **Opposite:** uneven
2 An even number can be divided by two.

evening
NOUN evenings
The evening is the time of day when the Sun goes down and it grows dark.

event
NOUN events
An event is something interesting or exciting that happens. *The fireworks display is a big **event** each year.*

eventually
ADVERB
If you do something eventually, you do it finally, after a long time.

ever
ADVERB
Ever means at any time. *Have you **ever** been on TV?*

evergreen
ADJECTIVE
An evergreen tree has green leaves all year round.

every
ADJECTIVE
Every means each one. *I play football **every** Saturday.*

everybody
Everybody or everyone means all people. ***Everybody** in my class likes chocolate.*

everything
Everything means all things. *He ate **everything** on his plate.*

everywhere
Everywhere means in all places. *I've looked **everywhere** for my phone, but I can't find it!*

evidence
NOUN
Evidence is proof that something has happened.

evil
ADJECTIVE
Someone who is evil is very wicked.

evolution
NOUN
Evolution is the way in which animals and plants change gradually over a very long time.

ewe
NOUN ewes
A ewe is a female sheep.

exact
ADJECTIVE
Something that is exact is completely right or accurate. *Do you know the **exact** number of people in your school?*

exaggerate
VERB exaggerates, exaggerating, exaggerated
If you exaggerate, you say that something is bigger or better than it really is.

exam
NOUN exams
An exam is an important test to find out how much you know about something. Exam is short for **examination**.

examine
VERB examines, examining, examined
If you examine something, you look at it very carefully. *She picked up the necklace and **examined** it.*

example
NOUN examples
If you give an example, you talk about one thing that is typical and shows what all the others are like. *A chimpanzee is an **example** of an ape.*

excellent
ADJECTIVE
Something that is excellent is extremely good. *This is an **excellent** piece of work.*

except
PREPOSITION
Except means not including one person or thing. *I like all vegetables **except** cabbage.*

Ewes don't usually have horns.
ewe

excited
ADJECTIVE
If you are excited, you feel happy because something good is happening or is going to happen soon. *I'm really **excited** about going on holiday.*
exciting (ADJECTIVE)
If something is exciting, you enjoy it and feel happy. *Going to the fair is **exciting**.*

exclamation
NOUN exclamations
An exclamation is something that you shout because you are very happy, angry, or surprised. In writing, you use an **exclamation mark** (**!**) after an exclamation.

excuse
NOUN excuses
An excuse is a reason you give for not doing something. *He had a good **excuse** for not doing his homework.*

exercise
NOUN exercises
1 Exercise is running or playing sport that you do to make you fit. *Tennis is good **exercise**.*
2 An exercise is a set of questions that you answer to practise something.

exhausted
ADJECTIVE
If you are exhausted, you are extremely tired. *After running a marathon, he was totally **exhausted**.*

a b c d Ee f g h i j k l m n o p q r s t u v w x y z

exhibition
NOUN exhibitions
An exhibition is a collection of things that are put on show in a public place, so that people can come and see them.

exist
VERB exists, existing, existed
Something that exists lives or can be seen in the real world. *Do you think that aliens **exist**?*

exit
NOUN exits
An exit is a way out of a building.

expand
VERB expands, expanding, expanded
When something expands, it gets bigger.

expect
VERB expects, expecting, expected
If you expect something to happen, you think that it will happen. *We didn't **expect** to win the competition.*

expensive
ADJECTIVE
Something that is expensive costs a lot of money.

experience
NOUN experiences
1 An experience is an important event that you remember for a long time. *Going on safari to Africa was a fantastic **experience**.*
2 If you have experience of doing something, you have done it before and so know about it. *My sister has a lot of **experience** of performing in shows.*

experiment
NOUN experiments
If you do an experiment, you do something to see what happens.

expert
NOUN experts
An expert is someone who knows a lot about a subject.

explain
VERB explains, explaining, explained
If you explain something, you give more information about it so that people can understand. *Can you **explain** how a rainbow forms?*
explanation (NOUN)
If you give an explanation of something, you explain it.

explode
VERB explodes, exploding, exploded
If something explodes, it blows up or bursts apart suddenly and makes a loud noise.
explosion (NOUN)
An explosion is a loud noise that happens when a bomb or something else explodes.

explore
VERB explores, exploring, explored
If you explore a place, you look around it for the first time. *Let's go and **explore** the garden.*

extinct
ADJECTIVE
If a type of animal is extinct, there are no more of that type of animal in the world. *The dodo is an **extinct** bird.*

experiment

extra
ADJECTIVE
Extra means more than is usual.

extraordinary
ADJECTIVE
Something that is extraordinary is very unusual and surprising. *I had never seen such an **extraordinary** creature before.*

extreme
ADJECTIVE
1 Extreme means very great. *We realised that we were in **extreme** danger.*
2 An extreme sport is a sport such as mountain biking that is very dangerous.
extremely (ADVERB)
Extremely means very. *That film was **extremely** boring!*

eye
NOUN eyes
Your eyes are the parts of your body that you see with.

eyesight
NOUN
Your eyesight is how well you can see. *Owls have very good **eyesight**.*

fable
NOUN fables
A fable is a story, often with animal characters, that tries to teach us something in an amusing way.

face
NOUN faces
Your face is the front of your head, where your eyes, nose, and mouth are.

fact
NOUN facts
A fact is a piece of information that people know is true. *We learned some interesting **facts** about the rainforest.*

factor
NOUN factors
In maths, a factor is a number that will divide exactly into another number. For example, 5 is a factor of 10.

factory
NOUN factories
A factory is a building where people make things using machines.

fade
VERB fades, fading, faded
If something fades, it becomes weaker or less bright. *The colour on my jeans has **faded**.*

fail
VERB fails, failing, failed
If you fail, you do not manage to do something successfully or well. *I hope I don't **fail** the spelling test.*
failure (NOUN)
If something is a failure, it does not work well or does not go as planned.

faint
VERB faints, fainting, fainted
1 When you faint, you become unconscious for a short time. *He **fainted** in the heat.*
ADJECTIVE fainter, faintest
2 If you feel faint, you feel dizzy.
3 A faint sound, smell, or taste is not very strong. *She heard a **faint** noise coming from the cupboard.*

fair
NOUN fairs
1 A fair is a place with rides, stalls, competitions, and games.
ADJECTIVE fairer, fairest
2 If something is fair, everyone is treated in the same way. *She's got more sweets than me – it's not **fair**!*
☛ **Opposite:** unfair
3 Fair weather is dry and sunny.
☛ **Be careful with spelling:**
fair *We went on rides at the **fair**.*
fare *How much is the bus **fare**?*

fairy
NOUN fairies
A fairy is a small, imaginary creature from stories. Fairies often have magical powers.

A fairy waves her wand.

fairy tale
NOUN fairy tales
A fairy tale is a story for young children in which magical things happen.

faith
NOUN
If you have faith in someone, you trust them. *I have **faith** in my doctor.*

faithful
ADJECTIVE
If someone is faithful to you, they keep helping you and supporting you, and you can trust them.

fake
ADJECTIVE
1 Something that is fake is not real. *Her coat was made of **fake** fur.*
VERB fakes, faking, faked
2 If you fake something such as a feeling or an illness, you are only pretending and do not really have that feeling or illness.

a b c d e Ff g h i j k l m n o p q r s t u v w x y z

falcon
NOUN falcons
A falcon is a bird with a sharp beak and claws. Falcons are good hunters and can fly very fast. *The **falcon** flew over the fields.*

fall
VERB falls, falling, fell, fallen
1 To fall means to drop to the ground. *I **fell** over while I was playing football.*
NOUN falls
2 If you have a fall, you lose your balance and drop to the ground.
3 Fall is the American name for autumn.

false
ADJECTIVE
1 Something that is false is not true. *He gave the police **false** information.*
2 Something that is false is not real. *He was wearing a **false** beard.*

familiar
ADJECTIVE
If something is familiar to you, you know it well. *I saw a **familiar** face in the crowd.*
☛ **Opposite:** unfamiliar

family
NOUN families
1 Your family is all the people who are related to you. *I come from a large **family**.*
2 A family of animals or plants is a group of them that are similar to each other and are related to each other. *Tigers belong to the cat **family**.*

famine
NOUN famines
If there is a famine, there is not enough food for people for a long period of time.

famous
ADJECTIVE
If someone is famous, a lot of people know them and recognize them. *One day I'm going to become a **famous** film star!*

*Keep cool with a **fan**.*

fan
NOUN fans
1 A fan is a person who likes and supports a person, a pop group, or a sports team.
2 A fan is something that moves air around to make you feel cooler.

fang
NOUN fangs
Fangs are the long, sharp, pointed teeth that some animals have.

fantastic
ADJECTIVE
Something that is fantastic is very good indeed. *We had a **fantastic** holiday.*

fantasy
NOUN fantasies
A fantasy is a story about magical things that are not real and not possible. *Do you like playing **fantasy** games on the computer?*

far
ADVERB farther, farthest or further, furthest
1 If you go far, you go a long way.
2 If something is far away, it is a long way away. *They live in a place **far** away from the city.*

fare
NOUN fares
The fare is the amount of money you pay to travel on a bus, train, or plane.
☛ **Be careful with spelling:**
fare *How much is the bus **fare**?*
fair *We went on lots of rides at the **fair**.*

farm
NOUN farms
A farm is a place where people grow crops or keep animals for meat or milk.

farmer
NOUN farmers
A farmer is someone who lives and works on a farm. *The **farmer** gets up very early to milk his cows.*

fascinate
VERB fascinates, fascinating, fascinated
If something fascinates you, you find it very interesting. *Dinosaurs **fascinate** me.*

fashion
NOUN fashions
Fashion is the type of clothes that people like to wear at a particular time. *Bright colours are in **fashion** at the moment.*
fashionable (ADJECTIVE)
Clothes that are fashionable are in fashion now.

fast
VERB fasts, fasting, fasted
1 When you fast, you do not eat food for a time, usually because of your religion. *Muslims **fast** during the month of Ramadan.*
ADJECTIVE faster, fastest
2 Something that is fast can move very quickly. *Are you a **fast** runner?*
3 If a clock is fast, it shows a later time than the real time. *That clock is **fast** – it says 8.15, but it's only eight o'clock.*
4 Fast food is food such as burgers that can be prepared and served quickly.
ADVERB
5 If you run fast, you run quickly. *We ran **fast** to catch the bus.*
6 If something is stuck fast, it is stuck firmly. *I can't open the window because it's stuck **fast**.*

fasten
VERB fastens, fastening, fastened
1 If you fasten things together, you tie or join them together. *She **fastened** the buttons on her coat.*
2 If someone fastens their gaze on another person, they look very hard at them. *She **fastened** her gaze on the clown.*

fat
NOUN fats
1 Fat is a substance that is stored under your skin.
2 Fat is an oily substance that people use in cooking. *You shouldn't eat too much **fat**.*
ADJECTIVE fatter, fattest
3 Someone who is fat has a lot of fat on their body.

father
NOUN fathers
Your father is your male parent.

fault
NOUN faults
1 If there is a fault in a machine, there is something wrong with it and it does not work properly.
2 If something is your fault, you made it happen, even though you probably didn't want it to happen. *It was my **fault** we were late.*
3 A fault is a large split in the Earth's surface.

favour
NOUN favours
If you do someone a favour, you do something kind that will help them.

favourite
ADJECTIVE
Your favourite thing or person is the one you like the best. *What's your **favourite** colour?*

fawn
NOUN fawns
A fawn is a young deer.

fear
NOUN fears
1 Fear is the feeling of being afraid.
VERB fears, fearing, feared
2 If you fear something, you are afraid of it.
fearless (ADJECTIVE)
Someone who is fearless is not at all afraid.

feast
NOUN feasts
A feast is a large meal that you have to celebrate something.

feather
NOUN feathers
A bird's feathers are the soft, light things that cover its body.

*As light as a **feather**...*

fed
☛ See **feed**.

fed up
ADJECTIVE
If you feel fed up, you feel sad and bored.

feed
VERB feeds, feeding, fed
1 If you feed a person or an animal, you give them food.
2 When animals feed, they eat food. *Caterpillars **feed** on leaves.*

a b c d e **Ff**

feel
VERB feels, feeling, felt
1 The way you feel is the mood you are in or the emotions that you have. *I **feel** happy today.*
2 If you feel something, you touch it with your hands or your body so that you know what it is like. ***Feel** the cat's lovely, soft fur.*

feeling
NOUN feelings
A feeling is an emotion, such as happiness, sadness, or anger.

fell
☛ See **fall**.

felt
☛ See **feel**.

female
ADJECTIVE
Female animals produce eggs or give birth to babies.

fence
NOUN fences
A fence is a barrier that separates one piece of land from another.

ferocious
ADJECTIVE
A ferocious animal is fierce and dangerous.

ferry
NOUN ferries
A ferry is a boat that carries people and cars across a small stretch of water.

festival
NOUN festivals
A festival is a celebration or special event, often with music and dancing.

fetch
VERB fetches, fetching, fetched
If you fetch something, you go and get it and bring it back. *The dog **fetched** the stick.*

fête
NOUN fêtes
A fête is an outdoor event where there are games, and stalls selling different things.

fever
NOUN fevers
If you have a fever, your body is very hot because you are ill. *I couldn't go to school because I had a **fever**.*

few
ADJECTIVE fewer, fewest
A few means a small number of people or things. *There are a **few** sweets left in the packet.*

fiction
NOUN
Stories that have been made up and are not true are called fiction. *Do you enjoy reading **fiction** or non-fiction?*
☛ **Opposite:** non-fiction

fiddle
VERB fiddles, fiddling, fiddled
If you fiddle with something, you touch it or move it. *You mustn't **fiddle** with the controls.*

fidget
VERB fidgets, fidgeting, fidgeted
If you fidget, you keep moving around in an annoying way.

field
NOUN fields
A field is an area of land where grass grows, crops are grown, or animals graze.

fierce
ADJECTIVE fiercer, fiercest
A fierce person or animal is violent and dangerous. *My dog looks **fierce**, but he's really very friendly.*
fiercely (ADVERB)
If you say or do something fiercely, you do it in a fierce way. *"Go away!" he shouted **fiercely**.*

fight
VERB fights, fighting, fought
1 When people fight, they hit each other or use weapons to try to hurt each other.
2 When people fight, they argue with each other.

s t u v w x y z

figure
NOUN figures
1 A figure is a single number such as 1, 2, or 3.
2 Your figure is the shape of your body.

file
NOUN files
1 A file is a folder that you keep important pieces of paper in.
2 A file on a computer is a place where you keep information.
3 If you walk in single file, you walk with one person behind the other.

fill
VERB fills, filling, filled
When you fill a container, you put as much into it as it can hold.

film
NOUN films
1 A film is a moving picture that tells a story and is shown on a screen. *We went to see a* ***film*** *at the cinema.*
VERB films, filming, filmed
2 When you film something, you take moving pictures of it.

filthy
ADJECTIVE
Something that is filthy is very dirty.

fin
NOUN fins
The fins on a fish are the parts that stick out from the sides of its body and help it to swim.

A shark's **fin** breaks the surface of the water.

fin

final
NOUN finals
1 A final is the last game in a competition, which decides who the winner is.
ADJECTIVE
2 The final thing is the last one. *This is the* ***final*** *week of term.*
finally (ADVERB)
If something happens finally, it happens in the end, after a long time. *We pushed and pushed, and the door* ***finally*** *opened.*

find
VERB finds, finding, found
When you find something that you are looking for, you see it.

fine
NOUN fines
1 A fine is an amount of money you have to pay as a punishment for doing something wrong.
ADJECTIVE finer, finest
2 Something that is fine is all right. *That jacket looks* ***fine****.*
3 Something that is fine is thin and light. *My hair is very* ***fine****.*
4 Fine weather is dry and sunny.

finger
NOUN fingers
Your fingers are the long, thin parts at the ends of your hands.

fingernail
NOUN fingernails
Your fingernails are the nails on your fingers.

fingerprints

fingerprint
NOUN fingerprints
A fingerprint is a mark that your finger leaves when it touches something. *The police found the thief's* ***fingerprints*** *on the table.*

finish
VERB finishes, finishing, finished
1 When something finishes, it ends.
2 When you finish something, you have done all of it. *I've now* ***finished*** *reading the book.*

fir
NOUN firs
A fir is a tall, evergreen tree that has thin leaves like needles.

fire
NOUN fires
1 A fire is a mass of heat, light, and flames when something is burning.
VERB fires, firing, fired
2 If someone fires a gun, they shoot with it.

fire engine
NOUN fire engines
A fire engine is a large vehicle that fire-fighters travel in to get to a fire.

fire-fighter
NOUN fire-fighters
A fire-fighter is someone whose job is to put out fires and rescue people in danger.

flag

*The **flags** have been put up for the festival.*

firework
NOUN fireworks
Fireworks are things that burn or explode in an attractive, colourful way when you light them.

firm
ADJECTIVE firmer, firmest
1 Something that is firm is hard and solid. *My bed is quite **firm**.*
2 If something is firm, it is fixed in place and you cannot move it.
3 If someone is firm, they are strict and will not change their mind.

first
ADJECTIVE
The first person or thing is the one before all the others.

first aid
NOUN
First aid is help that you give to someone who is hurt or becomes ill suddenly.

first person
NOUN
If you write a story in the first person, you write it using words like "I" and "me", rather than words like "he" or "she".

fish
NOUN fish or fishes
1 A fish is an animal that lives under water and breathes through gills.
VERB fishes, fishing, fished
2 When you fish, you use a net or rod to try to catch fish.

fist
NOUN fists
A fist is a shape that you make with your hand when you curl up your fingers and thumb tightly.

fit
VERB fits, fitting, fitted
1 If something fits, it is the right size for you to wear. *That dress **fits** you well.*
2 If something fits into a place, it is the right size for the place. *My clothes wouldn't all **fit** into the bag.*
ADJECTIVE fitter, fittest
3 If you are fit, you are well and healthy. *My dad goes running twice a week to keep **fit**.*
☛ **Opposite:** unfit

fix
VERB fixes, fixing, fixed
1 When you fix something, you mend it. *A person came to **fix** the television.*
2 If you fix something in place, you attach it there firmly. *I **fixed** the wheels onto the model.*

fizzy
ADJECTIVE fizzier, fizziest
A fizzy drink has a lot of bubbles in it.

flag
NOUN flags
A flag is a piece of cloth that is used as colourful decoration or has a design that represents a country.

flame
NOUN flames
Flames are the bright points of burning gas that you see in a fire.

flap
VERB flaps, flapping, flapped
1 If something flaps around, it moves about in the wind.
2 When birds flap their wings, they move them up and down.

flash
NOUN flashes
1 A flash is a sudden, bright light.
2 If something happens in a flash, it happens very fast.
VERB flashes, flashing, flashed
3 If something flashes, it shines brightly for a short time.

flat
ADJECTIVE flatter, flattest
1 Something that is flat is level and even. *You need a **flat** surface for painting.*
2 If a ball or tyre is flat, it has no air inside it.
3 A flat battery has no power left in it.
NOUN flats
4 A flat is a home that is on one floor of a larger building.

flavour
NOUN flavours
The flavour of food or drink is what it tastes like.

fleece
NOUN fleeces
A fleece is a jacket or top made of a warm, thick material.

flew
Flew is the past tense of the verb **fly**.
☛ **Be careful with spelling:**
flew *The bird **flew** away.*
flu *I feel ill – I think I've got **flu**.*

flick
VERB flicks, flicking, flicked
If you flick something, you tap it quickly with your finger so that it flies through the air. *She **flicked** the piece of paper into the bin.*

flight
NOUN flights
1 Flight is when something flies. *Some superheroes have the power of **flight**.*
2 A flight is a journey on an aeroplane.
3 A flight of stairs is a set of stairs.

fling
VERB flings, flinging, flung
If you fling something, you throw it suddenly and roughly. *She **flung** her bag down on the bed.*

flip
VERB flips, flipping, flipped
When you flip something, you turn it over quickly. *Let's **flip** a coin to see who goes first.*

flipper
NOUN flippers
1 Flippers are the flat limbs that sea creatures, such as dolphins and seals, use for swimming.
2 Divers wear flippers on their feet to help them move through the water.

float
VERB floats, floating, floated
If something floats, it stays on the surface of water and does not sink.

flock
NOUN flocks
A flock of birds or animals is a large group of them.

flood
NOUN floods
1 A flood happens when a large amount of water covers the land.
VERB floods, flooding, flooded
2 When a river floods, it spills out and covers the land around it.

floor
NOUN floors
1 The floor is the surface that you walk on inside a building.
2 A floor of a building is one level inside it. *I live on the sixth **floor**.*

flop
VERB flops, flopping, flopped
If you flop down, you sit down suddenly because you are tired. *He came in and **flopped** down on the sofa.*

flour
NOUN
Flour is a powder that is made by crushing wheat. You use flour to make bread and cakes.
☛ **Be careful with spelling:**
flour *You use **flour** to make cakes.*
flower *Look at those beautiful **flowers**!*

flow
VERB flows, flowing, flowed
1 Something that flows moves along steadily. *The river **flows** by our house.*
2 A continuous stream of people. *The crowd kept **flowing** along the road.*

flow chart
NOUN flow charts
A flow chart is a diagram that shows how one stage of something follows on from another.

flower
NOUN flowers
A flower is a colourful part of a plant from which seeds grow.
☛ **Be careful with spelling:**
flower *Look at those beautiful **flowers**!*
flour *You use **flour** to make cakes.*

flu
NOUN
Flu is an illness caused by a virus that makes you feel very ill and gives you a sore throat, a cough, and a runny nose. Flu is short for **influenza**.
☛ **Be careful with spelling:**
flu *I feel ill – I think I've got **flu**.*
flew *The bird **flew** away.*

fluffy
ADJECTIVE
Something that is fluffy is very soft and light.

fluid
NOUN fluids
A fluid is a liquid.

flung
☛ See **fling**.

flush
VERB flushes, flushing, flushed
1 If you flush, your face goes red, usually because you feel embarrassed.
2 When you flush a toilet, you clean it by making water move through it quickly.

flute
NOUN flutes
A flute is a musical instrument made of wood or metal. You hold it sideways in front of your mouth and play it by covering holes with your fingers and blowing across a hole at one end.

flute

flutter
VERB flutters, fluttering, fluttered
When something flutters, it flies gently. *A butterfly **fluttered** by.*

fly
NOUN flies
1 A fly is a very common insect that you often see in houses in the summer.
VERB flies, flying, flew, flown
2 If something flies, it moves through the air.

foal
NOUN foals
A foal is a baby horse.

foam
NOUN
Foam is a mass of small bubbles.

focus
VERB focuses, focusing, focused
When you focus a camera or a telescope, you change the controls slightly so that you can see through it more clearly.

fog
NOUN
Fog is a thick cloud that hangs in the air making it hard to see.
foggy (ADJECTIVE)
When it is foggy, there is fog in the air.

fold
VERB folds, folding, folded
When you fold something, you bend one part of it neatly over another. *He **folded** the card in half.*

folder
NOUN folders
1 A folder is a thin cardboard case to keep papers in.
2 A folder is a place on a computer where you can keep several files or documents.

follow
VERB follows, following, followed
1 If you follow someone, you go along behind them.
2 When you follow orders, you do as you are asked. *He **followed** the teacher's instructions.*

fond
ADJECTIVE
If you are fond of someone, you like them a lot.

food
NOUN
1 Food is what you eat to help you live and grow.
2 Something to think about is food for thought.

food chain
NOUN food chains
A food chain is a group of plants and animals that are connected because each one feeds on the next one in the chain.

fool
NOUN fools
A fool is a very silly or stupid person.
foolish (ADJECTIVE)
Someone who is foolish is silly and not sensible.

foot
NOUN feet
Your feet are the parts of your body that you stand on.

football
NOUN
Football is a game in which teams of players try to kick a ball into a net to score goals. The ball that they use is called a **football**.

Food

Eating a daily mixture of these foods will help your body to be healthy.

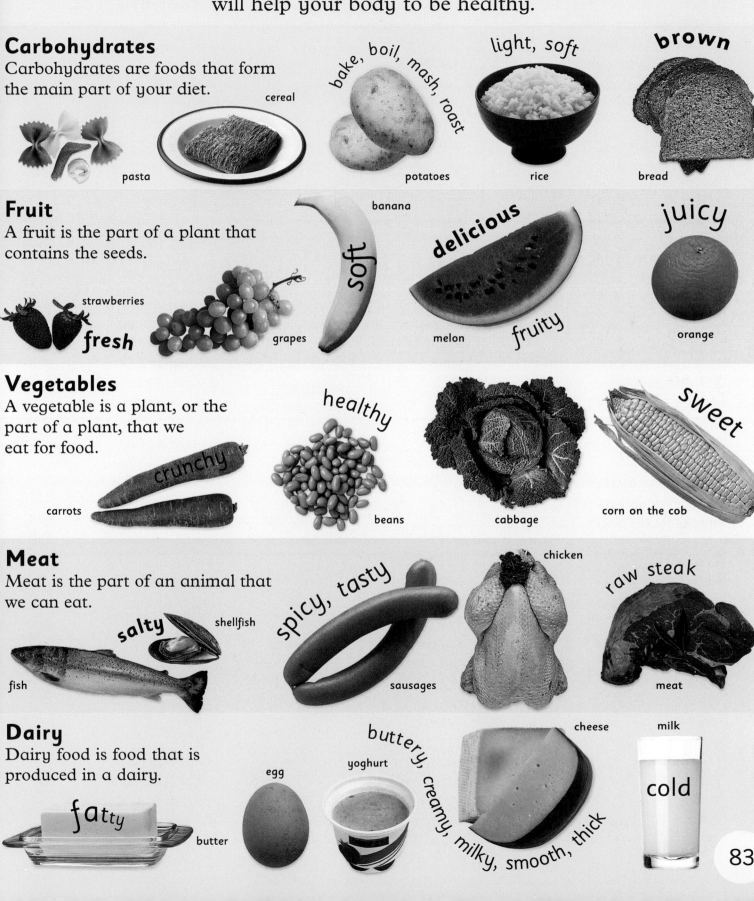

Carbohydrates

Carbohydrates are foods that form the main part of your diet.

Fruit

A fruit is the part of a plant that contains the seeds.

Vegetables

A vegetable is a plant, or the part of a plant, that we eat for food.

Meat

Meat is the part of an animal that we can eat.

Dairy

Dairy food is food that is produced in a dairy.

footprint
NOUN footprints
A footprint is a mark that your foot leaves on the ground.

forbid
VERB forbids, forbidding, forbade, forbidden
If you forbid someone to do something, you tell them they must not do it. *The teachers have* ***forbidden*** *us to play football on wet grass.*

force
NOUN forces
1 In science, a force is a power that pushes or pulls something.
2 A force is a group of people who fight or do a job together. *The police* ***force*** *makes sure the streets are safe.*
VERB forces, forcing, forced
3 If you force someone to do something, you make them do it.

forecast
NOUN forecasts
A weather forecast tells you what the weather is going to be like.

forehead
NOUN foreheads
Your forehead is the part of your face above your eyes.

foreign
ADJECTIVE
Something that is foreign comes from another country. *Can you speak any* ***foreign*** *languages?*

forest
NOUN forests
A forest is a large area where a lot of trees grow close together.

forget
VERB forgets, forgetting, forgot, forgotten
If you forget something, you do not remember it. *Don't* ***forget*** *to bring your sports kit tomorrow!*

forgive
VERB forgives, forgiving, forgave, forgiven
If you forgive someone, you stop being angry with them about something bad that they did.

fork
NOUN forks
1 A fork is a tool with sharp spikes. You use a fork to eat your food, and you use a big fork to dig in the garden.
2 A fork in a road is a place where it divides into two roads going in different directions.

fossil

An ancient animal shell has become a ***fossil.***

form
NOUN forms
1 A form is a piece of paper on which you have to answer questions and give information. *I filled in a* ***form*** *to join the library.*
2 One form of something is one type of it. *Trains are a* ***form*** *of transport.*

fort
NOUN forts
A fort is a building like a castle that has high walls to protect it from attack.

fortnight
NOUN fortnights
A fortnight is two weeks.

fortunate
ADJECTIVE
If you are fortunate, you are lucky.
☛ **Opposite:** unfortunate
fortunately (ADVERB)
Fortunately means luckily. ***Fortunately****, the weather was warm and sunny.*

fortune
NOUN
1 If you have good fortune, you are lucky.
☛ **Opposite:** misfortune
2 A fortune is a lot of money. *He won a* ***fortune*** *in the lottery.*

forward
ADVERB
If you move forward, you move in the direction that is in front of you. *He ran* ***forward*** *to meet us.*

fossil
NOUN fossils
A fossil is the remains of a plant or animal that died many years ago and has turned to stone.

fought
☛ See **fight**.

found
☛ See **find**.

fountain
NOUN fountains
A fountain is water that sprays up into the air, often through a statue.

fox

NOUN foxes

A fox is an animal with reddish-brown fur and a bushy tail. Foxes belong to the dog family and live in the country and in towns.

fraction

NOUN fractions

A fraction is a part of a whole number. *One-third is a **fraction**.*

fracture

NOUN fractures

A fracture is a crack or break in a bone.

fragile

ADJECTIVE

Something that is fragile is delicate and will break easily.

frame

NOUN frames

The frame on something is the part that goes around the edge and holds it in place. *She put the photo in a **frame** and hung it up.*

freckle

NOUN freckles

Freckles are small, light brown spots on some people's skin.

free

ADJECTIVE

1 If something is free, you do not have to pay for it. *With this magazine, you get a **free** game.*

2 If you are free, you are not locked up. *The prisoners were finally **free**.*

3 If you are free, you can do whatever you want.

freedom (NOUN)

If you have freedom, you are free to do what you want.

freeze

VERB freezes, freezing, froze, frozen

1 If something freezes, it becomes solid because it is so cold. *Water **freezes** and becomes ice.*

2 If you are freezing, you are very cold.

freezer

NOUN freezers

A freezer is a machine that freezes food so that you can store it and keep it fresh for a long time.

frequent

ADJECTIVE

Something that is frequent happens often. *There will be **frequent** showers in the afternoon.*

frequently (ADVERB)

If something happens frequently, it happens often.

fresh

ADJECTIVE fresher, freshest

1 Something that is fresh is new. *Start each story on a **fresh** page.*

2 Fresh food is not old or rotten, and is not frozen or tinned. *Would you like a lovely, **fresh** strawberry?*

3 Fresh water is not salty.

fridge

NOUN fridges

A fridge or refrigerator is a machine like a large, cold cupboard, that keeps food cool and fresh.

Fresh strawberries

friend

NOUN friends

1 A friend is someone that you like and who likes you.

2 A friend is someone who supports something. *He was a friend of the **opera**.*

friendly

ADJECTIVE friendlier, friendliest

Someone who is friendly is kind and helpful and shows that they like you.

☛ **Opposite:** unfriendly

frighten

VERB frightens, frightening, frightened

If something frightens you, it makes you feel scared.

frightened (ADJECTIVE)

If you feel frightened, you feel scared.

frightening (ADJECTIVE)

Something that is frightening makes you feel scared.

frog

NOUN frogs

A frog is a small animal that can swim and jump. Frogs are amphibians and live near water.

front

NOUN fronts

1 The front of something is the part that faces forward.

2 The promenade at the seaside is called a front. *They walked along the **front** and looked at the boats.*

a b c d e Ff g h i j k l m n o p q r s t u v w x y z

frost
NOUN frosts
Frost is ice that forms on the ground outside in very cold weather.
frosty (ADJECTIVE)
If the weather is frosty, there is frost on the ground.

frown
VERB frowns, frowning, frowned
When you frown, you move your eyebrows together and wrinkle your forehead to show that you are angry or puzzled.

froze
☛ See **freeze**.

frozen
ADJECTIVE
1 Something that is frozen is solid because it is very cold.
2 If you are frozen, you are very cold.

fruit
NOUN fruits
A fruit is the part of a plant that contains the seeds. A lot of fruits taste sweet, and we can eat them. Apples, pears, bananas, and oranges are all fruits.

fry
VERB fries, frying, fried
When you fry food, you cook it in hot fat. *We **fried** some eggs for breakfast.*

fuel
NOUN fuels
A fuel is something that you burn to give heat or power. Coal and oil are types of fuel.

full
ADJECTIVE fuller, fullest
If something is full, it has a lot of things inside and no room for any more. *I can't eat anymore – I'm **full**!*

full stop
NOUN full stops
A full stop is a dot that you put at the end of a sentence. After a full stop, you must use a capital letter to begin the next sentence.

fun
NOUN
If you have fun, you enjoy yourself. *The treasure hunt was great **fun**.*

funeral
NOUN funerals
A funeral is a ceremony that happens when someone has died.

funnel
NOUN funnels
1 A funnel is a tube that is wide at one end and narrow at the other. You use a funnel for pouring liquid through a small opening.
2 The funnel on a ship is a chimney.

funny
ADJECTIVE funnier, funniest
1 Something that is funny makes you laugh or smile.
2 Something that is funny is strange or odd. *What's that **funny** noise?*

fur
NOUN
Fur is the soft hair on an animal's body.
furry (ADJECTIVE)
A furry animal has thick fur.

furious
ADJECTIVE
If you are furious, you are very angry.
furiously (ADVERB)
If you say something furiously, you say it in a way that shows you are very angry. *"It's all your fault!" she shouted **furiously**.*

furniture
NOUN
Things such as chairs, beds, and cupboards are called furniture.

furniture

fuss
NOUN
If you make a fuss about something, you get angry or upset about it when it isn't necessary.

fussy
ADJECTIVE
Someone who is fussy only likes certain things. *My little sister is very **fussy** about food.*

future
NOUN
The future is the time that is to come. *In the **future** people might travel to Mars.*

Go!

gadget
NOUN gadgets
A gadget is a small, useful tool.

gain
VERB gains, gaining, gained
If you gain something, you get it. *I **gained** an extra point for getting all the answers right.*

galaxy
NOUN galaxies
A galaxy is a large group of stars. The Milky Way is a galaxy.

gale
NOUN gales
A gale is a strong wind.

gallery
NOUN galleries
A gallery is a large room where you can look at pictures on the walls.

gallop
VERB gallops, galloping, galloped
When a horse gallops, it runs very fast.

game
NOUN games
1 A game is something that you play for fun.
2 A game is a sports match in which you try to score points and beat other players.

gaming
NOUN
Gaming is playing computer games.

gang
NOUN gangs
A gang is a group of people who do things together.

gap
NOUN gaps
A gap is a hole or space between two things. *There was a narrow **gap** between the two buildings.*

garage
NOUN garages
1 A garage is a place where you keep a car.
2 A garage is a place where cars are mended.

garbage
NOUN
Garbage is rubbish that you no longer want or need.

garden
NOUN gardens
A garden is a piece of ground where you grow flowers, vegetables, and fruit.

garlic
NOUN
Garlic is a plant that is added to cooking to give a strong flavour to food.

gas
NOUN gases
A gas is a substance like air that is not a liquid or a solid.

garden
*Fabulous flowers grow in the **garden**.*

a b c d e f Gg h i j k l m n o p q r s t u v w x y z

gasp

VERB gasps, gasping, gasped

If you are gasping, you are breathing quickly because you are out of breath. *He rose to the surface of the water, **gasping** for air.*

gate

NOUN gates

A gate is a door in a fence that you can open and shut.

gather

VERB gathers, gathering, gathered

1 If you gather things, you collect them together.

2 When people gather together, they come together in a crowd. *Everyone **gathered** round to watch the magic tricks.*

gave

☛ See **give**.

gaze

VERB gazes, gazing, gazed

If you gaze at something, you stare at it for a long time. *She was **gazing** up at the stars.*

gear

NOUN gears

The gears on a bike or in a car are the parts that control how fast it goes or whether it goes forward or backward.

general

ADJECTIVE

Something that is general includes most people or things.

generally (ADVERB)

If something is generally true, it is usually true. *The bus is **generally** on time.*

generous

ADJECTIVE

Someone who is generous is kind and shares things with other people or gives people things.

genius

NOUN geniuses

A genius is someone who is very intelligent.

gentle

ADJECTIVE gentler, gentlest

If you are gentle, you are kind and careful not to hurt or damage things.

gently (ADVERB)

If you do something gently, you do it in a kind, gentle way. *I stroked the kitten's fur very **gently**.*

gentleman

NOUN gentlemen

Gentleman is a polite word for a man.

genuine

ADJECTIVE

Something that is genuine is real, and not false. *The glittering diamond ring is not a fake – it's **genuine**.*

geography

NOUN

Geography is the subject in which you study the Earth and the ways people live in the world.

germ

NOUN germs

A germ is a tiny living thing or particle that lives in the air or on things around us. It can infect us and make us ill.

get

VERB gets, getting, got

1 When you get something, you fetch it or someone gives it to you. *I **got** a new skateboard for my birthday.*

2 Get means to become. *I could see that my dad was **getting** annoyed.*

ghost

NOUN ghosts

A ghost is the spirit of a dead person. Some people believe they can see ghosts.

giant

NOUN giants

A giant is a huge person in fairy tales or stories.

gift

NOUN gifts

A gift is a present. *I wrote to my aunt to thank her for her kind **gift**.*

gift

gigabyte

NOUN gigabytes

A gigabyte is a unit that is used to measure the size of a computer's memory.

gigantic

ADJECTIVE

Something that is gigantic is very big. *The dragon had **gigantic** teeth.*

giggle

VERB giggles, giggling, giggled

When you giggle, you laugh a lot in a nervous or silly way. *He couldn't stop **giggling**.*

Ghosts and fantasy

All sorts of mysterious things haunt this page of spooky words.

a b c d e f Gg h

giraffe
NOUN giraffes
A giraffe is a very tall animal with a long neck. Giraffes live in Africa.

Giraffes have long necks.

giraffe

o p q r s t u v w x y z

girl
NOUN girls
A girl is a young female person. *It was an all-**girl** pop group.*

give
VERB gives, giving, gave, given
If you give something to someone, you hand it to them and let them have it. *Please will you **give** me some of your chocolate?*

glad
ADJECTIVE
If you feel glad, you feel happy. *I was **glad** to be back home.*
gladly (ADVERB)
If you do something gladly, you are happy to do it. *I will **gladly** share my lunch with you.*

gladiator
NOUN gladiators
A gladiator was a man who was trained to fight to entertain people in ancient Rome.

glamorous
ADJECTIVE
Someone who is glamorous is beautiful or handsome, and rich.

glance
VERB glances, glancing, glanced
If you glance at something, you look at it quickly. *I **glanced** up at the clock on the wall.*

glare
VERB glares, glaring, glared
If you glare at someone, you look at them in an angry way. *The man **glared** at me angrily.*

glass
NOUN glasses
1 Glass is a substance that you can see through. Windows and many bottles are made of glass.
2 A glass is a cup made of glass that you drink out of. *Would you like a **glass** of water?*
3 People wear glasses over their eyes to help them to see better. Glasses are pieces of special glass or plastic that make things look bigger, smaller, or clearer.

gleam
VERB gleams, gleaming, gleamed
If something gleams, it shines. *The stars **gleamed** in the darkness.*

glide
VERB glides, gliding, glided
If something glides along, it moves along smoothly. *A swan **glided** across the lake.*

glitter
verb glitters, glittering, glittered
If something glitters, it shines brightly. *The gold coins **glittered** in the sunlight.*

globe
NOUN globes
1 The globe is the world.
2 A globe is a model of the world.
global (ADJECTIVE)
Something that is global happens all over the world. *The Olympic Games is a **global** sports competition.*

Turn the **globe** to find China.

gloomy
ADJECTIVE
A gloomy place is dark. *We walked on through the **gloomy** forest.*

glorious
ADJECTIVE
Something that is glorious is lovely or wonderful.

glossary
NOUN glossaries
A glossary is a list of words and their meanings, often at the back of a book.

Shining ***goldfish*** *swim around a glass tank.*

glove
NOUN gloves
You wear gloves on your hands to keep them warm when the weather is cold.

glow
VERB glows, glowing, glowed
When something glows, it gives off a steady light. *The candle* ***glowed*** *in the darkness.*

glue
NOUN glues
Glue is a sticky substance that you use for sticking things together.

glum
ADJECTIVE
If you feel glum, you feel sad.

gnarled
ADJECTIVE
Something that is gnarled is old, bent, and twisted.

gnaw
VERB gnaws, gnawing, gnawed
When an animal gnaws on something, it chews it. *We gave the dog a bone to* ***gnaw*** *on.*

go
VERB goes, going, went, gone
If you go somewhere, you move so that you are there. *My sister's not here – she's* ***gone*** *to her friend's.*

goal
NOUN goals
1 The goal is the net or hoop that you aim the ball at to score points in a game. *The goalkeeper guarded the* ***goal****.*
2 A goal is something that you want to do. *My* ***goal*** *in life is to become a doctor.*

goat
NOUN goats
A goat is a farm animal. Goats are kept for their milk. A baby goat is called a **kid**.

god
NOUN gods
1 God is the name of the being that some people, such as Christians, Jews, and Muslims, worship and believe made the world.
2 A god is a being that people worship.

goggles
NOUN
Goggles are special glasses that you wear to protect your eyes.

gold
NOUN
Gold is a shiny, yellow metal that is very valuable.
golden (ADJECTIVE)
Something that is golden is made of gold or looks like gold.

goldfish
NOUN
A goldfish is a type of orange fish that some people keep as a pet.

golf
NOUN
Golf is a game that you play by hitting a small ball with a special stick called a **golf club**. The aim is to hit the ball into a series of holes in the ground.

gone
☛ See **go**.

good
ADJECTIVE better, best
1 Something that is good is pleasant and enjoyable. *Did you have a* ***good*** *holiday?*
2 Something that is good is well made or well done. *That's a* ***good*** *painting.*
3 If you are good at something, you can do it well. *She's* ***good*** *at maths.*

goodbye
You say goodbye to someone when you are going your separate ways, or sometimes at the end of a telephone conversation.

goods
NOUN
Goods are things that people buy and sell.

goose
NOUN geese
A goose is a large bird that lives near water. Farmers sometimes keep geese for their eggs and meat. A male goose is called a **gander**.

gorgeous
ADJECTIVE
1 Something that is gorgeous is very nice to look at or taste. *What a **gorgeous** cake!*
2 Someone who is gorgeous is very good-looking.

gorilla
NOUN gorillas
A gorilla is a large animal with dark fur that lives in rainforests in Africa. Gorillas are the largest and strongest apes in the world.

gorilla

got
☛ See **get**.

government
NOUN governments
The government is the group of people who run a country.

GPS
NOUN
GPS is a system for finding your way to a place on an electronic device such as a phone. GPS stands for **global positioning system**.

grab
VERB grabs, grabbing, grabbed
If you grab something, you take it or pick it up quickly and roughly. *He **grabbed** his coat and ran out of the room.*

graceful
ADJECTIVE
Someone who is graceful moves in a smooth, beautiful way. *Ballet dancers are very **graceful**.*
gracefully (ADVERB)
If you move gracefully, you move in a graceful way.

grade
NOUN grades
A grade is a mark that you get for a piece of work. *My **grades** have been much better this term.*

gradually
ADVERB
If something happens gradually, it happens slowly, little by little. *The water **gradually** ran out.*

graffiti
NOUN
Graffiti is writing and pictures that are scribbled on the walls of buildings.

grain
NOUN grains
1 Grain is the seeds of a cereal crop such as wheat or barley.
2 A grain of sand is one small piece of it.

gram
NOUN grams
You measure how much something weighs by saying how many grams it weighs.

grammar
NOUN
The rules that we use when we are writing or speaking a language are called grammar.

grand
ADJECTIVE grander, grandest
Something that is grand is big and impressive.

grandchild
NOUN grandchildren
Someone's grandchild is the child of their son or daughter.

grandparent
NOUN grandparents
Your **grandfather**, **grandad**, or **grandpa** is the father of your mother or father. Your **grandmother**, **grandma**, or **granny** is the mother of your mother or father. Your grandparents are the parents of your mother and father.

grape
NOUN grapes
A grape is a small, round fruit with green or black skin and soft, juicy flesh. Grapes can be used to make wine.

grapefruit
NOUN grapefruit or grapefruits
A grapefruit is a large, round, yellow fruit with a thick skin and a sour taste.

graph
NOUN graphs
A graph is a diagram that shows information about something.

graphics
NOUN
The graphics in the computer game are the pictures. *The **graphics** are amazing in this game!*

grass
NOUN grasses
Grass is a plant with thin, green leaves that grows on the ground in gardens, parks, and fields.

grasshopper
NOUN grasshoppers
A grasshopper is an insect with long legs that can jump very high.

*A **grasshopper** jumps far and high.*

grateful
ADJECTIVE
If you are grateful, you are glad that you have something or glad that someone has done something for you.

grave
NOUN graves
A grave is a place where a dead person is buried.

gravity
NOUN
Gravity is the natural force that pulls things down toward the Earth.

gravy
NOUN
Gravy is a hot sauce that you eat with meat.

graze
VERB grazes, grazing, grazed
1 When animals graze, they eat grass and plants.
2 If you graze your skin, you scrape it and make it bleed. *I fell and **grazed** my knee.*

grease
NOUN
Grease is a thick, oily substance.

great
ADJECTIVE greater, greatest
1 Great means very big. *We climbed on board the **great** ship.*
2 A great person is important and powerful.
3 Something that is great is very good. *That's a **great** idea!*

greedy
ADJECTIVE greedier, greediest
Someone who is greedy eats or wants more of something than they really need. *The **greedy** boy ate twice as much as anyone else.*

green
ADJECTIVE
Something that is green is the colour of grass.

greenhouse
NOUN greenhouses
A greenhouse is a building made of glass in which you grow plants.

greet
VERB greets, greeting, greeted
When you greet someone, you say hello to them.

grew
☛ See **grow**.

grey
ADJECTIVE
Something that is grey is the colour of clouds on a rainy day.

grid
NOUN grids
A grid is a pattern of straight lines that cross each other to form squares.

grill
NOUN grills
1 A grill is the part of a cooker where food is heated from above.
VERB grills, grilling, grilled
2 When you grill food, you cook it on a grill.

grin
VERB grins, grinning, grinned
When you grin, you give a big smile.

grind
VERB grinds, grinding, ground
When you grind something, you crush it into a powder.

grip
VERB grips, gripping, gripped
If you grip something, you hold on to it firmly.

groan
VERB groans, groaning, groaned
If you groan, you make a loud, deep sound because you are unhappy or in pain.

ground
NOUN
1 The ground is the surface of the Earth. *The apple fell to the **ground**.*
2 A sports ground is a place where a sport is played.
3 Ground is the past tense of **grind**.

group
NOUN groups
A group is a number of people who are doing something together.

grow
VERB grows, growing, grew, grown
1 When something grows, it gets bigger.
2 Grow means to become. *She was beginning to **grow** sleepy.*

growl
VERB growls, growling, growled
When an animal growls, it makes a low, angry sound in its throat. *The dog **growled** every time I came near.*

grown-up
VERB grown-ups
A grown-up is an adult.

growth
NOUN
Growth is the way in which plants and animals change as they become bigger and older.

grumble
VERB grumbles, grumbling, grumbled
If you grumble, you complain about something. *Everyone was **grumbling** that the water in the pool was too cold.*

grunt
VERB grunts, grunting, grunted
When a pig grunts, it makes a short, rough sound.

guarantee
NOUN guarantees
A guarantee is a written promise that if something you have bought goes wrong, it will be mended for you for free.

guard
NOUN guards
1 A guard is someone who watches and looks after a person or protects a place.
VERB guards, guarding, guarded
2 If you guard something, you keep it safe. *Our dog is **guarding** the house.*

Growth

All animals grow and change as they get older.

Hatching

The duck egg cracks.

One hour old
The duckling has just hatched.

Two days old
The duckling heads for the water. She's big enough for her first swim.

guess
VERB guesses, guessing, guessed
When you guess the answer to something, you say what you think it might be, although you do not know for sure. *We had to **guess** what she was holding.*

guest
NOUN guests
A guest is someone who stays at a house or a hotel.

guide
NOUN guides
1 A guide is someone whose job is to show people around places. *The **guide** took us around the museum.*
2 A guide to a place is a book with maps and information about the place.
VERB guides, guiding, guided
3 If you guide someone to a place, you show them the way there. *I **guided** the tourists to the main square in the town.*

guilty
ADJECTIVE
Someone who is guilty has done something wrong.

guitar
NOUN guitars
A guitar is a musical instrument with strings. You pluck the strings with your fingers to make different sounds.

gulp
VERB gulps, gulping, gulped
If you gulp down a drink, you drink it quickly. *He **gulped** down a big glass of water.*

guitar

gum
NOUN gums
1 Your gums are the parts inside your mouth around your teeth.
2 Gum is a sweet that you chew for a long time and do not swallow.

gun
NOUN guns
A gun is a weapon that fires metal bullets.

gurdwara
NOUN gurdwaras
A gurdwara is a temple where Sikhs go to pray.

gym
NOUN gyms
A gym is a large room where people can play sports or do exercise using special equipment.

gymnast
NOUN gymnasts
A gymnast is a person who does gymnastics.

gymnastics
NOUN
Gymnastics is a sport in which people do movements and jumps to show how strong and agile they are. *My friend is great at **gymnastics**.*

Three weeks old
The duckling has grown into a young duck. She still stays close to her mother.

The yellow feathers are falling out and white feathers are beginning to grow.

Fully grown
The duck is now a fully grown adult, ready to lay eggs and have ducklings of her own.

H

hole

habit
NOUN habits
A habit is something that you do a lot without thinking. *Biting your nails is a bad **habit**.*

habitat
NOUN habitats
A habitat is the natural place where an animal or plant lives and grows.

hack
VERB hacks, hacking, hacked
1 If you hack something to pieces you roughly cut it up.
2 If someone hacks into a computer, they get into it and use it illegally.
hacker (NOUN)
A hacker is someone who hacks into a computer.

had
☛ See **have**.

hail
NOUN
Hail is drops of frozen rain.

hair
NOUN
Hair grows on your head and body, and on the skin of other mammals.
hairy (ADJECTIVE)
Someone who is hairy has a lot of hair on their body.
☛ **Be careful with spelling:**
hair *She's got long, dark **hair**.*
hare *A **hare** looks like a big rabbit.*

hairdresser
NOUN hairdressers
A hairdresser is someone whose job is to cut people's hair.

Hajj
NOUN
The Hajj is a journey to the city of Mecca that all Muslims try to make at least once.

half
NOUN halves
1 If you divide something into two halves, you divide it into two equal parts. Each part is called one half.
2 Your half-brother or half-sister is a boy or girl who shares one parent with you.

hall
NOUN halls
1 A hall is a corridor or small room just inside the front door of a house.
2 A hall is a large room that people use for meetings and other events.

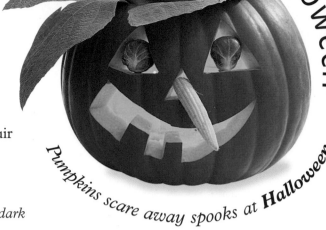

*Pumpkins scare away spooks at **Halloween**.*

Halloween
NOUN
Halloween is a festival on 31st October, when some people dress up as witches and ghosts.

ham
NOUN
Ham is meat from a pig that has been salted or smoked to keep it fresh.

hamburger
NOUN hamburgers
A hamburger is a flat, round piece of chopped beef that you usually eat in a bread roll. A hamburger is also called a **burger**.

hammer
NOUN hammers
A hammer is a tool with a heavy piece of metal on one end that you use to hit nails into wood.

hamster

NOUN hamsters

A hamster is a small animal that looks like a mouse with no tail. Some people keep hamsters as pets.

hand

NOUN hands

1 Your hands are the parts of your body at the ends of your arms that you use for gripping and holding things.

VERB hands, handing, handed

2 If you hand something to someone, you give it to them.

*A menorah (candlestick) used at **Hanukkah***

handbag

NOUN handbags

A handbag is a small bag in which a person carries money and other things.

handle

NOUN handles

1 A handle is the part of something that you hold in your hand.

VERB handles, handling, handled

2 If you handle something, you touch it or hold it in your hand. *I wouldn't like to **handle** a snake!*

handsome

ADJECTIVE

A handsome man or boy is attractive and pleasant to look at.

handstand

NOUN handstands

If you do a handstand, you put your hands on the ground and kick your legs up into the air.

handwriting

NOUN

Handwriting is writing that you do by hand, using a pen or pencil.

hang

VERB hangs, hanging, hung

If you hang something up, you fix it by the top so that the bottom part falls loosely down. *We **hung** our coats on the pegs.*

Hanukkah

NOUN

Hanukkah is the Jewish festival of lights held in winter.

happen

VERB happens, happening, happened

If something happens, it takes place. *Are you OK? What **happened**?*

happy

ADJECTIVE happier, happiest

If you are happy, you feel pleased.

☛ **Opposite:** unhappy

happily (ADVERB)

If you do something happily, you do it in a happy way. *We played **happily** together.*

happiness (NOUN)

Happiness is the feeling you have when you are happy.

harbour

NOUN harbours

A harbour is a sheltered place on the coast that is protected from rough water and stormy weather. Ships can safely come to a harbour to anchor before unloading their goods.

hard

ADJECTIVE harder, hardest

1 Something that is hard is solid and firm to touch. *The ground was dry and **hard**.*

2 Something that is hard is difficult to do. *These sums are **hard**.*

ADVERB

3 If you work hard, you work with a lot of effort.

hard disk

NOUN hard disks

The hard disk is fixed in a computer. It is the part where lots of information is stored.

hardly

ADVERB

If you can hardly do something, you can only just do it. *The writing was so small that I could **hardly** read it.*

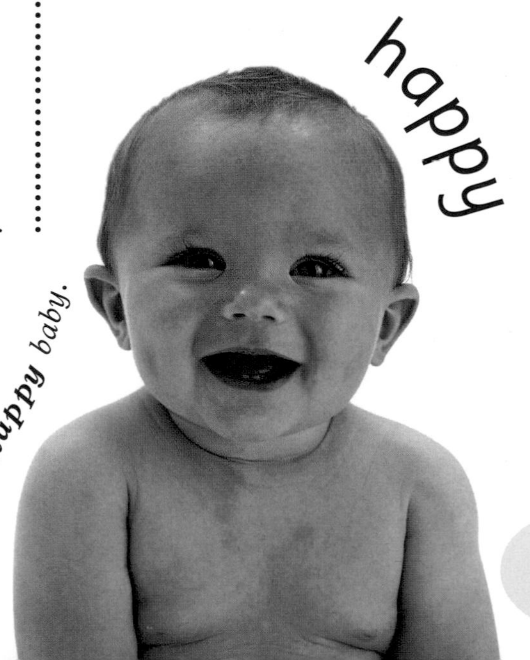

*I'm a **happy** baby.*

a b c d e

hare
NOUN hares
A hare is an animal that looks like a big rabbit. Hares can run fast and can hear very well with their long ears.
☛ **Be careful with spelling:**
hare *A **hare** is like a big rabbit.*
hair *She's got long, dark **hair**.*

A hawk hunts other birds in the sky.
hawk

i j k l m n o p q r s t u v w x y z

harm
NOUN
1 If you do harm to something, you damage it or hurt it.
VERB harms, harming, harmed
2 If you harm someone, you hurt them.
harmful (ADJECTIVE)
Something that is harmful can harm you. *Cars give off **harmful** chemicals.*
harmless (ADJECTIVE)
Something that is harmless will not harm you. *Most kinds of insects are **harmless**, but some can cause diseases.*

harvest
NOUN harvests
The harvest is the time when crops are cut and fruit and vegetables are picked.

hashtag
NOUN hashtags
A hashtag is the symbol (#) that you use in tweets.

hat
NOUN hats
A hat is something that you wear on your head.

hatch
VERB hatches, hatching, hatched
When an animal or bird hatches, it comes out of an egg and is born. *The chicks **hatched** today.*

hate
VERB hates, hating, hated
If you hate something, you have a strong feeling that you do not like it. *I never drink coffee because I **hate** it!*
hatred (NOUN)
Hatred is the feeling that you hate something or someone.

haunted
ADJECTIVE
A place that is haunted has ghosts or spirits in it.

have
VERB has, having, had
If you have something, it is yours or you own it.

hawk
NOUN hawks
A hawk is a bird of prey. It hunts other creatures for food.

hay
NOUN
Hay is dried grass that is fed to animals.

hay fever
NOUN
If you get hay fever, you sneeze a lot when there is pollen, sometimes from grass, in the air.

head
NOUN heads
1 Your head is the part of your body that contains your brain.
2 The head of a group of people is the leader. *Who is the **head** of your school?*

headache
NOUN headaches
If you have a headache, you have a pain in your head.

heading
NOUN headings
A heading is a title of a piece of writing.

headphones
NOUN
Headphones are small speakers that you wear over or in your ears to listen to music.

headteacher
NOUN headteachers
The headteacher in a school is the teacher who is in charge of the whole school. A man who does this is also called the **headmaster**, and a woman is called the **headmistress**.

heal
VERB heals, healing, healed
When a cut heals, it gets better.

healthy
ADJECTIVE healthier, healthiest
1 If you are healthy, you are well and not ill.
2 Things that are healthy are good for you. *A **healthy** diet includes lots of fruit and vegetables.*
☛ **Opposite:** unhealthy

heap
NOUN heaps
A heap is a pile of things lying on top of each other. *She left her clothes in a **heap** on the floor.*

hear
VERB hears, hearing, heard
If you can hear a sound, you notice it. *Did you **hear** that bird?*
☛ **Be careful with spelling:**
hear *I can **hear** music.*
here *Come **here**!*

heart
NOUN hearts
1 Your heart is the organ in your chest that pumps blood around your body.
2 A heart is a shape. People often draw hearts to show that they love someone.

heat
NOUN
1 When there is heat, something feels hot.
VERB heats, heating, heated
2 When you heat something, you make it warmer. *We **heated** some water.*

heaven
NOUN
Heaven is the happy place where some people believe you go to when you die.

heavy
ADJECTIVE heavier, heaviest
Something that is heavy weighs a lot.

helicopter

*A **helicopter** hovers high in the sky.*

hedge
NOUN hedges
A hedge is a line of bushes between two fields or gardens.

heel
NOUN heels
1 Your heel is the back part of your foot.
2 The heel on a shoe is the high part at the back.

height
NOUN heights
1 The height of something is how high it is.
2 Your height is how tall you are.

held
☛ See **hold**.

heavy

*The truck is **heavier** than the cat.*

helicopter
NOUN helicopters
A helicopter is a type of aircraft with large blades that spin round on top of it.

hello
You say hello to someone when you meet them.

helmet
NOUN helmets
A helmet is a strong hat that you wear to protect your head.

help
VERB helps, helping, helped
If you help someone, you do something for them.
helpful (ADJECTIVE)
Someone who is helpful helps you.
helpless (ADJECTIVE)
Someone who is helpless cannot look after themselves. *The tiny kittens were completely **helpless**.*

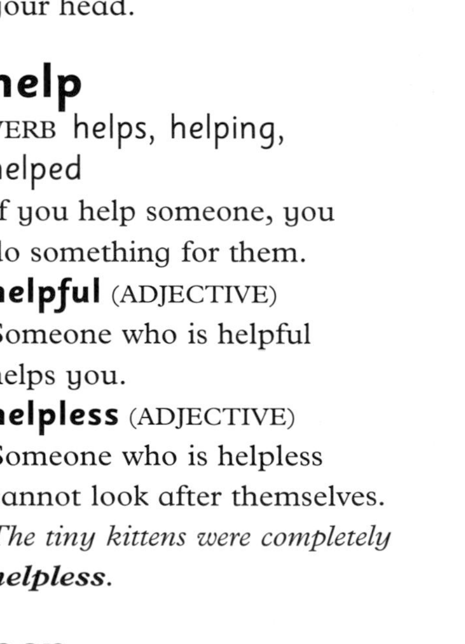

hen
NOUN hens
A hen is a female chicken.

a b c d e f g Hh i j k l m n o p q r s t u v w x y z

herb
NOUN herbs
A herb is a plant that people use to give flavour to food or to make medicines.

herbivore
NOUN herbivores
A herbivore is an animal that eats plants.

herd
NOUN herds
A herd of animals is a large group of them.

here
ADVERB
Here means in this place. *Do you live **here**?*
☛ **Be careful with spelling:**
here *Come **here**!*
hear *I can **hear** music.*

hero
NOUN heroes
1 A hero is a very brave man or boy. *You rescued my cat – you're my **hero**!*
2 The hero in a story is the man or boy that the story is about.

heroine
NOUN heroines
1 A heroine is a very brave woman or girl.
2 The heroine in a story is the woman or girl that the story is about.

hexagon
NOUN hexagons
A hexagon is a shape with six straight sides.

hibernate
VERB hibernates, hibernating, hibernated
When an animal hibernates, it goes to sleep for the winter.

hiccup
NOUN hiccups
If you have hiccups, you make sudden sounds in your throat by breathing in quickly. *You'll get **hiccups** if you drink too quickly.*

hide
VERB hides, hiding, hid, hidden
If you hide something, you put it in a place where people cannot see it. *I **hid** the map under my pillow.*

hieroglyphics
NOUN
Hieroglyphics is a type of writing in which you use pictures instead of words. The ancient Egyptians used hieroglyphics.

high
ADJECTIVE higher, highest
1 Something that is high in the air is a long way away from the ground.
2 Something high is very tall. *We had to climb over a **high** wall.*

highlight
VERB highlights, highlighting, highlighted
When you highlight words, you draw over them using a coloured pen or change their colour on a computer screen, so that you can see them more easily.

hijab
NOUN hijabs
A hijab is a covering that some Muslim women wear over their head, to cover their hair.

hill
NOUN hills
A hill is an area of high ground.

Hindu
NOUN Hindus
A Hindu is a person who follows **Hinduism**, an Indian religion. Hindus worship many gods, and believe that when people die, they are born again.

hip
NOUN hips
Your hips are the joints where your legs join onto your body.

hippopotamus
NOUN hippopotamuses or hippopotami
A hippopotamus, or hippo, is a very large animal that lives in Africa. They live in lakes or rivers, and eat water plants.

hire
VERB hires, hiring, hired
If you hire something, you pay to use it for a short time. *We **hired** bikes and rode around the lake.*

history
NOUN
History is a subject in which you study events in the past.

hit
NOUN hits
1 If something is a hit, people like it and it is successful. *The song was a big **hit**.*
VERB hits, hitting, hit
2 If you hit someone, you bang them with your hand. *That boy **hit** me!*
3 If you hit something, you knock it or bump into it. *In tennis, you have to **hit** the ball over the net.*

hi-tech
ADJECTIVE
Something that is hi-tech is very modern and uses computer technology. Hi-tech stands for **high technology**.

hive
NOUN hives
A hive is a box that bees live in.

hobby
NOUN hobbies
A hobby is something that you do for enjoyment in your spare time.

hockey
NOUN
Hockey is a game in which teams of players hit a ball with a curved stick and try to score goals.

hold
VERB holds, holding, held
1 When you hold something, you keep it in your hands. *Would you like to **hold** our new puppy?*
2 If something holds an amount, it can have that amount inside it. *This bottle will **hold** two litres of water.*

hole
NOUN holes
A hole is a gap or opening in something.
☛ **Be careful with spelling:**
hole *There's a **hole** in my shoe.*
whole *He ate a **whole** box of chocolates!*

Holi
NOUN
Holi is a Hindu festival of colours that takes place in spring.

holiday
NOUN holidays
A holiday is a time when you do not have to go to school or work. It's often a time when you go away.

hollow
ADJECTIVE
Something that is hollow has an empty space inside.

holly
NOUN
Holly is an evergreen plant with shiny evergreen leaves that are prickly and bright red berries.

holy
ADJECTIVE
Something that is holy is thought to be special because it is connected with religion.

home
NOUN homes
Your home is the place where you live.

home page
NOUN home pages
A home page is the main page on a website.

homework
NOUN
Homework is schoolwork that you do at home.

homograph
NOUN homographs
Homographs are words that are spelled the same way but are not said in the same way and have different meanings. For example, there are two homographs in the sentence: *Put down your **bow** and arrow before you **bow** to the king.*

holly

Horse

Here are some words about horses and horse equipment.

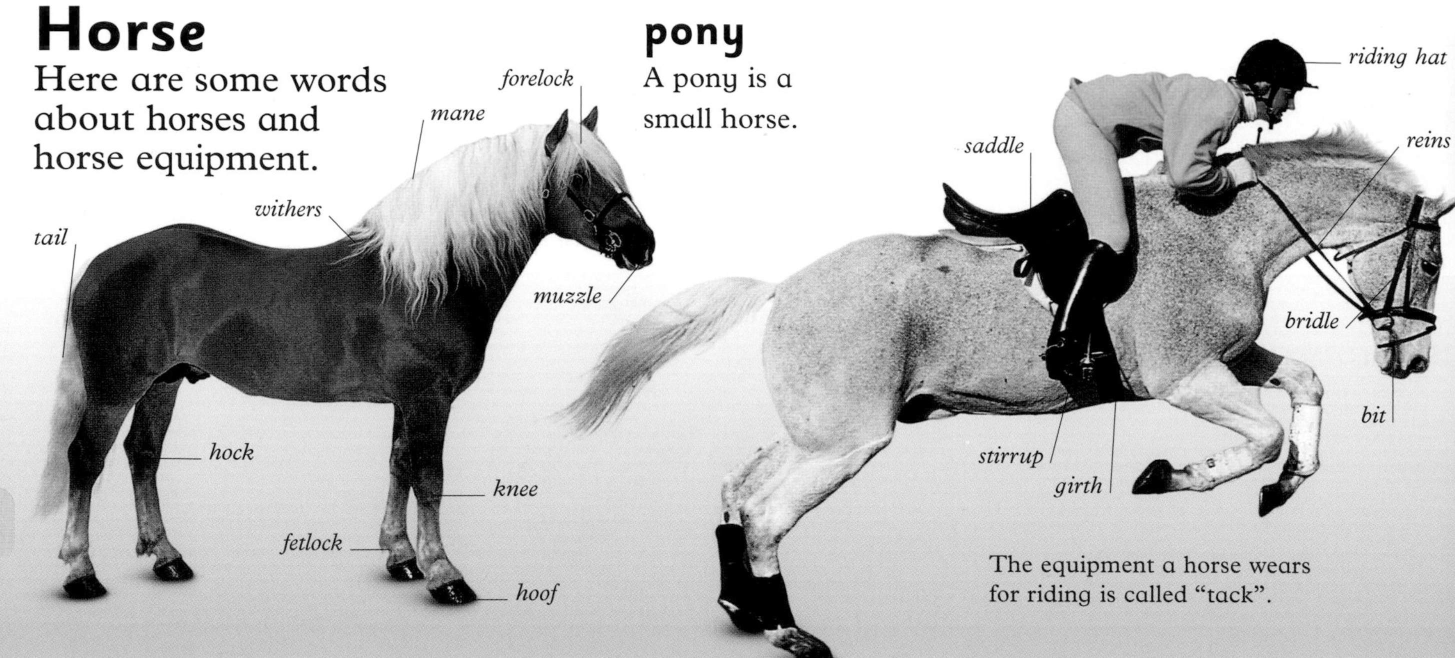

pony
A pony is a small horse.

The equipment a horse wears for riding is called "tack".

homophone
NOUN homophones
Homophones are words that sound the same but have different spellings and meanings. For example, there are two homophones in the sentence: *I can't **hear** you over **here**.*

honest
ADJECTIVE
Someone who is honest tells the truth and does not steal things.
☛ **Opposite:** dishonest

honey
NOUN
Honey is a sweet, sticky food that bees make.

hood
NOUN hoods
A hood is a part of a jacket or top that covers your head.

hoof
NOUN hoofs or hooves
The hooves of animals such as horses are their hard feet.

hook
NOUN hooks
A hook is a curved piece of metal. *I hung it on the coat **hook**.*

hoot
VERB hoots, hooting, hooted
1 When an owl hoots, it makes a loud sound.
2 When a car hoots, its horn makes a loud sound.

hop
VERB hops, hopping, hopped
When you hop, you jump on one leg.

hope
VERB hopes, hoping, hoped
If you hope that something will happen, you want it to happen.
hopeful (ADJECTIVE)
If you are hopeful, you hope something will happen. *I am **hopeful** that I will win.*
hopefully (ADVERB)
You use this word when you are hopeful that something will happen.

horn
NOUN horns
1 An animal's horns are the tough, pointed spikes on its head. *A rhinoceros has one **horn**.*
2 A horn is a musical instrument made of brass.
3 A horn is something that can make a loud warning noise.

horrible
ADJECTIVE
Something that is horrible is very unpleasant or frightening.

horror
NOUN
If something fills you with horror, it makes you feel shocked and frightened. *They watched in **horror** as the house burned down.*

horse
NOUN horses
A horse is a large animal that people use for riding and pulling carts.

mare
An adult female horse. The mother is also called the "dam".

stallion
An adult male horse. The father is also called the "sire".

a b c d e f g Hh i j k l m n o p q r s t u v w x y z

hose
NOUN hoses
A hose is a long flexible tube that water can go through. *A **hose** is useful for watering flowers or for putting out fires.*

hospital
NOUN hospitals
A hospital is a place where people go when they are sick or injured and need medical treatment by a doctor.

hot
ADJECTIVE hotter, hottest
1 Something that is hot has a very high temperature. *The bars of the heater are very **hot**.*
2 Hot food is very spicy.
3 Something that is hot is the latest craze. *He learned the **hottest** dance moves.*

hotel
NOUN hotels
A hotel is where people pay to eat a meal and stay the night.

hour
NOUN hours
An hour is 60 minutes. There are 24 hours in a day.

house
NOUN houses
A house is a building that people live in.

how
ADVERB
You can use "how" to ask questions or in sentences that explain something. ***How** did he do that magic trick?*

howl
VERB howls, howling, howled
1 If a wolf or dog howls, it makes a loud, high-pitched wailing sound.
2 If someone howls, they cry loudly, because of fear, anger or pain.
3 When a strong wind is blowing we can say that it is howling.

huddle
VERB huddles, huddling, huddled
If people huddle together, they stay close to each other because they are either cold or frightened.

*Baby rabbits **huddle** together for warmth.*

hug
VERB hugs, hugging, hugged
If you hug someone, you hold them in a loving way.

huge
ADJECTIVE
Something that is huge is very big. *That cake is **huge**!*

a b c d e f g Hh i j k l m n o p q r s t u v w x

hum
VERB hums, humming, hummed
When you hum, you sing with your lips closed.

human
NOUN humans
A human is a person: man, woman, or child. A human is also called a **human being**.

humid
ADJECTIVE
If the weather is humid, it is warm and damp.

humour
NOUN
If you have a sense of humour, you can tell when things are funny.

hump
NOUN humps
A hump is a large, round lump. Camels have humps on their backs.

hundred
NOUN hundreds
A hundred is the number 100.

hung
☛ See **hang**.

hump

hungry
ADJECTIVE
If you are hungry, you want to eat something.
hunger (NOUN)
Hunger is the feeling you have when you are hungry. *I was weak with **hunger**.*
hungrily (ADVERB)
If you eat hungrily, you eat quickly because you are very hungry.

hunt
VERB hunts, hunting, hunted
1 When animals or people hunt, they follow other animals to try and kill them for food. *Lions **hunt** in packs.*
2 If you hunt for something, you look everywhere because you are trying to find it. *The police are **hunting** for the criminal.*

hurl
VERB hurls, hurling, hurled
If you hurl something, you throw it as hard as you can. *She **hurled** the cushion across the room.*

hurricane
NOUN hurricanes
A hurricane is a violent storm with strong winds. Hurricanes can do a lot of damage to buildings.

hurry
VERB hurries, hurrying, hurried
When you hurry, you do things quickly. *He had to **hurry** to deliver the parcel on time.*

hurt
VERB hurts, hurting, hurt
1 If you hurt a part of your body, you injure it. *I **hurt** my leg when I fell.*
2 If somewhere hurts, you feel pain. *My broken arm **hurts**.*

husband
NOUN husbands
A person's husband is the man they are married to.

hush
NOUN
When there is hush, there is no noise where there was noise before. *There was a **hush** as the teacher came into the room.*

hut
NOUN huts
A hut is a small, wooden house.

hutch
NOUN hutches
A hutch is a small cage that you can keep a rabbit in.

hygiene
NOUN
Hygiene is keeping things clean. *Good **hygiene** is very important.*

hyphen
NOUN hyphens
A hyphen is a mark (-) that you use to join parts of words together. The word *hi-tech* has a hyphen.

I

ice
NOUN
Ice is frozen water.
icy (ADJECTIVE)
Something that is icy is very cold or covered in ice.
*I slipped on the **icy** path.*

iceberg
NOUN icebergs
An iceberg is a huge piece of ice floating in the sea.

ice cream

ice cream
NOUN ice creams
Ice cream is a sweet, frozen food that is made from cream or milk and flavoured with fruit, nuts, or chocolate.

ice hockey
NOUN ice hockey
Ice hockey is a game in which teams skate on ice and score goals by using a stick to hit a flat disk called a **puck** into a net.

ice rink
NOUN ice rinks
An ice rink is a large area of ice that people can skate on.

ice skate
NOUN ice skates
1 Ice skates are special boots with metal blades on the bottom that you wear when you are skating on ice.
VERB ice skates, ice skating, ice skated
2 When you ice-skate, you move over ice with ice skates on your feet.

ice skate

Ice skates help you to move over ice.

icicle
NOUN icicles
An icicle is a long, thin piece of ice that is hanging down from a surface.

icing
NOUN
Icing is a sweet substance that you put on the top of cakes, biscuits, or puddings.

icon
NOUN icons
An icon is a small picture on a computer or phone that you touch or click on if you want to use a program.

ICT
NOUN
ICT is the subject in which you study computers. ICT stands for **information and communication technology**.

idea
NOUN ideas
An idea is a thought that you have in your head.

ideal
ADJECTIVE
Something that is ideal is perfect in every way.

identical
ADJECTIVE
If things are identical, they are exactly the same.

a b c d e f g h Ii

identify
VERB identifies, identifying, identified
If you identify something, you can say exactly what it is. If you identify someone, you can say who they are.

idiot
NOUN idiots
An idiot is someone who is very silly or stupid.

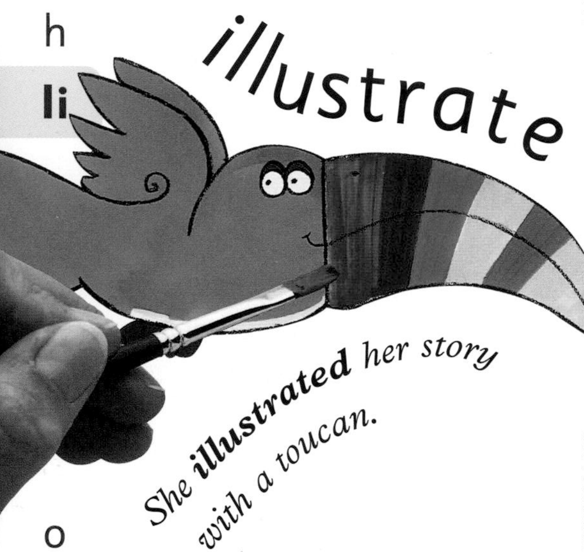
illustrate
She **illustrated** her story with a toucan.

o p q r s t u v w x y z

idle
ADJECTIVE
Someone who is idle is lazy.

igloo
NOUN igloos
An igloo is a round building made of snow and ice.

ignorant
ADJECTIVE
Someone who is ignorant does not know very much.

ignore
VERB ignores, ignoring, ignored
If you ignore someone, you take no notice of them. *I asked him where he was going, but he **ignored** me.*

ill
ADJECTIVE
If you feel ill, you do not feel well.
illness (NOUN)
If you get an illness, you become ill.

illegal
ADJECTIVE
If something is illegal, you are not allowed to do it because it is against the law.
☞ **Opposite:** legal

illustrate
VERB illustrates, illustrating, illustrated
If you illustrate a story, you draw pictures to go with it.
illustration (NOUN)
An illustration is a picture in a book.

image
NOUN images
An image is a picture of something or someone.

imaginary
ADJECTIVE
Something that is imaginary is not real and only exists in stories. *The unicorn is an **imaginary** animal.*

imagination
NOUN
If you use your imagination, you think of new ideas. *You need a good **imagination** to write stories.*

imagine
VERB imagines, imagining, imagined
When you imagine something, you picture it in your mind.
*I **imagined** a warm, sunny beach.*

imitate
VERB imitates, imitating, imitated
If you imitate someone, you copy them.

immediately
ADVERB
If you do something immediately, you do it very quickly, without waiting.
*We need to leave **immediately**.*

immigrate
VERB immigrates, immigrating, immigrated
When people immigrate, they come into a country in order to live there.
immigrant (NOUN)
An immigrant is someone who has come into a country in order to live there.

impatient
ADJECTIVE
Someone who is impatient quickly gets angry, especially if they have to wait. *The bus was late, and I was starting to get **impatient**.*
☞ **Opposite:** patient
impatiently (ADVERB)
If you say or do something impatiently, you do it in an impatient way. *"Hurry up!" she shouted **impatiently**.*

important
ADJECTIVE
1 If something is important, it means a lot to you.
*Winning this competition is very **important** to me.*
2 An important person has a lot of power.

impossible
ADJECTIVE
If something is impossible, you cannot do it. *It is **impossible** for people to fly like birds.*
☛ **Opposite:** possible

improve
VERB improves, improving, improved
If something improves, it gets better. *My spelling is **improving**.*
improvement (NOUN)
An improvement is a change that makes something better.

include
VERB includes, including, included
If you include something, you have it or put it with other things. *I'm going to **include** some pictures with my story.*

inconvenient
ADJECTIVE
If something is inconvenient, you find it difficult or annoying. *It's **inconvenient** having the sports field so far away from the school.*
☛ **Opposite:** convenient

incorrect
ADJECTIVE
Something that is incorrect is wrong. *I'm sorry, you are **incorrect**!*
☛ **Opposite:** correct

increase
VERB increases, increasing, increased
When a number or an amount increases, it gets bigger. *My pocket money **increases** every year.*
☛ **Opposite:** decrease

incredible
ADJECTIVE
If something is incredible, it is so strange that you find it difficult to believe.

independent
ADJECTIVE
Someone who is independent can do things for themselves and decide things for themselves.

index
NOUN indexes
An index is a list of all the things that are included in a book, with numbers for the pages where you can find each thing.

individual
NOUN individuals
1 An individual is a person.
ADJECTIVE
2 Something that is individual is for just one person. *There will be **individual** prizes and team prizes.*

indoors
ADVERB
Indoors means inside a building. *Let's go **indoors** now.*
☛ **Opposite:** outdoors

industry
NOUN industries
An industry is a business that makes things or sells things. *A lot of people work in the food **industry**.*

infant
NOUN infants
An infant is a very young child.

infection
NOUN infections
If you get an infection, a germ gets into your body and makes you ill.

infinity
NOUN
Infinity is a time, number, or place that never ends. *Looking at the night sky is like looking into **infinity**.*

inflate
VERB inflates, inflating, inflated
When you inflate something, you blow or pump air into it to make it bigger.
☛ **Opposite:** deflate

influence
VERB influences, influencing, influenced
If you influence someone, you change the way they think or behave.

inflate

*He **inflated** the balloon with air.*

Insect

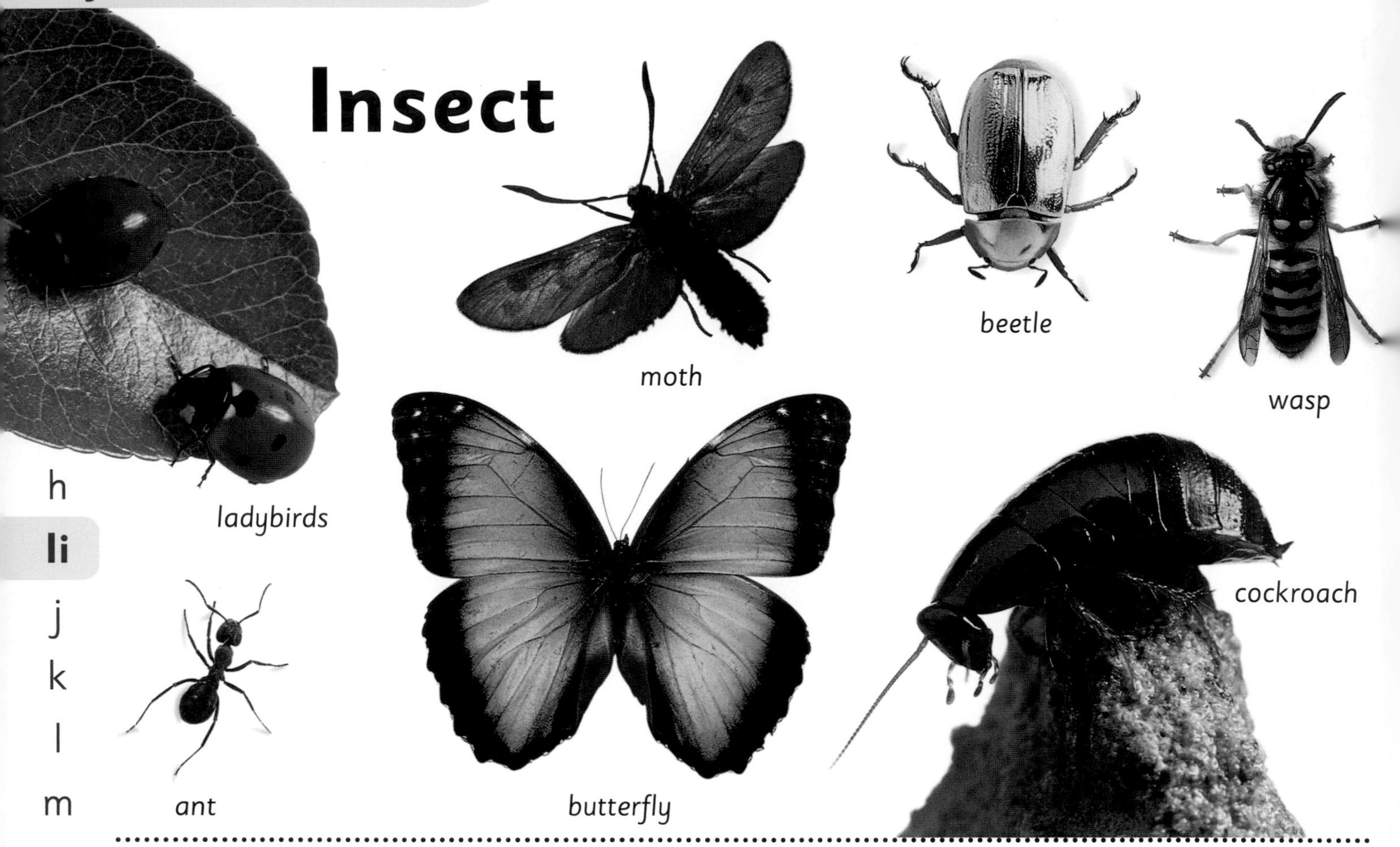

moth

beetle

wasp

ladybirds

cockroach

ant

butterfly

information
NOUN
Information is facts about something. *We had to find some **information** about Africa.*

ingredient
NOUN ingredients
Ingredients are things that you mix together to make something.

inhabitant
NOUN inhabitants
The inhabitants of a place are the people who live there.

inhaler
NOUN inhalers
An inhaler is a container with medicine in it. You breathe the medicine into your lungs. A lot of people who have asthma use inhalers.

initial
NOUN initials
Your initials are the first letters of your names.

injection
NOUN injections
If you have an injection, a doctor puts some medicine, or a vaccination, into your body using a needle.

injure
VERB injures, injuring, injured
If you injure a part of your body, you hurt it.
injured (ADJECTIVE)
If you are injured, you have hurt a part of your body.
injury (NOUN)
If you have an injury, you have hurt a part of your body.

ink
NOUN inks
Ink is a black or coloured liquid that you use for writing or drawing. It is also used in printers to print the words and pictures from a computer on a piece of paper.

innocent
ADJECTIVE
Someone who is innocent has not done anything wrong.

insect
NOUN insects
An insect is a small animal with six legs. Insects usually have wings and do not have a backbone. Flies, bees, beetles, and butterflies are all insects.

inside

NOUN insides

The inside of something is the part within it. *The **inside** of the building is really beautiful.*

insist

VERB insists, insisting, insisted

If you insist on doing something, you do it even though other people tell you not to. *He **insisted** on inviting all his friends to the party.*

inspect

VERB inspects, inspecting, inspected

If you inspect something, you check it carefully. *He **inspected** the apple and then took a bite.*

inspector (NOUN)

An inspector is someone whose job is to check things.

install

VERB installs, installing, installed

When you install something, you put it in a place so it is ready to use. *You can **install** this app on your phone or computer.*

instant

ADJECTIVE

Something that is instant happens straight away. *The show was an **instant** success.*

instantly (ADVERB)

If something happens instantly, it happens immediately. *I knew **instantly** that he was lying.*

instead

ADVERB

Instead means in the place of another person or thing. *I chose the red pen **instead** of the blue one.*

instruction

NOUN instructions

If someone gives you an instruction, they tell you what you should do. *Read the **instructions** before you use the machine.*

instrument

NOUN instruments

1 An instrument is something that you use for making music. *He plays two musical **instruments**.*

2 An instrument is a tool.

insult

VERB insults, insulting, insulted

If you insult someone, you call them names or say horrible things to them.

intelligent

ADJECTIVE

An intelligent person is clever and learns things quickly.

intelligence (NOUN)

Intelligence is the ability to learn things quickly.

interactive

ADJECTIVE

Something that is interactive is a thing in which you can control the way in which things happen. *I like playing **interactive** computer games.*

interest

VERB interests, interesting, interested

If something interests you, you like it and want to learn more about it.

interested (ADJECTIVE)

If you are interested in something, you want to learn more about it. *I'm **interested** in fossils.*

interesting (ADJECTIVE)

If something is interesting, it holds your attention and is not boring. *We watched an **interesting** documentary about whales.*

interjection

NOUN interjections

An interjection is a word such as "Hello" or "Goodbye" that you say on its own, not in a full sentence.

international

ADJECTIVE

Something that is international involves two or more different countries.

internet

NOUN

The internet is a system for linking computers from all over the world so information can be shared.

interrupt

VERB interrupts, interrupting, interrupted

If you interrupt someone, you stop them from talking or working. *Please don't **interrupt** while I'm speaking!*

interruption (NOUN)

An interruption is something that interrupts you while you are talking or working.

interval

NOUN intervals

1 An interval is a short break during a play or show.

2 An interval is the time between two things happening.

interview

NOUN interviews

An interview is a meeting where someone has to answer questions.

introduce

VERB introduces, introducing, introduced

When you introduce someone, you say their name and explain who they are.

introduction (NOUN)

The introduction is the part of a book or story that explains who the characters are or what the book will be about.

Ivy covered the old brick wall.

invade

VERB invades, invading, invaded

When people invade a country, they enter it and attack it.

invent

VERB invents, inventing, invented

If you invent something, you think of it and design it. *Who **invented** the telephone?*

invention (NOUN)

An invention is something that you invent.

inverted commas

NOUN

Inverted commas are the marks (' ') or (" ") used in writing to show what someone has said.

investigate

VERB investigates, investigating, investigated

If you investigate something, you try to find out about it. *The police are **investigating** yesterday's robbery.*

invisible

ADJECTIVE

If something is invisible, you cannot see it.

☛ **Opposite:** visible

invite

VERB invites, inviting, invited

If you invite someone to go with you somewhere, you ask them.

invitation (NOUN)

If you give someone an invitation, you invite them to an event.

involve

VERB involves, involving, involved

If you are involved in something, you take part in it. *She loved being **involved** the school play.*

iron

NOUN

1 Iron is a strong, heavy metal found in rocks. People use iron to make things such as tools and gates.

2 You use a hot iron to make clothes smooth after they have been washed.

Islam

NOUN

Islam is the Muslim religion. Muslims believe there is one God, Allah, and that Muhammad is His prophet.

island

NOUN islands

An island is a piece of land that is completely surrounded by water.

italics

NOUN

Italics are letters that are sloping *like this*.

itch

VERB itches, itching, itched

If your skin itches, it feels uncomfortable and you want to rub or scratch it.

ivy

NOUN ivies

Ivy is a woody evergreen plant that climbs up walls and trees or creeps along the ground.

jab
VERB jabs, jabbing, jabbed
If you jab someone, you poke him or her with your finger. *My friend* ***jabbed*** *me in the ribs to get my attention.*

jacket
NOUN jackets
A jacket is a short coat.

jackpot
NOUN jackpots
A jackpot is a very large amount of money that you can win. *The family won the lottery* ***jackpot****.*

jagged
ADJECTIVE
Something that is jagged has a lot of sharp points or rough edges.

jail
NOUN jails
A jail is a place where people are kept locked up.

jam
NOUN jams
1 Jam is a sweet food made with fruit and sugar. You spread jam on bread.
2 If there is a jam, a lot of people or cars are stuck and cannot move.

jar
NOUN jars
A jar is a glass container that you keep food in.

jaw
NOUN jaws
Your jaw is the bone in your chin that supports your mouth and allows it to open and close.

jazz
NOUN
Jazz is a type of popular music with strong rhythms.

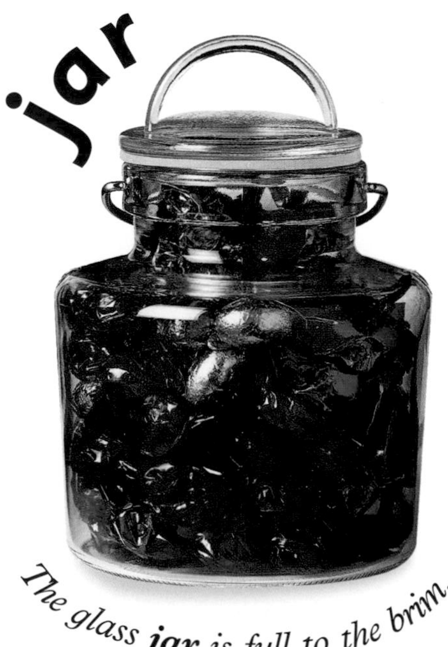

The glass ***jar*** *is full to the brim.*

jealous
ADJECTIVE
If you are jealous of someone, you feel angry because they have something that you would like. *He was* ***jealous*** *of his friend's new phone.*
jealousy (NOUN)
Jealousy is the feeling you have when you are jealous.

jeans

jeans
NOUN
Jeans are trousers made of a thick cotton.

jelly
NOUN jellies
Jelly is a soft, wobbly, sweet food made from fruit juice and sugar.

jellyfish
NOUN jellyfish or jellyfishes
A jellyfish is a sea animal that has a soft body and long, stinging tentacles.

jet
NOUN jets
1 A jet of water is a stream of water moving quickly through the air.
2 A jet is a fast aircraft.

Jew
NOUN Jews
A Jew is someone whose religion is Judaism.
Jewish (ADJECTIVE)
Someone who is Jewish follows the religion of Judaism.

a b c d e f g

jewel
NOUN jewels
A jewel is a precious stone that has been cut and polished. Diamonds, rubies, and emeralds are all jewels.

jewellery
NOUN
Jewellery is an object like a necklace, bracelet, or ring, that people wear on their bodies for decoration.

She wore simple ***jewellery*** *– just a gold heart.*

m n o p q r s t u v w x y z

jigsaw puzzle
NOUN jigsaw puzzles
A jigsaw puzzle is a game with a lot of different pieces that you have to fit together to make a picture. *We finished the big* ***jigsaw puzzle*** *on the rainy afternoon.*

job
NOUN jobs
1 A job is something that you have to do. *Your* ***job*** *is to collect up all the pencils.*
2 Your job is the work that you do to make money. *What* ***job*** *do you want to do when you grow up?*

jockey
NOUN jockeys
A jockey is a person who rides a horse in races.

jog
VERB jogs, jogging, jogged
When you jog, you run slowly and steadily.

join
VERB joins, joining, joined
1 When you join things, you fix them together.
2 When you join a club, you become a member of it.

joint
NOUN joints
A joint is a place in your body where two bones meet. Your knees and your elbows are joints.

joke
NOUN jokes
1 A joke is something that you say or do to make people laugh.
VERB jokes, joking, joked
2 If you are joking, you are not being serious but are saying or doing something just to make people laugh.

journalist
NOUN journalists
A journalist is someone who gathers news and writes about it in a newspaper or magazine, or talks about it on television.

journey
NOUN journeys
If you go on a journey, you travel somewhere.

joyful
ADJECTIVE
If you are joyful, you are very happy.

Judaism
NOUN
Judaism is the religion of Jewish people. Jews believe in one God and in the teachings of the Old Testament and the Talmud, the Jewish holy books.

judge
NOUN judges
1 A judge is the person in charge of a court, who decides how people should be punished when they have done something wrong.
2 The judge in a competition is the person who decides who the winner is.
VERB judges, judging, judged
3 When you judge something, you decide how good or bad it is. *Who is going to* ***judge*** *the dog competition?*

judo
NOUN
Judo is a sport in which two people fight using special movements to try and throw the other player to the ground.

jug
NOUN jugs
A jug is a container with a handle and a spout that you use for pouring liquids out of.

juggle
VERB juggles, juggling, juggled
When you juggle, you keep several objects in the air at the same time by throwing and catching them.

juice
NOUN juices
Juice is the liquid that you can squeeze out of fruit or vegetables.
juicy (ADJECTIVE)
Food that is juicy has a lot of juice in it. *We had some lovely **juicy** strawberries.*

jump
VERB jumps, jumping, jumped
When you jump, you throw yourself into the air. *Can you **jump** over that fence?*

jumper
NOUN jumpers
A jumper is a thick top often knitted from wool that you wear to keep warm.

juice

jungle
NOUN jungles
A jungle is a thick forest in a tropical part of the world.

junior
ADJECTIVE
Junior means for children. *We are going to have a **junior** football tournament.*

junk
NOUN
1 You can describe things that are broken or no use as junk. *Our garage is full of my dad's **junk**.*
2 Junk food is food that is not good for you because it contains a lot of fat or sugar.

jury
NOUN juries
A jury is a group of people who sit in a court and decide whether the person on trial is guilty or not guilty.

just
ADVERB
1 Just means exactly. *These shoes are **just** perfect for me!*
2 If something has just happened, it happened a short time ago. *My friends have **just** gone home.*
3 Just means only. *I **just** need to brush my teeth, and then I'll be ready to leave.*

jump

*Frogs can **jump** a long way to escape enemies.*

king

kangaroo
NOUN kangaroos
A kangaroo is a large Australian animal that hops on its strong back legs. Female kangaroos carry their young in a pouch.

karate
NOUN
Karate is a sport in which people fight using their hands and feet to kick and chop.

keen
ADJECTIVE
If you are keen on something, you like it a lot. *I'm a **keen** swimmer and I love the water.*

keep
VERB keeps, keeping, kept
1 If you keep something, you have it and do not give it away. *I **keep** my old bike in the shed.*
2 Keep means to remain. *Please **keep** still!*
3 If you keep doing something, you do not stop.

kennel
NOUN kennels
A kennel is a small hut for a dog to sleep in.

kept
☛ See **keep**.

ketchup
NOUN
Ketchup is a thick sauce, usually made with tomatoes. *I like **ketchup** on my chips.*

kettle
NOUN kettles
A kettle is a special container that you boil water in.

key
NOUN keys
1 A key is a piece of metal that has been cut into a special shape so that it will fit into a lock and open it.
2 The keys on a computer are the buttons that you press to work it.

keyboard
NOUN keyboards
1 The keyboard on a computer has keys that you press to work it.
2 A keyboard is a musical instrument like a piano that works with electricity.

kick
VERB kicks, kicking, kicked
When you kick something, you hit it with your foot.

kid
NOUN kids
1 A kid is a child.
2 A kid is a baby goat.

kidnap
VERB kidnaps, kidnapping, kidnapped
To kidnap someone means to take them away and keep them prisoner.

kill
VERB kills, killing, killed
If you kill something, you make it die. *She **killed** the wasp with a rolled-up newspaper.*

kilo
NOUN kilos
When you weigh something, you say how many kilos it weighs. A kilo is also called a **kilogram**. One kilo is 1,000 grams. *The bag of sugar weighs one **kilo**.*

kilometre
NOUN kilometres
When you say how far away a place is, you say how many kilometres away it is. One kilometre is 1,000 metres. *The park is five **kilometres** from here.*

kind
NOUN kinds
1 A kind of thing is a type or a sort of that thing. *There are lots of different **kinds** of bird.*
ADJECTIVE kinder, kindest
2 Someone who is kind helps others. *It was **kind** of you to help me with my homework.*
☛ **Opposite:** unkind
kindly (ADVERB)
If you do or say something kindly, you do it in a kind way.
kindness (NOUN)
Kindness is behaviour that is kind. *You should treat all animals with **kindness**.*

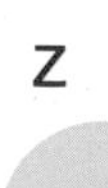

king
NOUN kings
A king is a man who rules a country.
kingdom (NOUN)
A kingdom is a land that is ruled by a king or queen.

kiss
VERB kisses, kissing, kissed
1 When you kiss someone, you touch them with your lips to show that you like them or love them.
NOUN kisses
2 A kiss is what you give someone when you kiss them. *Granny gave him a **kiss** on the cheek.*

kit
NOUN kits
1 A sports kit is a set of clothes that you wear to do sport.
2 A kit is a set of parts that you put together to make something. *She has a **kit** to make a model aeroplane.*

kitchen
NOUN kitchens
A kitchen is a room where people cook food.

kite
NOUN kites
A kite is a very light toy that you fly in the air on the end of a long string.

kitten
NOUN kittens
A kitten is a young cat.

knee
NOUN knees
Your knee is the part in the middle of your leg where you can bend it.

kneel
VERB kneels, kneeling, kneeled or knelt
When you kneel, you sit on your knees.

knew
☛ See **know**.

knife
NOUN knives
You use a knife for cutting things. It has a sharp blade and a handle that you hold.

knight
NOUN knights
A knight is a soldier from medieval times who rode a horse and wore armour.
☛ **Be careful with spelling:**
knight *A **knight** wears armour.*
night *It's dark at **night**.*

knit
VERB knits, knitting, knitted
When you knit, you make clothes and blankets from wool, using large needles.

knob
NOUN knobs
1 A knob is a round handle on a piece of furniture.
2 A knob is a button that you turn to make something work.

knock
VERB knocks, knocking, knocked
1 When you knock on a door, you rap on it with your hand. *He **knocked** on the door until someone opened it to let him in.*
2 If you knock something, you bump it by accident. *She **knocked** over the jug.*

knot
NOUN knots
A knot is a piece of string or rope that is twisted. You can also tie a knot to connect string or rope.
☛ **Be careful with spelling:**
knot *I've got to untie this **knot**.*
not *She's **not** here. She's away.*

know
VERB knows, knowing, knew, known
1 If you know something, you have it in your mind and understand it. *Do you **know** what the capital of France is?*
2 If you know someone, you have met them before.
☛ **Be careful with spelling:**
know *Do you **know** my name?*
no *There's **no** food left.*

knuckle
NOUN knuckles
Your knuckles are the joints in your fingers where the bones connect.

koala
NOUN koalas
A koala is a furry Australian animal that lives in eucalyptus trees. Koalas eat leaves and tree bark and sleep a lot.

Koran
NOUN
The Koran is the holy book of the religion of Islam.

koala

label
NOUN labels
A label is a small piece of paper or cloth that is fixed to something and gives you information about it.

laboratory
NOUN laboratories
A laboratory is a place where scientists work and do experiments.

lace
NOUN laces
1 Lace is thin material with small holes. It often decorates the edges of clothes.
2 The laces on your shoes are the pieces of string that you tie to fasten them.

ladder
NOUN ladders
A ladder is a tall frame with rungs or steps, which you use for climbing up or down.

lady
NOUN ladies
A lady is a polite term for a woman.

ladybird
NOUN ladybirds
A ladybird is a small, red beetle with black spots.

laid
☛ See **lay**.

lake
NOUN lakes
A lake is a large area of water surrounded by land.

lamb
NOUN lambs
1 A lamb is a young sheep.
2 Lamb is the meat from a young sheep.

lamp
NOUN lamps
A lamp is a small light that works by using electricity, oil, or gas.

land
NOUN lands
1 The land is the part of the world that is not covered by sea.
2 A land is a country. *He was the best dancer in the **land**.*
VERB lands, landing, landed
3 When something lands, it comes back to the ground after it has been in the air. *The plane **landed** in a field.*

lane
NOUN lanes
A lane is a narrow road.

language
NOUN languages
A language is all the words that people use to speak or write to each other.

lantern
NOUN lanterns
A lantern is a candle with a see-through case around it.

lap
NOUN laps
1 Your lap is the top part of your legs when you are sitting down. *The kitten curled up on my **lap**.*
2 One lap of a race track is one time right round it. *The runners were on the last **lap** of the race.*
VERB laps, lapping, lapped
3 When water laps against something, it splashes gently against it. *The waves **lapped** against the beach.*
4 When an animal laps up a drink, it drinks using its tongue.

laptop
NOUN laptops
A laptop is a small computer that you can carry around and use on your lap.

large
ADJECTIVE larger, largest
Something that is large is big.

larva
NOUN larvae
A larva is a young form of an insect, before it becomes the adult form. A caterpillar is the larva of a butterfly.

laser
NOUN lasers
A laser is a machine that produces a very thin beam of strong light. Doctors use lasers to perform some medical operations.

last
VERB lasts, lasting, lasted
1 How long something lasts is how long it takes before it is finished. *My riding lesson **lasts** an hour.*
ADJECTIVE
2 The last one is the only one left. *Do you want the **last** biscuit?*
3 Last night or last week means the one that has just finished. *We went to the cinema **last** night.*

late
ADJECTIVE later, latest
If you are late, you do something after the time when you should do it. *They were **late** for dinner.*

lately
ADVERB
Lately means recently. *I've been getting good marks at school **lately**.*

laugh
VERB laughs, laughing, laughed
When you laugh, you make a loud noise because you think that something is funny.

launch
VERB launches, launching, launched
To launch a boat means to move it into the water.

lava
NOUN
Lava is hot, liquid rock that comes out of a volcano when it erupts.

law
NOUN
The law is the set of rules that all the people who live in a country must obey. The law is usually made by the government of a country. *People who break the **law** can be sent to prison.*

lawn
NOUN lawns
A lawn is an area of grass in a garden or park.

lay
VERB lays, laying, laid
1 If you lay something somewhere, you put it there carefully. *We **laid** all our paintings out on the table.*
2 When a bird lays an egg, it produces it from its body.
3 Lay is the past tense of the verb **lie**.

layer
NOUN layers
A layer is an amount of something that covers a surface. *There was a thick **layer** of chocolate on top of the cake.*

lazy
ADJECTIVE lazier, laziest
Someone who is lazy does not want to work hard.

lead
NOUN leads
1 A lead is a thin strap or chain that you fix to a dog's collar so that you can hold it.
2 If you are in the lead, you are in first place in a race or competition. *She was in the **lead** all the way around the racetrack.*
VERB leads, leading, led
3 If you lead people to a place, you take them there. *He said that he would **lead** us to the treasure.*
4 If you lead a group of people, you are in charge of them.
leader (NOUN)
The leader of a group of people is the person in charge.

leaf
NOUN leaves
The leaves on a plant are the thin, flat, green parts that grow on the stem or branches.

leaflet
NOUN
leaflets
A leaflet is a piece of paper with information on it.

leak
NOUN leaks
A leak is a small hole or crack in something that lets liquid come out.

leaf

lean
VERB leans, leaning, leaned or leant
1 If you lean on something, you rest against it.
2 If something is leaning to one side, it bends to one side.

a b c d e f g h i j k Ll m n o p q r s t u v w x y z

leap
VERB leaps, leaping, leaped or leapt
When you leap, you jump high into the air. *The deer **leaps** over the fence and runs away.*

leap year
NOUN leap years
A leap year is a year that has 366 days instead of 365. There is a leap year every four years, and the extra day is 29th February.

leap
He leapt over the hurdle.

learn
VERB learns, learning, learned or learnt
When you learn about something, you find out about it and understand it. *We **learned** how to make a cake at school today.*

least
ADJECTIVE
The least amount is the smallest amount. *Let's see who can make the **least** mess.*

leather
NOUN
Leather is a material made from the skin of an animal. Shoes and bags are often made of leather.

leave
VERB leaves, leaving, left
1 When you leave a place, you go away from it. *I **leave** home at eight o'clock to come to school.*
2 If you leave something, you do not take it with you. *I **left** my swimming kit at school today.*
3 If you leave something alone, you do not touch it.

led
☛ See **lead**.

left
ADJECTIVE
1 Your left side is the side that is opposite your right side. *She writes with her **left** hand.*
VERB
2 Left is the past tense of the verb **leave**.

leg
NOUN legs
1 Your legs are the long parts of your body between your hips and your feet.
2 The legs on a piece of furniture are the parts that it stands on. *A chair has four **legs**.*

lemon

legal
ADJECTIVE
If something is legal, you are allowed to do it because it is within the law.
☛ **Opposite:** illegal

legend
NOUN legends
A legend is a very old story.

lemon
NOUN lemons
A lemon is a yellow fruit with a sour taste.

lemonade
NOUN
Lemonade is a sweet, fizzy drink traditionally made from lemons.

lend
VERB lends, lending, lent
If you lend something to someone, you let them have it or use it for a short time.

length
NOUN lengths
1 The length of something is how long it is. *We measured the **length** of the football field.*
2 A length of something is a long piece of it.

A lemon is a juicy, yellow fruit.

lent
☛ See **lend**.

leopard
NOUN leopards
A leopard is a large animal that lives in Africa and Asia and belongs to the cat family.

leotard
NOUN leotards
A leotard is a tight, stretchy outfit that you wear to do dancing or gymnastics.

less
ADJECTIVE
If you have less of something, you do not have as much. *I've got **less** chocolate than you!*

lesson
NOUN lessons
A lesson is a time when someone teaches you something. *I have a piano **lesson** today.*

let
VERB lets, letting, let
If you let someone do something, you allow them to do it. *My dad **let** me use his computer.*

letter
NOUN letters
1 A letter is one of the symbols that we use to write words. There are 26 letters in the English alphabet.
2 A letter is a message that you write on paper and send to someone.

lettuce
NOUN lettuces
A lettuce is a vegetable with large green leaves that people eat in salads.

level
NOUN levels
1 A level is a position on a scale. *I really want to get to the next **level** in this game.*
ADJECTIVE
2 Something that is level is flat.
3 Things that are level are the same height.
4 If people are level in a game, they have the same number of points.

liar
NOUN liars
A liar is someone who tells lies and does not tell the truth.

library
NOUN libraries
A library is a place where you can go to borrow books and other things.

lick
VERB licks, licking, licked
When you lick something, you touch it with your tongue.

lid
NOUN lids
A lid is a cover on a jar or box.

lie
VERB lies, lying, lied
1 When you lie, you say something that you know is untrue. *My brother **lied** when he said that I broke the window.*
VERB lies, lying, lay, lain
2 When you lie down, you rest with all your body flat on a bed or on the ground. *I **lay** down on my bed and fell asleep.*

life
NOUN lives
1 If there is life in a place, there are living things there. *Is there **life** on Mars?*
2 Your life is the time that you are alive. *I'll remember this moment all my **life**!*

lifeboat
NOUN lifeboats
A lifeboat is a boat that goes out to rescue people at sea.

life cycle
NOUN life cycles
The life cycle of an animal is the way in which it is born, lives, has babies, and dies.

lift
NOUN lifts
1 A lift is a machine that carries people up or down inside a building.
2 A lift is a ride in someone else's car. *You should never accept **lifts** from strangers.*
VERB lifts, lifting, lifted
3 When you lift something up, you pick it up.

light

NOUN lights
1 A light is something that shines to help you see in the dark. *I had to turn on the **light** so I could see.*
VERB lights, lighting, lit
2 When you light something, you make it catch fire. *We **lit** a candle so that we could see.*
ADJECTIVE lighter, lightest
3 Something that is light does not weigh much. *Your bag is very **light**.*
4 A light colour is not very dark. *Her dress was **light** blue.*

lighthouse

NOUN lighthouses
A lighthouse is a tall tower with a bright, flashing light. The light warns ships that there are dangerous rocks near the coast.

lightning

NOUN
Lightning is a flash of light in the sky during a thunderstorm.

like

VERB likes, liking, liked
1 If you like someone, you get on well with them. *I **like** our new teacher.*
2 If you like something, you enjoy it or think it is nice. *Do you **like** orange juice?*
ADJECTIVE
3 If one thing is like another, it is similar to it. *He looks **like** his brother.*

likely

ADJECTIVE
If something is likely, it will probably happen.
☛ **Opposite:** unlikely

limit

NOUN limits
A limit is a level or an amount that people should not go past. *There is a **limit** of two bags per person.*

limp

VERB limps, limping, limped
When you limp, you walk in an uneven way because you have hurt one of your legs.

line

NOUN lines
1 A line is a long, thin mark. *Draw a **line** with your pencil.*
2 A line of things is a straight row of them. *There was a long **line** of people waiting to get into the museum.*

link

NOUN links
1 A link is something that joins or connects things.
2 A link on the internet is an address that you can click on to take you to a page on a website.

lion

NOUN lions
A lion is a large, fierce animal that belongs to the cat family. A female lion is called a **lioness**.

lighthouse

lip

NOUN lips
Your lips are the soft edges around your mouth.

liquid

NOUN liquids
A liquid is a substance, such as water, that you can pour.

list

NOUN lists
When you make a list, you write down the names of people or things one after the other. *We need to make a **list** of everyone in the team.*

listen

VERB listens, listening, listened
When you listen, you pay attention and hear something.

lit

☛ See **light**.

litre

NOUN litres
You measure how much liquid you have by saying how many litres you have.

litter

NOUN
1 Litter is rubbish that people have left lying around.
2 A litter is a number of baby animals, such as kittens or piglets, born at the same time.

little

ADJECTIVE
1 Something that is little is small.
2 If you only have a little of something, you do not have much. *I only have a **little** water left.*

live
VERB lives, living, lived
1 When you live, you are alive. *My grandfather* ***lived*** *to an old age.*
2 The place where you live is the place that is your home.

live
ADJECTIVE
1 Something that is live is living. *I've never seen a* ***live*** *scorpion.*
2 A live television show is not recorded but is shown while it is actually taking place.

lively
ADJECTIVE
Someone who is lively is active and has a lot of energy.

living room
NOUN living rooms
A living room is a room in which you sit and chat or watch television.

lizard
NOUN lizards
A lizard is a reptile, usually with four legs and a long tail. Many lizards live in warm countries and eat insects.

load
NOUN loads
1 A load is an amount of something that you carry.
2 If you have loads of things, you have a lot of them.
VERB loads, loading, loaded
3 When you load things into a vehicle, you put them in so that you can take them somewhere.
4 When you load a computer program, you put it onto a computer.

loaf
NOUN loaves
A loaf of bread is a large chunk of bread that you can cut into slices.

local
ADJECTIVE
Something that is local is close to the place where you live. *Why don't you join your* ***local*** *sports club?*

lock
NOUN locks
1 A lock keeps a door or box shut. You need a key to open a lock.
VERB locks, locking, locked
2 When you lock something, you shut it by turning a key in a lock.

loft
NOUN lofts
A loft is a small room at the top of a house, where you can store things.

log
NOUN logs
A log is a thick piece of a tree's trunk or branch. *Let's put another* ***log*** *on the fire.*

logo
NOUN logos
A logo is a small picture or sign that a company uses on its products. *The company's* ***logo*** *is a panda riding a bicycle.*

lollipop
NOUN lollipops
A lollipop is a sweet on a stick that you lick. A lollipop is also called a **lolly**.

lonely
ADJECTIVE lonelier, loneliest
If you feel lonely, you feel sad because you are alone.

long
ADJECTIVE longer, longest
1 Something that is long measures a lot in length.
2 Something that is long goes on for a large amount of time.

Two ***lizards*** *sunbathing*

look
VERB looks, looking, looked
1 When you look at something, you use your eyes to see it. ***Look*** *at the stars!*
2 The way something looks is the way it appears. *The water* ***looked*** *cold.*

Delicious ***lollipops*** *are lovely to lick.*

a b c d e f g h i j k **Ll** m n o p q r s t u v w x y z

loose
ADJECTIVE looser, loosest
1 If something is loose, it is not held firmly in place.
2 Loose clothes are baggy.
loosen (VERB)
If you loosen something, you make it less tight.

lorry
NOUN lorries
A lorry is a large vehicle for carrying goods by road.

lose
VERB loses, losing, lost
1 When you lose something, you cannot find it. *I've* ***lost*** *my shoe.*
2 If you lose a game or battle, you are defeated.

lot
NOUN lots
If you have a lot of things, you have a large number or a large amount.

lottery
NOUN lotteries
A lottery is a game in which people win a prize if they choose the right numbers. *What would you do if you won the* ***lottery****?*

loud
ADJECTIVE louder, loudest
Something that is loud makes a lot of noise.
loudly (ADVERB)
If you speak loudly, you speak in a loud voice.

lounge
NOUN lounges
A lounge is a room in which you sit and chat or watch television.

love
VERB loves, loving, loved
1 If you love someone, you like them a lot.
2 If you love something, you like it or enjoy it a lot. *I* ***love*** *strawberry ice cream!*

lovely
ADJECTIVE lovelier, loveliest
Something that is lovely is very nice.

low
ADJECTIVE lower, lowest
Something that is low is near the ground.
lower (VERB)
When you lower something, you move it nearer to the ground. *The crane* ***lowered*** *the roof into position.*

lower case
ADJECTIVE
Lower case letters are small letters, not capital letters.

loyal
ADJECTIVE
If you are loyal to someone, you keep supporting them.

luck
NOUN
Luck is something that happens by chance. *It was bad* ***luck*** *that it started to rain.*
luckily (ADVERB)
If something happens luckily, something good happens, by chance. *I lost my phone, but* ***luckily*** *I found it again.*
lucky (ADJECTIVE)
If you are lucky, something good happens to you by chance. *I think we were* ***lucky*** *to win that game!*

luggage
NOUN
Your luggage is the cases and bags that you take with you when you travel.

luggage

lump
NOUN lumps
A lump of something is a piece of it. *He moulded the* ***lump*** *of clay into a teapot.*

lunar
ADJECTIVE
Lunar means to do with the moon. *You can see some* ***lunar*** *rocks in the museum.*

lunch
NOUN lunches
Lunch is a meal that you eat in the middle of the day.

lung
NOUN lungs
Your lungs are the organs inside your body that you use for breathing.

luxury
NOUN luxuries
A luxury is something expensive that you do not really need.

machine
NOUN machines
A machine has moving parts and uses power to make things or do a job.

mad
ADJECTIVE madder, maddest
1 Someone who is mad is crazy or very silly. *You're **mad** to swim in the sea in the winter!*
2 If you are mad, you are very angry.
3 If you are mad about something, you like it a lot. *My sister's **mad** about animals.*

made
☞ See **make**.

magazine
NOUN magazines
A magazine is a thin book with pictures and stories. Magazines are often produced once a week or once a month.

magic
NOUN
When someone does magic, they do clever things that seem to be impossible.

magician
NOUN magicians
A magician is someone who has magical powers or does clever magic tricks.

magnet
NOUN magnets
A magnet is a piece of iron that attracts metals with iron or steel in them.
magnetic (ADJECTIVE)
Something that is magnetic is a magnet.

magnificent
ADJECTIVE
Something that is magnificent is wonderful. *The castle is a **magnificent** old building.*

mail
NOUN
Mail is letters and parcels that are delivered to people's homes and offices.
☞ **Be careful with spelling:**
mail *A postman delivers the **mail**.*
male *Is your guinea pig **male** or female?*

main
ADJECTIVE
The main thing is the most important one.

major
ADJECTIVE
A major thing is big and important. *Scientists have made a **major** discovery.*

majority
NOUN majorities
A majority is most people. *The **majority** of us voted to have longer playtimes.*

make
VERB makes, making, made
1 When you make something, you build it or create it. *Let's **make** a snowman!*
2 If you make someone do something, you force them to do it. *Our teacher **made** us tidy up.*
3 If you make up a story or name, you invent it.

make-up
NOUN
When you wear make-up, you wear colours on your face to make yourself look nice or to make yourself look different.

male
ADJECTIVE
Most male animals cannot produce eggs or give birth to babies.
☞ **Be careful with spelling:**
male *Is your guinea pig **male** or female?*
mail *A postman delivers the **mail**.*

mammal
NOUN mammals
A mammal is an animal that has hair on its body and is warm-blooded. Female mammals feed their young with milk. Cows, lions, whales, and people are all mammals.

man
NOUN men
A man is an adult male person.

manage
VERB manages, managing, managed
1 The person who manages a shop or business is in charge of it. *She **manages** a shop and has two assistants to help her.*
2 If you manage to do something, you do it even though it is difficult. *We **managed** to swim across the bay.*
manager (NOUN)
A manager is someone who is in charge of a shop or business.

mango
NOUN mangoes
A mango is a large fruit with golden-yellow flesh that grows in hot countries. *My dad makes delicious **mango** smoothies.*

manner
NOUN manners
1 The manner in which you do something is the way in which you do it. *My next-door neighbour always greets me in a friendly **manner**.*
2 Your manners are the way you behave when you are with other people. *It's bad **manners** to shout across the room.*

many
ADJECTIVE
Many means a large number of people or things. *There were so **many** people at the carnival that I couldn't find my sister.*

map
NOUN maps
A map is a drawing of a place. Maps show where towns and cities, roads, rivers, and mountains are.

marathon
NOUN marathons
A marathon is a very long running race. A marathon is 42.19 km (26 miles 385 yards) long.

marble
NOUN marbles
1 Marble is a hard stone that people sometimes use for building.
2 Marbles are small, glass balls that children play with.

*I won lots of multi-coloured **marbles**.*

Marine life

Spectacular marine life makes its home in the sea.

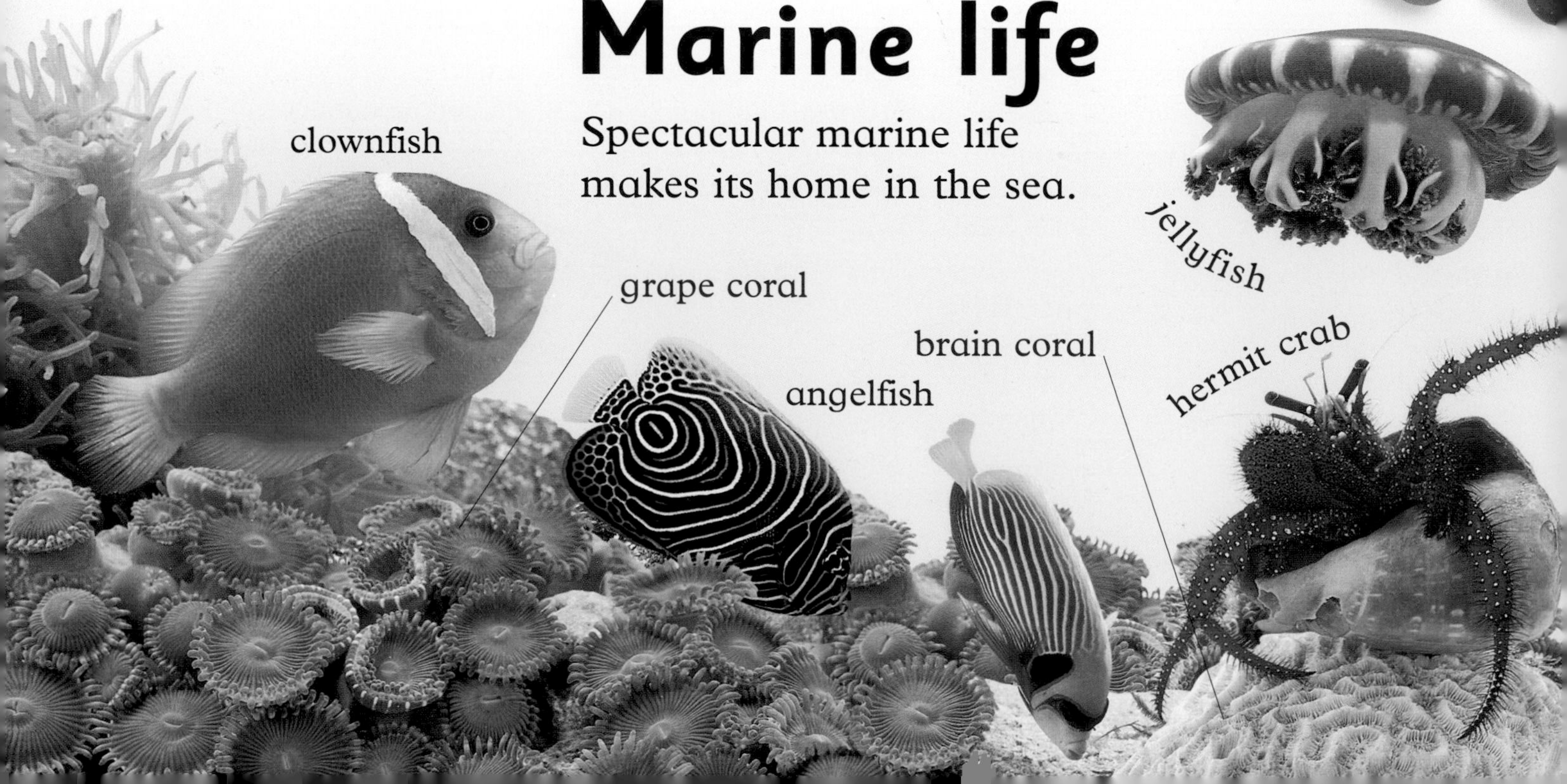

clownfish
grape coral
jellyfish
brain coral
angelfish
hermit crab

march

VERB marches, marching, marched

When you march, you walk with quick, regular steps, like a soldier. *The band **marched** in time to the music.*

margarine

NOUN

Margarine is a soft substance made from vegetable oils. You spread it on bread like butter.

margin

NOUN margins

A margin is an empty space with no writing at the side of a piece of paper.

marine

ADJECTIVE

Marine animals live in the sea. Marine life is life in the sea. *We saw brightly coloured fish and other amazing **marine** animals when we went snorkelling.*

mark

NOUN marks

1 A mark is a scratch or stain on something. *There were some dirty **marks** on his clothes.*

2 Your mark in a test is the number you get that shows how well you have done.

market

NOUN markets

A market is a place with stalls where you can buy things.

marmalade

NOUN marmalades

Marmalade is jam made from fruit such as oranges and lemons.

marry

VERB marries, marrying, married

When you marry someone, you become their husband or wife.

married (ADJECTIVE)

Someone who is married has a husband, or wife.

marsupial

NOUN marsupials

A marsupial is an animal that carries its babies in a special pouch. Kangaroos and koalas are marsupials.

marvellous

ADJECTIVE

Something that is marvellous is very good. *This is a **marvellous** new invention!*

mash

VERB mashes, mashing, mashed

When you mash food, you crush it so that it becomes soft and smooth. *My brother's favourite food is **mashed** potatoes.*

mask

NOUN masks

You wear a mask over your face to hide it or protect it. *My sister and I wore scary **masks** at Halloween.*

a b c d e f g h i j k l Mm n o p q r s t u v w x y z

massive
ADJECTIVE
Something that is massive is very big. *They used a **massive** crane to lift the ship out of the water.*

mat
NOUN mats
1 A mat is a small carpet.
2 A table mat is a small piece of material or wood that you put under a hot plate on a table.

match
NOUN matches
1 A match is a game between two teams of people. *I'm playing in a hockey **match** on Saturday.*
2 A match is a small stick that you strike against a rough surface to make a flame.
VERB matches, matching, matched
3 If things match, they look the same or go well together. *This jacket **matches** my trousers.*

material
NOUN materials
1 Material is cloth. *My costume was made of a shiny **material**.*
2 A material is something that you use to make or build things. *Wood is a good **material** to use to build a tree house.*

mathematics
NOUN
Mathematics is the subject in which you study numbers and shapes. Mathematics is often called **maths**.

matter
VERB matters, mattered
If something matters, it is important. If it does not matter, it is not important. *Don't worry, it doesn't **matter** if you lose the game.*

mattress
NOUN mattresses
The mattress on a bed is the soft, thick part that you lie on.

maximum
NOUN
The maximum number or amount is the biggest possible. *This box holds a **maximum** of 12 pencils.*

may
VERB
1 You ask if you may do something when you are asking permission to do it. *Please **may** we go outside to play?*
2 If something may happen, it is possible that it will happen. *It **may** rain later.*

mayor
NOUN mayors
A mayor is a person who has been chosen to be in charge of a town or city.

maze
NOUN mazes
A maze is a system of paths in which it is difficult to find your way around.

*I got lost in the **maze**.*

maze

meal
NOUN meals
When you have a meal, you eat food. *What time do you have your evening **meal**?*

mean
VERB means, meaning, meant
1 If you ask what something means, you want someone to explain it to you.
2 If you mean what you are saying, you are not joking.
ADJECTIVE meaner, meanest
3 If someone is mean, they do something unkind or unpleasant. *That was a **mean** trick!*
4 Someone who is mean does not like to spend money or give things to people. *He was too **mean** to buy us an ice cream.*

meaning
NOUN meanings
The meaning of something is what it is about or what it means. *She didn't understand the **meaning** of the joke.*

meanwhile
ADVERB
Meanwhile means while something else is happening.

measure
VERB measures, measuring, measured
When you measure something, you find out how big it is. *Can you help me **measure** my height?*
measurement (NOUN)
A measurement is a number or result that you get when you measure something.

War **medals** are given to people for being brave.

meat
NOUN
Meat is the part of an animal that we can eat.
☛ **Be careful with spelling:**
meat *Some people don't eat* ***meat****.*
meet *Let's* ***meet*** *in the park.*

medal
NOUN medals
A medal is a round piece of metal on a ribbon that is given to you when you win a competition or when you have done something very brave.

media
NOUN
The media is television, radio, and newspapers.

medical
ADJECTIVE
Medical problems or treatments are to do with people's health.

medicine
NOUN medicines
Medicine is a special liquid or pill that you take to make you better when you are ill.

medium
ADJECTIVE
Something that is medium is not very big and not very small. It is in the middle.

meet
VERB meets, meeting, met
When you meet someone, you see them and talk to them. *I'll* ***meet*** *you at the cinema at six o'clock.*

megabyte
NOUN megabytes
You say how big a computer's memory is by saying how many megabytes it has.

melon
NOUN melons
A melon is a large, round fruit with a tough skin and soft, sweet flesh.

Melons *have sweet, juicy flesh.*

melt
VERB melts, melting, melted
When something melts, it turns from a solid into a liquid because it has become hot. *Chocolate will* ***melt*** *if you leave it in sunlight.*

member
NOUN members
A member of a club is a person who belongs to it. *You can only use the tennis courts if you are a* ***member*** *of the tennis club.*

memory
NOUN memories
1 If you have a good memory, you can remember things easily. If you do not have a good memory, you forget things.
2 Your memories are things that you remember from the past. *The photos brought back happy* ***memories*** *of our holiday.*

men
☛ See **man**.

a b c d e f g h i j k l Mm n o p q r s t u v w x y z

a b c d e f g h i j k l Mm n o p q r s t u v w x y

mend
VERB mends, mending, mended
If you mend something that is broken, you fix it.

mental
ADJECTIVE
When you do mental arithmetic, you do sums in your head, without writing them down.

mention
VERB mentions, mentioning, mentioned
If you mention something, you talk about it a little bit but not very much.

menu
NOUN menus
1 The menu in a restaurant is the list of things you can buy to eat there.
2 A menu on a computer is a list of things you can choose from.

mercy
NOUN
If you show mercy to someone, you do not hurt or punish them.

mermaid
NOUN mermaids
In stories, a mermaid is a sea creature that has the body of a woman and the tail of a fish.

merry
ADJECTIVE merrier, merriest
If you are merry, you are happy and cheerful. *The room was filled with **merry** laughter.*

mess
NOUN messes
If a place is in a mess, it is dirty or untidy. *There was a lot of **mess** after they had finished cooking.*
messy (ADJECTIVE)
If a place is messy, it is dirty or untidy. *Your bedroom is always **messy**!*

message
NOUN messages
If you leave a message for someone, you leave some written or recorded words for them to tell them something.

met
☛ See **meet**.

metal
NOUN metals
A metal is a hard substance that is found in rocks. Iron, gold, and copper are all metals.

meteorite
NOUN meteorites
A meteorite is a piece of rock that falls to Earth from space without burning up. A piece of rock that burns up as it enters the Earth's atmosphere is called a **meteor**.

method
NOUN methods
The method you use to do something is the way in which you do it.

metre
NOUN metres
When you say how long something is, you say how many metres it is. *A kilometre is the same as 1,000 **metres**.*

mice
☛ See **mouse**.

microchip
NOUN microchips
A microchip is a small piece of equipment that carries information a computer can read.

microphone
NOUN microphones
You speak or sing into a microphone to make your voice sound louder.

microscope
NOUN microscopes
A microscope is a piece of equipment that you can look through to make very small things look bigger.

mice

*Three little **mice** scampering along*

microwave
NOUN
A microwave is an oven that cooks food quickly by passing electrical waves through it.

midday
NOUN
Midday is 12 o'clock in the middle of the day.

middle
NOUN middles
The middle of something is the part near the centre. *His house is in the **middle** of a forest.*

midnight
NOUN
Midnight is 12 o'clock at night.

might
VERB
If something might happen, it is possible that it will happen. *It **might** snow later.*

migrate
VERB migrates, migrating, migrated
When people or animals migrate, they move from one place to another, over long distances. *The whales **migrated** thousands of kilometres to find food.*
migrant (NOUN)
A migrant is someone who has moved to live in a different country.

mild
ADJECTIVE milder, mildest
1 A mild soap or shampoo is not very strong and will not hurt your skin.
2 Mild weather is warm.

mile
NOUN miles
When you say how far away a place is, you say how many miles away it is.

milk
NOUN
Milk is the white liquid that mammals produce to feed their babies. You can use cow's milk to make butter, cream, yoghurt, and cheese.

milkshake
NOUN milkshakes
A milkshake is a sweet drink that is made with milk.

millennium
NOUN millennia or millenniums
A millennium is one thousand years.

milkshake
A delicious strawberry ***milkshake***

millimetre
NOUN millimetres
You can measure how long something is by saying how many millimetres it is. You use millimetres for measuring short lengths.

million
NOUN millions
A million is a thousand thousands (1,000,000).

millionaire
NOUN millionaires
A millionaire is a very rich person who has money and property worth more than a million pounds or dollars.

mime
VERB mimes, miming, mimed
When you mime, you pretend to do an action without speaking.

mind
NOUN minds
1 Your mind is the way that you think and remember things.
2 If you change your mind, you change something that you had already decided. *I've changed my **mind** – I don't want to go shopping now.*
VERB minds, minding, minded
3 If you mind about something, it annoys you or upsets you. If you do not mind, it does not bother you. *I don't **mind** if you borrow my phone.*

mine
NOUN mines
A mine is a deep hole in the ground where coal or metals are dug out of rock.

a b c d e f g h i j k l Mm n o p q r s t u v w x y z

minor
ADJECTIVE
A minor thing is not very important.

mint
NOUN mints
A mint is a type of sweet.

minus
Minus is a word you use when you are taking one number away from another number. The symbol for minus is "–". *Eight **minus** five equals three.*

minute
NOUN minutes
A minute is 60 seconds. There are 60 minutes in an hour.

minute
ADJECTIVE
Something that is minute is very small.

miracle
NOUN miracles
If something that happens is a miracle, it is wonderful because you did not think that it was possible.

mirror
NOUN mirrors
A mirror is a shiny piece of glass. When you look into a mirror, you see yourself.

misbehave
VERB misbehaves, misbehaving, misbehaved
If someone misbehaves, they behave in a bad or naughty way.

mischief
NOUN
If you get into mischief, you do silly things or play tricks on people for fun.
mischievous (ADJECTIVE)
Someone who is mischievous likes to have fun by playing tricks on people. *The boy had a **mischievous** look in his eye.*

miserable
ADJECTIVE
If you are miserable, you are very sad.

*A fish **mobile** hangs from a hook.*

miss
VERB misses, missing, missed
1 If you miss something, you do not hit it when you are trying to. *He threw the ball at the target, but he **missed** it.*
2 If you miss someone, you are sad because they are not there.
3 If you miss school, you do not go to school. *I **missed** a lot of school days when I was ill.*

mist
NOUN mists
Mist is a cloud that hangs in the air close to the ground and makes it difficult to see things.
misty (ADJECTIVE)
When it is misty, there is mist in the air.

mistake
NOUN mistakes
If you make a mistake, you do something wrong.

mix
VERB mixes, mixing, mixed
If you mix things together, you put them together.

mixture
NOUN mixtures
A mixture is a number of different things that you have put or mixed together.

moan
VERB moans, moaning, moaned
If you moan about something, you complain about it.

mobile
NOUN mobiles
1 A mobile is a toy for a baby. You put it high up, and small things hang down from it and move around in the air.
ADJECTIVE
2 If something is mobile, you can move it around.

mobile phone
NOUN mobile phones
A mobile phone is a phone that you can carry around with you.

model
NOUN models
1 A model is a small copy of something. *He likes **model** aeroplanes.*
2 A model is someone who wears clothes to show people what they will look like.

modern
ADJECTIVE
Something that is modern is new and uses the latest ideas.

modest
ADJECTIVE
Someone who is modest does not like boasting about good things that they have done.

mole
NOUN moles
1 A mole is a small, furry animal that lives in underground tunnels. Moles eat worms and insects and they are almost blind.
2 A mole is a small, dark patch on your skin.

moment
NOUN moments
A moment is a short time. *I'll be back in a* ***moment****.*

money
NOUN
Money is the coins and notes that you use to buy things.

monitor
NOUN monitors
A monitor is a computer screen.

monkey
NOUN monkeys
A monkey is a small animal that is found in many countries. Most monkeys live in trees and eat fruit, although some eat insects and other small animals. *We saw three kinds of* ***monkey*** *at the zoo.*

monster
NOUN monsters
In stories, a monster is a very big, fierce creature.

month
NOUN months
A month is a period of time between 28 and 31 days. There are 12 months in a year. *December is my favourite* ***month*** *of the year.*

mood
NOUN moods
If you are in a good mood, you are happy. If you are in a bad mood, you are cross.
moody (ADJECTIVE)
Someone who is moody is often angry and upset.

Moon / moon
NOUN moons
You can see the Moon shining in the sky at night. The Moon moves round the Earth once every 28 days. Some other planets in our Solar System also have moons.

Do you think there's a man in the ***Moon****?*

mop
NOUN mops
You use a mop for cleaning floors. A mop has a long handle and bits of soft material on the end, which you rub over the floor.

more
ADJECTIVE
If you have more of something, you have a greater amount. *She's got* ***more*** *cake than me!*

monkey

A mischievous ***monkey*** *lives in the tree.*

a b i j k l **Mm**

morning
NOUN mornings
The morning is the early part of the day, ending at midday.

mosque
NOUN mosques
A mosque is a building where Muslims go to pray.

mosquito
NOUN mosquitoes or mosquitos
A mosquito is a small insect like a fly. Mosquitoes can bite you, and some mosquitoes carry serious diseases.

most
ADJECTIVE
The most is the greatest amount. *The player with the **most** points is the winner.*

moth
NOUN moths
A moth is an insect that looks like a butterfly and flies around at night.

mother
NOUN mothers
Your mother is your female parent.

***Moths** flutter around the lamp.*

motor
NOUN motors
A motor is a machine that gives power to something so that it can move or work.

motorbike
NOUN motorbikes
A motorbike is a large bike with a motor, or an engine.

motorway
NOUN motorways
A motorway is a large road that people can drive fast on.

mountain
NOUN mountains
A mountain is a very high hill.

mouse
NOUN mice
1 A mouse is a small, furry animal with a long tail. Mice have large front teeth, which they use to gnaw food.
2 The mouse on a computer is the part that you move around with your hand to move things on the screen.

moustache
NOUN moustaches
A man's moustache is hair that grows on his top lip if he does not shave.

mouth
NOUN mouths
1 Your mouth is the opening in your face that you use for eating and talking.
2 The mouth of a river is the place where it meets the sea.

*I love riding my speedy **motorbike***

motorbike

move
VERB moves, moving, moved
1 When something moves, it goes from one place to another.
2 When you move something, you take it from one place to another.

movie
NOUN movies
A movie is a film that you watch.

mow
VERB mows, mowing, mowed
When you mow grass, you cut it.

much
ADJECTIVE
Much means a lot. *We don't have **much** money left.*

mud
NOUN
Mud is soil that has become wet and sticky.
muddy (ADJECTIVE)
Something that is muddy is covered with mud.

muddle
NOUN muddles
If things are in a muddle, they are untidy or not well organized.

muffin
NOUN muffins
A muffin is a small cake.

mug
NOUN mugs
A mug is a large cup.

multiply
VERB multiplies, multiplying, multiplied
When you multiply a number, you add it to itself several times. The symbol for multiply is "x". *Nine* ***multiplied*** *by five equals 45.*

murder
VERB murders, murdering, murdered
To murder someone means to kill them deliberately.

murmur
VERB murmurs, murmuring, murmured
If you murmur, you speak in a low, quiet voice.

muscle
NOUN muscles
Your muscles are the strong parts that cover your bones and help you to move and lift things.

museum
NOUN museums
A museum is a place where you can go to see interesting things from the past.

mushroom
NOUN mushrooms
A mushroom is like a plant with no leaves that grows in the wild. You can eat some types of mushroom, but other types are poisonous.

mushroom

music
NOUN
You make music by singing or playing instruments.
musical (ADJECTIVE)
A musical instrument is an instrument you use to play music.
musician (NOUN)
A musician is someone who sings or plays a musical instrument.

Muslim
NOUN Muslims
A Muslim is someone whose religion is Islam.

must
VERB
If you must do something, you have to do it. *You* ***must*** *pay before you go into the disco.*

mustard
NOUN
Mustard is a spicy sauce that you eat with meat.

mutter
VERB mutters, muttering, muttered
If you mutter, you talk in a low voice. *I can't hear when you* ***mutter****.*

mystery
NOUN mysteries
If something is a mystery, people cannot understand or explain it. *His disappearance is still a* ***mystery****.*
mysterious (ADJECTIVE)
If something is mysterious, people cannot understand it or explain it.

myth
NOUN myths
A myth is a very old story, often involving gods and magic.

She played some beautiful ***music*** *on her trumpet.*

music

a b c d e f g h i j k l Mm n o p q r s t u v w

a
b
c
d
e
f
g
h
i
k
l
m
Nn
o
p
q
r
s
t
u
v
w
x
y
z

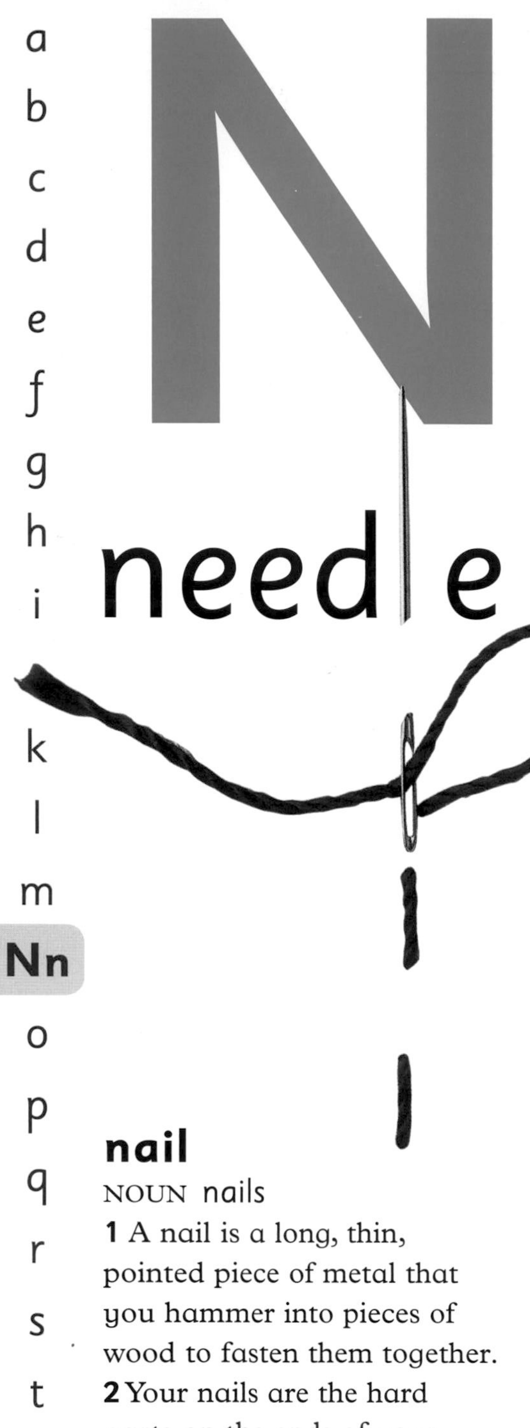

nail
NOUN nails
1 A nail is a long, thin, pointed piece of metal that you hammer into pieces of wood to fasten them together.
2 Your nails are the hard parts on the ends of your fingers and toes.

naked
ADJECTIVE
If you are naked, you are not wearing any clothes.

name
NOUN names
Your name is what you are called.

nap
NOUN naps
If you have a nap, you have a short sleep.

narrator
NOUN narrators
A narrator is a person who tells a story.

narrow
ADJECTIVE narrower, narrowest
Something that is narrow is not very wide. *We climbed up the* ***narrow*** *mountain path.*

nasty
ADJECTIVE nastier, nastiest
Someone who is nasty is unkind to others. *Don't be* ***nasty*** *to your sister!*

nation
NOUN nations
A nation is a country.
national (ADJECTIVE)
Something that is national involves a whole country. *We took part in a* ***national*** *tennis tournament.*

natural
ADJECTIVE
Something that is natural is made by nature, not by people. *Wool is a* ***natural*** *material.*

nature
NOUN
Nature is all the things in the world that are not made by people, such as the weather, animals, plants, and the sea.

naughty
ADJECTIVE naughtier, naughtiest
Someone who is naughty behaves badly.

navy
NOUN
1 The navy is the part of the military that fights at sea.
2 Navy blue is a very dark blue colour.

near
PREPOSITION
If you are near a place, you are close to it. *They live* ***near*** *the airport.*

nearly
ADVERB
Nearly means almost.
It's ***nearly*** *bedtime.*

neat
ADJECTIVE neater, neatest
If something is neat, it is tidy and not messy.
neatly (ADVERB)
If you arrange things neatly, you arrange them in a tidy way.

necessary
ADJECTIVE
If something is necessary, you need to have it or do it.
It is ***necessary*** *to clean your teeth every day.*
☛ **Opposite:** unnecessary

neck
NOUN necks
Your neck is the part of your body that joins your head to the rest of your body.

necklace
NOUN necklaces
A necklace is a chain or string of beads that you wear around your neck as a piece of jewellery.

nectar
NOUN
Nectar is a sweet liquid inside flowers. Bees collect nectar to make honey.

need
VERB needs, needing, needed
If you need something, you have to have it. *All animals **need** food to live.*

needle
NOUN needles
1 A needle is a thin, pointed piece of metal that you use for sewing.
2 A knitting needle is a plastic or metal stick that you use for knitting.
3 Needles on a pine tree are thin, pointed leaves.

neighbour
NOUN neighbours
Your neighbours are the people who live near you.
neighbourhood (NOUN)
Your neighbourhood is the area where you live.

nephew
NOUN nephews
Your nephew is the son of your brother or sister.

nervous
ADJECTIVE
If you are nervous about something, you are slightly worried or frightened about what is going to happen. *I was **nervous** about singing in the concert.*
nervously (ADVERB)
If you do something nervously, you do it in a nervous way. *She walked **nervously** to the front of the classroom.*

nest
NOUN nests
A nest is a home that a bird or animal builds out of leaves, twigs, or grass. *Crows build their **nests** high up in trees.*

nest

*A bird laid four eggs in her **nest**.*

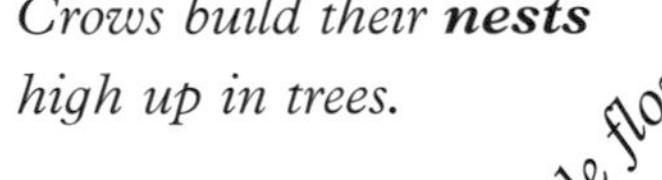

*Hummingbirds drink **nectar** from inside flowers.*

nectar

net
NOUN nets
A net is a piece of material with a lot of small holes. People use nets to catch fish.

netball
NOUN
Netball is a game in which teams of players try to throw a ball through a high net to score goals.

nettle
NOUN nettles
A nettle is a plant with leaves that sting you if you touch them.

network
NOUN networks
A network is a group of computers that are all connected to each other.

a b c d e f g h i j k l m **Nn** o p q r s t u v w x y z

new
ADJECTIVE newer, newest
1 If something is new, it has only just been made or you have only just bought it. *Do you like my **new** shirt?*
2 If you go to a new place, you go to a place where you have not been before. *We're moving house, so I'll be going to a **new** school.*

news
NOUN
The news is information about things that are happening in the world. *Do you watch the **news** on television?*

newspaper
NOUN newspapers
A newspaper is a group of articles about the news, printed on paper or published on the internet.

next
ADJECTIVE
1 The next person or thing is the one that comes straight after this one. *Who is the **next** person in the queue?*
2 The next room or house is the one nearest to you. *My brother sleeps in the **next** room.*

nibble
VERB nibbles, nibbling, nibbled
When you nibble food, you eat it by taking very small bites.

Chipmunks love **nibbling** nuts.
nibble

nice
ADJECTIVE nicer, nicest
1 Something that is nice is pleasant. *We had a **nice** day by the sea.*
2 A nice person is kind to other people.

nickname
NOUN nicknames
A nickname is a short, friendly name that you call someone instead of their proper name. *William's **nickname** is Bill.*

niece
NOUN nieces
Your niece is the daughter of your brother or sister.

night
NOUN nights
Night is the time between sunset and sunrise when the sky is dark.
☛ **Be careful with spelling:**
night *It's dark at **night**.*
knight *A **knight** wears armour.*

nightdress
NOUN nightdresses
A nightdress is a dress that girls and women wear to sleep in. A nightdress is also called a **nightie**.

nightmare
NOUN nightmares
A nightmare is a bad, frightening dream.

nobody
PRONOUN
Nobody or **no one** means not a single person.

nocturnal
ADJECTIVE
Nocturnal animals are active at night. *Bats are **nocturnal**.*

nod
VERB nods, nodding, nodded
When you nod your head, you move it up and down. *I asked if she was OK, and she **nodded**.*

noise
NOUN noises
A noise is a sound that you can hear, especially a loud, unpleasant one. *He was making a lot of **noise**.*
noisy (ADJECTIVE)
Something that is noisy makes a loud noise.

none
PRONOUN
None means not any. *I had spent all my money, so I had **none** left.*

nonsense
NOUN
Nonsense is words that have no meaning. *You're talking **nonsense**!*

Night life

Many animals are active at night. Here are some words to describe night life.

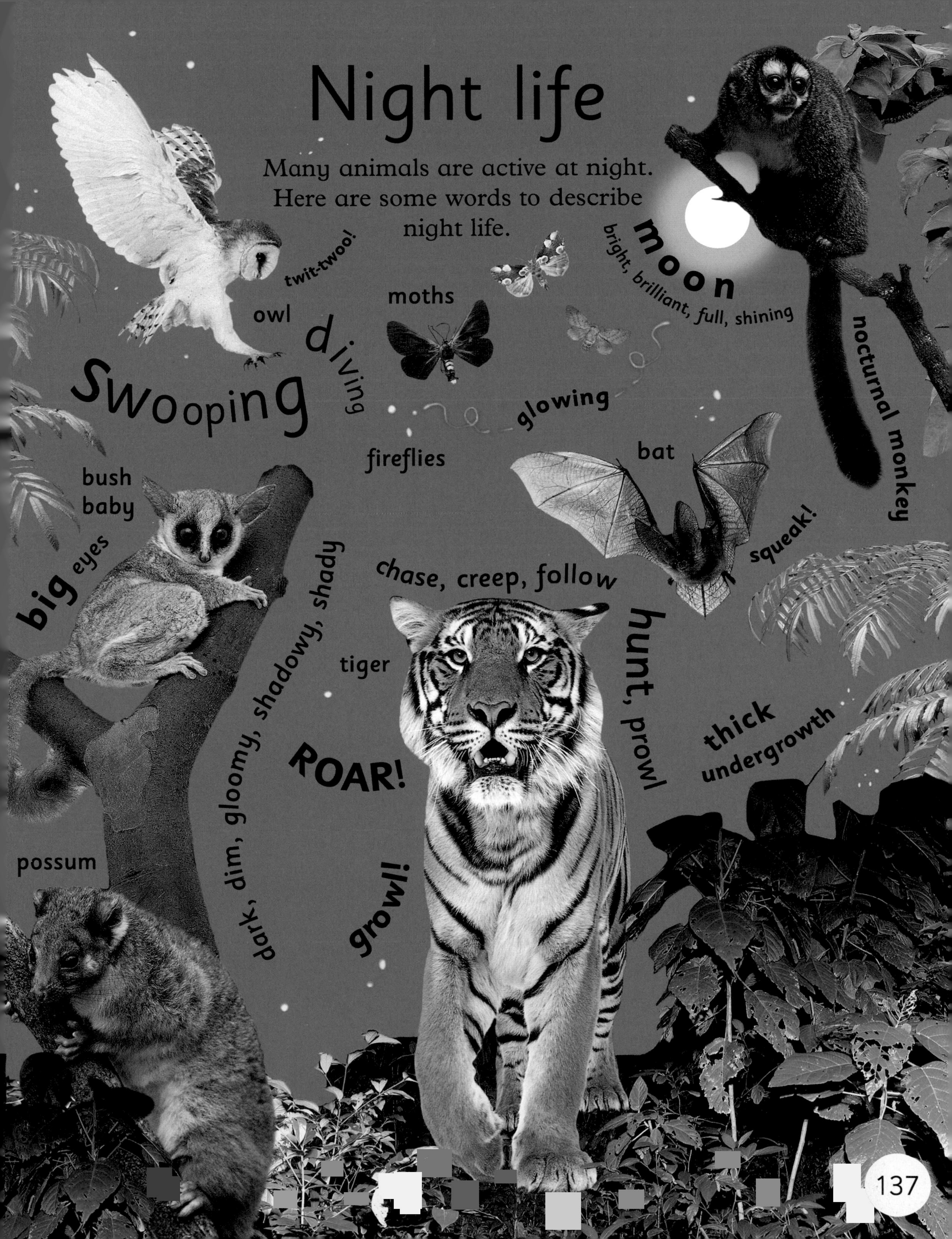

a b c d e f g h i j k l m **Nn** o y z

noon
NOUN
Noon is 12 o'clock in the middle of the day.

normal
ADJECTIVE
If something is normal, it is how you expect it to be. *The doctor took my temperature and it was **normal**.*

north
NOUN
North is one of the directions on a compass. If you keep going north, you will come to the **North Pole**, which is the farthest point north on Earth.

nose
NOUN noses
Your nose is the part of your face that you smell and breathe with. The two holes in your nose are called nostrils.

*The puppy has a wet **nose**.*

nosy
ADJECTIVE nosier, nosiest
Someone who is nosy tries to find out about things that do not concern them. *Don't be so **nosy**!*

note
NOUN notes
1 A note is a short message that you write to someone.
2 A note is a piece of paper money. *My uncle gave me a £20 **note**.*
3 A musical note is a single sound in a piece of music.

nothing
PRONOUN
1 Nothing means not anything. *There's **nothing** to worry about.*
2 Nothing is the number zero.

notice
NOUN notices
1 A notice is a sign that you put up on a wall to tell people about something.
2 If you take notice of something, you pay attention to it. If you take no notice, you do not pay attention. *Take no **notice** of them if they tease you.*
VERB notices, noticing, noticed
3 If you notice something, you see it or become aware of it. *Did you **notice** what the man was wearing?*

nought
NOUN noughts
Nought is the number zero.

noun
NOUN nouns
A noun is a word that is the name of something, such as "cat", "paper", or "happiness".

novel
NOUN novels
A novel is a book that tells a story. *I've read all the Harry Potter **novels**.*

nowhere
ADVERB
Nowhere means not in any place. *There was **nowhere** to hide.*

nudge
VERB nudges, nudging, nudged
If you nudge someone, you push or poke them gently because you want to get their attention.

nuisance
NOUN nuisances
A nuisance is something that annoys you.

numb
ADJECTIVE
If a part of your body is numb, you cannot feel it.

number
NOUN numbers
A number is a figure that you use for counting.

nurse
NOUN nurses
A nurse is someone who is trained to look after ill people.

nursery
NOUN nurseries
1 A nursery is a place where young children are looked after.
2 A nursery is a place where people grow and sell trees and plants.

nut
NOUN nuts
1 A nut is a hard fruit that grows on a tree. We can eat some types of nut.
2 A nut is a small piece of metal with a hole in it that you can twist onto a bolt to fasten something.

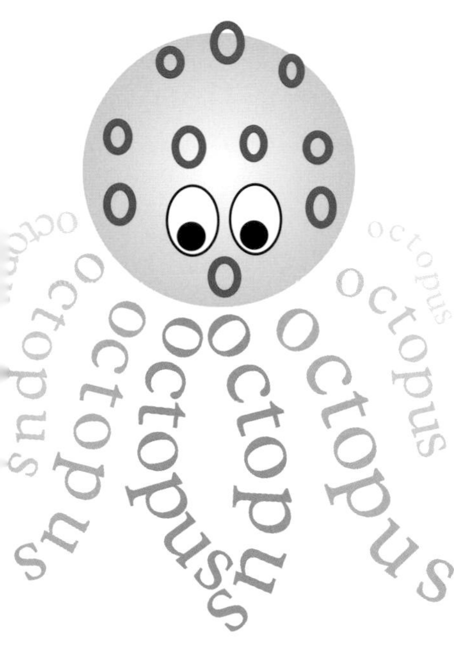

oak
NOUN oaks
An oak is a type of large tree. Oak trees produce nuts that are known as acorns.

oar
NOUN oars
Oars are long poles with flat ends that you use for rowing a boat.

oats
NOUN
Oats are grown as a crop by farmers. Oats are cooked with water or milk to make a breakfast dish called porridge.

obey
VERB obeys, obeying, obeyed
When you obey someone, you do what they have told you to do.
obedient (ADJECTIVE)
If you are obedient, you do what you have been told to do. *What an **obedient** dog!*

object
NOUN objects
1 An object is anything you can see or touch that is not alive.
2 The object of a sentence is the person or thing that receives the action of the verb. *"An apple" is the object in the sentence: The boy ate **an apple**.*

oblong
NOUN oblongs
An oblong is a shape that has four straight sides. An oblong is not square, but has two long sides and two short sides.

obstacle
NOUN obstacles
An obstacle is something that gets in your way. *He had to jump over ten **obstacles** to win the race.*

obvious
ADJECTIVE
If something is obvious, you can see or understand it very easily. *It was **obvious** that he was not telling the truth.*
obviously (ADVERB)
If something is obviously true, you can easily see that it is true. *She was **obviously** very nervous.*

occur
VERB occurs, occurring, occurred
1 When something occurs, it happens. *When did the accident **occur**?*
2 If something occurs to you, you think of it.

ocean
NOUN oceans
An ocean is a very large sea.

o'clock
ADVERB
You say what time it is by saying what number it is o'clock. *We must leave the house by three **o'clock**.*

octagon
NOUN octagons
An octagon is a shape with eight straight sides.

o'clock

a b c d e f g h i j k l m n Oo p q r s t u v w x y z

octopus
NOUN octopuses
An octopus is a sea animal with eight long arms called tentacles.

odd
ADJECTIVE odder, oddest
1 Something that is odd is strange. *He wore **odd** clothes!*
2 Odd socks or shoes do not go together as a pair.
3 An odd number cannot be divided by two. *Three and seven are **odd** numbers.*

offer
VERB offers, offering, offered
If you offer something to someone, you ask them if they want it. *He **offered** her grapes.*

office
NOUN offices
An office is a place where people work at desks.

officer
NOUN officers
1 An officer is a member of the police.
2 In the army, navy, or airforce, an officer is someone who gives orders to other people.

often
ADVERB
Often means many times. *We **often** go swimming at the weekend.*

oil
NOUN
1 Oil is a thick, black liquid that is found underground. We use oil to make petrol and plastics.
2 Oil is a thick, clear liquid used in cooking. It comes from plant seeds or the fruit of olive trees.

ointment
NOUN ointments
An ointment is a substance that you put on your skin when it is sore to make it better.

odd
Why are you wearing odd socks?

old
ADJECTIVE older, oldest
1 Something that is old was made a long time ago. *We found some **old** toys in the attic.*
2 Someone who is old has lived for a long time. *My grandma is quite **old** now.*

old-fashioned
ADJECTIVE
Something that is old-fashioned is not new or modern. *He drives an **old-fashioned** car.*

onion
NOUN onions
An onion is a round vegetable with a strong taste and smell. The smell of onions sometimes makes your eyes water.

online
ADJECTIVE
When you are online, you are working on a computer that is connected to the internet.

only
ADJECTIVE
An only child has no brothers or sisters.

open
VERB opens, opening, opened
1 When you open a door, you move it to go through it.
2 When you open something, you take the lid or wrapping off it. *May I **open** my presents now?*
ADJECTIVE
3 Something that is open is not closed or shut. *Come in, the door is **open**.*

operation
NOUN operations
If you have an operation, doctors cut open your body to remove something or make something better.

opinion
NOUN opinions
Your opinion is what you think about something. *In my **opinion**, he is the best footballer in the world.*

opportunity
NOUN opportunities
An opportunity is a chance to do something interesting or exciting. *He had the **opportunity** to go to Europe for the summer.*

onions

opposite
NOUN opposites

1 The opposite of something is the thing that is most different from it. *Tall is the* ***opposite*** *of short.*

ADJECTIVE

2 The opposite side is the other side. *I saw my friend on the* ***opposite*** *side of the river.*

optician
NOUN opticians

An optician is someone who tests people's eyes and sells glasses.

optimistic
ADJECTIVE

If you are optimistic, you think that something good will happen.

oral
ADJECTIVE

An oral test is one in which you listen and speak, but do not write things down.

orange
NOUN oranges

1 An orange is a juicy fruit with a tough skin.

ADJECTIVE

2 Something that is orange is the colour you make by mixing red and yellow.

orang-utan
NOUN orang-utans

An orang-utan is a large ape with long fur that lives in tropical forests in Southeast Asia.

orbit
VERB orbits, orbiting, orbited

To orbit a planet, moon, or the Sun, means to travel around it. *The Earth* ***orbits*** *the Sun.*

orchard
NOUN orchards

An orchard is a field or large area of land in a garden where fruit trees are grown.

orchestra
NOUN orchestras

An orchestra is a large group of musicians who play a wide variety of different musical instruments together. They are directed by a conductor.

order
NOUN orders

1 If you give someone an order, you tell them that they must do something.

2 The order things are in is the way they are arranged one after the other. *The words in this dictionary are in alphabetical* ***order****.*

VERB orders, ordering, ordered

3 If you order someone to do something, you tell them they must do it. *"Stand still!" he* ***ordered****.*

4 If you order something in a shop or restaurant, you ask for it. *We* ***ordered*** *a pizza for dinner.*

ordinary
ADJECTIVE

Something that is ordinary is not different or special or particularly interesting in any way. *Everything was very quiet: nothing out of the ordinary happened.*

organ
NOUN organs

1 An organ is a musical instrument with a keyboard and large air pipes.

2 The organs in your body are the parts such as your heart, brain, and liver that each do a particular job.

organic
ADJECTIVE

Organic food is grown in a natural way, without using strong chemicals.

organize
VERB organizes, organizing, organized

1 If you organize something, you plan it and arrange for it to happen. *We helped to* ***organize*** *the school fête.*

2 When you organize things, you arrange them neatly.

orang-utan

Orang-utans *live in trees.*

a b c d e f g h i j k l m n Oo p q r s t u v w x y z

original
ADJECTIVE
Something that is original is new and has not been copied.

orphan
NOUN orphans
An orphan is a child whose parents have died.

ostrich
NOUN ostriches
An ostrich is a tall bird from Africa that can run very fast but cannot fly.

other
ADJECTIVE
The other person or thing is the second one. *I've found one sock, but I can't find the* ***other*** *one.*

otter
NOUN otters
An otter is a furry animal with a long tail. Otters live near water and catch fish to eat.

ought
VERB
If you ought to do something, you should do it. *You* ***ought*** *to go to bed now.*

outdoors
ADVERB
Outdoors means not inside a building. *If the weather is good we usually play* ***outdoors*** *in the summer.*

outline
NOUN outlines
The outline of something is its shape.

outside
NOUN
The outside of something is the part at the edge, not the part in the middle. *They painted the* ***outside*** *of the house green.*

oval
NOUN ovals
An oval is a shape that looks like a long circle.

oven
NOUN ovens
An oven is the part of a cooker in which you can bake cakes and roast meat.

overboard
ADVERB
If someone falls overboard, they fall out of a boat into the water.

overhear
VERB overhears, overhearing, overheard
If you overhear something, you hear other people talking about it. *I* ***overheard*** *her say that she failed the maths test.*

overseas
ADVERB
If you go overseas, you go to another country. *My father travels a lot* ***overseas****.*

overtake
VERB overtakes, overtaking, overtook, overtaken
If you overtake someone, you go past them so that you are in front of them.

overweight
ADJECTIVE
Someone who is overweight is too heavy.

owe
VERB owes, owing, owed
If you owe money to someone, they have lent it to you and you need to pay it back. *My brother* ***owes*** *me money.*

owl
NOUN owls
An owl is a bird that hunts at night for mice and other small animals. Owls have good hearing and can see well in the dark.

own
VERB owns, owning, owned
If you own something, it belongs to you. *Do you* ***own*** *a bicycle?*
owner (NOUN)
The owner of something is the person it belongs to. *Who is the* ***owner*** *of this shop?*

oxygen
NOUN
Oxygen is a gas that is in the air around us. You cannot see, smell, or taste oxygen. Living things need oxygen in order to live.

owl

P

pack
NOUN packs
1 A pack of animals is a large group of them. *A **pack** of dogs roams the woods.*
2 A pack of cards is a set of cards that you use for playing games.
VERB packs, packing, packed
3 When you pack things, you put them into a suitcase or a box so that you can take them somewhere.

package
NOUN packages
A package is a parcel.
packaging (NOUN)
Packaging is the paper or box that something is wrapped in when you buy it.

packet
NOUN packets
A packet is a box or bag that you buy things in.

pad
NOUN pads
1 A pad of paper is a set of sheets that are joined together at one end.
2 A helicopter pad is a place where helicopters land and take off.

paddle
NOUN paddles
1 A paddle is a special pole with flat ends that you use to move a boat or canoe through water.
VERB paddles, paddling, paddled
2 When you paddle, you walk around in shallow water.

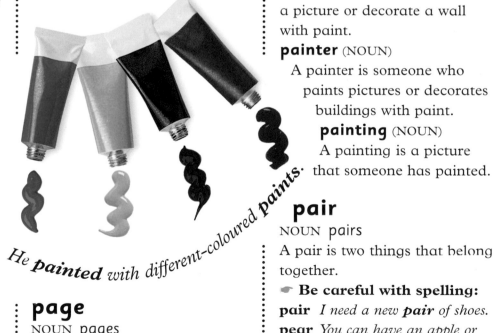

*He **painted** with different-coloured **paints**.*

page
NOUN pages
A page is one side of a piece of paper in a book or magazine, or one screen on a website.

paid
☛ See **pay**.

pail
NOUN pails
A pail is a bucket.
☛ **Be careful with spelling:**
pail *He was carrying a **pail** of water.*
pale *Are you OK? You look a bit **pale**.*

pain
NOUN pains
If you have a pain, a part of your body hurts.
painful (ADJECTIVE)
If a part of your body is painful, it hurts.

paint
NOUN paints
1 Paint is a coloured liquid that you use for making pictures or decorating walls.
VERB paints, painting, painted
2 When you paint, you make a picture or decorate a wall with paint.
painter (NOUN)
A painter is someone who paints pictures or decorates buildings with paint.
painting (NOUN)
A painting is a picture that someone has painted.

pair
NOUN pairs
A pair is two things that belong together.
☛ **Be careful with spelling:**
pair *I need a new **pair** of shoes.*
pear *You can have an apple or a **pear**.*

*She bought a new **pair** of shoes.*

palace
NOUN palaces
A palace is a large house where a king or queen lives.

pale
ADJECTIVE paler, palest
1 A pale colour is not very dark or bright. *She was wearing **pale** blue trousers.*
2 If you look pale, you look white because you are ill.
☛ **Be careful with spelling:**
pale *Are you OK? You look a bit **pale**.*
pail *He was carrying a **pail** of water.*

palm
NOUN palms
1 The palm of your hand is the inside part of your hand.
2 A palm tree is a type of tree that mainly grows in hot countries.

pan
NOUN pans
A pan is a metal container that you cook food in.

pancake
NOUN pancakes
A pancake is a flat cake made of eggs, flour, and milk, that you cook in a frying pan. To turn it over, you can toss it.

*Toss a **pancake**.*

pancake

panda
NOUN pandas
A panda is a large black and white animal in the bear family that lives in the mountain forests of China. Pandas mainly eat bamboo shoots.

panic
VERB panics, panicking, panicked
If you panic, you feel so frightened that you cannot think what you should do.
*I **panicked** when I realized I had got on the wrong train.*

pant
VERB pants, panting, panted
When you pant, you breathe quickly through your mouth because you are out of breath.
*We were all **panting** by the time we got to the top of the hill.*

pantomime
NOUN pantomimes
A pantomime is a traditional play that children often watch at Christmas. A pantomime tells a fairy story and has music, singing, and jokes.

pants
NOUN
Pants are a small item of clothing that you wear under your trousers or skirt.

paper
NOUN papers
Paper is a thin material made from wood, which you use for writing and drawing on.

parachute
NOUN parachutes
A parachute is a large piece of cloth that opens over someone's head when they jump out of a plane. A parachute stops you falling too quickly.

parade
NOUN parades
A parade is a line of people marching in the street to celebrate something.

paragraph
NOUN paragraphs
A paragraph is one section in a long piece of writing. You begin each paragraph on a new line.

parallel
ADJECTIVE
Parallel lines continue side by side, always the same distance away from each other.

parcel
NOUN parcels
A parcel is something that is wrapped up in paper.

parent
NOUN parents
Your parents are your father and mother.

At the park

There are lots of things to see and do in a park.

open air

playground

climb

catch, kick, throw... a ball

fun

games

green

flying disc

monkey bars

slide

hanging

swinging

run

jump

see-saw

meet friends

skateboard

do tricks

dog

fetch

The park is... grassy, leafy, airy

You can... chat, laugh, joke play, have a picnic

path

flowers

plants

a b c d e f g h i j k l m n o **Pp** q r s t u v w x y z

park
NOUN parks
1 A park is an area of grass and trees, where people can go to sit or play.
VERB parks, parking, parked
2 When you park a car, you leave it in a safe place.

parrot
NOUN parrots
A parrot is a large, colourful bird that lives in tropical forests and eats fruits and seeds.

part
NOUN parts
One part of something is one bit or piece of it. *I really liked the first **part** of the film.*

partner
NOUN partners
1 Your partner is the person you work or do an activity with.
2 Someone's partner is a person they are in a relationship with.

party
NOUN parties
When people have a party, they come together to have fun and celebrate something.

pass
VERB passes, passing, passed
1 When you pass something, you go past it. *You will **pass** the school on your way to the station.*
2 If you pass something to someone, you give it to them. *Please could you **pass** me a pencil?*
3 When you pass the ball to someone in a game, you throw it or kick it to them.
4 If you pass an exam, you are successful in it.

passage
NOUN passages
A passage is a corridor.
*An underground **passage** leads to the beach.*

passenger
NOUN passengers
The passengers in a vehicle are the people who are travelling in it but are not driving it.

Passover
NOUN
Passover is a Jewish festival that takes place in the spring.

passport
NOUN passports
A passport is an official document that allows you to travel to different countries.

past
NOUN
The past is the time that has already gone. *In the **past**, some people lived in castles.*

pasta
NOUN
Pasta is an Italian food made from flour and water. Pasta is made into a lot of different shapes, and you usually eat it with sauce.

paste
VERB pastes, pasting, pasted
When you paste something into a computer document, you add it after you have cut it from another document or from somewhere else in the same document.

pastry
NOUN
Pastry is a mixture made of flour, water, and fat that is baked to make pies and tarts.

pat
VERB pats, patting, patted
When you pat an animal, you touch it gently.

patch
NOUN patches
A patch is a small piece of material that you sew over a hole in your clothes.

path
NOUN paths
1 A path is a narrow track that you can walk along.
2 A path can be the direction that something moves. *He followed the **path** of the tornado.*

*There is a lot of different-shaped **pasta**.*

patient
NOUN patients
1 A patient is someone who is ill and is being treated by a doctor or nurse.
ADJECTIVE
2 If you are patient, you can wait calmly without getting cross.
☛ **Opposite:** impatient
patiently (ADVERB)
If you do something patiently, you do it in a patient way. *We waited **patiently** for the show to begin.*

pattern
NOUN patterns
A pattern is a design of shapes and colours.
patterned (ADJECTIVE)
Something that is patterned has a pattern on it. *He was wearing a bright, **patterned** shirt.*

pause
VERB pauses, pausing, paused
When you pause, you stop what you are doing for a while.

pavement
NOUN pavements
The pavement is the surface that you walk on at the side of a road.

paw
NOUN paws
Paws are the soft feet with claws that animals such as dogs and cats have.

pay
VERB pays, paying, paid
When you pay for something, you give someone money for it so that you can have it.

The shapes
make a pretty
pattern
pattern.

PC
NOUN PCs
A PC is a personal computer.

pea
NOUN peas
A pea is a small, round, green vegetable.

peace
NOUN
When there is peace, there is no war, fighting, or noise.
peaceful (ADJECTIVE)
A peaceful place is quiet and makes you feel relaxed.
☛ **Be careful with spelling:**
peace *Go away and leave me in **peace**!*
piece *Would you like a **piece** of cake?*

peach
NOUN peaches
A peach is a sweet, round fruit with a soft skin, yellow flesh, and a large stone inside.

peacock
NOUN peacocks
A peacock is a large bird. Male peacocks have very long, colourful tails, with eye-like markings, which they can raise up in the air to display.

peanut
NOUN peanuts
Peanuts are small nuts that grow under the ground.

pear
NOUN pears
A pear is a fruit that is thin at one end and round at the other. Pears have a sweet, juicy flesh.
☛ **Be careful with spelling:**
pear *Take an apple or a **pear**.*
pair *I need a new **pair** of shoes.*

pearl
NOUN pearls
A pearl is a smooth, shiny object that grows inside an oyster. Pearls are used to make jewellery.

pebble
NOUN pebbles
A pebble is a small, smooth, round stone.

peck
VERB pecks, pecking, pecked
When a bird pecks something, it hits or bites it with its beak.

peacock
*A **peacock** puts on a colourful display.*

a b c d e f g h i j k l m n o **Pp** q r s t u v w x y z

peculiar
ADJECTIVE
Something that is peculiar is strange and not normal. *What's that **peculiar** smell?*

pedal
NOUN pedals
A pedal is a part of a machine that you press with your foot to make it go.

peel
VERB peels, peeling, peeled
When you peel fruit or vegetables, you remove the skin.

peep
VERB peeps, peeping, peeped
When you peep at something, you look at it quickly.

peer
VERB peers, peering, peered
If you peer at something, you look at it carefully for a long time. *I **peered** out into the darkness, but I couldn't see anything.*

peg
NOUN pegs
A peg is a small piece of metal or plastic for hanging things on.

pelican
NOUN pelicans
A pelican is a large waterbird that lives in warm countries. It has a pouch under its beak, which it uses to catch and hold fish.

pen
NOUN pens
1 You use a pen for writing. It is long and thin, and filled with ink.
2 A pen is a fenced area that is used to keep animals in.

pencil
NOUN pencils
You use a pencil for writing and drawing. It is long and thin, and has a dark material in the middle.

penguin
NOUN penguins
A penguin is a large black and white bird that cannot fly but is a very good swimmer. Most penguins live near the South Pole. They swim underwater and catch fish and squid to eat.

pentagon
NOUN pentagons
A pentagon is a shape with five straight sides.

people
☛ See **person**.

pepper
NOUN peppers
1 Pepper is a black or white spice that you add to food to give it flavour.
2 A pepper is a bright green, yellow, orange, or red vegetable.

percussion
NOUN
Percussion instruments are musical instruments that you play by banging them or hitting them.

perfect
ADJECTIVE
Something that is perfect is just right and has nothing wrong with it.

percussion

*She made a **percussion** instrument out of pencils.*

perform
VERB performs, performing, performed
When you perform, you put on a show for other people. *We **performed** a play for our parents.*
performance (NOUN)
A performance is a play or show that you perform for other people.

perfume
NOUN perfumes
Perfume is a sweet-smelling liquid that you put on your skin so that you smell nice.

perhaps
ADVERB
Perhaps means maybe.

period
NOUN periods
A period of time is a length of time. *A fortnight is a* ***period*** *of two weeks.*

permission
NOUN
If someone gives you permission to do something, they say that you are allowed to do it. *The teacher gave us* ***permission*** *to go out and play.*

person
NOUN persons or people
A person is a man, woman, or child.

personal
ADJECTIVE
Personal things are items that belong just to you.

persuade
VERB persuades, persuading, persuaded
If you persuade someone to do something, you make them agree to do it. *We* ***persuaded*** *Dad to take us bowling.*

pest
NOUN pests
A pest is an insect or animal that is a nuisance to people.

pester
VERB pesters, pestering, pestered
If you pester someone, you keep annoying them until they give you something that you want.

pet
NOUN pets
A pet is a tame animal that you keep and look after.

petal
NOUN petals
Petals are the parts of a flower that may have bright colours or scent to attract insects.

petrified
ADJECTIVE
If you are petrified, you are so frightened that you cannot move. *I'm* ***petrified*** *of spiders.*

petrol
NOUN
Petrol is a liquid that is used as fuel to make engines work.

pharaoh
NOUN pharaohs
A pharaoh was the head of the government and a king in Ancient Egypt.

phone
NOUN phones
A phone is a machine that you use to talk to someone who is in a different place. A phone is also called a **telephone**. A **mobile phone** is one you carry around with you.

photo
NOUN photos
A photo is a picture that you take with a camera. A photo is also called a **photograph**. *I've got loads of* ***photos*** *on my phone.*

photographer (NOUN)
A photographer is someone whose job is taking photos.

photocopy
NOUN photocopies
A photocopy is a copy that you make of a picture or piece of writing, by putting it into a special machine that takes a photograph of it.

Pharaohs *ruled Egypt for 3,000 years.*

piano
NOUN pianos
A piano is a large musical instrument with black and white keys. You press down the keys to make different musical notes.

pick
VERB picks, picking, picked
1 When you pick something, you choose it. *Who are you going to **pick** to be in your team?*
2 When you pick a flower or fruit, you take it off the plant where it is growing.
3 When you pick something up, you lift it up in your hand.

picnic
NOUN picnics
When you have a picnic, you go to a nice place and eat a meal outside.

piano

picnic

*They had a **picnic** in the park.*

picture
NOUN pictures
A picture is something that you have drawn or painted.

pie
NOUN pies
A pie is made with meat or fruit that is covered in pastry and baked in an oven.

piece
NOUN pieces
A piece of something is a bit of it. *Can I have a **piece** of your pizza?*
☛ **Be careful with spelling:**
piece *Would you like a **piece** of cake?*
peace *Go away and leave me in **peace**!*

pig
NOUN pigs
A pig is an animal with a short snout and a curly tail. Pork, ham, and bacon come from the meat of pigs.

pigeon
NOUN pigeons
A pigeon is a large bird that you often see in towns and in the countryside.

pile
NOUN piles
A pile of things is a lot of them all lying on top of each other.

pill
NOUN pills
A pill is a small piece of medicine that you swallow whole.

pillow
NOUN pillows
A pillow is a cushion that you rest your head on in bed.

pilot
NOUN pilots
A pilot is someone who controls and flies a plane or helicopter.

pin
NOUN pins
A pin is a small, pointed piece of metal that you use to fasten pieces of cloth together.

pinch
VERB pinches, pinching, pinched
If you pinch someone, you squeeze their skin with your finger and thumb.

pine
NOUN pines
A pine tree is a type of evergreen tree that has cones and thin needles for leaves.

pineapple
NOUN pineapples
A pineapple is a fruit with a tough, brown skin and sweet, yellow flesh.

pink
ADJECTIVE
Something that is pink is the colour that you make by mixing red and white together.

pint
NOUN pints
A pint is an amount of liquid that is just over half a litre.

pipe
NOUN pipes
A pipe is a tube that liquid or gas can go through.

pirate
NOUN pirates
A pirate is someone who attacks and robs ships at sea.

pitch
NOUN pitches
A pitch is an area where you play a game or sport.

pity
NOUN
1 If you feel pity for someone, you feel sorry for them.
2 If something is a pity, it is a shame that it has happened. *It's a **pity** we had to cancel our picnic because of the weather.*

pizza
NOUN pizzas
A pizza is a flat piece of dough with tomato, cheese, and other foods on top.

place
NOUN places
1 A place is a building, town, or piece of land.
VERB places, placing, placed
2 When you place something somewhere, you put it there. *He **placed** the books on the table.*

plain
ADJECTIVE
Something that is plain is ordinary and not fancy.
☛ **Be careful with spelling:**
plain *She was wearing a **plain** green dress.*
plane *Have you ever flown in a **plane**?*

pirate
*He dressed as a **pirate** for the party.*

plan
NOUN plans
1 A plan is a drawing of a building or town. *We looked at the **plan** of the museum.*
2 A plan is an idea you have of how you are going to do something. *I've got a **plan** for how we can catch the thieves.*
VERB plans, planning, planned
3 When you plan something, you decide how you are going to do it.

*Would you like a slice of **pizza**?*

plane
NOUN planes
A plane is a vehicle that can travel through the air and carry passengers or goods. A plane is also called an **aeroplane**.
☛ **Be careful with spelling:**
plane *Have you ever flown in a **plane**?*
plain *She was wearing a **plain** green dress.*

a b c d e f g h i j k l m n o Pp q r s t u v w x y z

planets

planet
NOUN planets
A planet is a huge object in space that revolves around the Sun. The eight planets in our Solar System are Mercury, Venus, Earth, Mars, Jupiter, Saturn, Uranus, and Neptune.

plank
NOUN planks
A plank of wood is a long, flat piece of wood.

plant
NOUN plants
1 A plant is something that grows in soil. Grass, flowers, and trees are all plants.
VERB plants, planting, planted
2 When you plant something, you put it into the soil so that it will grow.

plaster
NOUN plasters
A plaster is a small piece of sticky material that you put over a cut in your skin to keep it clean.

plate
NOUN plates
A plate is a flat dish that you eat food off.

play
NOUN plays
1 A play is a story that people perform for others.
VERB plays, playing, played
2 When you play a game or sport, you take part in it.
3 When you play a musical instrument, you use it to make music.
player (NOUN)
A player is someone who plays a game, sport, or musical instrument.

pleasant
ADJECTIVE
If something is pleasant, you like it and enjoy it. *We had a very **pleasant** day at the seaside.*

please
You say please when you are asking for something politely. ***Please** can I have some more pudding?*

pleased
ADJECTIVE
If you are pleased about something, you are happy about it. *He was very **pleased** with his presents.*

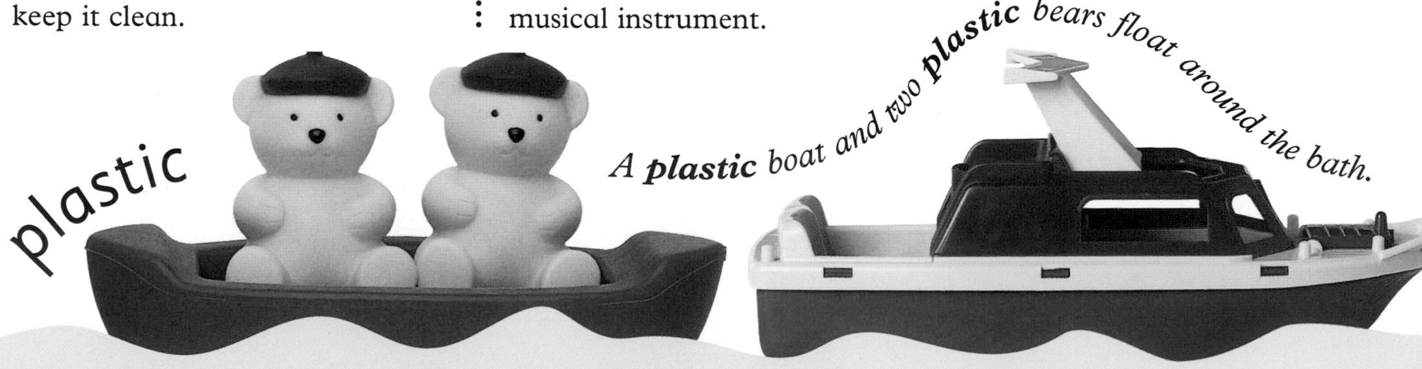

plastic
A **plastic** boat and two **plastic** bears float around the bath.

plastic
NOUN plastics
Plastic is a light material that is used to make all sorts of different things. A lot of toys are made of plastic.

playground
NOUN playgrounds
A playground is an outdoor area where children can play.

plenty
NOUN
If you have plenty of something, you have enough of it. *You've already got **plenty** of sweets!*

plot
NOUN plots
1 The plot in a book or film is the story.
2 A plot is a piece of land for growing things. *This is our vegetable* ***plot****.*

plough
NOUN ploughs
A plough is a large farm tool that cuts and turns the soil so it's ready for planting crops.

plug
NOUN plugs
1 The plug in a sink or bath is the part that you put in the hole to keep the water in.
2 The plug on a piece of electrical equipment is the part you put into a socket to connect it to the electricity supply.

plum
NOUN plums
A plum is a fruit with a smooth skin and soft, juicy flesh.

plump
ADJECTIVE plumper, plumpest
Someone or something that is plump is quite fat.

plural
NOUN plurals
The plural of a word is the form that you use for two or more things or people. *The* ***plural*** *of baby is babies.*

plus
Plus is a word you use when you are adding one number to another number. The symbol for plus is "+". *Eight* ***plus*** *two equals ten.*

pocket
NOUN pockets
A pocket is a part of a piece of clothing where you can keep small things. *Put your money in your* ***pocket****.*

podcast
NOUN podcasts
A podcast is a radio programme that you can download from the internet.

poem
NOUN poems
A poem is a short piece of writing that uses language in a clever way. Poems use rhythms and sometimes rhymes.
poet (NOUN)
A poet is someone who writes poems.
poetry (NOUN)
Poetry is a general name for poems.

point
NOUN points
1 A point is a thin, sharp part on the end of an object.
2 You get points in a game by scoring goals or doing things well. The person with the most points wins the game.
3 The point of something is the reason why you are doing it. *I can't see the* ***point*** *of watching the same film again!*
VERB points, pointing, pointed
4 If you point at something, you show where it is with your finger.
pointed (ADJECTIVE)
Something that is pointed has a thin, sharp part at one end.

poison
NOUN poisons
Poison is a substance that will kill you or make you ill if it gets inside your body.
poisonous (ADJECTIVE)
Something that is poisonous has poison in it.

poke
VERB pokes, poking, poked
If you poke something, you push it with your finger or a stick.

polar bear
NOUN polar bears
A polar bear is a large, white animal that lives in Arctic regions. Polar bears eat other animals, such as seals and fish.

pole
NOUN poles
1 A pole is a long, thin, round piece of wood or metal.
2 The **North Pole** is the part of the Earth that is farthest north. The **South Pole** is the part of the Earth that is farthest south.

police
NOUN
The police are men and women who make sure that people do not break the law. They also arrest people who have broken the law.

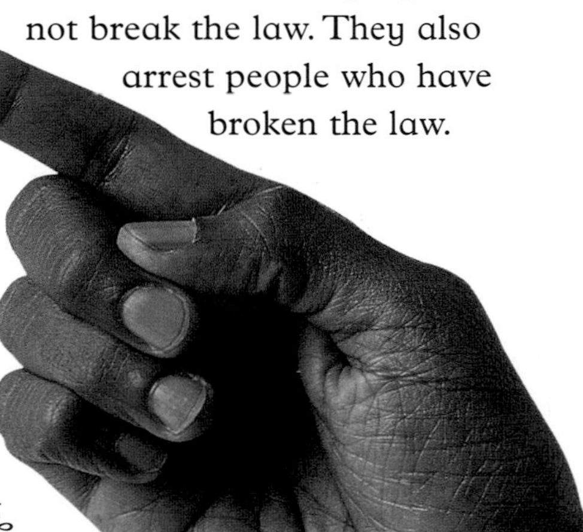
He ***pointed*** *out the* ***planets*** *in the sky.*

polish
NOUN
1 Polish is a cream or liquid that you rub onto something to make it shine.
VERB polishes, polishing, polished
2 If you polish something, you rub it so that it shines. *You ought to **polish** your shoes.*

polite
ADJECTIVE
If you are polite, you speak and behave in a pleasant way to other people.
☛ **Opposite:** impolite
politely (ADVERB)
If you say or do something politely, you do it in a polite way. *She smiled **politely**.*

pollen
NOUN
Pollen is a fine, yellow powder in the middle of flowers. Pollen makes people with hay fever sneeze.

pollution
NOUN
Pollution is dirt in the air, water, and land around us. *Cars cause a lot of **pollution** in cities.*

pond
NOUN ponds
A pond is a small area of fresh water.

*Car fumes cause **pollution**.*

*He **popped** the green balloon.*

pony
NOUN ponies
A pony is a small horse.

pool
NOUN pools
1 A pool is a small area of water. *It's interesting to look in the rock **pools** at the seaside.*
2 A pool is a place that has been filled with water so that people can swim in it.

poor
ADJECTIVE poorer, poorest
1 Someone who is poor does not have very much money.
2 Something that is poor is not very good. *This piece of work is very **poor**.*
3 Poor means unlucky. *That **poor** animal looks miserable in a cage.*

pop
NOUN
1 Pop music is modern, popular music.
VERB pops, popping, popped
2 If a balloon pops, all the air suddenly comes out of it.

popcorn
NOUN
Popcorn is made by heating seeds of corn until they puff up.

poppy
NOUN poppies
A poppy is a wild flower with delicate red petals.

popular
ADJECTIVE
If something is popular, a lot of people like it.
☛ **Opposite:** unpopular

pork
NOUN
Pork is meat from a pig.

porridge
NOUN
Porridge is a breakfast food made by cooking oats.

port
NOUN ports
A port is on a coast or river where ships can load and unload.

portable
ADJECTIVE
If something is portable, you can carry it around easily.

portrait
NOUN portraits
A portrait is a picture of a person.

position
NOUN positions
1 Your position is the way you are standing, sitting, or lying. *Are you in a comfortable **position**?*
2 The position of something is where it is. *Find our **position** on the map.*

positive
ADJECTIVE
If you are positive about something, you are sure about it. *I'm **positive** that I didn't leave my phone on the bus.*

possible
ADJECTIVE
If something is possible, it can be done or it can happen. *It is **possible** to swim without using your arms.*
☛ **Opposite:** impossible
possibility (NOUN)
If there is a possibility that something can happen, it is possible that it can happen.
possibly (ADVERB)
If something can possibly happen, it is possible that it can happen. *You can't **possibly** swim all that way!*

post
NOUN posts
1 The post is the letters and parcels that are delivered to people's homes every day.
2 A post is a tall piece of wood or stone fixed into the ground.
VERB posts, posting, posted
3 When you post a letter, you address it, then send it to someone so that it will be delivered to their home.

postcard
NOUN postcards
A postcard is a small piece of card with a picture on one side, sometimes a view of the place you are staying at. On the other side, you write a message and the address of the person you want to sent it to in the post.

poster
NOUN posters
A poster is a large picture or notice that you put on a wall as an advertisement or for decoration.

post office
NOUN post offices
A post office is a place where you go to buy stamps and materials for packaging, as well as send letters and parcels.

pot
NOUN pots
A pot is a container that you put things in.

potato
NOUN potatoes
A potato is a vegetable that you can boil, roast, fry, or bake. *These mashed **potatoes** are delicious.*

*She likes collecting **postcards**.*
postcards

*He **poured** some juice into his glass.*
pour

pottery
NOUN
Pottery is a general name for objects that are made of clay and are dried and baked in a kiln. Mugs, plates, and vases can all be made from clay.

pounce
VERB pounces, pouncing, pounced
To pounce means to jump forward suddenly and try to catch something. *The cat **pounced** on the mouse.*

pour
VERB pours, pouring, poured
1 When you pour a liquid, you tip up the container it is in so that the liquid comes out. *I **poured** some orange juice into my glass.*
2 When liquid pours out of something, it comes out very quickly. *Water was **pouring** out of the broken pipe.*

a b c d e f g h i j k l m n o **Pp** q r s t u v w x y z

powder
NOUN
A powder is a mass of very fine, dry grains.

power
NOUN powers
1 Someone who has power can tell other people what they should do.
2 The powers that you have are the things that you are able to do. *In some stories, people have special **powers** and can do magical things.*
3 Power is the energy that a machine needs in order to work. *The battery has run out of **power**.*

powerful
ADJECTIVE
Something that is powerful is very strong. *That car has a **powerful** engine.*

practice
NOUN
Practice is when you do something over and over again so that you become better at it. *You need a lot of **practice** to be a good goalkeeper.*

practise
VERB practises, practising, practised
When you practise something, you do it over and over again so that you become better at it. *You need to **practise** every day to play the trumpet well.*

praise
VERB praises, praising, praised
If you praise someone, you tell them that they have done well.

pram
NOUN prams
A pram is a small bed on wheels, in which you can push a baby along.

prawn
NOUN prawns
A prawn is a small sea creature that you can cook and eat. Prawns are pink when they have been cooked.

pray
VERB prays, praying, prayed
When you pray, you talk to a god.
prayer (NOUN)
When you say a prayer, you talk to a god.
☛ **Be careful with spelling:**
pray *They **pray** to God every day.*
prey *Lions can run fast to catch their **prey**.*

precious
ADJECTIVE
Something that is precious is worth a lot of money, or is very special to someone.

predator
NOUN predators
A predator is an animal that hunts and kills other animals. *Deer use their speed to escape from their **predators**.*

prefer
VERB prefers, preferring, preferred
If you prefer something, you like it better than other things. *Which shirt do you **prefer**, the blue one or the red one?*

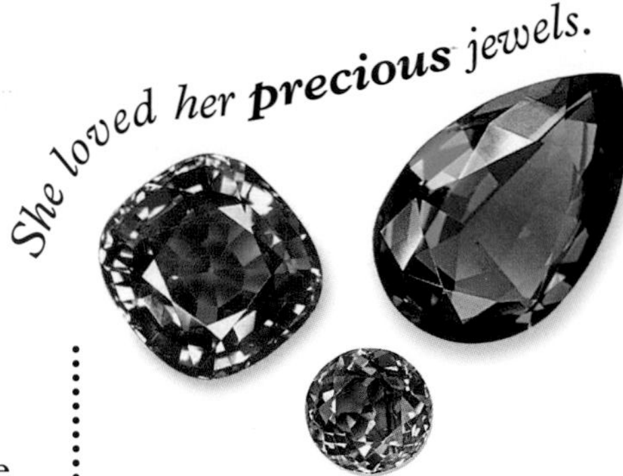
*She loved her **precious** jewels.*

prefix
NOUN prefixes
A prefix is a group of letters that you add to the front of a word to change its meaning. For example, you can add the prefix "un-" to words like "happy" and "comfortable" to make words with an opposite meaning – "unhappy" and "uncomfortable".

prehistoric
ADJECTIVE
Prehistoric means from the time long ago, before people started writing things down. *Dinosaurs lived in **prehistoric** times.*

prepare
VERB prepares, preparing, prepared
When you prepare something, you get it ready. *We need to **prepare** some sandwiches for lunch.*
preparation (NOUN)
Preparation for something means getting ready for it. *We were all busy with **preparations** for the party.*

preposition
NOUN prepositions
A preposition is a word such as "on" or "in" that we use in front of a noun. There are two prepositions in the following sentence: *He was sitting **on** a chair **in** the garden.*

present
NOUN
1 The present is the time that is happening now. *The story takes place in the* ***present****.*
2 A present is something that you give to someone.
VERB presents, presenting, presented
3 If you present something to someone, you give it to them as a prize. *He* ***presented*** *the trophy to the winner.*
ADJECTIVE
4 If you are present, you are in a place.

president
NOUN presidents
A president is someone who is in charge of a country, a company, or a college.

press
NOUN
1 The press is newspapers and magazines. *A photographer came from the* ***press*** *to take a picture of us.*
VERB presses, pressing, pressed
2 When you press something, you push it.

pretend
VERB pretends, pretending, pretended
When you pretend, you say or do things that are not really true, either to have fun or to trick people. *She wasn't really upset – she was only* ***pretending****.*

pretty
ADJECTIVE prettier, prettiest
Someone or something that is pretty is nice to look at.

prevent
VERB prevents, preventing, prevented
To prevent something from happening means to stop it from happening. *The barrier* ***prevented*** *anyone from falling down the hole.*

prey
NOUN
An animal's prey is the animal that it hunts and eats.
☛ **Be careful with spelling:**
prey *Lions can run fast to catch their* ***prey****.*
pray *They* ***pray*** *to God every day.*

price
NOUN prices
The price of something is the amount of money you have to pay to buy it.

prickly
ADJECTIVE
Something that is prickly has a lot of sharp points on it.

prime minister
NOUN prime ministers
A prime minister is someone who is in charge of a country.

prime number
NOUN prime numbers
A prime number is a number that can only be divided by 1 and by itself: 3, 5, and 7 are all prime numbers.

prince
NOUN princes
A prince is the son or grandson of a king or queen.

princess
NOUN princesses
A princess is the daughter or granddaughter of a king or queen.

print
VERB prints, printing, printed
1 When you print letters, you write them separately, rather than joining them up.
2 If words are printed, they are put onto paper by a machine, rather than being written by someone.
printer (NOUN)
A printer is a machine that prints words and pictures onto paper from a computer.

prison
NOUN prisons
A prison is a building where people are kept as a punishment when they have broken the law.
prisoner (NOUN)
A prisoner is someone who is being kept in a prison.

prickly

This ***prickly*** *cactus has* ***pretty*** *flowers.*

private
ADJECTIVE
If something is private, it belongs to one person and other people must not touch it, look inside it, or use it. *My diary is **private**.*

prize
NOUN prizes
A prize is something that you win.

*The third **prize** is a yellow rosette.*

probably
ADVERB
If something will probably happen, it is very likely that it will happen.

problem
NOUN problems
A problem is something that makes things difficult for you.

produce
VERB produces, producing, produced
1 If you produce something, you make it appear.
2 To produce things means to make them. *This factory **produces** cars.*

professional
ADJECTIVE
Someone who is professional earns money by doing something, rather than doing it just for fun. *Would you like to be a **professional** dancer?*

profit
NOUN profits
A profit is money that you make for yourself when you sell something.

program
NOUN programs
A program is a set of instructions that tells a computer how to do a task.

programme
NOUN programmes
1 A programme is a show on television or radio.
2 A programme is a small book that gives you information about an event. *He looked at the **programme** to see who was on stage first.*

*The magician **produced** a rabbit out of his hat.*

progress
NOUN
When you make progress, you get better at something. *You have made good **progress** with your English this year.*

project
NOUN projects
A project is a big piece of work in which you find out a lot of information and do a lot of work on a subject. *We're doing a **project** on the Vikings.*

promise
VERB promises, promising, promised
If you promise to do something, you say you will definitely do it.

pronoun
NOUN pronouns
A pronoun is a word such as "he", "she", or "it" that you use instead of a noun. There are two pronouns in the sentence: ***He** picked up the apple and ate **it**.*

pronunciation
NOUN pronunciations
The pronunciation of a word is the way in which it is said.

proof
NOUN
If you have proof that something happened, you have something that shows it really happened.

proper
ADJECTIVE
1 Proper means correct. *This is the **proper** way to hit a golf ball.*
2 A proper noun is a noun that is the name of a person or place such as "George" and "Africa".

property
NOUN
If something is your property, it belongs to you.

protect
VERB protects, protecting, protected
If you protect someone, you keep them safe.

proud
ADJECTIVE prouder, proudest
If you are proud of something, you are pleased with it and think that it is good. *He was **proud** of his painting.*
proudly (ADVERB)
If you do something proudly, you do it in a way that shows you are proud. *"I made this boat myself," he said **proudly**.*

prove
VERB proves, proving, proved
To prove that something is true means to show that it is definitely true.

proverb
NOUN proverbs
A proverb is a short saying that gives you a piece of advice. *"Many hands make light work" is a **proverb**.*

prowl
VERB prowls, prowling, prowled
To prowl means to move around quietly and secretly. *The tiger **prowled** around the tree.*

public
ADJECTIVE
Something that is public is open to everybody.

pudding
NOUN puddings
A pudding is a sweet food that you eat at the end of a meal.

puddle
NOUN puddles
A puddle is a shallow pool of rainwater on the ground.

puff
NOUN puffs
A puff of wind or smoke is a small amount of it that is suddenly blown along.

pull
VERB pulls, pulling, pulled
When you pull something, you move it toward you. *We **pulled** the sledge across the snow.*

pump
NOUN pumps
A pump is a machine that pushes liquids or gases into or out of something.

pumpkin
NOUN pumpkins
A pumpkin is a large, round, orange fruit with seeds in the middle. It can be used for sweet and savoury dishes. Children make pumpkins into lanterns at Halloween. Adults help to hollow them out and carve a face.

punch
VERB punches, punching, punched
If you punch someone, you hit them with your fist.

punctuation
NOUN
Punctuation is a group of marks such as full stops and question marks that you use when you are writing.

puncture
NOUN punctures
A puncture is a hole that lets the air out of something. *My tyre has a **puncture**.*

*She trod in a **puddle**.*

puddle

a b c d e f g h i j k l m n o **Pp** q r s t u v w x y z

punish
VERB punishes, punishing, punished
To punish someone means to make them suffer in some way because they have done something wrong.
punishment (NOUN)
A punishment is something you do to someone because they have done something wrong. *As a **punishment**, you will have to stay inside at lunch time.*

pupil
NOUN pupils
1 The pupils in a school are the children who go to that school.
2 Your pupils are the small, dark circles in the middle of your eyes.

puppet
NOUN puppets
A puppet is a doll or animal figure that you move by pulling on its strings or moving your hand inside it.

puppy
NOUN puppies
A puppy is a young dog.

puppets

pure
ADJECTIVE purer, purest
Something that is pure is not mixed with anything else. *Her ring was made of **pure** gold.*

purple
ADJECTIVE
Something that is purple is the colour made by mixing red and blue together.

purse
NOUN purses
A purse is a small bag that you carry money in.

push
VERB pushes, pushing, pushed
When you push something, you use your hands to move it away from you. *I tried to **push** the door open, but it was locked.*

pushchair
NOUN pushchairs
A pushchair is a small chair on wheels, in which you can push a small child.

put
VERB puts, putting, put
When you put something somewhere, you move it so that it is there. *I **put** the biscuits back in the cupboard.*

puzzle
NOUN puzzles
1 A puzzle is a game in which you have to find an answer to a difficult problem or question.
2 If something is a puzzle, no one can understand it or explain it.

pyjamas
NOUN
Pyjamas are a loose top and trousers that you wear in bed.

pyramid
NOUN pyramids
1 A pyramid is a large, stone building that was made in Ancient Egypt to bury a dead king or queen.
2 A pyramid is a solid shape that has a square base and four triangular sides that join in a point at the top.

python
NOUN pythons
A python is a large snake that is found in hot countries. Pythons kill their prey by wrapping themselves around the animal and squeezing it to death.

Q

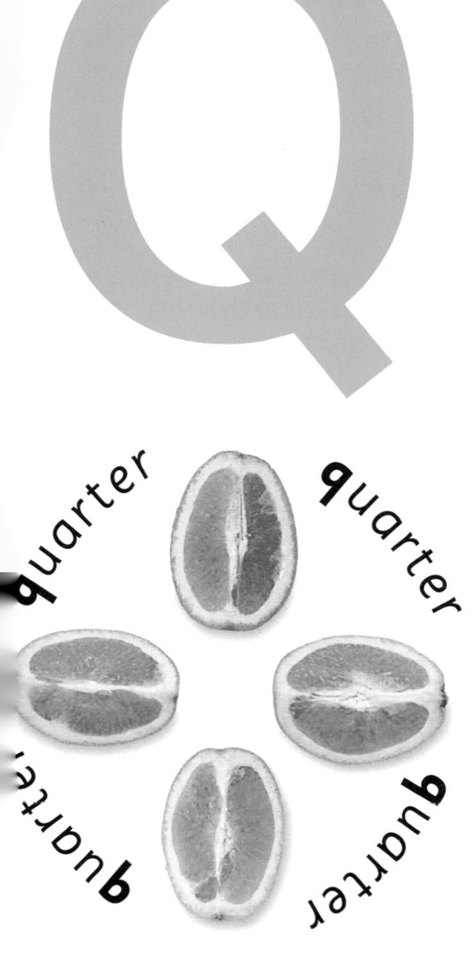

qualify
VERB qualifies, qualifying, qualified
If you qualify in a competition, you get enough points to go to the next part of the competition. *If we win this game, we'll **qualify** for the finals.*

quality
NOUN qualities
The quality of something is how good or bad it is. *It's cheap, but the **quality** isn't very good.*

quantity
NOUN quantities
A quantity is an amount. *I was amazed at the **quantity** of food he had bought.*

quarrel
VERB quarrels, quarrelling, quarrelled
When people quarrel, they shout at each other because they are angry with each other.

quarry
NOUN quarries
A quarry is a place where stone is dug out of the ground.

quarter
NOUN quarters
If you divide something into four quarters, you divide it into four equal parts. Each part is called one quarter. *Two **quarters** make one half.*

queen
NOUN queens
A queen is a woman who rules a country.

quest
NOUN quests
A quest is a long journey in which you are searching for something. *I began my **quest** to find my missing cat.*

question
NOUN questions
When you ask a question, you ask someone something because you want to know the answer.
question mark (NOUN)
A question mark is a mark (**?**) that you use after a question in writing.
questionnaire (NOUN)
A questionnaire is a set of questions that you ask people so that you can collect information about something.

queue
NOUN queues
A queue is a line of people who are waiting for something.

quick
ADJECTIVE quicker, quickest
Something that is quick does not take long. *It was a **quick** journey.*
quickly (ADVERB)
If you do something quickly, you do it in a way that does not take long. *I **quickly** ran to get help.*

quiet
ADJECTIVE quieter, quietest
If it is quiet in a place, there is no noise. If you are quiet, you do not make any noise.
quietly (ADVERB)
If you do something quietly, you do it without making any noise. *I tiptoed **quietly** out of the room.*

quilt
NOUN quilts
A quilt is a thick cover that you put on a bed.

quit
VERB quits, quitting, quitted
If you quit a computer game or program, you leave it. If you quit doing something, you stop doing it.

quite
ADVERB
1 Quite means fairly. *I am **quite** good at running.*
2 Quite means completely. *You are **quite** right.*

quiz
NOUN quizzes
A quiz is a game in which people answer questions to get points.

a b c d e f g h i j k l m n o p q **Rr** s t u v w x y z

R

ring ring ring ring ring ring

rabbi
NOUN rabbis
A rabbi is a Jewish religious leader.

rabbit
NOUN rabbits
A rabbit is a small, furry animal. Rabbits live underground in burrows and eat grass.

race
NOUN races
A race is a competition to see who can go the fastest.

*Two furry **rabbits** twitch their noses.*

rack
NOUN racks
A rack is a special shelf for putting things on.

racket
NOUN rackets
1 A racket is a bat that you use to play tennis and badminton.
2 A racket is a very loud, annoying noise. *He was making a terrible **racket** with his drums.*

radar
NOUN
Radar is a way of finding out where a ship or plane is by using radio waves.

radiator
NOUN radiators
A radiator is a heater attached to a wall.

radio
NOUN radios
A radio is a machine that you use to listen to programmes that are broadcast.

raffle
NOUN raffles
When there is a raffle, people buy tickets with numbers on, and if their number is chosen, they win a prize.

raft
NOUN rafts
A raft is a small, flat boat that is made from logs, which are tied together.

rag
NOUN rags
A rag is a small, torn piece of cloth. *The children were dressed in **rags**.*

rage
NOUN
Rage is very great anger. *She slammed the door in a **rage**.*

rail
NOUN rails
1 A rail is a long metal or wooden bar. *Hold onto the **rail** as you climb.*
2 If you travel by rail, you travel on a train.

railway
NOUN railways
1 A railway line is the two metal bars that trains travel along.
2 If you travel on the railways, you travel on a train.

rain
NOUN
1 Rain is water that falls from the clouds in drops.
VERB rains, raining, rained
2 When it rains, water falls from the clouds.
☛ **Be careful with spelling:**
rain *We can't play outside in the **rain**.*
reign *The king **reigns** over his kingdom.*
rein *You hold the **reins** when you ride a horse.*

rainbow
NOUN rainbows
A rainbow is an arc of colours that appears in the sky when the sun shines during rain.

rainbow
A rainbow shines between the clouds.

raindrop
NOUN raindrops
A raindrop is one drop of rain.

rainforest
NOUN rainforests
A rainforest is a hot, wet jungle that grows in tropical countries.

raise
VERB raises, raising, raised
If you raise something, you lift it up. *He **raised** his hand to answer the question.*

raisin
NOUN raisins
A raisin is a dried grape that you can eat or use in cooking.

rake
NOUN rakes
A rake is a tool that you use in the garden to gather up leaves into a pile or to smooth over soil.

Ramadan
NOUN
Ramadan is a time each year when Muslims do not eat between the time the Sun comes up in the morning and the time it sets at night.

ramp
NOUN ramps
A ramp is a slope that you go up or down. *We drove up a **ramp** to the boat.*

ran
☛ See **run**.

ranch
NOUN ranches
A ranch is a farm in America where cattle are kept.

rang
☛ See **ring.**

range
NOUN ranges
A range of things is a lot of different things. *There is a **range** of activities for children at the campsite.*

rap
NOUN
Rap is a type of poetry with a strong rhythm, that you speak to music.

rapid
ADJECTIVE
Rapid means quick. *We ate a **rapid** lunch before we left.*
rapidly (ADVERB)
If something happens rapidly, it happens quickly. *The water was rising quite **rapidly**.*

rare
ADJECTIVE rarer, rarest
If something is rare, you do not see it very often. *Wild tigers are now **rare**.*

rash
NOUN rashes
If you have a rash, you have red, itchy spots on your skin.

raspberry
NOUN raspberries
A raspberry is a juicy, red fruit that grows on a plant.

rat
NOUN rats
A rat is an animal that looks like a big mouse. Rats have strong front teeth, which they use to gnaw food.

rate
NOUN rates
The rate at which something happens is how quickly it happens.

rather
ADVERB
1 Rather means quite. *He looked **rather** sad.*
2 If you would rather have or do something, you would prefer to have or do that thing. *I don't want to go to the cinema – I would **rather** stay at home.*

*We picked some **raspberries** for tea.*

a b c d e f g h i j k l m n o p q Rr s t u v w x y z

rattle

NOUN rattles

1 A rattle is a baby's toy that makes a noise when you shake it.

VERB rattles, rattling, rattled

2 When something rattles, it makes a loud noise.

raw

ADJECTIVE

Raw food has not been cooked. *Some **raw** vegetables are very good for you.*

ray

NOUN rays

A ray of light is a beam of light.

razor

NOUN razors

A razor is a sharp blade that people use for removing hair from their face or body.

reach

VERB reaches, reaching, reached

1 If you reach towards something, you stretch out your hand to touch it.

2 If you reach a place, you arrive there. *What time will we **reach** London?*

react

VERB reacts, reacting, reacted

When you react to something that has happened, you say or do something because it has happened. *When his bike was stolen, he **reacted** by bursting into tears.*

reaction (NOUN)

Your reaction to something is the way that you react to it.

read

VERB reads, reading, read

When you read, you look at words that are written down and understand them.

ready

ADJECTIVE

If you are ready, you are prepared and so you can do something. *Are you **ready** to leave?*

real

ADJECTIVE

Something that is real is true, and is not false. *Is that **real** gold?*

reach

*He finally **reached** the top of the hill.*

realize

VERB realizes, realizing, realized

When you realize that something is true, you quickly understand it. *I suddenly **realized** that we were lost.*

really

ADVERB

1 Really means very. *The film was **really** funny.*

2 Really means actually. *Is it **really** true that you're leaving?*

reason

NOUN reasons

The reason why something happens is the thing that causes it to happen. *Can you explain the **reason** why you hit your brother?*

reasonable

ADJECTIVE

Something that is reasonable is fair and sensible.

receipt

NOUN receipts

A receipt is a piece of paper that shows you have paid for something.

receive

VERB receives, receiving, received

When you receive something, someone gives it or sends it to you.

recent

ADJECTIVE

Something that is recent happened only a short time ago.

recently (ADVERB)

If something happened recently, it happened a short time ago. *I visited my grandma **recently**.*

recipe

NOUN recipes

A recipe is a set of instructions that tell you how to cook something.

recite

VERB recites, reciting, recited

When you recite a poem, you say it out loud without reading it.

recognize
VERB recognizes, recognizing, recognized

If you recognize someone, you know who they are. If you recognize something, you know what it is. *I **recognized** my friend's coat on the hook.*

recommend
VERB recommends, recommending, recommended

If you recommend something, you tell other people that it is good. *I would really **recommend** this film.*

record
NOUN records

1 The record for doing something is the fastest, best, or most that it has ever been done. *He holds the world **record** for the 100 metres.*

2 A record is a piece of information that is written down. *She kept a **record** of the day's events in her diary.*

record
VERB records, recording, recorded

1 When you record sound or pictures, you store them on film, disc, or digitally. *I **recorded** a video of my dog on my phone.*

2 If you record information, you write it down.

recorder
NOUN recorders

A recorder is a small musical instrument that you blow into. You make different notes by covering different holes with your fingers.

recover
VERB recovers, recovering, recovered

When you recover, you get better after you have been ill.

rectangle
NOUN rectangles

A rectangle is a shape that has four straight sides. It is not square, but has two equal long sides and two equal short sides.

rectangular (ADJECTIVE)
Something that is rectangular is the shape of a rectangle.

recycle
VERB recycles, recycling, recycled

To recycle things means to use them again, often by turning them into new things. Glass, plastics, paper, and metal can all be recycled.

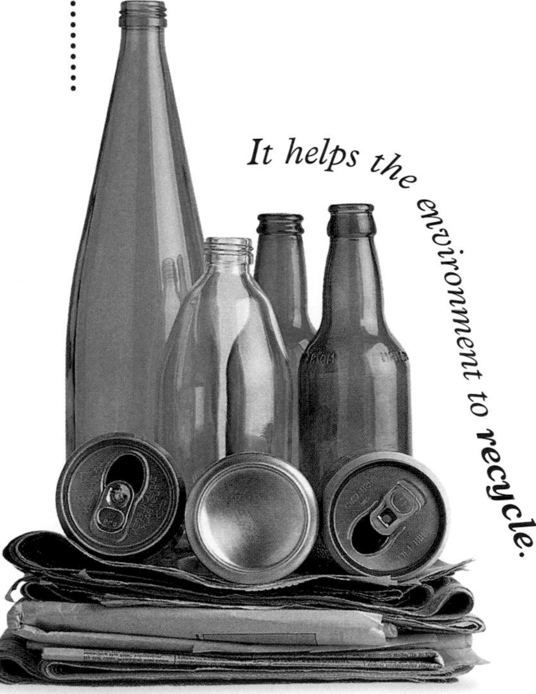

It helps the environment to ***recycle.***

red
ADJECTIVE

Something that is red is the colour of blood.

reduce
VERB reduces, reducing, reduced

If you reduce something, you make it smaller. *The shop **reduced** the price of all its trainers.*

refer
VERB refers, referring, referred

If you refer to something, you mention it.

referee
NOUN referees

The referee in a game is the person who watches the game and makes sure that people follow all the rules.

reference
ADJECTIVE

Reference books give you information.

reflect
VERB reflects, reflecting, reflected

If something is reflected in a mirror or in water, you can see an image of it. *The trees were **reflected** in the lake.*

reflection (NOUN)
A reflection is an image of something in a mirror or in water.

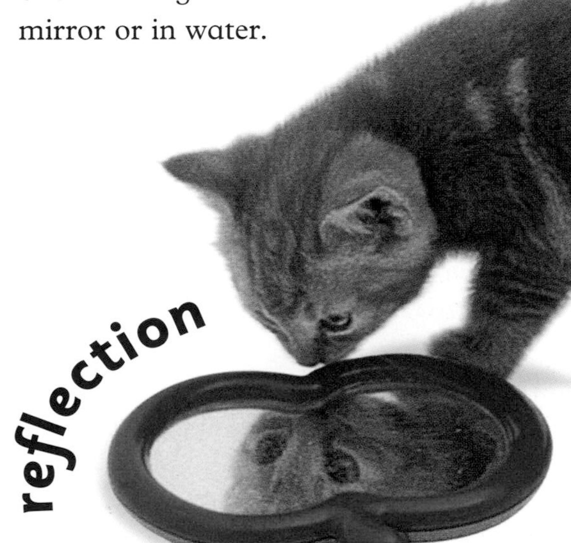

reflection

a b c d e f g h i j k l m n o p q Rr s t u v w x y z

refreshing
ADJECTIVE
If something is refreshing, it makes you feel fresh and less tired.

refreshments
NOUN
Refreshments are things to eat and drink. *We had some **refreshments** after playing football.*

refrigerator
NOUN refrigerators
A refrigerator is a machine that keeps food and drink cool and fresh. A refrigerator is also called a **fridge**.

refugee
NOUN refugees
A refugee is someone who has left their own country because of a war.

refuse
VERB refuses, refusing, refused
If you refuse to do something, you say that you will not do it. *He **refused** to give her the ball.*

register
NOUN registers
A register is a book in which you keep a list of names. *The teacher put a tick next to my name in the **register**.*

regret
VERB regrets, regretting, regretted
If you regret doing something, you are sorry that you did it. *I **regretted** shouting at my friends.*

regular
ADJECTIVE
Something that is regular happens every day or every week at the same time.
regularly (ADVERB)
If you do something regularly, you do it often.

rehearse
VERB rehearses, rehearsing, rehearsed
When you rehearse something, you practise it before you do it in front of people.

reign
VERB reigns, reigning, reigned
When someone reigns, they are the king or queen of a country.
☛ **Be careful with spelling:**
reign *The king **reigns** over his kingdom.*
rain *We can't play outside in the **rain**.*
rein *You hold the **reins** when you ride a horse.*

rein
NOUN reins
Reins are leather straps that you use to control a horse when you are riding it.
☛ **Be careful with spelling:**
rein *You hold the **reins** when you ride a horse.*
rain *We can't play outside in the **rain**.*
reign *The king **reigns** over his kingdom.*

reindeer
NOUN reindeer or reindeers
A reindeer is a deer with large antlers that lives in cold, Arctic regions.

related
ADJECTIVE
People who are related belong to the same family.
relative (NOUN)
Your relatives are the people who are in your family. These people are also called your **relations**.

relax
VERB relaxes, relaxing, relaxed
When you relax, you rest and feel comfortable. *I just wanted to **relax** in front of the fire and read my book.*
relaxed (ADJECTIVE)
If you feel relaxed, you feel calm and comfortable.
relaxing (ADJECTIVE)
Something that is relaxing helps you to feel calm and comfortable. *We listened to some **relaxing** music.*

relay
NOUN relays
A relay is a race in which a team of people each run or swim one part of the race.

reindeer

release
VERB releases, releasing, released
To release someone means to let them go free. To release something means to let go of it. *They **released** the prisoner from the prison.*

relief
NOUN
If something is a relief, you are glad that it has happened because it means you can stop worrying. *It was a **relief** when the exam was over.*
relieved (ADJECTIVE)
If you feel relieved, you feel happy and no longer worried about something. *He was **relieved** when he found his lost cat.*

religion
NOUN religions
A religion is a set of beliefs and ideas about God or gods.
religious (ADJECTIVE)
Religious ideas or events are ideas or events to do with religion.

reluctant
ADJECTIVE
If you are reluctant to do something, you do not want to do it. *He was **reluctant** to cross the old bridge in case it fell down.*

rely
VERB relies, relying, relied
If you rely on someone, you need them and depend on them to do things for you. *Young birds **rely** on their parents for food.*

remain
VERB remains, remaining, remained
1 If you remain in a place, you stay there.
2 To remain means to stay. *She **remained** calm while everyone else panicked.*
remainder (NOUN)
In maths, the remainder is the number that is left over when you divide one number into another. *Nine divided by four is two, with a **remainder** of one.*

remark
NOUN remarks
A remark is something that you say.

remember
VERB remembers, remembering, remembered
If you remember something, you think about it again. *She suddenly **remembered** she had left her bag on the bus.*

remind
VERB reminds, reminding, reminded
To remind someone of something means to make them think about it again.

remote control
NOUN remote controls
A remote control is a machine that you hold in your hand and use to control another machine such as a television.

remove
VERB removes, removing, removed
If you remove something, you take it off or take it away.

rent
NOUN
Rent is money that you pay each week to live in a house or flat.

repair
VERB repairs, repairing, repaired
When you repair something, you mend it.

repeat
VERB repeats, repeating, repeated
If you repeat something, you say it again.

replace
VERB replaces, replacing, replaced
If you replace something that is old or broken, you change it for a new one.

*He **released** the balloon.*

a b c d e f g h i j k l m n o p q Rr s t u v w x y z

To the rescue

If you are in danger, one of these vehicles will come to the rescue.

reply

VERB replies, replying, replied

If you reply, you say something when someone has spoken to you or asked you a question. *"How old are you?" I asked. "Ten," he **replied**.*

reply (NOUN)

A reply is an answer. *I called his name, but there was no **reply**.*

report

NOUN reports

A report is a piece of writing that gives information about things that have happened.

reporter (NOUN)

A reporter is someone who writes news reports or goes on TV to tell people about things that have happened.

reptile

NOUN reptiles

A reptile is a cold-blooded animal that has dry, scaly skin. Most reptiles lay eggs. Crocodiles, snakes, lizards, and tortoises are all reptiles.

rescue

VERB rescues, rescuing, rescued

If you rescue someone, you save them from danger.

research

NOUN

1 When you do research, you find out information about something.

VERB researches, researching, researched

2 When you research something, you find out information about it. *I **researched** volcanoes for my geography homework.*

resource

NOUN resources

A resource is something that people can use. *Oil is a natural **resource**.*

respect

NOUN

If you have respect for someone, you admire them. *I have a lot of **respect** for my teacher.*

responsible

ADJECTIVE

1 If someone is responsible, they are sensible and can be trusted.

2 If you are responsible for doing something, it is your job.

responsibility (NOUN)

If something is your responsibility, it is your job to do it.

rest

NOUN

1 A rest is a time when you are relaxing and not working.

2 The rest is all the people and things that are left over. *He ate most of the cake, and I ate the **rest**.*

restaurant

NOUN restaurants

A restaurant is a place where you can pay to eat a meal.

result

NOUN results

1 The result in a game is the score at the end of the game.

2 The result of something is what happens because of it.

return
VERB returns, returning, returned

1 To return to a place means to go back there. *We **returned** home after school.*

2 If you return something to someone, you give it back to them. *Can I borrow your book? I'll **return** it to you next week.*

reveal
VERB reveals, revealing, revealed

If you reveal something, you uncover it so that people can see it.

revenge
NOUN

Revenge is when you do something unpleasant to someone because they have hurt or upset you.

reverse
VERB reverses, reversing, reversed

When you reverse, you go backwards in a car.

revise
VERB revises, revising, revised

If you revise for an exam, you look at your previous work to prepare for it.

reward
NOUN rewards

If you give someone a reward, you give them money or something nice because they have done something good. *They offered a **reward** to anyone who found their cat.*

rhinoceros
NOUN rhinoceroses

A rhinoceros is a large animal that has thick skin and either one or two horns on its nose.

rhyme
NOUN rhymes

1 A rhyme is a poem in which the last words of some lines have the same sound.

VERB rhymes, rhyming, rhymed

2 If words rhyme, they end in the same sound. *"Eat" **rhymes** with "feet".*

rhythm
NOUN rhythms

A rhythm is a regular beat in music, dancing, or poetry.

ribbon
NOUN ribbons

A ribbon is a piece of coloured material that you use for tying up a present.

rice
NOUN

Rice is a plant that grows in warm, wet climates. You can cook and eat the white or brown seeds of the rice plant.

rich
ADJECTIVE richer, richest

Someone who is rich has a lot of money. *He ran a succesful business which made him **rich**.*

riddle
NOUN riddles

A riddle is a difficult puzzle that has a clever or funny answer.

ride
VERB rides, riding, rode, ridden

1 When you ride a horse or bicycle, you sit on it and make it move along. *I **ride** my bike to school.*

2 When you ride on a bus, train, or other vehicle, you sit on it while it moves.

ridiculous
ADJECTIVE

Something that is ridiculous is very silly or strange. *We can't stay up all night – that's a **ridiculous** idea!*

rhinoceros

a b c d e f g h i j k l m n o p q Rr s t u v w x y z

right
ADJECTIVE
1 Your right side is the side that is opposite your left side. *He kicks with his **right** foot.*
2 Something that is right is correct. *That's the **right** answer.*
3 Something that is right is fair and good. *It's not **right** that she should have all the sweets.*
4 A right angle is an angle of 90 degrees, like the angles in a square.
☛ **Be careful with spelling:**
right *That's the **right** answer.*
write *Which hand do you **write** with?*

ring
NOUN rings
1 A ring is a piece of jewellery that you wear on your finger.
VERB rings, ringing, rang, rung
2 When a bell rings, it makes a pleasant sound because you have hit it or shaken it. *The school bell **rings** at the end of lessons.*
3 If you ring someone, you phone them. *I have tried to **ring** her three times today.*

rinse
VERB rinses, rinsing, rinsed
If you rinse something, you wash it in clean water after you have washed it with soap.

rip
VERB rips, ripping, ripped
If you rip a piece of paper or cloth, you tear it. *He **ripped** the letter in half.*

ripe
ADJECTIVE riper, ripest
Fruit that is ripe is soft and ready to eat.

rise
VERB rises, rising, rose, risen
To rise means to go upward.

risk
NOUN risks
A risk is a danger that something bad might happen. *There was a **risk** that I might fall.*

rival
NOUN rivals
Your rival is the person you are against in a game or competition.

river
NOUN rivers
A river is a large stream of water that flows into another river, a lake, or the ocean.

road
NOUN roads
A road is a wide, smooth path that cars and other vehicles can drive along.
☛ **Be careful with spelling:**
road *We drove along the main **road**.*
rode *I **rode** my bike to school yesterday.*

roar
VERB roars, roaring, roared
1 When an animal roars, it makes a loud, deep, rumbling noise. *The angry lion **roared**.*
2 If someone roars, they shout loudly. *"Sit down!" he **roared**.*

rock

roast
VERB roasts, roasting, roasted
When you roast meat or vegetables, you cook them in a hot oven or over a fire.

rob
VERB robs, robbing, robbed
To rob someone means to steal things from them. *Some thieves **robbed** the bank.*
robber (NOUN)
A robber is someone who robs people.
robbery (NOUN)
A robbery is a crime in which a person or place is robbed. *The bank had lots of money stolen from it in the **robbery**.*

robin
NOUN robins
A robin is a small bird with a red breast.

robot
NOUN robots
A robot is a machine that can do jobs that a person usually does.

rock
NOUN rocks
1 A rock is a big stone.
2 Rock is the hard material that mountains are made of.
3 Rock music is music with a strong rhythm.

rocket
NOUN rockets
1 A rocket is a long, thin spacecraft.
2 A rocket is a type of firework that shoots into the sky and explodes.

Robots

Robots can perform many different jobs. Here are some words to describe them.

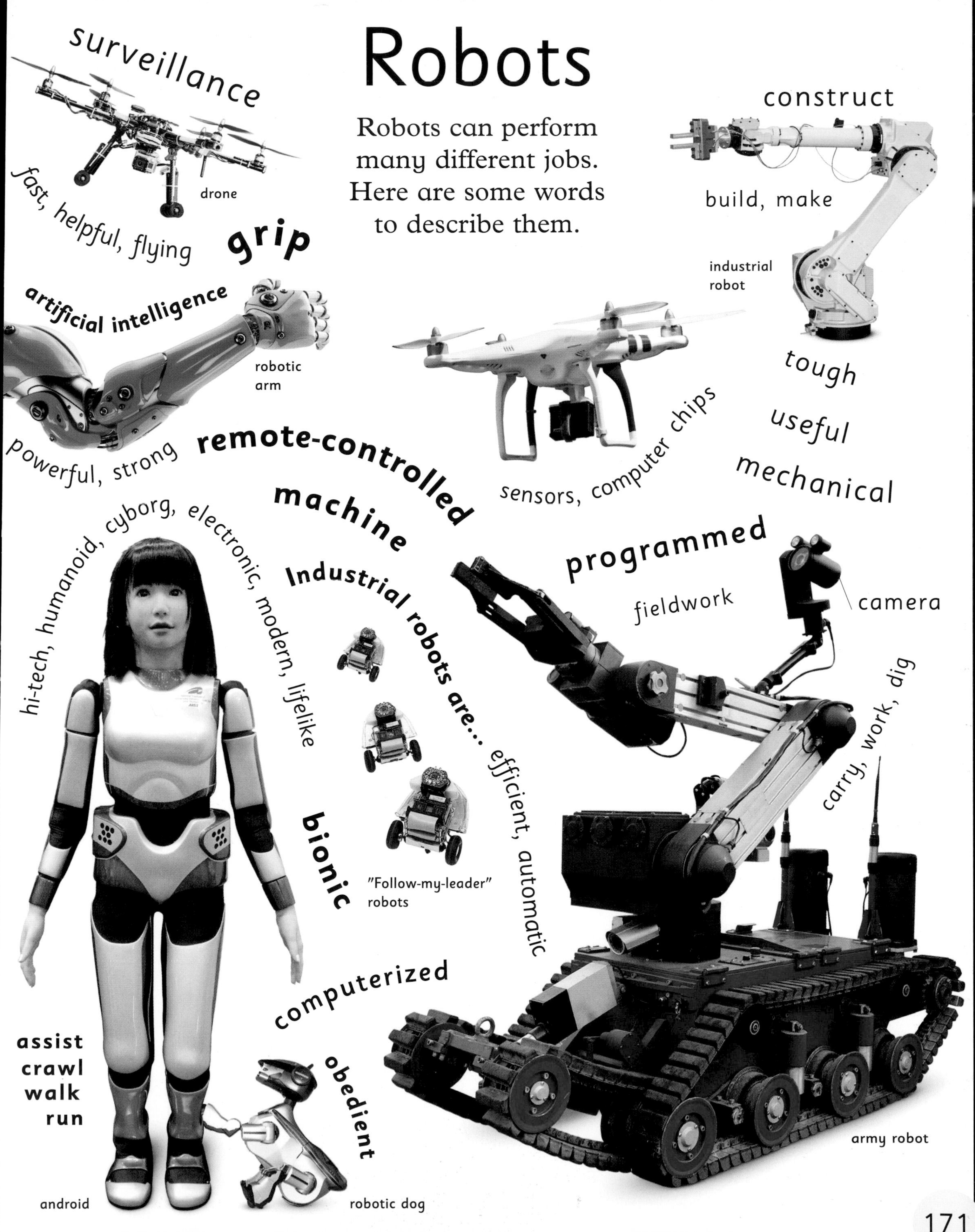

drone

industrial robot

robotic arm

"Follow-my-leader" robots

army robot

android

robotic dog

a b c d e f g h i j k l m n o p q Rr s t u v w x y z

rod
NOUN rods
A rod is a thin piece of wood or metal.

rode
☛ See **ride**.

rodent
NOUN rodents
A rodent is an animal with long front teeth for gnawing food. Rats, mice, and squirrels are rodents.

roll
NOUN rolls
1 A roll of paper or cloth is an amount of it that has been wound onto a tube.
2 A bread roll is a small, round piece of bread.
VERB rolls, rolling, rolled
3 When something rolls, it moves along by turning over and over.

roller-skate
NOUN roller-skates
Roller-skates are a type of boots with two rows of wheels attached to the bottom.

roof
NOUN roofs
1 The roof on a building is the sloping part on top of it.
2 The roof of your mouth or a cave is the curved top part inside it.

room
NOUN rooms
1 The rooms in a building are the separate parts inside the building.
2 If there is room for something, there is enough space for it.

root
NOUN roots
The roots of a plant are the parts that grow underground.
☛ **Be careful with spelling:**
root *Trees have very deep **roots**.*
route *What's the quickest **route** from here to your house?*

rope
NOUN ropes
A rope is a piece of thick, strong string or wire.

rose
NOUN roses
1 A rose is a type of flower that grows on a prickly bush.
2 Rose is the past tense of **rise**. *The balloon **rose** into the air.*

*He tugged on the **rope**.*

rope

rot
VERB rots, rotting, rotted
When something rots, it is no longer fresh and it goes bad and starts to break down.
rotten (ADJECTIVE)
Something that is rotten is no longer fresh, but has gone bad.

rough
ADJECTIVE rougher, roughest
1 Something that is rough is not smooth or even. *The sea is very **rough**.*
2 A rough amount is not exact. *That's only a **rough** guess.*
roughly (ADVERB)
Roughly means more or less, but not exactly. *There are **roughly** 30 children in each class.*

round
ADJECTIVE
Something that is round is shaped like a circle.

roundabout
NOUN roundabouts
1 A roundabout is a circle in the middle of the road where several roads meet. Cars must drive round the roundabout.
2 A roundabout is a machine at a fair or playground that you sit on and go round in a circle.

rounders
NOUN
Rounders is a game in which two teams try to hit a ball and then run around four posts called bases to score points.

route
NOUN routes
Your route is the way that you go to get from one place to another. *I always take the same **route** to school.*
☛ **Be careful with spelling:**
route *What's the quickest **route** from here to your house?*
root *Trees have very deep **roots**.*

row
NOUN rows
A row is an angry argument.

row
NOUN rows
1 A row of things is a line of them.
VERB rows, rowing, rowed
2 When you row a boat, you make it move with oars.

royal
ADJECTIVE
Royal means to do with a king or queen. *The **royal** family lives in a palace.*

rub
VERB rubs, rubbing, rubbed
When you rub something, you move your hand backwards and forwards over it. *She **rubbed** her wet hair with a towel.*

rucksack
NOUN rucksacks
A rucksack is a bag that you carry on your back. *I put my books and lunch into a **rucksack** before school.*

rude
ADJECTIVE
Someone who is rude talks or behaves in a way that is not polite. *He was told off for being **rude** to the teacher.*
rudely (ADVERB)
If you say or do something rudely, you do it in a rude way. *He stuck his tongue out **rudely**.*

rug
NOUN rugs
1 A rug is a small carpet.
2 A rug is a soft blanket. *We sat on a **rug** while we ate our picnic.*

row

*He pulled a **row** of colourful toys.*

rubber
NOUN rubbers
1 Rubber is a soft, stretchy material. Car tyres are made of rubber.
2 You use a rubber to remove something that you have written with a pencil. *He used a **rubber** to remove the mistake in his answer.*

rubbish
NOUN
Rubbish is things that you throw away because you do not want them. *She threw the **rubbish** into the bin.*

rugby
NOUN
Rugby is a game in which teams of players throw and kick an oval ball, and try to score points by running over a line with it or kicking it between goal posts.

ruin
NOUN ruins
1 The ruins of a building are the broken parts that remain after it has been destroyed.
VERB ruins, ruining, ruined
2 To ruin something means to spoil it.

rule
NOUN rules
1 A rule is an instruction that tells you what you must and must not do. *Do you know the **rules** of cricket?*
VERB rules, ruling, ruled
2 To rule a country means to be in charge of it.

ruler
NOUN rulers
1 A ruler is a straight piece of wood, metal, or plastic that you use for measuring and drawing straight lines.
2 A ruler is a person, such as a king or queen, who rules a country.

run
VERB runs, running, ran, run
1 When you run, you go fast by moving your legs quickly. *I want to **run** a marathon one day.*
2 If you run something, you organize it. *Who **runs** the school shop?*
runner (NOUN)
A runner is someone who runs. *Are you a fast **runner**?*

rush
VERB rushes, rushing, rushed
If you rush, you run or do something quickly. *I **rushed** home to tell my mum the good news.*

rust
NOUN
Rust is a brown substance that forms on old metal.
rusty (ADJECTIVE)
Something that is rusty has rust on it. *His car was old and **rusty**.*

a b c d e f g h i j k l m n o p q r Ss t u v w x y z

S

shade

sack
NOUN sacks
A sack is a large, strong bag.

sad
ADJECTIVE sadder, saddest
If you are sad, you are not happy.
sadly (ADVERB)
If you say or do something sadly, you do it in a sad way. *"We lost the game 3-0," he said **sadly**.*
sadness (NOUN)
Sadness is the feeling you have when you are sad. *There was **sadness** in her voice.*

saddle
NOUN saddles
The saddle on a horse or bicycle is the seat that you sit on.

safari
NOUN safaris
A safari is a trip to hunt or watch wild animals, usually in Africa.

safe
NOUN safes
1 A safe is a metal container that you can lock, in which you keep money and valuable things.
ADJECTIVE safer, safest
2 If you are safe, you are not hurt and not in danger. *At last we reached the shore and were **safe** again.*
3 Something that is safe is not dangerous. *All the fairground rides are perfectly **safe**.*
☛ **Opposite:** unsafe
safely (ADVERB)
If you do something safely, you do it in a safe way. *It's important to learn how to cycle **safely**.*
safety (NOUN)
Safety is keeping people safe. *You must wear a seatbelt for **safety**.*

said
☛ See **say**.

sail
NOUN sails
1 A sail is a large piece of material on a boat that catches the wind and helps to move the boat along.
VERB sails, sailing, sailed
2 When you sail, you travel across water in a ship or boat. *We **sailed** across to a small island.*
sailor (NOUN)
A sailor is someone who sails on a boat.
☛ **Be careful with spelling:**
sail *Can you **sail** a boat?*
sale *Are these toys for **sale**?*

salad
NOUN salads
A salad is a mixture of raw vegetables or fruit.

salary
NOUN salaries
Someone's salary is the money that they earn for doing their job.

sale
NOUN sales
1 If something is for sale, you can buy it.
2 When there is a sale, things are sold for less money than usual. *I always buy my clothes in the **sales**.*
☛ **Be careful with spelling:**
sale *Are these toys for **sale**?*
sail *Can you **sail** a boat?*

salmon
NOUN
A salmon is a large fish that you can eat.

***Sailing** boats have colourful **sails**.*

salt
NOUN
Salt is a white powder that people add to meat and vegetables to improve the flavour. Salt is found in the sea and in rocks.
salty (ADJECTIVE)
Food that is salty tastes of salt.

salute
VERB salutes, saluting, saluted
When you salute, you put the side of your hand next to your head as a sign of respect to someone.

same
ADJECTIVE
If two things are the same, they look or sound like each other. *She was wearing the **same** dress as me.*

sample
NOUN samples
A sample is a small amount of something that you can try.

sand
NOUN
Sand is very small grains of broken rock that you find on beaches or in deserts.

sandal
NOUN sandals
Sandals are open shoes with straps that fasten round your feet.

sandwich
NOUN sandwiches
A sandwich is slices of bread with a filling placed between them.

sang
☛ See **sing**.

sank
☛ See **sink**.

sari
NOUN saris
A sari is a type of dress that women in India and other parts of Asia traditionally wear. It is made from a long piece of cloth that is wrapped around the body.

sat
☛ See **sit**.

satellite
NOUN satellites
1 A satellite is an object that is in orbit around a larger object in space. The satellites of planets are called moons.
2 A satellite is a machine in orbit around the Earth, which receives and transmits radio and television signals.

satellite dish
NOUN satellite dishes
A satellite dish is a round, metal dish attached to a building, which can receive television signals sent by satellite.

satisfactory
ADJECTIVE
If something is satisfactory, it is good enough, but not very good.

satnav
NOUN
Satnav is a way of finding your way using information that is transmitted from satellites. Satnav is short for **satellite navigation**. *Have you got a **satnav** in your car?*

satsuma
NOUN satsumas
A satsuma is a fruit that looks and tastes like a small, sweet orange. Satsumas do not have pips and are easy to peel.

sauce
NOUN sauces
A sauce is a liquid that you eat with food. Gravy, ketchup, and mayonnaise are all types of sauce.

saucepan
NOUN saucepans
A saucepan is a metal container that you cook food in.

saucer
NOUN saucers
A saucer is a small, shallow plate that you put a cup on.

sausage
NOUN sausages
A sausage is a mixture of chopped meat inside a long tube of thin skin. *My favourite kind of **sausage** is a hot dog.*

a b c d e f g h i j k l m n o p q r **Ss** t u v w x y z

save
VERB saves, saving, saved
1 If you save someone, you take them away from danger. *The firefighter **saved** him from the burning house.*
2 If you save something, you do not waste it. ***Save** power – turn off the light!*
3 If you save a document on a computer, you give an instruction to the computer to keep a copy of it.
4 If you save money, you keep it so that you can use it later. *He **saved** up for a year to buy his bicycle.*
savings (NOUN)
Your savings are money that you are keeping to use later.

saw
1 Saw is the past tense of **see**.
NOUN saws
2 A saw is a tool that you use for cutting wood. It has a blade with sharp teeth.
VERB saws, sawing, sawed
3 When you saw wood, you cut it using a saw.

say
VERB says, saying, said
When you say something, you speak words. *"Hurry up!" I **said**.*

scale
NOUN scales
1 The scales on a fish are hard pieces of skin on its body.
2 You use scales to measure how much things weigh.
scaly (ADJECTIVE)
Scaly skin is skin that is dry, hard, and flaking off.

scarecrow

A scarecrow scares away birds.

scanner
NOUN scanners
A scanner is a machine that copies writing or pictures from a page and sends them to a computer.

scar
NOUN scars
A scar is a mark that stays on your skin after a wound has healed.

scare
VERB scares, scaring, scared
If something scares you, it makes you feel afraid.
scared (ADJECTIVE)
If you are scared, you are afraid. *Are you **scared** of spiders?*
scary (ADJECTIVE)
Something that is scary makes you feel afraid. *That film's too **scary** for me!*

scarecrow
NOUN scarecrows
A scarecrow is a figure made from sticks and old clothes and is used to scare birds, including crows, away from crops.

scarf
NOUN scarves
You wear a scarf around your neck to keep you warm.

scatter
VERB scatters, scattering, scattered
To scatter things means to spread them in many different directions.

scene
NOUN scenes
1 The scene of something is the place where it happens. *Clues were found at the **scene** of the crime.*
2 A scene in a play or film is one part of it.
3 A scene is a picture of something. *The card showed a winter **scene**.*
scenery (NOUN)
The scenery is everything that you can see around you. *We stood on top of the mountain and admired the **scenery**.*

scent
NOUN scents
1 The scent of a person or animal is the smell that they leave behind them. *The dog followed the **scent**.*
2 Scent is perfume.

school
NOUN schools
A school is a place where children go to learn.

science
NOUN sciences
Science is the subject in which you study things in the world around you, such as water, electricity, light, metals, plants, and animals.
scientist (NOUN)
A scientist is someone who studies science.

science fiction
NOUN
Science fiction is stories or films about things that happen in the future or in space. *My brother likes pirate stories, but I prefer* ***science fiction****.*

scissors
NOUN
You use scissors for cutting things such as paper, cloth, and hair. Scissors have two blades that move apart and then together again.

scold
NOUN scolds, scolding, scolded
To scold someone means to speak to them in an angry way because they have done something wrong. *The teacher* ***scolded*** *me for being late.*

scooter
NOUN scooters
A scooter is a toy with two wheels that you can ride around on. You stand on the scooter and use one foot to push yourself along.

score
VERB scores, scoring, scored
When you score a point or goal in a game, you get it. *I* ***scored*** *two goals in the last game.*

scowl
VERB scowls, scowling, scowled
When you scowl, you make your face look angry. *The man* ***scowled*** *at us angrily.*

scrap
NOUN scraps
1 A scrap is a small piece of something.
2 Scrap is anything that is broken, worn out, or not useful any more. *The cars were sold as* ***scrap****.*

scrape
VERB scrapes, scraping, scraped
To scrape something means to scratch it or pull something sharp across it. *I* ***scraped*** *the mud off my shoes.*

I whizz along on my scooter.
scooter

DK findout!

screen

scratch
VERB scratches, scratching, scratched
1 If you scratch something, you make a small cut on it.
2 When you scratch, you rub your skin with your nails.

scream
VERB screams, screaming, screamed
When you scream, you shout or cry in a loud voice because you are frightened or in pain.

screech
VERB screeches, screeching, screeched
When you screech, you shout or cry loudly. *"The water's freezing!" she* ***screeched****.*

screen
NOUN screens
1 A screen is a flat surface on which pictures or films can be shown.
2 The screen on a computer or television is the part where the picture or writing appears.
screenshot (NOUN)
A screenshot is a picture that is taken from the screen of a computer or phone. *I'll send you a* ***screenshot*** *of the website.*

a b c d e f g h i j k l m n o p q r **Ss** t u v w x y z

screw
NOUN screws
A screw is a pointed piece of metal, like a nail.
screwdriver (NOUN)
A screwdriver is a tool that you use to fix a screw into something by turning it round and round.

scribble
VERB scribbles, scribbling, scribbled
When you scribble, you write or draw something in a very messy way. *My little brother **scribbled** all over the wallpaper in his bedroom.*

script
NOUN scripts
The script of a play is all the words that the characters say.

sculpture
NOUN sculptures
A sculpture is a statue or model made out of stone or wood.

sea
NOUN seas
The sea is the salt water that covers a large amount of the Earth's surface. *Whales are large animals that live in the **sea**.*
seabed (NOUN)
The seabed is the bottom of the sea.
seagull (NOUN)
A seagull is a large bird that lives near the sea.
seaside (NOUN)
The seaside is the land next to the sea. *In the summer, we will visit the **seaside**.*

seal
NOUN seals
1 A seal is a sea animal with fur and flippers that lives in the sea. Seals eat fish and are excellent swimmers.
VERB seals, sealing, sealed
2 When you seal something, you close it tightly.

seal

***Seals** dive deep in the **sea** to catch fish.*

search
VERB searches, searching, searched
If you search for something, you look for it carefully. *He **searched** for his ball in the long grass.*

search engine
NOUN search engines
A search engine is a computer program that you use to search for something on the internet.

season
NOUN seasons
1 Seasons are the different parts that a year is divided into. Our four seasons are spring, summer, autumn, and winter.
2 A sport's season is the time of year when people play that sport. *The football **season** starts today.*

seat
NOUN seats
A seat is something that you sit on.
seatbelt (NOUN)
A seatbelt is a strap that you fasten around your body when you are in a car.

second
NOUN seconds
1 A second is a very short period of time. There are 60 seconds in one minute.
ADJECTIVE
2 The second person or thing is the one that comes after the first one.

secret
NOUN secrets
If something is a secret, only a few people know about it.
secret agent (NOUN)
A secret agent is a spy.
secretly (ADVERB)
If you do something secretly, you do it so that other people do not know about it.

secretary
NOUN secretaries
A secretary is a person who works in an office and helps someone else by making business appointments, writing letters, and keeping records. Secretaries are now often called personal assistants, or PAs.

see
VERB sees, seeing, saw, seen
When you see something, you notice it with your eyes.

seed
NOUN seeds
A seed is a small, hard object that is made by a plant. You can put a seed in the ground and it will grow into a new plant.

seek
VERB seeks, seeking, sought
When you seek something, you try to find it.

seem
VERB seems, seeming, seemed
To seem means to appear. *Are you OK? You **seem** upset.*

seen
☛ See **see**.

seesaw
NOUN seesaws
A seesaw is a balancing toy. Children play on a seesaw by sitting at either end of a board and rocking up and down.

seize
VERB seizes, seizing, seized
If you seize something, you take hold of it suddenly. *The thief **seized** her bag.*

select
VERB selects, selecting, selected
If you select something, you choose it.
selection (NOUN)
A selection is a number of things you can choose from. *The shop has an amazing **selection** of sweets.*

selfie
NOUN selfies
A selfie is a photo that you take of yourself. *My sister's new phone is great for taking **selfies**.*

selfish
ADJECTIVE
If you are selfish, you only care about yourself and not about other people. *He was **selfish** and never shared his toys.*
☛ **Opposite:** unselfish

sell
VERB sells, selling, sold
When you sell something, you give it to someone and they give you money in return. *I **sold** my old bike to my friend.*

semicircle
NOUN semicircles
A semicircle is half a circle.

semi-final
NOUN semi-finals
A semi-final is a game or match to decide who will play in the final of a competition.

send
VERB sends, sending, sent
When you send something to someone, you arrange for it to be delivered to them in the post or using the internet. *I'll **send** you some photos of my new puppy.*

senior
ADJECTIVE
Someone who is senior to you is older than you or more important than you.

sense
NOUN senses
1 The five senses are the five ways in which we can receive information about the world around us. The five senses are sight, hearing, touch, smell, and taste.
2 If someone has sense, they are able to make good, sensible decisions. *I'm glad you had the **sense** to bring an umbrella.*
3 If something makes sense, it seems sensible or right.

sensible
ADJECTIVE
Someone who is sensible does the right thing and does not do silly or stupid things.
sensibly (ADVERB)
If you behave sensibly, you behave in a sensible way.

sensitive
ADJECTIVE
1 Something that is sensitive reacts very quickly to things around it. *I'm careful which soaps I use because my skin is **sensitive**.*
2 Someone who is sensitive becomes upset easily.

sent
☛ See **send**.

sentence
NOUN sentences
1 A sentence is a group of words that make sense together. Sentences start with a capital letter and end with a full stop.
2 A sentence is a punishment that is given to someone by a judge in a law court.

separate
*The red buttons are **separate** from the other buttons.*

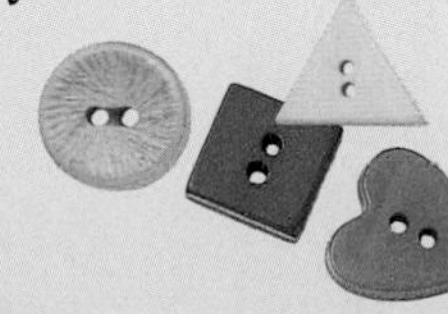

separate
VERB separates, separating, separated
1 When you separate things, you take them apart from each other.
ADJECTIVE
2 Things that are separate are not joined to each other or not with each other.

a b c d e f g h i j k l m n o p q r Ss t u v w x y z

a b c d e f g h i j k l m n o p q r Ss t u v w x y z

sequence
NOUN sequences
A sequence is a number of things that follow each other in order.

series
NOUN
1 A series of things is a number of them that follow one another in order.
2 A television series is a television programme that is shown in regular episodes.

serious
ADJECTIVE
1 If something is serious, people need to think and talk about it carefully. *Missing so much school is a very **serious** matter.*
2 Someone who is serious is not smiling or laughing. *The teacher came in looking **serious**.*
3 If something is serious, it is worrying and could be dangerous.
seriously (ADVERB)
If someone is seriously hurt, they are badly hurt.

servant
NOUN servants
A servant is a person who works for another person in their home.

serve
VERB serves, serving, served
1 When you serve someone, you help them by giving them something that they want or need. *The waiter will **serve** you at your table.*
2 When you serve in a game like tennis, you start the game by hitting the ball to your opponent.

*It is his turn to **serve**.*

serve

service
NOUN services
1 The service in a shop or restaurant is how quick and helpful the staff are.
2 A service is something that is provided for people to use if they want to.

set
NOUN sets
1 A set of things is a group of things that belong together. *Have you got a chess **set**?*
VERB sets, setting, set
2 When something sets, it goes hard. *The glue took a long time to **set**.*
3 When the Sun sets, it goes down in the evening. *The Sun **sets** in the west.*
4 When you set a timer or an alarm, you change the controls so that it will go off at a particular time. *I **set** my alarm for seven o'clock.*
5 When you set someone work, you give it to them. *The teacher **set** the class some homework.*

settle
VERB settles, settling, settled
1 If you settle down, you stop moving around and sit or lie quietly. *The teacher told us to **settle** down and get on with our work.*
2 When you settle an argument, you stop arguing and agree on who is right. *In the end, Dad **settled** the argument for us.*

Shape up!
Here are some common shapes and their names.

square

rectangle/
oblong

triangle

semicircle

circle

several
ADJECTIVE
Several means quite a lot of people or things. ***Several** people waved as they walked past.*

severe
ADJECTIVE
Something that is severe is very bad. *Our ferry was cancelled because of the **severe** weather.*

sew
VERB sews, sewing, sewed, sewn
When you sew, you join pieces of cloth together using a needle and thread.
☛ **Be careful with spelling:**
sew *Can you **sew** this button back on?*
sow *You usually **sow** seeds in the spring.*

sex
NOUN sexes
Male and female are the two sexes that people and animals are divided into.

shade
NOUN shades
1 If you are in the shade, you are in a cool place where the Sun's light and heat cannot reach. *She sat in the **shade** to read.*
2 Different shades of a colour are all the same colour, but are different because some are darker or lighter than others. *I have three red T-shirts, but they're all different **shades** of the colour.*
3 Shades are sunglasses.

shadow
NOUN shadows
A shadow is a dark shape that is made when something blocks the light.

shake
VERB shakes, shaking, shook, shaken
1 When something shakes, it moves roughly up and down or from side to side. *The bus was **shaking** and rattling as it drove along.*
2 When you shake something, you move it roughly up and down. ***Shake** the tin before opening it.*
3 If you are shaking, you cannot stop your body from moving because you are cold or frightened.

shall
VERB
I shall do something means that I will do it. *I **shall** go shopping later.*

shallow
ADJECTIVE
Something that is shallow is not very deep. *We paddled in the **shallow** water.*

shame
NOUN
1 If something is a shame, it is sad. *It's a **shame** you can't come.*
2 Shame is the feeling you have when you know that you have done something wrong and feel bad about it.

shampoo
NOUN shampoos
Shampoo is a soapy liquid that you use for washing your hair.

shape
NOUN shapes
You can say what shape something is by saying whether it is a circle, a square, or a triangle.
shaped (ADJECTIVE)
If something is shaped like an object, it has the shape of that object. *Her pencil case was **shaped** like a banana.*

pentagon hexagon octagon star diamond

share
VERB shares, sharing, shared
1 When people share something, they take it in turns to use it. *We haven't got enough cups so we'll have to* ***share****.*
2 When people share something, they divide it up and give some to each person. *I hope you're going to* ***share*** *your chocolate with everyone.*

shark
NOUN sharks
A shark is a large fish with rows of sharp teeth. Sharks live in both cold and warm seas and eat fish or small water animals.

sharp
ADJECTIVE sharper, sharpest
1 Something that is sharp has a thin edge or pointed end that can cut things. *Careful – that knife is* ***sharp****!*
2 If you have sharp eyes or ears, you are good at seeing or hearing things.
sharpen (VERB)
If you sharpen a knife, you make it sharper.

shatter
VERB shatters, shattering, shattered
If something shatters, it breaks into very small pieces. *The mirror fell to the floor and* ***shattered*** *into tiny pieces.*

shave
VERB shaves, shaving, shaved
When you shave, you remove hair from your body with a razor.

shed
NOUN sheds
1 A shed is a small building that you keep things in.
VERB sheds, shedding, shed
2 To shed something means to lose it because it drops off. *Some trees* ***shed*** *all their leaves in autumn.*

sheep
NOUN
A sheep is an animal with a thick, woolly coat that is kept on farms to produce meat and wool.

sheer
ADJECTIVE
1 A sheer drop does not slope but goes straight down.
2 Sheer means complete. *She smiled with* ***sheer*** *pleasure when she saw all the presents.*

sheet
NOUN sheets
1 A sheet is a large piece of cloth that you put on a bed.
2 A sheet of something is a large, flat piece of it.

shelf
NOUN shelves
A shelf is a piece of wood attached to a wall that you can put things on.

Sharks have very ***sharp*** *teeth.*

shark

shell
NOUN shells
A shell is a hard part that covers and protects something. Eggs, nuts, and animals such as snails, crabs, and tortoises have shells.

shells

We collected some ***shells****.*

shelter
NOUN shelters
1 A shelter is a place that protects you from the weather or from danger. *The doorway provided a **shelter** from the rain.*
VERB shelters, sheltering, sheltered
2 When you shelter somewhere, you stay there so that you are safe from the weather or danger.

shepherd
NOUN shepherds
A shepherd is someone who looks after a flock of sheep.

sheriff
NOUN sheriffs
In America, a sheriff is a person whose job is to make sure that people do not break the law in their area.

shield
NOUN shields
1 A shield is a strong piece of metal or leather that soldiers used to carry in battle to protect their bodies.
VERB shields, shielding, shielded
2 To shield something means to protect it. *She **shielded** her eyes from the Sun.*

shin
NOUN shins
Your shins are the front parts of your legs below your knees.

shine
VERB shines, shining, shone
When something shines, it gives out light and looks bright.
shiny (ADJECTIVE)
Something that is shiny looks bright.

The **sheriff** wears a **shiny** badge.

ship
NOUN ships
A ship is a large boat.

shipwreck
NOUN shipwrecks
When there is a shipwreck, a ship is destroyed at sea.

shirt
NOUN shirts
A shirt is a piece of clothing that you wear on the top half of your body. Shirts usually have buttons down the front.

shiver
VERB shivers, shivering, shivered
When you shiver, your body keeps moving because you are cold or frightened.

shock
NOUN shocks
1 If something is a shock, it happens suddenly and surprises you a lot.
2 If you get an electric shock, electricity goes through your body and hurts you.
VERB shocks, shocking, shocked
3 If something shocks you, it surprises you and upsets you.

shocked
ADJECTIVE
If you are shocked by something, you are surprised and upset by it. *I was **shocked** by a story I saw on the news this morning.*

shoe
NOUN shoes
You wear shoes on your feet to protect them and keep them warm.
shoelace (NOUN)
A shoelace is a cord that fastens a shoe.

Her **shoe** has **shoelaces**.

shone
☛ See **shine**.

shook
☛ See **shake**.

shoot
VERB shoots, shooting, shot
1 To shoot someone means to fire at them with a gun or other weapon.
2 When you shoot in a ball game such as football or basketball, you try to score a goal or point.

a b c d e f g h i j k l m n o p q r **Ss** t u v w x y z

shop
NOUN shops
1 A shop is a place where you can go to buy things.
VERB shops, shopping, shopped
2 When you shop, you go to the shops to buy things.

shore
NOUN shores
The shore is the land at the edge of the sea or a lake.

short
ADJECTIVE shorter, shortest
1 Something that is short is not very long. *__Short__ hair is fashionable at the moment.*
2 Something that is short does not last long. *The film was __short__.*
3 If you are short of something, you do not have enough of it. *Our school is __short__ of money.*
shorten (VERB)
If you shorten something, you make it shorter.

shorts
NOUN
Shorts are short trousers that usually finish just above your knees. *I wear __shorts__ to school during the summer.*

shot
1 Shot is the past tense of **shoot**.
NOUN shots
2 A shot is a photo. *That's a lovely __shot__ of you!*
3 In tennis, a shot is a hit of the ball. In football or basketball, a shot is an attempt to score a goal or point. *That was a brilliant __shot__!*
4 If you fire a shot at something, you shoot at it.

should
VERB
If you should do something, you ought to do it. *We __should__ do our homework before we play.*

shoulder
NOUN shoulders
Your shoulder is the place below your neck where your arms join your body.

shout
NOUN shouts
1 A shout is a loud call. *We heard a __shout__ from the garden.*
VERB shouts, shouting, shouted
2 When you shout, you speak or call out loudly. *"Go away!" she __shouted__.*

show
NOUN shows
1 A show is something that people perform for others to watch.
VERB shows, showing, showed, shown
2 If you show something to someone, you let them see it. *He __showed__ me some of his photos.*
3 If you show someone how to do something, you explain it to them and do it so that they can watch it and learn. *Can you __show__ me how to get to the next level in the game?*

shower
NOUN showers
1 If you have a shower, you wash your body by standing under a fine spray of water.
2 If there is a shower, it rains for a short time.

shrank
☛ See **shrink**.

shred
NOUN shreds
A shred of something is a small, narrow strip of it. *My shirt was torn to __shreds__.*

show

She introduced the performers at the start of the __show__.

shuffle

shriek
VERB shrieks, shrieking, shrieked
If you shriek, you shout or cry out in a high-pitched voice because you are excited or afraid. *She **shrieked** when she saw the mouse.*

shrill
ADJECTIVE shriller, shrillest
A shrill sound is sharp and high.

shrink
VERB shrinks, shrinking, shrank, shrunk
When something shrinks, it becomes smaller. *My jumper **shrank** in the wash.*

shrug
VERB shrugs, shrugging, shrugged
When you shrug, you raise your shoulders to show that you do not care or do not know.

shuffle
VERB shuffles, shuffling, shuffled
1 When you shuffle cards, you mix them around to change the order they are in.
2 If you shuffle along, you walk slowly, dragging your feet along the ground.

shut
VERB shuts, shutting, shut
1 If you shut something, you close it.
2 When you shut down your computer, you close the programs you have been using and switch it off.

shy
ADJECTIVE shyer, shyest
Someone who is shy is nervous and frightened when they meet and talk to new people.

sick
ADJECTIVE sicker, sickest
1 If you are sick, food comes up out of your stomach and out of your mouth.
2 If you are sick, you do not feel well.

side
NOUN sides
1 The sides of something are the parts at the edges. *Triangles have three **sides**.*
2 The side of something is the part on the left or right of it.
3 A side is a team of people who are competing against another group. *Which **side** are you on?*

sideways
ADVERB
If you move sideways, you move to the side, not forward or backward. *Crabs walk **sideways**.*

sieve
NOUN sieves
A sieve is a container with a lot of tiny holes in it. You pour things into a sieve to separate solids from liquids, or fine grains from larger pieces.

sigh
VERB sighs, sighing, sighed
When you sigh, you let out a long, deep breath slowly because you are tired or sad.

sight
NOUN
1 Your sight is your ability to see things. *She lost her **sight** in an accident.*
2 A sight is something that you can see. *The old ship was an amazing **sight** as it sailed up the river.*
☛ **Be careful with spelling:**
sight *Bats have no **sight**.*
site *We stayed at a camp **site**.*

sign
NOUN signs
1 A sign is a picture or symbol that represents something. *The **sign** for a dollar is $.*
2 If you give someone a sign, you move your body in order to tell them something. *He nodded his head as a **sign** that he agreed.*
3 A sign is a public notice that gives people information. *There was a "No Entry" **sign** by the gate.*
VERB signs, signing, signed
4 When you sign something, you write your name on it. *The author **signed** copies of her book.*
sign language (NOUN)
Sign language is a way of talking to people by moving your hands in special ways. People who cannot hear often use sign language.

signal
NOUN signals
1 If you give someone a signal, you move a part of your body or use an object in order to tell the person something. *When you are cycling, you put out one arm as a* ***signal*** *that you are going to turn left or right.*
2 A signal is a series of radio waves that can carry information. *I couldn't call you because there was no* ***signal*** *for my phone.*

signature
NOUN signatures
Your signature is your special way of writing your own name. *My mother wrote her* ***signature*** *at the bottom of the form.*

Sikh
NOUN Sikhs
A Sikh is someone whose religion is Sikhism.

A silly clown shows off on a unicycle.

silent
ADJECTIVE
Something that is silent does not make any noise. A place that is silent has no noise in it.
silence (NOUN)
When there is silence, there is no noise. *The teacher called for* ***silence****.*
silently (ADVERB)
If you do something silently, you do it with no noise.

silk
NOUN silks
Silk is a type of thin, soft cloth that is made from threads spun by small creatures called **silkworms**.

silly
ADJECTIVE sillier, silliest
Something that is silly is not very sensible.

silver
NOUN
Silver is a shiny, white-coloured metal that is very valuable. Silver is used for making coins and jewellery.

similar
ADJECTIVE
Things that are similar are almost the same, but not exactly the same.

simple
ADJECTIVE simpler, simplest
1 Something that is simple is easy to understand or solve. *The teacher gave us some* ***simple*** *sums to do for homework.*
2 Something that is simple is plain, and not decorated. *I chose a* ***simple*** *design for my costume.*

sincere
ADJECTIVE
Someone who is sincere is honest and tells the truth. *She was* ***sincere*** *when she said she was sorry.*
sincerely (ADVERB)
You write "Yours sincerely" at the end of a polite letter, before you finish it by signing your name.

sing
VERB sings, singing, sang, sung
When you sing, you make a musical sound with your voice. *I'm too shy to* ***sing*** *in front of other people.*
singer (NOUN)
A singer is someone who sings. *When I grow up, I want to be a pop* ***singer****.*

single
ADJECTIVE
Single means for only one person. *They booked two* ***single*** *rooms and one double at the hotel.*

singular
NOUN
The singular of a word is the form that you use for only one thing or person. "Child" is a singular form, and "children" is a plural form.

sink
NOUN sinks
1 A sink is a basin with taps that you can wash things in.
VERB sinks, sinking, sank, sunk
2 When something sinks, it goes down below the surface of water. *The stone* ***sank*** *to the bottom of the pond.*

sip
VERB sips, sipping, sipped
When you sip a drink, you drink it slowly, with small mouthfuls. *I **sipped** my smoothie slowly.*

sir
NOUN
A word you use when you are speaking to a man politely. *I'm sorry, **sir**.*

siren
NOUN sirens
A siren is a small machine that makes a loud noise to warn people about something. *We heard a police car's **siren**.*

sister
NOUN sisters
Your sister is a girl who has the same mother and father as you.

sit
VERB sits, sitting, sat
1 When you sit, you rest your body by supporting your weight on your bottom, rather than on your feet.
2 If something is sitting somewhere, it is there. *I left my book **sitting** on the kitchen table.*

site
NOUN sites
A site is an area of ground. *You mustn't play on the building **site**.*
☛ **Be careful with spelling:**
site *We stayed at a camp **site**.*
sight *Bats have no **sight**.*

sitting room
NOUN sitting rooms
A sitting room is a room in which you sit and chat or watch television.

situation
NOUN situations
A situation is everything that is happening in a particular place at a particular time. *You should call for help if you are in a dangerous **situation**.*

size
NOUN sizes
The size of something is how big it is. *These shoes are the wrong **size**.*

skate
VERB skates, skating, skated
When you skate, you slide along on a hard surface, wearing special shoes with blades or wheels. *Shall we go **skating** this afternoon?*

skateboard
NOUN skateboards
A skateboard is a small board on wheels that people stand on to ride along.
skateboarding (NOUN)
Skateboarding is riding on a skateboard. ***Skateboarding** is great fun!*

skeleton
NOUN skeletons
Your skeleton is all the bones in your body. There are more than 200 bones in a human skeleton.

sketch
NOUN sketches
A sketch is a rough drawing. *Here's a **sketch** of the next painting I'm going to do.*

ski
VERB skis, skiing, skied
When you ski, you move over snow on two long, thin sticks called skis.

skid
VERB skids, skidding, skidded
If a car or bike skids, it slides because the road is wet or slippery. *The car **skidded** on the ice.*

ski
*I enjoy whizzing downhill on **skis**.*

skill
NOUN
If you have skill, you can do something very well. *You need a lot of **skill** to be a professional tennis player.*
skilful (ADJECTIVE)
Someone who is skilful has a lot of skill. *He's a very **skilful** football player.*
skilfully (ADVERB)
If you do something skilfully, you do it with a lot of skill.

skin
NOUN skins
1 Your skin is the part of you that covers all your body.
2 The skin on a vegetable or fruit is the part on the outside.

skinny
ADJECTIVE skinnier, skinniest
Someone who is skinny is very thin.

skip
VERB skips, skipping, skipped
1 When you skip along, you run along and hop lightly from one foot to another. *She **skipped** down the road cheerfully.*
2 When you skip, you jump over a turning rope.

skirt
NOUN skirts
A skirt is a piece of clothing that a woman or girl wears. It fastens around her waist and can be short or long.

skull
NOUN skulls
Your skull is the bony case that protects your brain.

sky
NOUN skies
The sky is the air above us.

skyscraper
NOUN skyscrapers
A skyscraper is a very tall building.

slack
ADJECTIVE
Something that is slack is not stretched tight. *Keep the rope tight – don't let it go **slack**.*

slam
VERB slams, slamming, slammed
If you slam a door, you shut it with a loud bang.

slang
NOUN
Slang is words and phrases that people use when they are laughing and joking together, but not when they are writing or speaking politely.

slave
NOUN slaves
A slave is someone who is owned by another person and has to work for them.

sledge
NOUN sledges
A sledge is a vehicle with a smooth bottom that you sit on to move across snow or ice.

sleep
VERB sleeps, sleeping, slept
When you sleep, you rest with your eyes closed, and your body and mind are not active.
sleepy (ADJECTIVE)
If you are sleepy, you feel as if you want to sleep.

sleet
NOUN
Sleet is a mixture of snow and rain.

skydiving

***Skydiving** is a daring and exciting sport.*

skydiving
NOUN
Skydiving is a sport in which people jump out of an aeroplane wearing a parachute that opens after they have been falling for a short while.

slant
VERB slants, slanting, slanted
If something slants, it slopes and is not flat or straight.

slap
VERB slaps, slapping, slapped
If you slap someone, you hit them with the palm of your hand.

sleeve
NOUN sleeves
The sleeves on a piece of clothing are the parts that cover your arms.

sleigh
NOUN sleighs
A sleigh is a large sledge that is pulled by animals.

slept
☛ See **sleep**.

slice
NOUN slices
A slice of something is a thin piece of it. *Would you like a **slice** of cake?*

slide
NOUN slides
1 A slide is a large toy for children to play on. You climb up some steps and then slide down it.
VERB slides, sliding, slid
2 To slide means to move smoothly along. *She **slid** across the ice.*

slight
ADJECTIVE slighter, slightest
Slight means very small. *There's a **slight** chance that we might go to America this year.*
slightly (ADVERB)
Slightly means a little bit. *I was **slightly** annoyed with him.*

slim
ADJECTIVE slimmer, slimmest
Someone who is slim is thin.

slimy
ADJECTIVE
Something that is slimy feels wet and sticky.

sling
NOUN slings
A sling is a piece of material that you put around an injured arm to support it.

slip
VERB slips, slipping, slipped
1 If you slip, your foot slides on the floor and you nearly fall. *I **slipped** on the ice.*
2 If you slip something into a place, you put it there gently. *He **slipped** some money into my hand.*

slipper
NOUN slippers
Slippers are soft, comfortable shoes that you wear indoors.

slippery
ADJECTIVE
Something that is slippery is smooth or wet, and difficult to grip.

*Two **slippery** newts*

slit
NOUN slits
A slit is a long, narrow hole or cut in something.

slither
VERB slithers, slithering, slithered
When a snake slithers, it slides along the ground.

slogan
NOUN slogans
A slogan is a phrase that is used to advertise something.

slope
NOUN slopes
1 A slope is a piece of land that is not flat, but goes up or down. *They rolled the ball down the **slope**.*
VERB slopes, sloping, sloped
2 If something slopes, it is not flat but goes up or down at one end.

slot
NOUN slots
A slot is a small, narrow opening for putting something in. *She put a coin in the **slot**.*

slow
ADJECTIVE slower, slowest
Something that is slow takes a long time to do something or get somewhere. *The school bus is always **slow**.*
slowly (ADVERB)
If you do something slowly, you do it in a slow way and do not hurry. *I usually read quite **slowly**.*

slug
NOUN slugs
A slug is a small, soft, and slimy animal with no legs. ***Slugs** have eaten all the lettuces I planted in my garden.*

sly
ADJECTIVE slyer, slyest
Someone who is sly does things in a secret, sneaky way. *I don't trust my cousin – he's very **sly**.*

smack
VERB smacks, smacking, smacked
To smack someone means to hit them.

a b c d e f g h i j k l m n o p q r Ss t u v w x y z

small
ADJECTIVE smaller, smallest
Something that is small is not very big.

smart
ADJECTIVE smarter, smartest
1 Someone who is smart is clever.
2 Someone who looks smart is wearing clean, neat clothes.
3 A smart machine can make some decisions for itself.

smartphone
NOUN smartphones
A smartphone is a mobile phone that lets you get on the internet.

smash
VERB smashes, smashing, smashed
To smash something means to break it into lots of pieces.

smell
NOUN smells
1 Your sense of smell is your ability to smell things.
2 The smell that something has is what it is like when you sniff it. *The flower had a lovely* ***smell.***
3 If something smells, you can notice it by sniffing with your nose. *Your feet* ***smell!***
VERB smells, smelling, smelled or smelt
4 When you smell something, you use your nose to find out what it is like. *I* ***smelled*** *the cheese to check if it was fresh.*
smelly (ADJECTIVE)
Something that is smelly has an unpleasant smell.

smile
VERB smiles, smiling, smiled
When you smile, you show that you are happy by moving your mouth so that it turns upward at the sides.

smoke
NOUN
Smoke is the black or white gas that comes from a fire.

Snails

Snails *leave a trail of slime behind them.*

smooth
ADJECTIVE smoother, smoothest
Something that is smooth is flat and even, with no sharp bumps or lumps.
You need a nice ***smooth*** *surface for skateboarding.*

smoothie
NOUN smoothies
A smoothie is a thick drink that is made by crushing fruit or vegetables and adding milk, yoghurt, or ice cream.

smuggle
VERB smuggles, smuggling, smuggled
If you smuggle something into a place or out of a place, you move it there secretly.
We ***smuggled*** *cookies into my bedroom for a midnight feast.*
smuggler (NOUN)
A smuggler is someone who brings things into a country in a way that is against the law.

snack
NOUN snacks
A snack is a small amount of food that you eat between meals or have instead of a meal.

snail
NOUN snails
A snail is a small, slimy animal with no legs and a hard shell.

snake
NOUN snakes
A snake is a long, thin animal with no legs. Some snakes are venomous, which means they have poison in their fangs. Others kill by squeezing their prey tightly.

snap
VERB snaps, snapping, snapped
1 If you snap your fingers, you move them together so that they make a noise.
2 If something snaps, it breaks suddenly. *I was worried the rope might* ***snap.***
3 If you snap at someone, you shout at them in an angry way. *"Can't you see that I'm busy?" she* ***snapped.***

snarl
VERB snarls, snarling, snarled
When an animal snarls, it growls fiercely and shows its teeth. *The guard dog* ***snarled*** *at us.*

snatch
VERB snatches, snatching, snatched
If you snatch something, you take hold of it quickly. *I **snatched** my coat and ran out of the house.*

sneak
VERB sneaks, sneaking, sneaked
If you sneak somewhere, you go there in a quiet or secret way. *He **sneaked** out of the room when no one was looking.*

sneeze
VERB sneezes, sneezing, sneezed
When you sneeze, air comes out of your nose suddenly.

sniff
VERB sniffs, sniffing, sniffed
1 When you sniff, you breathe in noisily through your nose. *Stop **sniffing** and blow your nose!*
2 If you sniff something, you smell it. *Dogs find out about things by **sniffing** them.*

snore
VERB snores, snoring, snored
If you snore, you breathe noisily as you sleep.

snow
NOUN
1 Snow is soft, white flakes of ice that fall from the clouds in cold weather.
VERB snows, snowing, snowed
2 When it snows, snow falls from the clouds. *It's been **snowing** for days.*

snowball
NOUN snowballs
A snowball is a ball of snow that you make with your hands and throw at people for fun.

snowboard
NOUN snowboards
A snowboard is a large, flat board that you use for sliding over snow.
snowboarding (NOUN)
Snowboarding is riding on a snowboard.

snowdrift
NOUN snowdrifts
A snowdrift is snow that has been blown into a pile by the wind. *The car was stuck in a **snowdrift**.*

snowflake
NOUN snowflakes
A snowflake is one piece of snow that falls from the clouds.

snowman
NOUN snowmen
A snowman is a figure of a person that you make out of snow.

snug
ADJECTIVE
If you are snug, you are warm and comfortable. *The cat looked very **snug** curled up inside the basket.*

soak
VERB soaks, soaking, soaked
To soak something means to make it very wet. *My brother **soaked** me with his water pistol.*
soaking (ADJECTIVE)
Something that is soaking is very wet. *My clothes are **soaking**!*

soap
NOUN soaps
1 You use soap for cleaning your body.
2 A soap is a television series that tells the story of the everyday lives of a group of people. A soap is also called a **soap opera**.

soar
VERB soars, soaring, soared
If something soars, it goes high up into the air. *An eagle **soared** above us.*

sob
VERB sobs, sobbing, sobbed
If you sob, you cry noisily. *"You don't understand!" he **sobbed**.*

soccer
NOUN
Soccer is another name for football.

*The children made a **snowman**.*

a b c d e f g h i j k l m n o p q r Ss t u v w x y z

a b c d e f g h i j k l m n o p q r Ss t u v w x y z

sock
NOUN socks
A sock is a piece of clothing that you wear on your foot.

socket
NOUN sockets
A socket is a place on a wall where you can put an electric plug.

sofa
NOUN sofas
A sofa is a long, comfortable chair for two or three people.

soft
ADJECTIVE softer, softest
1 Something that is soft is not hard or firm. *What a lovely **soft** bed!*
2 Something that feels soft feels smooth.
3 A soft sound is not very loud. *She spoke in a **soft** voice.*
softly (ADVERB)
If you speak softly, you speak quietly. *"It's OK," she said **softly**.*

software
NOUN
Software is the programs that you put into a computer to make it work.

soggy
ADJECTIVE
Something that is soggy is wet and soft. *She lifted the **soggy** biscuit out of her drink.*

soil
NOUN
Soil is earth in which plants can grow. *The bush's roots had grown deep into the **soil**.*

solar
ADJECTIVE
Solar means to do with the Sun. *We wore special sunglasses when we watched the **solar** eclipse.*
solar panel (NOUN)
A solar panel collects heat from the Sun and uses it to make energy.
Solar System (NOUN)
The Solar System is the Sun and all the planets that move around it. The eight planets in the Solar System are Mercury, Venus, Earth, Mars, Jupiter, Saturn, Uranus, and Neptune.

soldier
NOUN soldiers
A soldier is someone who fights as part of an army.

sole
NOUN soles
1 The sole of your foot is the bottom part of your foot.
2 The sole of a shoe is the bottom part of it.

solid
NOUN solids
1 A solid is a substance that is hard and is not a liquid or gas. Ice and rock are solids.
ADJECTIVE
2 Something that is solid is made of the same thing all the way through and is not hollow. *This cat is carved from a **solid** block of wood.*
3 Something that is solid is strong and well made. *They built a **solid** wall around the castle.*

solo
NOUN solos
A solo is a performance that you give on your own. *Are you going to sing a **solo**?*

solve
VERB solves, solving, solved
When you solve a problem or mystery, you understand it and find the answer to it.

*A row of toy **soldiers***

some
ADJECTIVE
Some means a small number or amount. ***Some** people in my class have got pets.*

somebody
PRONOUN
Somebody or **someone** means a person. ***Somebody** has stolen my chocolate!*

something
PRONOUN
Something means a thing. *There's **something** in my drink!*

sometimes
ADVERB
Sometimes means at some times, but not always.

son
NOUN sons
Someone's son is their male child.

song
NOUN songs
A song is a piece of music with words that you sing.

soon
ADVERB
Soon means after a short time. *It will **soon** be lunchtime.*

sore
ADJECTIVE
If a part of your body is sore, it hurts. *My arm was **sore** after I fell.*

sorry
ADJECTIVE sorrier, sorriest
If you are sorry, you feel unhappy because of something that you have done. *I'm **sorry** that I broke your window.*

sort
NOUN sorts
1 One sort of thing is one type. *What **sort** of books do you like?*
VERB sorts, sorting, sorted
2 To sort things means to arrange them into different types or groups. *I **sorted** all my games into ones I still played and ones I didn't.*

sought
☛ See **seek**.

sound
NOUN sounds
A sound is something that you can hear.

souvenir
NOUN souvenirs
A souvenir is something that you keep to remind you of a person or place.

sow
VERB sows, sowing, sowed, sown
When you sow seeds, you put them in the soil so that they will grow into plants.
☛ **Be careful with spelling:**
sow *You usually **sow** seeds in the spring.*
sew *Can you **sew** this button back on?*

*Cymbals make a loud **sound**.*

soup
NOUN soups
Soup is a liquid food that is made with meat or vegetables.

sour
ADJECTIVE
Something that is sour has a sharp taste, like a lemon.

south
NOUN
South is one of the directions on a compass. If you keep going south, you will come to the **South Pole**, which is the farthest part south on Earth.

space
NOUN
1 Space is the area around the Earth, where all the stars and planets are found.
2 A space is a place that is empty. *We left a **space** for your chair.*
spacecraft (NOUN)
A spacecraft or **spaceship** is a vehicle that can travel in space.
space station (NOUN)
A space station is a large spacecraft that stays in orbit around the Earth. Astronauts can stay in the space station to study space.

spade

NOUN spades

A spade is a tool that you use for digging.

spaghetti

NOUN

Spaghetti is a type of long, thin pasta.

spare

ADJECTIVE

Something that is spare is extra, and you can use it if you need to.

spark

NOUN sparks

A spark is a tiny piece of fire or a tiny flash of electricity.

sparkle

VERB sparkles, sparkling, sparkled

If something sparkles, it shines in the light. *The water **sparkled** in the moonlight.*

spat

☛ See **spit**.

speak

VERB speaks, speaking, spoke, spoken

When you speak, you say words.

speaker

NOUN speakers

A speaker is a part of a radio, TV, or music player that sound comes out of.

spear

NOUN spears

A spear is a long weapon with a sharp point that you throw by hand.

special

ADJECTIVE

Something that is special is different and better than other things. *Today is a **special** day because it's my birthday.*

special effects (NOUN)

Special effects are images in films that are created using computers or clever ways of filming to make the film more exciting.

spectacular

ADJECTIVE

Something that is spectacular is very exciting. *The ski jumpers did some **spectacular** jumps.*

speech

NOUN speeches

1 Speech is the ability to speak. *Animals do not have the power of **speech**.*

2 A speech is a talk that someone gives to an audience. *The headteacher made a **speech** at the end of sports day.*

speech bubble (NOUN)

A speech bubble is a circle that you can add above someone's head in a picture to show what they are saying.

speech marks (NOUN)

Speech marks are special marks (" ") or (' ') that you use in writing to show words that someone speaks. There are speech marks in the sentence: *"Hello," she said.*

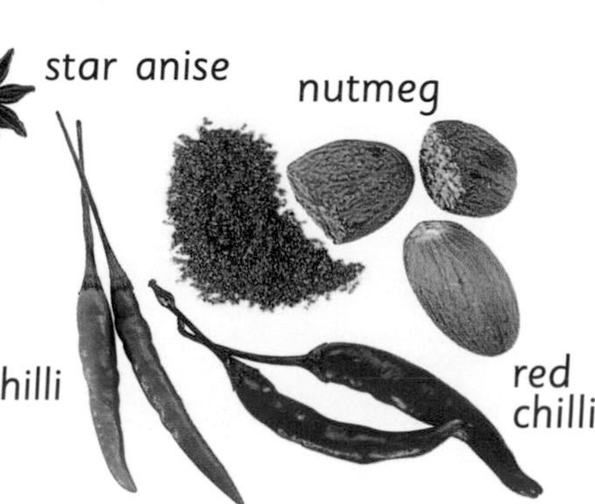

speed

NOUN speeds

The speed of something is how fast it is moving. *The train was travelling at a **speed** of 200 km per hour.*

spell

NOUN spells

1 A spell is a set of words that are supposed to have a magic power. *The witch cast a **spell** on her.*

VERB spells, spelling, spelled or spelt

2 The way you spell a word is the letters you use to write it. *How do you **spell** "special"?*

spellchecker (NOUN)

A spellchecker is a computer program that checks spellings and highlights mistakes.

spelling (NOUN)

The spelling of a word is the way it is spelled. *We've got a **spelling** test tomorrow.*

spend

VERB spends, spending, spent

1 When you spend money, you use it to buy things. *I've **spent** all my pocket money.*

2 When you spend time doing something, you use the time to do it. *We **spent** two weeks camping in the forest.*

spice

NOUN spices

A spice is something that you add to food to make it taste nice. Spices are made from the dried parts of plants.

spicy (ADJECTIVE)

Spicy food has a strong flavour because it has spices in it.

Space
Lost in space!
Here are some words to help you find your way around.
Sun
scorching
flaming
fiery
galaxy
turning
twisting
spinning
Zooming
rocket
mission
space probe
space tourism
spacewalking
space explorer
astronaut
Earth
oxygen
dry
dusty
rocky
empty
Moon
low gravity
lunar mission
weightlessness
spacecraft
Space Shuttle
International Space Station
planets in the Solar System
Mercury
Venus
Earth
Mars
Jupiter
Saturn
Uranus
Neptune

spider
NOUN spiders
A spider is a small animal with eight legs. Spiders spin nets of thin, sticky threads called webs, which they use to trap insects for food.

spill
VERB spills, spilling, spilled or spilt
If you spill something, you let it fall out of the container it is in. *I nearly **spilt** my drink.*

spin
VERB spins, spinning, spun
1 To spin means to turn around quickly. *The dancers were **spinning** round and round.*
2 To spin a thread or web means to make it. *I watched the spider **spin** a web.*

spine
NOUN spines
1 Your spine is the row of small bones in your back.
2 Spines are stiff, sharp points on an animal or on a plant.

spit
VERB spits, spitting, spat
If you spit, you force something out of your mouth. *She **spat** out the rotten apple.*

spiteful
ADJECTIVE
Someone who is spiteful is deliberately nasty to other people.

splash
VERB splashes, splashing, splashed
When you splash water, you hit it so that it flies up into the air. *Please don't **splash** water in my face!*

splinter
NOUN splinters
A splinter is a thin, sharp piece of wood or glass.

split
VERB splits, splitting, split
1 If you split something, you divide it into parts. *I **split** the biscuit in half and gave one half to my friend.*
2 If something splits, it tears or breaks. *The bag **split** open.*

spoil
VERB spoils, spoiling, spoiled or spoilt
1 If you spoil something, you damage it or destroy it so that you cannot use it any more. *Don't draw on that book – you'll **spoil** it.*
2 To spoil a child means to give them too much, so that they always expect to get what they want.

spoke
☛ See **speak**.

sponge
NOUN sponges
A sponge is a soft material that soaks up a lot of water. You use sponges for cleaning or washing things.

Sport
Here are some sports and the equipment you need to play them.

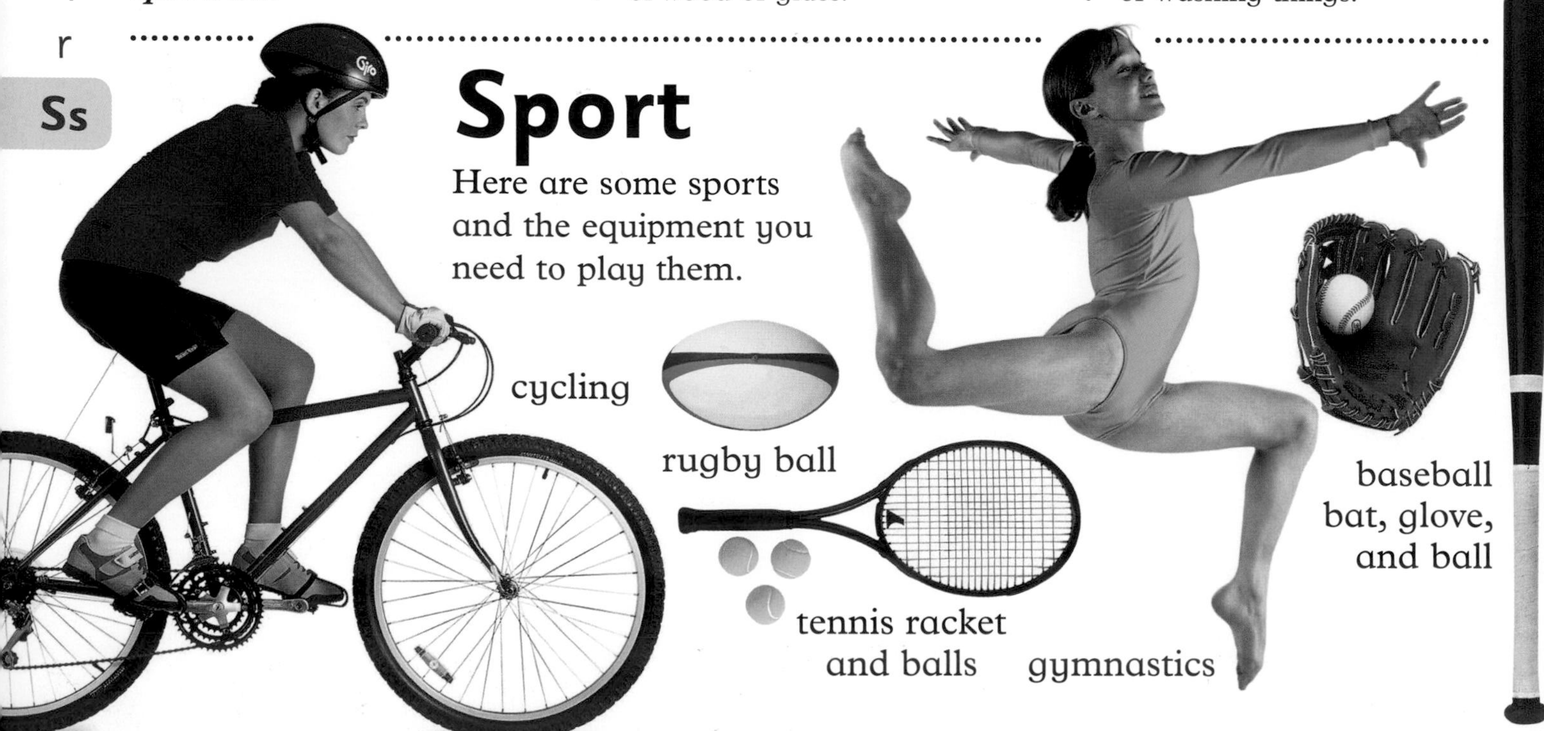
cycling

rugby ball

tennis racket and balls

gymnastics

baseball bat, glove, and ball

sponsor
VERB sponsors, sponsoring, sponsored
If you sponsor someone, you promise to give them money for a charity if they do something.

spooky
ADJECTIVE spookier, spookiest
A spooky place is frightening because it makes you think about ghosts.

spoon
NOUN spoons
A spoon is a tool with a small bowl at one end. You use a spoon for eating or stirring food.

sport
NOUN sports
A sport is something that you do to have fun and keep your body fit. Football, running, and golf are all sports.
sporty (ADJECTIVE)
Someone who is sporty enjoys doing sport and is good at it.

spot
NOUN spots
1 A spot is a small, round mark. *There were a few **spots** of paint on the floor.*
2 A spot is a small, red mark on your skin.
3 A spot is a place. *It was a perfect **spot** for a picnic.*
VERB spots, spotting, spotted
If you spot something, you see it. *We **spotted** a fox in our back garden.*

spout
NOUN spouts
The spout on a jug or teapot is the part that you pour liquid out of.

sprain
VERB sprains, spraining, sprained
If you sprain a part of your body, you hurt it. *I fell and **sprained** my wrist.*

sprang
☛ See **spring**.

spray
VERB sprays, spraying, sprayed
If you spray water onto something, you cover it with fine drops of water. *We **sprayed** the plants with water.*

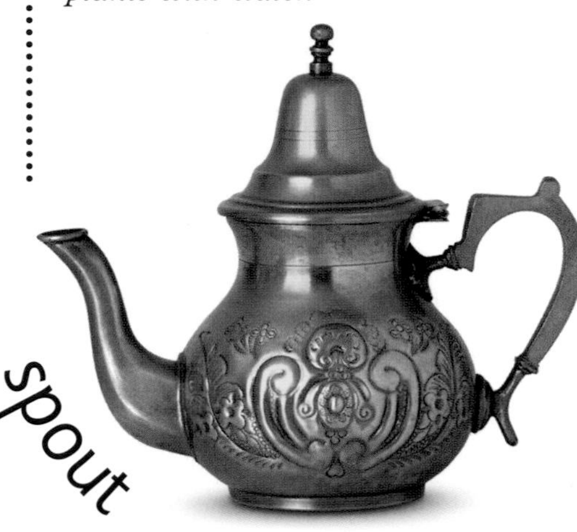
spout

spread
VERB spreads, spreading, spread
1 If you spread something out, you open it out. *We **spread** the blanket out on the ground and sat down.*
2 When you spread butter on bread, you put it all over the bread.

football

table tennis bat and ball

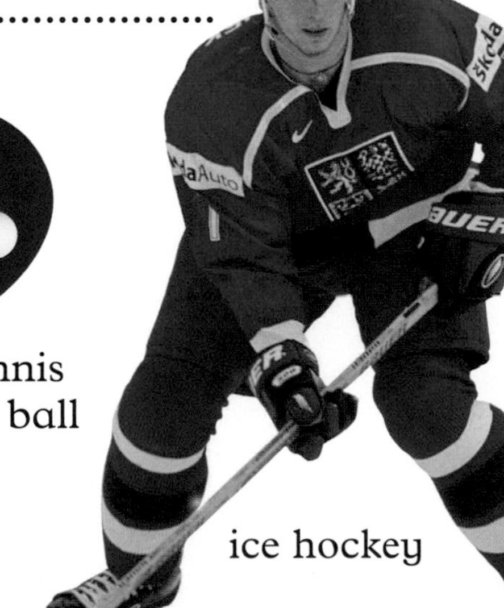

ice hockey

American football helmet

American football

golf club and balls

swimming

a b c d e f g h i j k l m n o p q r **Ss** t u v w x y z

a b c d e f g h i j k l m n o p q r Ss t u v w x y z

spring
NOUN springs

1 Spring is one of the four seasons. Spring follows winter and comes before summer. It is the time when the weather becomes warmer and many plants start to grow. *I look forward to the daffodils blooming in **spring**.*

2 A spring is a coil of thin metal that jumps back into shape after it has been stretched, bent, or squashed.

VERB springs, springing, sprang, sprung

3 When you spring, you jump upward in a lively way. ***She sprang** out of bed.*

sprint
VERB sprints, sprinting, sprinted

When you sprint, you run very fast. *I **sprinted** toward the bus stop.*

sprung
☛ See **spring**.

spun
☛ See **spin**.

spy
NOUN spies

A spy is a person who gathers information in secret. *The **spy** broke into the building in the middle of the night.*

squabble
VERB squabbles, squabbling, squabbled

When people squabble, they argue with each other. *My brothers are always **squabbling** over what to watch on TV!*

square
NOUN squares

A square is a shape with four equal sides and four right angles.

square number (NOUN)

A square number is a number that you get when you multiply a number by itself. For example, 9 is a square number because 3 x 3 = 9.

squirrel

squash
NOUN

1 Squash is a sweet drink made with fruit juice and sugar.

VERB squashes, squashing, squashed

2 If you squash something, you crush it so that it becomes flat. *My banana got **squashed** at the bottom of my bag.*

squeak
VERB squeaks, squeaking, squeaked

To squeak means to make a short, high sound, like the sound a mouse makes. *The wheel **squeaked** every time it went round.*

squeal
VERB squeals, squealing, squealed

To squeal means to make a long, high sound. *The girls **squealed** when I sprayed them with water.*

squeeze
VERB squeezes, squeezing, squeezed

If you squeeze something, you press it hard. *I **squeezed** the tube of toothpaste.*

squirrel
NOUN squirrels

A squirrel is a small, furry animal with a long, bushy tail. Squirrels eat nuts and berries.

squirt
VERB squirts, squirting, squirted

When you squirt liquid, you make it shoot out in a thin jet. *I accidentally **squirted** some orange juice into my eye.*

stab
VERB stabs, stabbing, stabbed

To stab something means to push something sharp into it.

stable
NOUN stables

A stable is a building where horses are kept.

stack
NOUN stacks

A stack is a pile of things, one on top of another. *There was a **stack** of books on the teacher's desk.*

stadium
NOUN stadiums or stadia

A stadium is a sports ground with seats all around for spectators.

staff
NOUN

The staff in a school, shop, or business are the people who work there.

stag
NOUN stags
A stag is an adult male deer. *We saw a beautiful **stag** on our trip to the countryside.*

stage
NOUN stages
1 A stage is a platform that people stand on to perform plays and shows.
2 One stage of something is one part of it. *We made the long journey in several **stages**.*

stagger
VERB staggers, staggering, staggered
If you stagger along, you walk in an unsteady way, nearly falling over. *I got up and **staggered** to the window.*

stain
NOUN stains
A stain is a dirty mark on something. *The old carpet was covered in **stains**.*

stair
NOUN stairs
Stairs are steps.
☛ **Be careful with spelling:**
stair *I went up the **stairs**.*
stare *You shouldn't **stare** at people.*

stale
ADJECTIVE
Food that is stale is not fresh. *They gave us water and some **stale** bread.*

stairs

stalk
NOUN stalks
The stalk of a flower or leaf is the part that joins it to the plant.

stall
NOUN stalls
A stall is a table where people show their goods and sell them at a market.

stammer
VERB stammers, stammering, stammered
If you stammer, you find it difficult to speak and you repeat the sounds at the beginning of words. *"I d-d-don't know," he **stammered**.*

stamp
NOUN stamps
1 A stamp is a sticker that you put on an envelope or parcel to show that you have paid for it to be delivered.
VERB stamps, stamping, stamped
2 If you stamp your foot, you bang it down on the ground.

stand
VERB stands, standing, stood
When you are standing, your feet are on the ground and your body is upright.

stank
☛ See **stink**.

star
NOUN stars
1 Stars are the tiny lights we see in the sky at night. The nearest star to Earth is the Sun.
2 A star is a shape with five or more points.
3 A star is a famous person.

stare
VERB stares, staring, stared
If you stare at something, you look at it for a long time.
☛ **Be careful with spelling:**
stare *You shouldn't **stare** at people.*
stair *I went up the **stairs**.*

start
NOUN starts
1 The start of something is when it begins.
VERB starts, starting, started
2 To start means to begin. *The runners lined up, ready to **start** the race.*

startle
VERB startles, startling, startled
If something startles you, it gives you a surprise or a shock. *The sudden movement **startled** him.*

starve
VERB starves, starving, starved
If someone is starving, they do not have enough food to live.

statement
NOUN statements
A statement is a sentence that tells you something rather than asking you a question or ordering you to do something.

station
NOUN stations
1 A station is a place where buses and trains stop.
2 A station is a building used by the police or fire brigade.

statue
NOUN statues
A statue is a model of a person or animal made from stone, wood, or metal.

stay
VERB stays, staying, stayed
1 If you stay in a place, you remain there.
2 If you stay in a place, you live there for a short time.
3 If something stays the same, it remains that way. *It **stayed** sunny all week.*

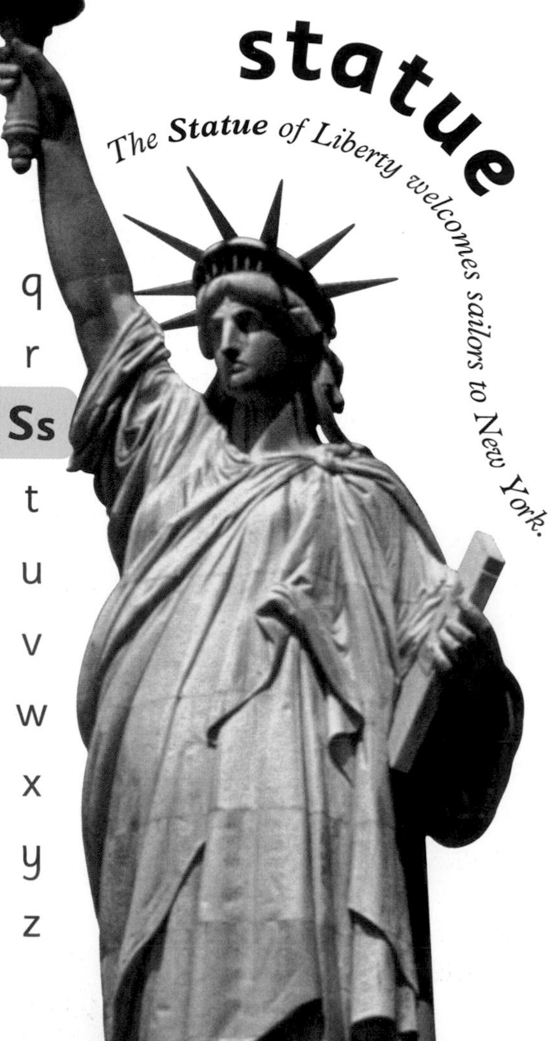

statue

*The **Statue** of Liberty welcomes sailors to New York.*

steady
ADJECTIVE steadier, steadiest
1 If something is steady, it is firm and does not move. *Hold the ladder **steady** while I climb up.*
2 Something that is steady continues without getting faster or slower. *We rode along at a **steady** speed.*

steak
NOUN steaks
A steak is a thick slice of fish or meat, usually beef.

steal
VERB steals, stealing, stole, stolen
To steal something means to take something that does not belong to you. *Thieves have **stolen** some paintings from the museum.*
☛ **Be careful with spelling:**
steal *Some people **steal** things from shops.*
steel *Wood is not as strong as **steel**.*

steam
NOUN
Steam is the gas that water turns into when it boils.

steel
NOUN
Steel is a hard, strong metal.
☛ **Be careful with spelling:**
steel *Wood is not as strong as **steel**.*
steal *Some people **steal** things from shops.*

steep
ADJECTIVE steeper, steepest
A steep hill or slope goes up or down sharply.

steer
VERB steers, steering, steered
When you steer something, you control the direction it goes in. *She **steered** her bicycle into the driveway.*

stem
NOUN stems
The stem of a plant is the main stalk that grows up out of the soil.

step
NOUN steps
1 When you take a step, you put one foot in front of the other and move forward.
2 A step is one of the parts of a staircase or a ladder on which you put your feet. *I sat on the bottom **step**, waiting for you to return.*

stem

stepbrother
NOUN stepbrothers
Your stepbrother is a boy who is not your real brother but whose father or mother has married your father or mother.

stepfather
NOUN stepfathers
Your stepfather is a man who is married to your mother but is not your real father. *My **stepfather** is an amazing cook.*

stepmother

NOUN stepmothers

Your stepmother is a woman who is married to your father but is not your real mother.

stepsister

NOUN stepsisters

Your stepsister is a girl who is not your real sister but whose father or mother has married your father or mother.

stereo

NOUN stereos

A stereo is a machine that you use for playing music.

stick

NOUN sticks

1 A stick is a long, thin piece of wood.

VERB sticks, sticking, stuck

2 If you stick things together, you glue or fasten them together. *I* ***stuck*** *the picture onto the front of my book.*

3 If you stick something sharp or pointed into an object, you push it in. *I* ***stuck*** *a pin into the map and said, "That's where I want to go."*

4 If something sticks out, part of it hangs out from a place. *There was a piece of paper* ***sticking*** *out of his pocket.*

sticker

NOUN stickers

A sticker is a small piece of paper with glue on one side.

sticky

ADJECTIVE stickier, stickiest

If something is sticky, it stays on your fingers when you touch it.

stiff

ADJECTIVE stiffer, stiffest

Something that is stiff does not bend or move easily. *The handle was too* ***stiff****, and I couldn't move it.*

still

ADJECTIVE

1 Something that is still is not moving or making any sound.

ADVERB

2 Still means even now. *Are you* ***still*** *watching the film?*

3 Still means even so. *I don't like toothpaste, but I* ***still*** *have to use it.*

sting

VERB stings, stinging, stung

If an insect stings you, it pricks your skin and hurts you.

stink

VERB stinks, stinking, stank, stunk

If something stinks, it smells bad. *Your feet* ***stink****!*

stir

VERB stirs, stirring, stirred

When you stir something, you mix it around with a spoon.

stole, stolen

See **steal**.

stomach

NOUN stomachs

1 Your stomach is the part inside your body where food goes after you have eaten it.

2 Your stomach is the outside part of your body below your chest.

A wasp ***sting*** *is very painful.*

Sting

stone

NOUN stones

1 Stone is the hard material that rocks are made of. *They made a statue out of* ***stone****.*

2 A stone is a small, loose piece of rock.

stood

See **stand**.

stool

NOUN stools

A stool is a chair with no back or arms.

stop

VERB stops, stopping, stopped

1 When something stops, it is no longer moving or no longer happening. *The train* ***stopped*** *suddenly.*

2 If you stop doing something, you no longer do it. *Please* ***stop*** *shouting!*

3 If you stop someone from doing something, you do not allow them to do it. *The man* ***stopped*** *the boy from running into the road.*

stopwatch

NOUN stopwatches

A stopwatch is a watch that you can start and stop to measure how much time something takes.

a b c d e f g h i j k l m n o p q r Ss t u v w x y z

store
NOUN stores
1 A store is a large shop.
VERB stores, storing, stored
2 When you store things, you put them away and keep them until you need them.

storm
NOUN storms
When there is a storm, there is a strong wind and heavy rain, hail, or snow.
stormy (ADJECTIVE)
When the weather is stormy, there is a storm. *It isn't safe to go out in a boat in **stormy** weather.*

story
NOUN stories
A story tells you about things that have happened to someone. Some stories are about real people and are true, and some are about imaginary people and are not true.

straight
ADJECTIVE straighter, straightest
Something that is straight is not bent or curved.
straighten (VERB)
If you straighten something, you make it straight.

stranded
ADJECTIVE
If you are stranded in a place, you are stuck there and are unable to leave.

strange
ADJECTIVE stranger, strangest
Something that is strange is not normal, or not how you expect it to be.

stranger
NOUN strangers
A stranger is a person you do not know.

strap
NOUN straps
A strap is a strip of leather or cloth that you use for fastening or holding things. *The **strap** on my satchel has broken.*

straw
NOUN straws
1 Straw is stalks of dried wheat that you put on the ground for animals to lie on.
2 A straw is a small hollow tube that you use for drinking through. *I drank my milkshake through a bendy **straw**.*

strawberry
NOUN strawberries
A strawberry is a small, red fruit that is soft and sweet. *We grew **strawberries** in our back garden this year.*

stray
ADJECTIVE
A stray dog or cat lives outside and does not have a home. *She fed the **stray** cat that turned up in her garden.*

stream
NOUN streams
A stream is a small river. *The water in the **stream** looked clean enough to drink.*

street
NOUN streets
A street is a road in a city or town. *What is the name of the **street** you live in?*

strength
NOUN
Strength is how strong something or someone is.
strengthen (VERB)
To strengthen something means to make it stronger.

stress
NOUN
If you are under stress, you have a lot of things that you are worried about.
stressful (ADJECTIVE)
Something that is stressful makes you feel worried.

stretch
VERB stretches, stretching, stretched
1 When you stretch something, you pull it so that it becomes longer or bigger.
2 When you stretch out a part of your body, you reach out with it as much as you can.

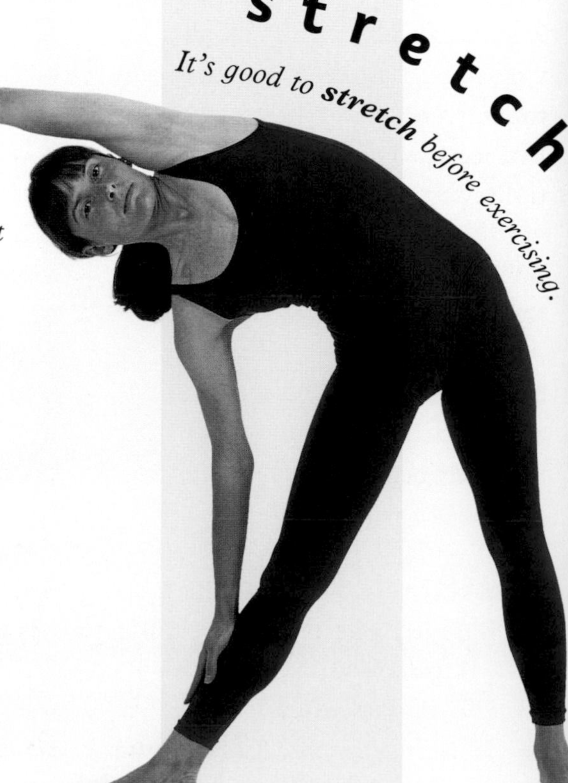

stretch
*It's good to **stretch** before exercising.*

strict

ADJECTIVE stricter, strictest
Someone who is strict makes people behave well and do the things they are told to do. *Teachers in the past were very **strict**.*

strike

NOUN strikes
1 When there is a strike, people refuse to work because they are unhappy or angry about something or because they want more money for doing their job.
VERB strikes, striking, struck
2 To strike something means to hit it. *The tree was **struck** by lightning.*
3 When a clock strikes, it makes a sound. *The clock **struck** ten.*

string

NOUN strings
1 String is thin cord or rope. *The cat chased the piece of **string**.*
2 The strings on a guitar or violin are the parts that you touch to make a sound.
I tuned the guitar by tightening its strings.

strip

NOUN strips
A strip is a long, narrow piece of something. *We cut **strips** of coloured paper to make the decorations.*

stripe

NOUN stripes
Stripes are narrow bands of colour.
striped (ADJECTIVE)
Something that is striped or **stripy** has a pattern of stripes on it.

stroke

VERB strokes, stroking, stroked
When you stroke an animal, you rub it gently with your hand.

stroll

VERB strolls, strolling, strolled
When you stroll along, you walk slowly in a relaxed way. *They **strolled** through the woods.*

strong

ADJECTIVE stronger, strongest
1 Something that is strong is tough and will not break easily.
2 Someone who is strong has a powerful body. *Elephants are very **strong**.*
3 A strong smell or flavour is easy to notice.

struck

☛ See **strike**.

struggle

VERB struggles, struggling, struggled
If you struggle to do something, you try very hard to do it. *The dog **struggled** to get free, but the ropes were too strong.*

stubborn

ADJECTIVE
Someone who is stubborn is determined to have their own way and will not change their mind.
stubbornly (ADVERB)
If you say or do something stubbornly, you do it in a stubborn way. *He **stubbornly** refused to get up.*

stuck

☛ See **stick**.

student

NOUN students
A student is someone who is studying at school, college, or university.

studio

NOUN studios
1 A studio is a room where an artist or photographer works. *The artist painted my portrait in her **studio**.*
2 A studio is a room where television programmes are made.

study

VERB studies, studying, studied
1 When you study a subject, you learn about it. *We're **studying** the Romans this term at school.*
2 If you study something, you look at it carefully. *She **studied** the flower through a magnifying glass.*

*The house is decorated with **stripy** wallpaper.*

a b c d e f g h i j k l m n o p q r Ss t u v w x y z

stuff
NOUN
Stuff is things. *There was **stuff** all over the floor.*

stuffy
ADJECTIVE
A room that is stuffy smells bad because there is no fresh air in it.

stumble
VERB stumbles, stumbling, stumbled
If you stumble, you trip and almost fall.

stump
NOUN stumps
A stump is a short part of a tree that is left behind after the rest has been cut off.

stung
☛ See **sting**.

stunk
☛ See **stink**.

stunt
NOUN stunts
A stunt is something clever and dangerous that someone does in a film or performance. *The **stunt** involved jumping over 15 cars on a motorbike.*

stupid
ADJECTIVE stupider, stupidest
Someone who is stupid is not very clever.
stupidity (NOUN)
Stupidity is stupid behaviour.
stupidly (ADVERB)
If you do something stupidly, you do it in a stupid way. *I **stupidly** forgot to take my sports kit to school.*

stutter
VERB stutters, stuttering, stuttered
If you stutter, you find it difficult to speak and you repeat the sounds at the beginning of words.

style
NOUN styles
A style is a shape or design of something. *The dress is a nice colour, but I don't like the **style**.*

subject
NOUN subjects
1 A subject is one thing that you are talking, writing, or learning about. *History and maths are my favourite **subjects** at school.*
2 The subject of a sentence is the person or thing that is the "do-er" of the verb. *"The boy" is the subject in the sentence: **The boy** ate an apple.*

submarine
NOUN submarines
A submarine is a boat that can travel underwater.

substance
NOUN substances
A substance is a material. *There was a sticky **substance** on the table.*

substitute
NOUN substitutes
A substitute is a player who joins in a game if someone else is hurt or tired.

subtract
VERB subtracts, subtracting, subtracted
When you subtract numbers, you take one away from the other. *Can you **subtract** five from eight?*
subtraction (NOUN)
When you do subtraction, you take one number away from another.

*A **submarine** dives to the depths of the sea.*

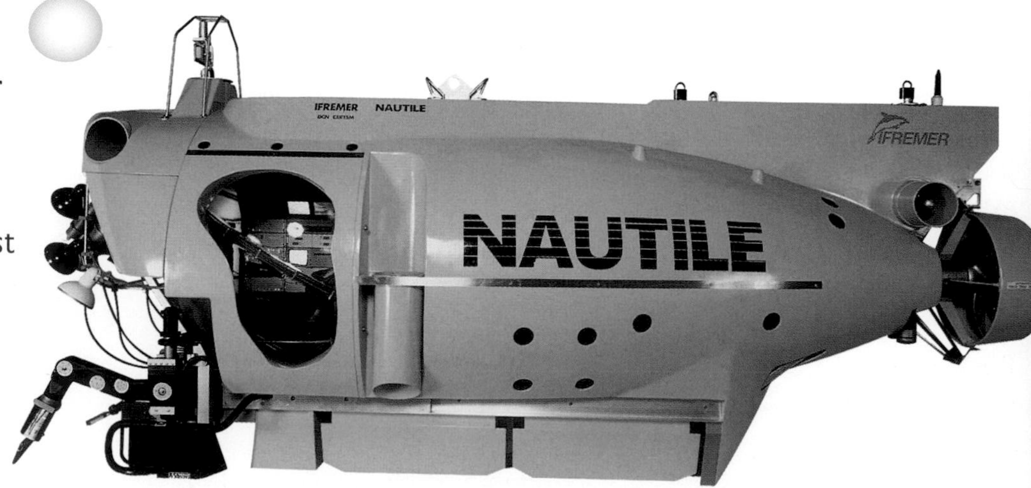

submarine

subway
NOUN subways
A subway is an underground tunnel that people use to walk under a road.

succeed
VERB succeeds, succeeding, succeeded
If you succeed, you do or achieve something well. *I'm sure you will **succeed** in all your exams.*

success
NOUN successes
If something is a success, it works well. *His magic act was a great **success**.*
successful (ADJECTIVE)
If you are successful, you manage to do something well.
successfully (ADVERB)
If you do something successfully, you do it well.

suck
VERB sucks, sucking, sucked
When you suck something, you hold it in your mouth and pull on it with your mouth. *She **sucked** the juice out of an orange.*

sudden
ADJECTIVE
Something that is sudden happens quickly, when you are not expecting it. *We heard a **sudden** loud bang coming from downstairs.*
suddenly (ADVERB)
If something happens suddenly, it happens quickly, when you are not expecting it. *He **suddenly** fell over.*

suffer
VERB suffers, suffering, suffered
1 If you are suffering, you are in pain.
2 If you are suffering from an illness, you have the illness.

sufficient
ADJECTIVE
Sufficient means enough.

suffix
NOUN suffixes
A suffix is a group of letters that you add to the end of a word to change its meaning. For example, you can add the suffix "-ly" to words like "careful" and "sudden" to make adverbs – "carefully" and "suddenly".

sugar
NOUN
Sugar is a substance that you add to food and drinks to make them taste sweet.

suggest
VERB suggests, suggesting, suggested
If you suggest something, you mention it and say that you think it is a good idea. *I **suggested** going to the park to ride our bikes.*
suggestion (NOUN)
A suggestion is an idea that you suggest.

suit
NOUN suits
1 A suit is a jacket and skirt or a jacket and trousers that go together.
VERB suits, suiting, suited
2 If something suits you, it looks nice when you wear it.

suitable
ADJECTIVE
If something is suitable, it is right for a particular purpose. *These boots are **suitable** for walking over rough ground.*
☛ **Opposite:** unsuitable

suitcase
NOUN suitcases
A suitcase is a large bag that you use for carrying clothing and other things when you travel. *She packed her **suitcase** for the holiday.*

sulk
VERB sulks, sulking, sulked
When you sulk, you are quiet because you are in a bad temper. *Please stop **sulking** – it's beginning to annoy me.*
sulky (ADJECTIVE)
If you are sulky, you are quiet because you are in a bad temper.

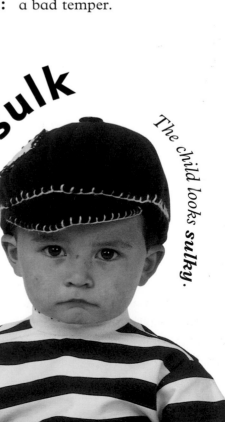

sulk

*The child looks **sulky**.*

a b c d e f g h i j k l m n o p q r Ss t u v w x y z

sum

NOUN sums

1 The sum of two numbers is the total that they add up to. *The **sum** of three and seven is ten.*

2 When you do a sum, you add, subtract, multiply, or divide numbers.

3 A sum of money is an amount of money.

summer

NOUN summers

Summer is one of the four seasons. Summer follows spring and comes before autumn. It is the warmest season of the year.

Sun / sun

NOUN

1 You can see the Sun shining in the sky during the day. The Sun is the star that is at the centre of the **Solar System**.

2 If you are in the sun, you are in the light and heat that we get from the Sun.

sunbathe

VERB sunbathes, sunbathing, sunbathed

When you sunbathe, you sit in the sun so that your skin becomes darker.

sunburn

NOUN

Sunburn is red, painful skin that you can get if you spend too long in the sun.

sunflower

NOUN sunflowers

A sunflower is a tall plant with large, yellow flowers. The seeds can be eaten or used to make cooking oil.

sung

☛ See **sing**.

sunglasses

NOUN

Sunglasses are glasses with dark lenses that you wear to protect your eyes from bright sunlight. Sunglasses are also called shades. *I've bought a pair of **sunglasses** for my holiday.*

sunk

☛ See **sink**.

sunlight

NOUN

Sunlight is the light from the Sun.

Sunflowers always face the Sun.

sunflower

sunny

ADJECTIVE sunnier, sunniest

If the weather is sunny, the Sun is shining and there are no clouds in the sky. *Today is the **sunniest** day of the year so far.*

sunrise

NOUN sunrises

Sunrise is the time when the Sun comes up in the morning.

sunscreen

NOUN

Sunscreen is a special cream that you put on your skin to protect it from the Sun and stop it from burning. *I always put on **sunscreen** when I go to the seaside in summer.*

sunset

NOUN sunsets

Sunset is the time when the Sun goes down in the evening.

sunshine

NOUN

Sunshine is bright light and heat from the Sun.

super

ADJECTIVE

Super means wonderful. *We had a **super** time.*

superb

ADJECTIVE

Superb means extremely good. *This is a **superb** game!*

superhero

NOUN superheroes

A superhero is a character in a story who has special powers and uses them to help people or solve crimes.

Supersonic planes go faster than the speed of sound.

supermarket
NOUN supermarkets
A supermarket is a large shop that sells food and other things.

supersonic
ADJECTIVE
A supersonic plane travels faster than the speed of sound.

superstar
NOUN superstars
A superstar is someone who is very famous.

superstition
NOUN superstitions
A superstition is an old belief that an action can bring good luck or bad luck.
superstitious (ADJECTIVE)
Someone who is superstitious believes in old superstitions.

supper
NOUN suppers
Supper is a meal that you eat in the evening.

supple
ADJECTIVE
Someone who is supple can bend their body a lot.

support
VERB supports, supporting, supported
1 To support someone or something means to hold them up and stop them from falling.
2 To support someone or something means to help them and encourage them. *Which football team do you **support**?*

suppose
VERB supposes, supposing, supposed
If you suppose that something is true, you think that it is true, but you do not know for certain. *I **suppose** this must be his phone.*

sure
ADJECTIVE
If you are sure about something, you are certain about it. *I am **sure** you will enjoy the film.*
☛ **Opposite:** unsure

surf
VERB surfs, surfing, surfed
1 When you go surfing, you balance on a special board and ride on waves as they begin to break near the seashore.
2 When you surf the internet, you search it to find information.

surface
NOUN surfaces
The surface of something is the top or outside of it. *The table has a shiny **surface**.*

surfboard

A surfer rides his *surfboard*.

surfboard
NOUN surfboards
A surfboard is a board that you use for surfing on waves.

surname
NOUN surnames
Your surname is your last name, which shows what family you belong to.

surprise
NOUN surprises
1 If something is a surprise, it happens when you do not expect it. *We want the party to be a **surprise**.*
VERB surprises, surprising, surprised
2 If something surprises you, it happens when you do not expect it. *I was **surprised** by the horrible weather.*
surprised (ADJECTIVE)
If you are surprised by something, you were not expecting it. *I was really **surprised** when I won the competition.*

surrender
VERB surrenders, surrendering, surrendered
If you surrender, you give yourself up. *The kidnappers finally **surrendered** to the police.*

surround
VERB surrounds, surrounding, surrounded
To surround a place means to be all around it. *The police **surrounded** the building.*

survive
VERB survives, surviving survived
If you survive, you do not die. *Luckily, everyone **survived** the crash.*

suspect
VERB suspects, suspecting, suspected
If you suspect that something is true, you think it might be true but you are not sure.

suspicious
ADJECTIVE
1 If you are suspicious of someone, you think that they might have done something bad.
2 A suspicious person behaves in a strange way and makes you think they might be doing something wrong. *We saw a **suspicious** character climbing into the house.*

swallow
NOUN swallows
1 A swallow is a small black and white bird with a forked tail.
VERB swallows, swallowing, swallowed
2 When you swallow food, you make it go down your throat and into your stomach.

swam
☛ See **swim**.

swan
NOUN swans
A swan is a large bird with a long neck that lives in and around water.

swap
VERB swaps, swapping, swapped
To swap something means to give it to someone in return for something else. *He **swapped** his computer game for her tennis racket.*

swarm
NOUN swarms
A swarm of insects is a large number of them flying together. *A **swarm** of bees can be dangerous.*

swear
VERB swears, swearing, swore, sworn
If you swear, you say rude and unpleasant words. *She told us never to **swear**.*

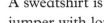

sweat
NOUN
1 Sweat is the salty liquid that comes out of your skin when you are hot. *She was covered in **sweat** after running in the race.*
VERB sweats, sweating, sweated
2 When you sweat, liquid comes out of your skin to cool you down when you are hot.

sweatshirt
NOUN sweatshirts
A sweatshirt is a thick, cotton jumper with long sleeves.

sweep
VERB sweeps, sweeping, swept
When you sweep a floor, you clean it using a brush.

sweet
NOUN sweets
1 A sweet is a small snack that you eat. It tastes sweet and is made with sugar.
ADJECTIVE sweeter, sweetest
2 Something that is sweet tastes of sugar. *Grapes are very **sweet**.*
3 Someone who is sweet is very kind. *It was **sweet** of you to bring me flowers.*

sweetcorn
NOUN
Sweetcorn is the sweet, yellow seeds of a corn plant that you can eat as a vegetable.

swept
☛ See **sweep**.

swim
VERB swims, swimming, swam, swum
When you swim, you use your arms and legs to move through water. *We **swam** from the boat to the shore.*
swimmer (NOUN)
A swimmer is someone who can swim.

swimming costume
NOUN swimming costumes
A swimming costume is a piece of clothing that a girl or woman wears to go swimming.

swimming pool
NOUN swimming pools
A swimming pool is a large area of water where people can go to swim.

swimming trunks
NOUN
Swimming trunks are a piece of clothing that a boy or man wears to go swimming.

swing
NOUN swings
1 A swing is a seat hung from ropes or chains. You sit on it and move backward and forward.
VERB swings, swinging, swung
2 To swing means to move backward and forward in the air. *The rope was **swinging** from side to side.*

switch
NOUN switches
A switch is a button or lever that you use to turn a machine on and off.

swollen
ADJECTIVE
If a part of your body is swollen, it is bigger than usual.

swoop
VERB swoops, swooping, swooped
To swoop means to move suddenly downward through the air. *The eagle **swooped** down on its prey.*

sword
NOUN swords
A sword is a weapon with a long, sharp blade and a handle.

swore
☛ See **swear**.

swum
☛ See **swim**.

swung
☛ See **swing**.

*The little girl **swings** to and fro.*

syllable
NOUN syllables
A syllable is a part of a word made up of a single sound. The word “computer” has three syllables.

symbol
NOUN symbols
A symbol is a picture or sign that represents something. *The dove is a **symbol** of peace.*

symmetrical
ADJECTIVE
If something is symmetrical, it has two halves that match each other exactly.

sympathy
NOUN
If you give someone sympathy, you show that you care about them and feel sorry for them. *Everyone gave me a lot of **sympathy** when I broke my arm.*
sympathetic (ADJECTIVE)
If you are sympathetic to someone, you show that you care about them and feel sorry for them.

synagogue
NOUN synagogues
A synagogue is a building where Jews go to pray.

synonym
NOUN synonyms
A synonym is a word that means the same as another word. “Large” is a synonym of “big”, and “little” is a synonym of “small”.

syrup
NOUN syrups
Syrup is a sweet, sticky liquid that you can eat. *I poured a little **syrup** on my pancake.*

system
NOUN systems
If things work together in a system, they work together in an organized way.

a b c d e f g h i l m n o p q r Ss t u v w x y z

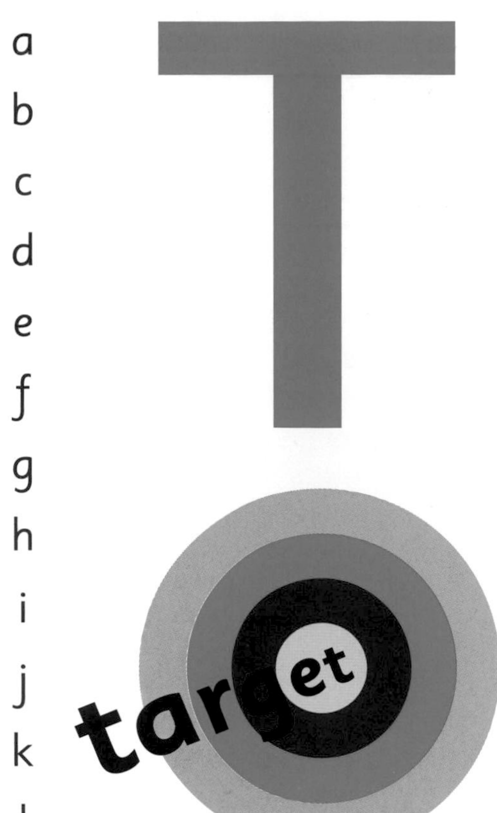

table
NOUN TABLES
1 A table is a piece of furniture with a flat surface and legs underneath to support it.
2 A table is a way of showing information in lists and columns.

tablet
NOUN tablets
1 A tablet is a small, solid piece of medicine that you swallow whole.
2 A tablet is a small computer that you can carry around with you and use by touching the screen.

table tennis
NOUN
Table tennis is a game in which you hit a small ball across a large table that has a net across the middle.

tackle
VERB tackles, tackling, tackled
1 If you tackle someone in a game such as football, you try to get the ball from them.
2 If you tackle a difficult job, you start doing it.

tadpole
NOUN tadpoles
A tadpole is a young frog or toad that has no legs and lives in water.

tail
NOUN tails
An animal's tail is the part of it that sticks out at the end of its body.
☛ **Be careful with spelling:**
tail *This cat has a long **tail**.*
tale *Do you like reading fairy **tales**?*

tailor
NOUN tailors
A tailor is a person who makes suits and other clothes for people.

take
VERB takes, taking, took, taken
1 When you take something, you remove it from a place. *Someone has **taken** my pen.*
2 When you take something somewhere, you move it to that place.
3 When you take someone somewhere, you bring them with you to that place.
4 When you take one number away from another, you subtract it.
5 When a plane or rocket takes off, it goes up into the air.

takeaway
NOUN takeaways
A takeaway is a meal that you buy in a restaurant to eat at home. *We didn't have time to cook so we bought a **takeaway**.*

*A lizard has a long **tail**.*

tale
NOUN tales
A tale is a story.
☛ **Be careful with spelling:**
tale *Do you like reading fairy **tales**?*
tail *This cat has a long **tail**.*

talent
NOUN talents
A talent is a natural ability that you have to do something well. *She has a **talent** for dancing.*
talented (ADJECTIVE)
Someone who is talented is good at doing something. *My brother is a **talented** musician.*

talk
VERB talks, talking, talked
When you talk, you say words to someone.
talkative (ADJECTIVE)
Someone who is talkative talks a lot. *Try not to be so **talkative** in class.*

tall
ADJECTIVE taller, tallest
1 Something that is tall is very high. *There are very **tall** buildings in the city.*
2 Someone who is tall has a long body. *Who is the **tallest** in your class?*

Talmud
NOUN
The Talmud is a book that has information about the Jewish religion.

tambourine
NOUN tambourines
A tambourine is a musical instrument that you hold in your hand and shake or tap to make a rhythm.

tambourine

tame
ADJECTIVE tamer, tamest
A tame animal is used to being with people and so is not fierce, and is not afraid of people.

tan
NOUN tans
1 When you get a tan, your skin goes brown because it has been in the sun.
VERB tans, tanning, tanned
2 When you tan, your skin goes brown in the sun.

tangle
VERB tangles, tangling, tangled
If something gets tangled, it gets twisted and tied into messy knots. *My hair always gets **tangled** when I go swimming.*

tank
NOUN tanks
1 A tank is a large container for keeping liquid in.
2 A tank is a heavy vehicle with guns that moves along on metal belts instead of wheels.

tap
NOUN taps
1 You turn a tap on to allow water to flow out.
VERB taps, tapping, tapped
2 If you tap something, you hit it gently. *I **tapped** on the door and then opened it.*

tape
NOUN tapes
A tape is a long, narrow strip of cloth or plastic. *We held a **tape** across the finishing line of the race.*

tape measure
NOUN tape measures
A tape measure is a tape with centimetres or inches marked on it, that you use for measuring things.

target
NOUN targets
A target is something that you try to hit when you are shooting or throwing something.

tart
NOUN tarts
A tart is a pie that has pastry on the bottom and a filling inside that is often fruit.

task
NOUN tasks
A task is a job or piece of work that you have to do. *Our first **task** was to find wood for a fire.*

taste
NOUN
1 Taste is one of your body's five senses, which you use to find out the flavour of something.
2 The taste of something is what it is like when you put it in your mouth. *Do you like the **taste** of chocolate?*
VERB tastes, tasting, tasted
3 When you taste something, you put it in your mouth to see what it is like. *Would you like to **taste** the soup?*
4 The way something tastes is what it is like when you put it in your mouth. *The ice cream **tasted** delicious!*
tasty (ADJECTIVE)
Something that is tasty has a nice taste. *I had a really **tasty** pizza.*

I used a tape measure to measure my height.

a b c d e f g h i j k l m n o p q r s Tt u v w x y z

taught
☛ See **teach**.

tax
NOUN taxes
Tax is money that everyone has to pay to the government.

taxi
NOUN taxis
A taxi is a car that you can hire to travel in by paying the driver money.

tea
NOUN teas
Tea is a drink that you make by pouring boiling water onto the dried leaves of the tea plant.

teach
VERB teaches, teaching, taught
When you teach someone something, you tell them about it or show them how to do it. *She **teaches** us maths.*
teacher (NOUN)
A teacher is someone who helps people to learn about things.

team
NOUN teams
A team is a group of people who work or play sports together.

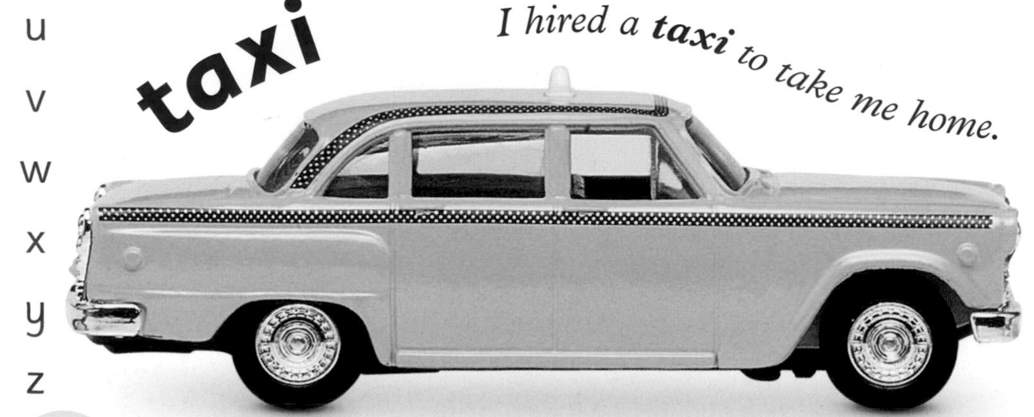

taxi
I hired a taxi to take me home.

tear
NOUN tears
Tears are drops of salty water that come from your eyes when you cry.

tear
VERB tears, tearing, tore, torn
When you tear paper or cloth, you make a hole or split in it.

tease
VERB teases, teasing, teased
If you tease someone, you say things to annoy them in a playful way.

technology
NOUN
Technology is science and machines that people use in everyday life.

teddy bear
NOUN teddy bears
A teddy bear is a soft toy in the shape of a bear.

teenager
NOUN teenagers
A teenager is a young person between the ages of 13 and 19.

teeth
☛ See **tooth**.

telephone
NOUN telephones
A telephone is a machine that you use to talk to someone who is in a different place. Telephone is often shortened to **phone**.

telescope
NOUN telescopes
A telescope makes things that are far away look bigger. You can look through a telescope to look at the stars and planets.

telescope

television
NOUN televisions
A television is a machine that receives signals that are broadcast and turns them into pictures and sound. Television is often shortened to **TV**.
televise (VERB)
If an event is televised, it is filmed and shown on television.

tell
VERB tells, telling, told
1 If you tell someone something, you speak to them about it or give them information about it. *He won't **tell** us where the treasure is!*
2 If you can tell the time, you can look at a clock or watch and understand what time it shows.

temper
NOUN tempers
1 Your temper is the mood you are in.
2 If you are in a temper, you are very angry. *She threw the book across the room in a* ***temper****.*

temperature
NOUN temperatures
1 When you measure temperature, you measure how hot or cold something is.
2 If you have a temperature you are hot and have a fever.

temple
NOUN temples
A temple is a building where people go to worship.

temporary
ADJECTIVE
Something that is temporary only lasts for a short time.

tender
ADJECTIVE
1 Food that is tender is soft and easy to chew.
2 If a part of your body is tender, it hurts when you touch it.
3 Someone who is tender is gentle and loving.

tennis
NOUN
Tennis is a game in which you use a racket to hit a ball over a net and score points if your opponent cannot hit it back.

tense
NOUN tenses
A tense is one of the different forms of a verb that tell you whether an action is in the present, past, or future. *The past* ***tense*** *of "tell" is "told".*

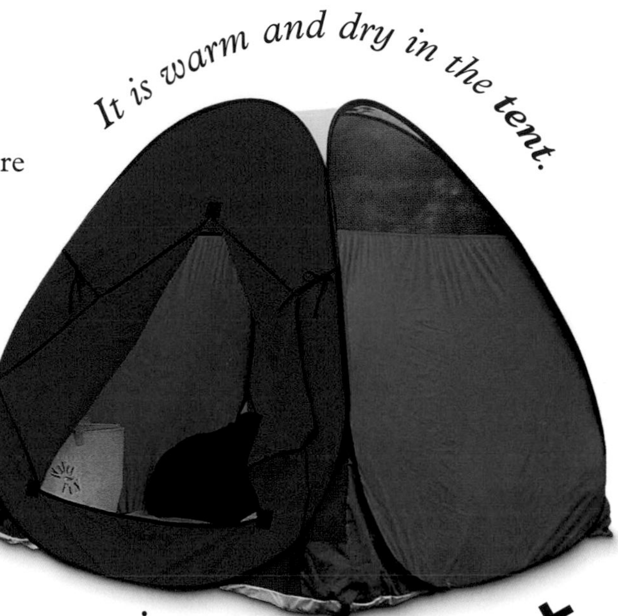
It is warm and dry in the tent.
tent

tent
NOUN tents
A tent is a shelter that is made of cloth and supported with poles and ropes. You sleep in a tent when you go camping.

term
NOUN terms
A school term is one of the periods of time during a year when schools are open for teaching.

terrible
ADJECTIVE
Something that is terrible is very bad or horrible. *Losing 3-0 was a* ***terrible*** *result for us.*

terrify
VERB terrifies, terrifying, terrified
If something terrifies you, it makes you feel very scared. *The thought of flying* ***terrifies*** *me!*
terrified (ADJECTIVE)
If you are terrified, you are very scared. *My sister is* ***terrified*** *of snakes.*
terrifying (ADJECTIVE)
Something that is terrifying is very scary. *It was* ***terrifying*** *being out at sea in the storm.*

terrorist
NOUN terrorists
A terrorist is someone who kills or injures people or uses bombs to try to make a government change its mind.

test
NOUN tests
1 When you do a test, you answer questions to show how much you know.
VERB tests, testing, tested
2 If you test something, you try it or use it to see what it is like.

test

text
NOUN texts
1 A text is a piece of writing. *I read an interesting **text** about elephants.*
2 A text or a text message is a message that you send to someone using a mobile phone.
VERB texts, texting, texted
3 When you text someone, you send them a text message. ***Text** me when you've finished your homework.*

thank
VERB thanks, thanking, thanked
If you thank someone, you say you are grateful to them for something they have done. *I **thanked** everyone for their presents.*

thaw
VERB thaws, thawing, thawed
When something that is frozen thaws, it melts. *The snow started to **thaw** in the sunshine.*

theatre
NOUN theatres
A theatre is a building where people perform plays and shows for other people to watch.

theme
NOUN themes
A theme is an idea or subject.

theme park
NOUN theme parks
A theme park is a place where people go to ride on large machines for fun.

then
ADVERB
Then means after that. *We went swimming and **then** we had lunch.*

there
ADVERB
There means in that place. *Hang your coat up over **there**.*

thermometer
NOUN thermometers
You use a thermometer to measure temperatures.

*I checked the temperature with a **thermometer**.*

thesaurus
NOUN
thesauruses or thesauri
A thesaurus is a book that lists groups of words with similar meanings.

thick
ADJECTIVE
thicker, thickest
1 Something that is thick is wide.
2 Thick clothes are warm because they are made of heavy material. *I wore a **thick** jumper.*
3 A liquid that is thick is not very watery and does not flow easily. *This paint is very **thick**.*

thief
NOUN thieves
A thief is a person who steals things.

thigh
NOUN thighs
Your thighs are the top parts of your legs.

thin
ADJECTIVE thinner, thinnest
1 Something that is thin is not very wide. *The walls are **thin** so we can hear everything they say.*
2 Someone who is thin is not very fat.
3 A liquid that is thin is very watery and flows easily.

thing
NOUN things
A thing is something that is not alive.

think
VERB thinks, thinking, thought
When you think, you use your mind to have ideas or opinions. *She was **thinking** about what she would eat for lunch.*

third person
NOUN
If you write a story in the third person, you write it using words like "he" and "she", rather than words like "I" or "me".

thirsty
ADJECTIVE thirstier, thirstiest
If you are thirsty, you want to drink something.

*She was so **thirsty**, she finished her drink in one gulp.*

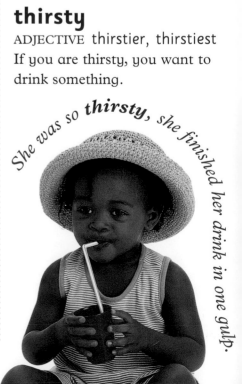

thorn
NOUN thorns
A thorn is a sharp spike on a plant. *Some roses have sharp **thorns**.*

throne

thought
NOUN thoughts
1 A thought is an idea that you have in your mind.
2 See **think**.

thoughtful
ADJECTIVE
If you are thoughtful, you are kind and think about other people's feelings. *It was **thoughtful** of you to remember my birthday.*

thousand
NOUN thousands
A thousand is ten hundreds (1,000).

thread
NOUN threads
A thread is a thin string that you use for sewing.

threaten
VERB threatens, threatening, threatened
If you threaten to do something unpleasant, you say you will do it. *His mother **threatened** to send him to bed if he didn't behave.*

threw
☛ See **throw**.

thrill
NOUN thrills
If something gives you a thrill, it gives you a strong feeling of excitement.
thrilled (ADJECTIVE)
If you are thrilled about something, you are very pleased about it. *I was **thrilled** with my presents.*
thrilling (ADJECTIVE)
Something that is thrilling is very exciting. *The final was a **thrilling** game.*

throat
NOUN throats
Your throat is the back of your mouth, where you swallow.

throne
NOUN thrones
A throne is a special chair that a king or queen sits on.

throw
VERB throws, throwing, threw, thrown
1 When you throw something, you hold it in your hand and then let go and push it through the air. *Quick, **throw** the ball to me!*
2 If you throw something away, you put it in the bin because you do not want it.

thumb
NOUN thumbs
Your thumb is the short, thick finger on the side of your hand. *The child sucked its **thumb**.*

thump
VERB thumps, thumping, thumped
If you thump someone, you hit them hard. *He **thumped** the table with his hand.*

thunder
NOUN
Thunder is the loud, rumbling sound that you hear during a storm. *The flash of lightning was quickly followed by the sound of **thunder**.*

throw

*She **threw** the ball a long way.*

a b c d e f g h i j k l m n o p q r s **Tt** u v w x y z

Time

Telling the time

We measure time in hours, minutes, and seconds. Most traditional clocks have two hands to tell us the time. The short hand tells us the hours; the long hand tells us the minutes.

There are 60 minutes in one hour.

There are five minutes between each number on a clockface.

24-hour clock

Digital clocks tell us the time in numbers. Because there are 24 hours in the day, digital clocks can tell us whether the time is in the morning or in the afternoon.

thunderstorm

NOUN thunderstorms

A thunderstorm is a storm that has thunder and lightning.

tick

NOUN ticks

1 A tick is a mark that you put beside something to show that it is correct.

VERB ticks, ticking, ticked

2 When a clock ticks, it makes a clicking sound.

ticket

NOUN tickets

A ticket is a piece of paper that shows that you have paid to do something. *He bought four **tickets** for the concert.*

tickle

VERB tickles, tickling, tickled

When you tickle someone, you touch their skin lightly and make them laugh.

tide

NOUN tides

The tide is the regular movement of the sea toward the shore and away from it. *We went down to the beach when the **tide** was out.*

tidy

VERB tidies, tidying, tidied

1 When you tidy a room, you put everything away in its proper place. *We need to **tidy** the kitchen before mum gets home.*

ADJECTIVE tidier, tidiest

2 If a place is tidy, it is neat and everything is in its proper place. *My bedroom is never **tidy**.*

☛ **Opposite:** untidy

tiger

tie

NOUN ties

1 A tie is a thin strip of material that you wear around your neck, under the collar of a shirt.

2 If there is a tie, two people or teams have the same number of points. *The football game ended in a **tie**.*

VERB ties, tying, tied

3 When you tie something, you fasten it with a knot or bow. *She **tied** her shoelaces.*

tiger

NOUN tigers

A tiger is a large, fierce, stripy animal that lives in Asia. Tigers belong to the cat family and hunt at night for their food.

tight

ADJECTIVE tighter, tightest

1 A tight piece of clothing fits your body closely. *These trousers are a bit too **tight**.*

2 A tight knot is fastened firmly and is not loose.

30 minutes past the hour is half past.
half past nine
09.30

15 minutes to the hour is quarter to.
quarter to ten
09.45

12:00 is noon

21:00 is 9 o'clock at night

p.m. (afternoon)

09:00 10:00 11:00 12:00 13:00 14:00 15:00 16:00 17:00 18:00 19:00 20:00 21:00 22:00 23:00 00:00

tights
NOUN
Tights are a stretchy piece of clothing that women and girls wear over their legs and bottom. *She put on a pair of **tights** to keep her legs warm.*

till
NOUN tills
A till is a machine that people use in shops to keep money in and add up how much things cost.

time
NOUN times
1 Time is all the hours, days, and years in the past, present, and future. *He wished that he could travel back in **time**.*
2 The number of times that you do something is how often you do it. *I go swimming three **times** a week.*
3 One number times another number is the two numbers multiplied together. *What's three **times** four?*

timetable
NOUN timetables
A timetable is a list of times when things happen. *We looked at the bus **timetable** to see when the next bus would arrive.*

timid
ADJECTIVE
Someone who is timid is not very brave. *The bird was **timid** and flew away when I moved.*

tin
NOUN tins
1 Tin is a light, silvery metal.
2 A tin is a metal container. *He opened a **tin** of soup using a tin-opener.*

tinsel
Tinsel is a thin strip of shiny, glittery material that you use for decorating a room.

tiny
ADJECTIVE tinier, tiniest
Something that is tiny is very small. *Baby kangaroos are **tiny**.*

tip
NOUN tips
1 The tip of something is its narrow, pointed end.
2 A tip is a little piece of advice that helps you to do something.
3 If you give someone a tip, you give them a small, extra amount of money when they have done something for you.
VERB tips, tipping, tipped
4 If you tip something, you move it so that it is not upright.

tiptoe
VERB tiptoes, tiptoeing, tiptoed
When you tiptoe, you walk slowly and quietly on your toes.

tired
ADJECTIVE
If you feel tired, you feel that you want to sleep.

tissue
NOUN tissues
A tissue is a piece of thin paper that you blow your nose on.

a b c d e f g h i j k l m n o p q r s **Tt** u v w x y z

title
NOUN titles
1 The title of a book, film, or painting is what it is called.
2 Someone's title is the part of their name that shows their rank or job. "Dr", "Mrs", and "Lord" are all titles.

toad
NOUN toads
A toad is an animal that looks like a large frog. Toads are amphibians but usually live on land.

toast
NOUN
Toast is bread that has been grilled on both sides until it is crisp and brown.

toboggan
NOUN toboggans
A toboggan is a sledge for sliding over snow.

today
Today is this day. *I'm going to the zoo* ***today***.

toddler
NOUN toddlers
A toddler is a young child who is just learning to walk.

toe
NOUN toes
Your toes are the five separate parts at the end of each foot.

toffee
NOUN toffees
A toffee is a type of chewy sweet.

together
ADVERB
When people do something together, they do it with each other. *Shall we walk to school* ***together***?

toilet
NOUN toilets
A toilet is a large bowl that flushes and that you use for getting rid of waste from your body.

told
☛ See **tell**.

tomato
NOUN tomatoes
A tomato is a soft, juicy, red fruit that you can eat raw or cooked.

tomorrow
Tomorrow is the day after today. *We're going on holiday* ***tomorrow***.

tongue
NOUN tongues
Your tongue is the part inside your mouth that you can move and which you use for talking and for tasting food.

He used his ***tools*** *to mend the shed.*

Tomatoes *are often used in salads.*

tonight
Tonight is the evening and night of today. *We're doing our school concert* ***tonight***.

too
ADVERB
1 Too means also. *Can I come to the cinema* ***too***?
2 Too much or too many means more than you need.

took
☛ See **take**.

tool
NOUN tools
A tool is something that you hold in your hand and use to do a job.

tooth
NOUN teeth
1 Your teeth are the hard, white things inside your mouth, which you use for biting and chewing.
2 The teeth on a comb or saw are the pointed parts.
toothbrush (NOUN)
A toothbrush is a small brush that you use to clean your teeth.
toothpaste (NOUN)
Toothpaste is a special cream that you use to clean your teeth.

top
NOUN tops
1 The top of something is the highest part of it.
2 A top is a lid.
3 A top is a piece of clothing that you wear on the top part of your body.

topic
NOUN topics
A topic is a subject that you learn about or talk about. *Our history **topic** is the Romans.*

torch
NOUN torches
A torch is a small lamp that you hold in your hand.

tore, torn
☛ See **tear**.

tornado
NOUN tornadoes or tornados
A tornado is a violent, whirling wind that causes great damage to land and buildings.

tortoise
NOUN tortoises
A tortoise is an animal with a hard shell that moves slowly and hides inside its shell when it is in danger.

toss
VERB tosses, tossing, tossed
1 When you toss something, you throw it.
2 When you toss a coin, you throw it into the air and guess which side will face upward when it lands.

total
NOUN totals
1 The total is the amount that you get when you add numbers together. *The **total** of two, three, and four is nine.*
ADJECTIVE
2 Total means complete. *We were left in **total** darkness.*
totally (ADVERB)
Totally means completely. *I was **totally** exhausted!*

touch
VERB touches, touching, touched
When you touch something, you put your hand on it. *Please do not **touch** any of the paintings.*

tough
ADJECTIVE tougher, toughest
1 Something that is tough is strong and will not break easily.
2 Something that is tough is difficult. *We had to do some **tough** maths questions.*

tour
NOUN tours
A tour is a trip to visit a lot of different places. *We went on a **tour** of the city.*

tourist
NOUN tourists
A tourist is a person who travels and visits places for pleasure.

tournament
NOUN tournaments
A tournament is a competition. *We're playing in a rugby **tournament** next weekend.*

tow
VERB tows, towing, towed
To tow a vehicle means to pull it along behind another vehicle. *The truck **towed** the car to the garage.*

towel
NOUN towels
A towel is a piece of soft material that you use for drying your body.

tower
NOUN towers
1 A tower is a tall, thin building.
2 To tower over someone means to be much taller than them.

tortoise *The **tortoise** moved slowly along the ground.*

a b c d e f g h i j k l m n o p q r s Tt u v w x y z

town

NOUN towns

A town is a place with houses and other buildings, where people live, work, and shop. A town is smaller than a city but larger than a village.

toy

NOUN toys

A toy is something that you play with.

trace

VERB traces, tracing, traced

When you trace a picture, you copy it by putting a sheet of thin paper over it and drawing around the outline.

track

NOUN tracks

1 A track is a mark that a person or animal leaves as they walk along. *The fox left **tracks** in the snow.*

2 A track is a path or rough road.

3 A track is a piece of ground that has lines marked on it so that it can be used for races.

tractor

NOUN tractors

A tractor is a vehicle that people use on farms.

tradition

NOUN traditions

A tradition is something that people have done in the same way for many years.

traditional (ADJECTIVE)

If something is traditional, people do it as a tradition. *It is **traditional** for the bride to wear a white dress.*

traffic

NOUN

The traffic on a road is all the cars, buses, lorries, and other vehicles on it. *There was a lot of **traffic** on the bridge.*

traffic lights (NOUN)

Traffic lights are different-coloured lights that tell drivers when they must stop and when they can go.

tragedy

NOUN tragedies

A tragedy is a very sad event, for example one in which people die or are hurt.

trail

NOUN trails

A trail is a narrow path. *We followed a nature **trail** through the woods.*

train

NOUN trains

1 A train is a vehicle that travels on railway lines.

VERB trains, training, trained

2 When you train, you practise sports skills. *She **trains** for three hours a day.*

3 When you train someone, you teach them to do something. *He **trained** his dog to sit.*

trainer

NOUN trainers

Trainers are shoes that you wear for running or doing sport.

tram

NOUN trams

A tram is a vehicle like a bus that goes along rails in the road in some cities.

trampoline

NOUN trampolines

A trampoline is a piece of equipment that you can bounce on. *We spent hours jumping on the **trampoline**.*

translate

VERB translates, translating, translated

When you translate something, you change it into a different language. *I **translated** the poem from English into French.*

transport

NOUN

1 Transport is a way of carrying goods or people from one place to another. Different methods of transport are used to travel on land, on water, and in the air. *My favourite method of **transport** is flying.*

VERB transports, transporting, transported

2 To transport people or things means to take them from one place to another. *The goods were **transported** by train.*

trap

NOUN traps

1 A trap is a machine or trick that you use to catch someone.

VERB traps, trapping, trapped

2 When you trap a person or animal, you catch them and hold them so that they cannot get away.

trapped (ADJECTIVE)

If someone is trapped, they cannot escape from a place. *The **trapped** man had to be rescued.*

Transport

This collection of words will be helpful on any journey.

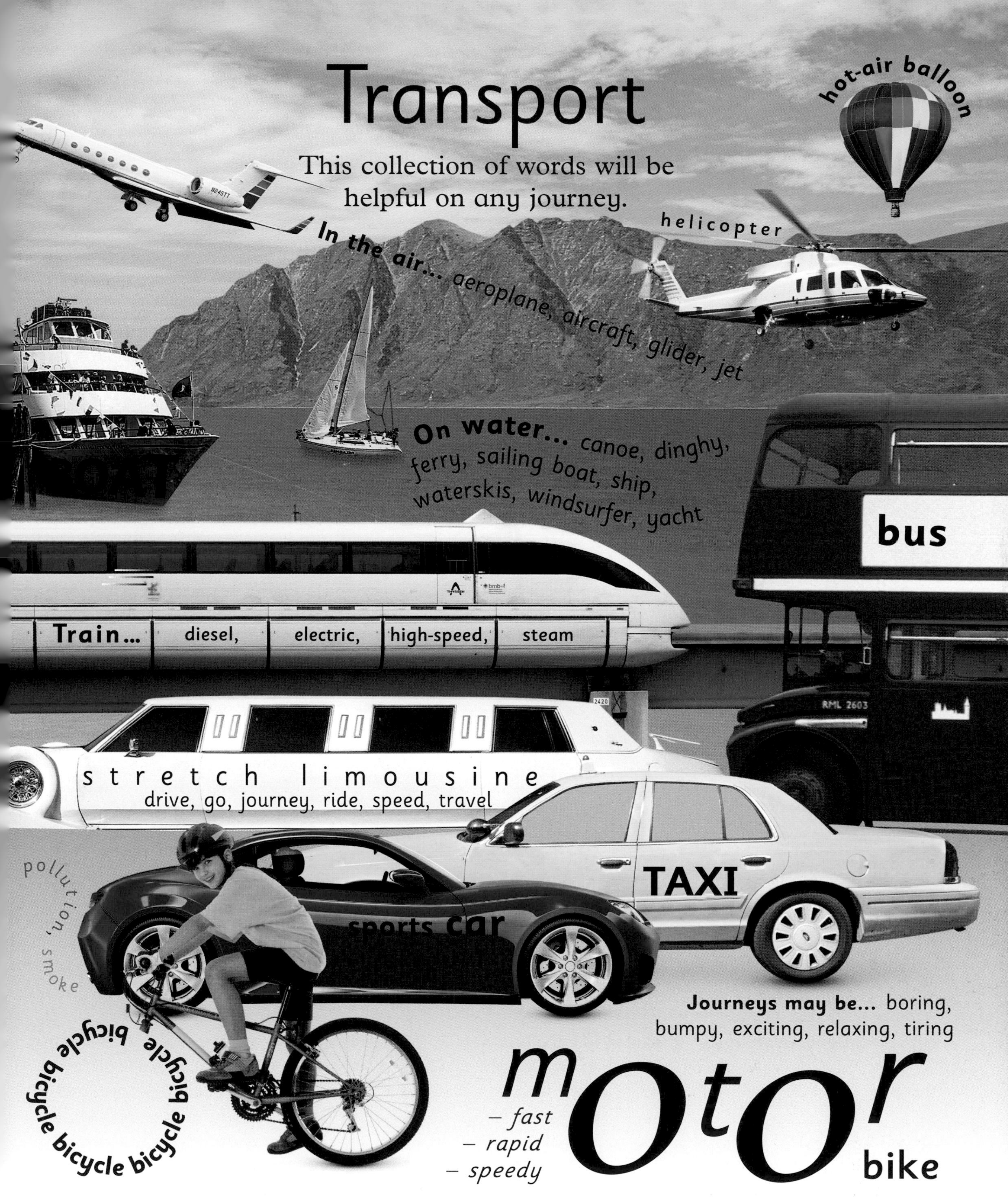

hot-air balloon

helicopter

In the air... aeroplane, aircraft, glider, jet

On water... canoe, dinghy, ferry, sailing boat, ship, waterskis, windsurfer, yacht

bus

Train... diesel, electric, high-speed, steam

stretch limousine

drive, go, journey, ride, speed, travel

pollution, smoke

TAXI

sports car

Journeys may be... boring, bumpy, exciting, relaxing, tiring

bicycle bicycle bicycle bicycle bicycle

motor bike

– *fast*
– *rapid*
– *speedy*

On land... bike, bus, car, caravan, coach, lorry, taxi, train, truck, van

a b c d e f g h i j k l m n

travel

VERB travels, travelling, travelled

When you travel, you go from one place to another. *We **travelled** around the lakes and mountains on holiday.*

tray

NOUN trays

A tray is a flat board that you use for carrying food and drinks.

tread

VERB treads, treading, trod, trodden

When you tread on something, you put your foot on it. *Mind that you don't **tread** on a thorn in bare feet.*

tree

*Leaves fall off the **trees** in autumn.*

treasure

NOUN

Treasure is a large amount of gold, jewels, or other valuable things.

treat

NOUN treats

1 A treat is something special that someone gives you or does for you. *My dad took us to the fair as a birthday **treat**.*

VERB treats, treating, treated

2 The way you treat someone is the way you behave toward them, for example whether you are kind or nasty to them. *She **treats** her pet hamster well.*

3 To treat someone means to try to make them better when they are ill or hurt.

treatment (NOUN)

Treatment is something that a doctor gives you or does to you to make you better. *He was taken to hospital for **treatment**.*

tree

NOUN trees

A tree is a tall plant with a trunk, branches, and leaves.

tremble

VERB trembles, trembling, trembled

When you tremble, you shake because you are cold or afraid.

tremendous

ADJECTIVE

Something that is tremendous is very good.

trendy

ADJECTIVE trendier, trendiest

Trendy clothes are modern and fashionable.

trial

NOUN trials

A trial is an event where a prisoner is questioned in court, and the court decides if the prisoner is guilty or not guilty of a crime.

triangle

NOUN triangles

1 A triangle is a shape that has three straight sides.

2 A triangle is a musical instrument in the shape of a triangle, which you hit with a small metal bar.

triangular (ADJECTIVE)

Something that is triangular is in the shape of a triangle.

trick

NOUN tricks

1 A trick is something clever or skilful that you do to entertain people. *I love watching magic **tricks**.*

2 If you play a trick on someone, you tell them something untrue for fun.

VERB tricks, tricking, tricked

3 If you trick someone, you tell them something untrue for fun.

tricycle

NOUN tricycles

A tricycle is a vehicle with three wheels that you ride by turning the pedals with your feet.

trim

VERB trims, trimming, trimmed

When you trim something, you cut the edges off it to make it neat. *My sister **trimmed** my hair.*

trip
NOUN trips
1 A trip is a journey. *We went on a school **trip**.*
VERB trips, tripping, tripped
2 If you trip, you catch your foot on something and fall over.

trod, trodden
☛ See **tread**.

troll
NOUN trolls
1 In stories, a troll is a fierce giant.
2 On the internet, a troll is someone who says mean or unkind things to other people.

trolley
NOUN trolleys
A trolley is a small cart on wheels that you use for carrying things.

trombone
NOUN trombones
A trombone is a large, brass musical instrument. You make different notes by sliding a long tube backward and forward.

troops
NOUN
Troops are soldiers.

trophy
NOUN trophies
A trophy is a cup, medal, or other prize that you receive when you win a competition.

tropical
ADJECTIVE
Tropical means from the hot, wet part of the world near the Equator.

trot
VERB trots, trotting, trotted
To trot means to run slowly. *The horse **trotted** away slowly.*

trouble
NOUN troubles
When there is trouble, people get angry and bad things happen. *If you smash that window, you'll be in **trouble**!*

trousers
NOUN
You wear trousers on the lower half of your body. Trousers fasten around your waist and have a separate part for each leg.

trout
NOUN trouts
A trout is a type of fish that people often eat.

truce
NOUN truces
A truce is an agreement to stop fighting a war.

truck
NOUN trucks
A truck is a lorry that people use for carrying goods.

true
ADJECTIVE
Something that is true really happened and is not made up.
☛ **Opposite:** untrue

trumpet
NOUN trumpets
A trumpet is a small, brass musical instrument. You make different notes by pressing down different buttons.

trunk
NOUN trunks
1 The trunk of a tree is the main part that grows up out of the ground.
2 An elephant's trunk is its long nose.
3 A trunk is a large box that you can keep things in.

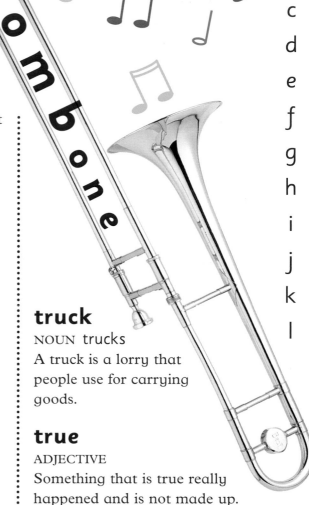

a b c d e f g h i j k l m n o p q r s Tt u v w x y z

trust
VERB trusts, trusting, trusted
If you trust someone, you believe that they are honest and will not steal from you or lie to you.

truth
NOUN
The truth is things that are true. *Do you always tell the* ***truth****?*
truthful (ADJECTIVE)
Someone who is truthful tells the truth and does not tell lies.

try
VERB tries, trying, tried
1 If you try to do something, you make an effort to do it. *He* ***tried*** *to climb up the tree but it was too difficult.*
2 If you try something, you use it or test it to see if it works. *Can I* ***try*** *your skateboard?*
3 If you try something, you eat or drink some of it to see if you like it. *Would you like to* ***try*** *one of my biscuits?*

T-shirt
NOUN T-shirts
A T-shirt is a shirt with short sleeves, no buttons, and usually a round neck.

tub
NOUN tubs
A tub is a plastic container. *We bought a small* ***tub*** *of ice cream.*

tube
NOUN tubes
1 A tube is a hollow pipe.
2 A tube is a narrow container for cream or paste. You squeeze the tube to get the cream or paste out.

tuck
NOUN tucks, tucking, tucked
1 When you tuck clothes in, you push them neatly inside another piece of clothing. ***Tuck*** *your shirt into your trousers.*
2 If you tuck someone up in bed, you cover their body up so that they are warm and comfortable.

tug
VERB tugs, tugging, tugged
If you tug something, you pull it roughly. *My sister was* ***tugging*** *at my sleeve.*

tumble
VERB tumbles, tumbling, tumbled
If you tumble, you fall down and roll over. *She* ***tumbled*** *down the hill.*

tumble-drier
NOUN tumble-driers
A tumble-drier is a machine that dries clothes by turning them around in warm air.

tummy
NOUN tummies
Your tummy is your stomach.

tuna
NOUN
Tuna is a kind of fish that you can eat.

tune
NOUN tunes
A tune is a set of musical notes that go together nicely. *Can you play a* ***tune*** *on the piano?*

tunnel
NOUN tunnels
A tunnel is an underground passage.

turban
NOUN turbans
A turban is a long piece of material that some people wear around their heads as a hat.

turkey
NOUN turkeys
A turkey is a type of large bird that is kept on farms for its meat.

turn
NOUN turns
1 If it is your turn to do something, you are the person who must do it next. *It's your* ***turn*** *to wash up.*
VERB turns, turning, turned
2 When something turns, it moves round.
3 When you turn, you change the direction you are looking or going in.
4 To turn means to become. *His fingers* ***turned*** *blue with the cold.*

turnip
NOUN turnips
A turnip is a round, white vegetable.

tusk
NOUN tusks
Tusks are the long, pointed teeth that stick out of the mouths of some animals, such as elephants.

TV
NOUN TVs
A TV is a **television**.

tweet
NOUN tweets
A tweet is a short message that someone posts on the website Twitter.

twice
ADVERB
If you do something twice, you do it two times.

twig
NOUN twigs
A twig is a very small branch of a tree.

twin
NOUN twins
Twins are two children who are born to the same mother at the same time.

twinkle
VERB twinkles, twinkling, twinkled
If something twinkles, it shines and sparkles. *The stars **twinkled** in the sky.*

twist
VERB twists, twisting, twisted
If you twist something, you turn it round. *I **twisted** the top off the jar.*

twist

*The baker **twisted** the bread before he put it in the oven.*

type
NOUN types
1 One type of thing is one sort of thing. *They sell two **types** of bread.*
VERB types, typing, typed
2 When you type, you write something by pressing down the letters on a typewriter or computer keyboard.

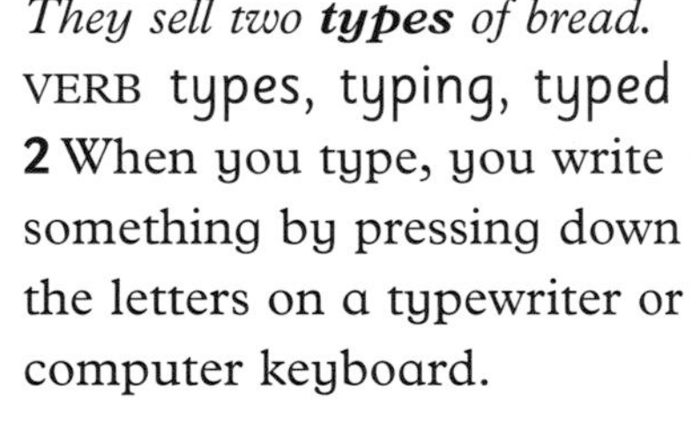

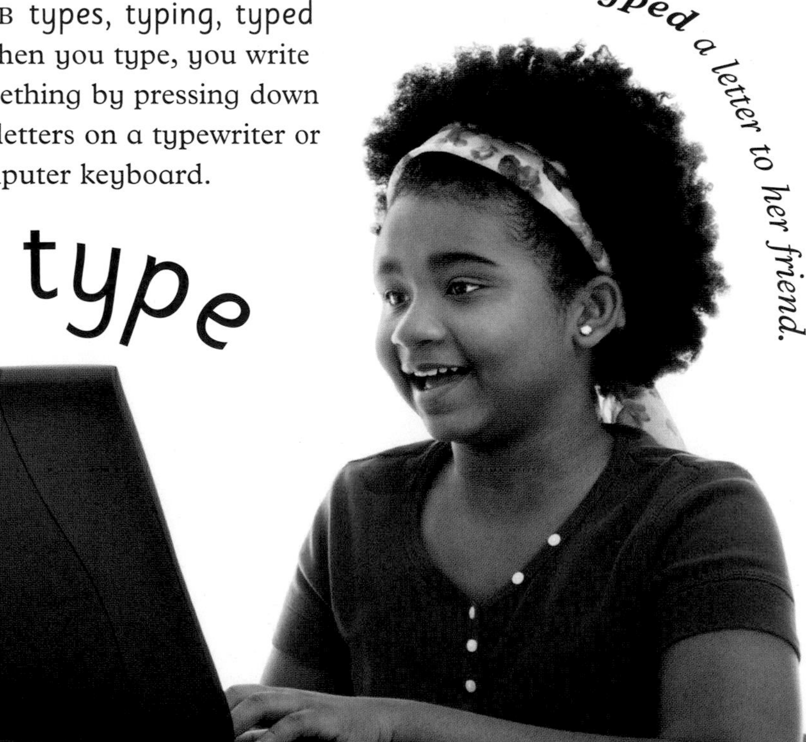

type

*She **typed** a letter to her friend.*

typhoon
NOUN typhoons
A typhoon is a violent tropical storm.

typical
ADJECTIVE
Something that is typical is like all other things of the same kind, and is not unusual or different. *They lived in a **typical** city street.*

tyre
NOUN tyres
A tyre is a circle of rubber with air inside it. A tyre goes around a wheel, on a car or bicycle.

U

upside

umop

ugly
ADJECTIVE uglier, ugliest
Something that is ugly is not nice to look at.

umbrella
NOUN umbrellas
An umbrella is a cover that you hold over your head to keep you dry when it rains.

umpire
NOUN umpires
An umpire is someone who makes sure that players follow the rules of a game or sport.

unable
ADJECTIVE
If you are unable to do something, you cannot do it. *I was so tired that I was **unable** to move.*
☛ **Opposite:** able

unbelievable
ADJECTIVE
If something is unbelievable, it is so strange that it is difficult to believe it is true.

uncle
NOUN uncles
Your uncle is the brother of one of your parents, the husband or partner of your aunt, or sometimes a friend of your parents.

uncomfortable
ADJECTIVE
1 If you are uncomfortable, your body hurts or does not feel relaxed. *I was **uncomfortable** on the hard chair.*
2 Something that is uncomfortable causes you pain or does not feel nice on your body. *These shoes are really **uncomfortable**.*
☛ **Opposite:** comfortable

My umbrella keeps me dry in the rain.
umbrella

unconscious
ADJECTIVE
If you are unconscious, you are in a very deep sleep and people cannot wake you up. People sometimes become unconscious after they have been hit on the head.
☛ **Opposite:** conscious

uncover
VERB uncovers, uncovering, uncovered
When you uncover something, you take off a thing that has been covering it, so that people can see it. *The archaeologists **uncovered** a Roman mosaic.*

undercover
ADJECTIVE
If you do something in an undercover way, you do it secretly, without telling people what you are doing. *The police were working on an **undercover** investigation.*

underground
ADJECTIVE
1 Something that is underground is below the ground. *A secret **underground** tunnel connects the two houses.*
NOUN
2 The underground is a railway that runs under the ground in some cities. *We can take the **underground** to get there.*

undergrowth
NOUN
The undergrowth in a forest is all the bushes and plants that grow under the trees. *It was hard to walk in the thick **undergrowth**.*

underline
VERB underlines, underlining, underlined
When you underline something, you draw a line under it. *Don't forget to **underline** the title of your story.*

underneath
NOUN
The underneath of something is the part that is not on top.

understand
VERB understands, understanding, understood
If you can understand something, you know what it means or how it works. *Did you **understand** the question?*

underwater
ADJECTIVE
Something that is underwater is under water in a sea or river. *We found an **underwater** cave.*

underwear
NOUN
You wear underwear next to your skin, under your other clothes.

undo
VERB undoes, undoing, undid, undone
When you undo something, you untie it. *It was difficult to **undo** the knot in the rope, but I eventually undid it.*

undress
VERB undresses, undressing, undressed
When you undress, you take your clothes off. *I **undressed** quickly and jumped into the lake – the water was very cold.*
☛ **Opposite:** dress

unemployed
ADJECTIVE
Someone who is unemployed does not have a job. *My uncle was **unemployed** for a year before starting his new job.*
☛ **Opposite:** employed

uneven
ADJECTIVE
Something that is uneven is not smooth or level. *I tried to ride my skateboard, but the road was too uneven.*
☛ **Opposite:** even

uneventful
ADJECTIVE
If something is uneventful, nothing exciting or interesting happens. *It was an **uneventful** day.*

unexpected
ADJECTIVE
If something is unexpected, you did not expect it to happen. *Everyone left the beach because of the **unexpected** rain.*
☛ **Opposite:** expected

unfair
ADJECTIVE
If something is unfair, some people are treated better than others or given more of something than others. *It's **unfair** that she's got three sweets and I only have two!*
☛ **Opposite:** fair

unfit
ADJECTIVE
If you are unfit, you are not very healthy and not used to doing exercise. *I'm too **unfit** to run a marathon!*
☛ **Opposite:** fit

underwater

*Fish blowing bubbles **underwater***

a b c d e f g h i j k l m n o p q r s t Uu v w x y z

a b c d e f g h i j k l m n o p q r s t **Uu** v w x y z

unfortunate
ADJECTIVE
If something is unfortunate, it happens because of bad luck. *It was **unfortunate** that it rained on sports day.*
☛ **Opposite:** fortunate
unfortunately (ADVERB)
If something happens unfortunately, it happens because of bad luck. ***Unfortunately,** I was ill so I couldn't go to the party.*

ungrateful
ADJECTIVE
If someone is ungrateful, they do not thank a person for helping them or giving them something.
☛ **Opposite:** grateful

unhappy
ADJECTIVE unhappier, unhappiest
If you are unhappy, you are sad about something. *She is **unhappy** because she failed the exam.*
☛ **Opposite:** happy

unhealthy
ADJECTIVE
1 If you are unhealthy, you are ill. *You need to get some rest – you look **unhealthy**.*
2 Things that are unhealthy are bad for you. *It's **unhealthy** to eat snacks all the time.*
☛ **Opposite:** healthy

unicorn
NOUN unicorns
A unicorn is a mythical animal that looks like a horse and has one long horn on its forehead.

unicycle
NOUN unicycles
A unicycle is a bicycle with only one wheel, which people use for performing acrobatic tricks.

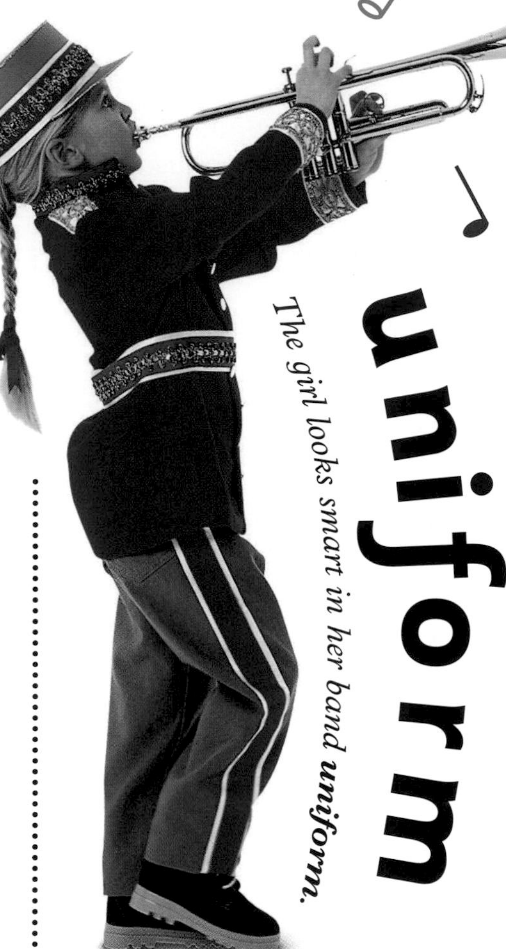

*The girl looks smart in her band **uniform.***

uniform
NOUN uniforms
A uniform is a set of clothes that people wear to show that they belong to a certain school or group, or that they do a certain job. *We don't wear a **uniform** at my school.*

unique
ADJECTIVE
If something is unique, it is the only one of its kind and there is no other that is exactly like it. *Every snowflake is **unique**.*

unit
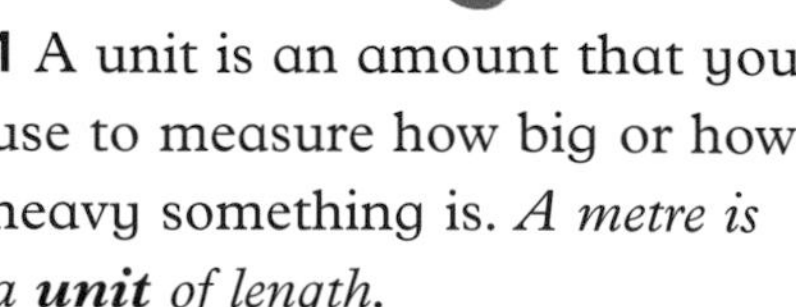
NOUN units
1 A unit is an amount that you use to measure how big or how heavy something is. *A metre is a **unit** of length.*
2 In maths, when you do sums you sometimes work in hundreds, tens, and units. A unit means one.

unite
VERB unites, uniting, united
If people unite, they join together to do something. *We all **united** to stop bullying in our school.*

Universe
NOUN
The Universe is all of space and everything in it. The Universe includes the Earth, the other planets, and all the stars.

university
NOUN universities
A university is a place where students can go to study after they have left school.

unkind
ADJECTIVE
Someone who is unkind is cruel to other people and does nasty things to them. *She's sometimes **unkind** to her little sister.*
☛ **Opposite:** kind

unknown
ADJECTIVE
If something is unknown, people do not know about it. *Motorways were **unknown** in the 19th century.*

unleaded
ADJECTIVE
Unleaded petrol does not have any lead in it, and so is not so bad for the environment.

unlikely
ADJECTIVE
If something is unlikely, it will probably not happen. *It is **unlikely** that they will win the competition twice in a row.*
☛ **Opposite:** likely

unload
VERB unloads, unloading, unloaded
When you unload things from a vehicle, you take them out.

unlock
VERB unlocks, unlocking, unlocked
When you unlock something, you open the lock on it. *He **unlocked** the door and went inside.*
☛ **Opposite:** lock

unlucky
ADJECTIVE unluckier, unluckiest
1 If you are unlucky, something bad happens to you. *How **unlucky** to break your arm!*
2 Something that is unlucky brings bad luck. *Some people think it's **unlucky** to walk under ladders.*
☛ **Opposite:** lucky

unnecessary
ADJECTIVE
If something is unnecessary, you do not need to do it. *It's **unnecessary** to wear your coat inside.*
☛ **Opposite:** necessary

unpack
VERB unpacks, unpacking, unpacked
When you unpack things, you take them out of a suitcase or box.
☛ **Opposite:** pack

unpleasant
ADJECTIVE
Something that is unpleasant is not nice. *There was an **unpleasant** smell coming from the cellar.*
☛ **Opposite:** pleasant

unsafe
ADJECTIVE
If something is unsafe, it is dangerous and not safe.
☛ **Opposite:** safe

unscrew
VERB unscrews, unscrewing, unscrewed
When you unscrew something, you loosen it by turning it or by undoing screws on it. *She **unscrewed** the numbers from the door.*

untidy
ADJECTIVE untidier, untidiest
If a place is untidy, it is in a mess. *Her room was always **untidy**.*
☛ **Opposite:** tidy

untie

untie
VERB unties, untying, untied
When you untie rope or string, you undo the knots in it. *She **untied** the rope and rowed away.*
☛ **Opposite:** tie

untrue
ADJECTIVE
If something is untrue, it is not true. *His story about finding buried treasure was **untrue**.*
☛ **Opposite:** true

unused
ADJECTIVE
Something that is unused has never been used.

*I **unlocked** my new padlock.*
unlock

a b c d e f g h i j k l m n o p q r s t **Uu** v w x y z

unusual
ADJECTIVE
Something that is unusual is not normal or ordinary. *It is **unusual** to have snow in July.*
☛ **Opposite:** usual

unwell
ADJECTIVE
If you are unwell, you are ill. *I was feeling a bit **unwell** so I went home.*
☛ **Opposite:** well

unwilling
ADJECTIVE
If you are unwilling to do something, you do not want to do it.
☛ **Opposite:** willing

unwise
ADJECTIVE
Something that is unwise is not a good or sensible thing to do. *It is **unwise** to swim out of your depth in the sea.*

unwrap
VERB unwraps, unwrapping, unwrapped
When you unwrap something, you take the wrapping or covering off it. *Can I **unwrap** my presents now?*
☛ **Opposite:** wrap

upbringing
NOUN
Your upbringing is the way that your parents bring you up.

update
VERB updates, updating, updated
To update something means to change it so that it has the most recent information. *We **update** our website every week.*

upgrade
VERB upgrades, upgrading, upgraded
If you upgrade something such as a computer, you improve it, often by adding new parts to it.

upload
VERB uploads, uploading, uploaded
When you upload information or photos, you copy them from your computer or phone onto the internet.

upper case
ADJECTIVE
Upper case letters are capital letters.

upright
ADVERB
Something that is upright is sitting or standing up straight. *The dog stood **upright** on its hind legs.*

uproar
NOUN
If there is an uproar, there is a lot of noise and confusion.

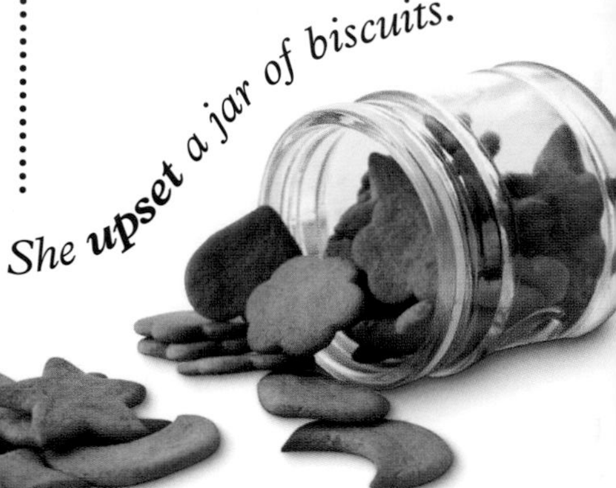

*She **upset** a jar of biscuits.*

upset
VERB upsets, upsetting, upset
1 To upset someone means to make them feel unhappy. *The other children **upset** her by not letting her play with them.*
2 If you upset something, you knock it over. *The cat **upset** the vase of flowers.*
ADJECTIVE
3 If you are upset, you feel unhappy and cry. *I was really **upset** when my pet hamster died.*

upside down
ADVERB
When something is upside down, it is the wrong way up and the top part of it is underneath. *He hung the picture **upside down**.*

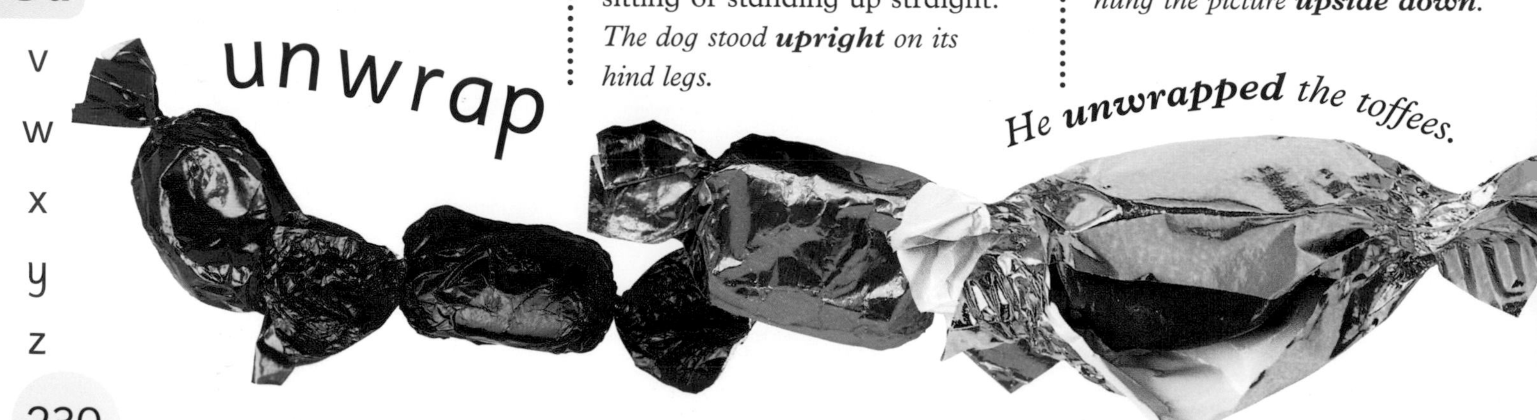

unwrap

*He **unwrapped** the toffees.*

upstairs
ADVERB
If you go upstairs, you go to a higher floor in a building. *She went **upstairs** to her bedroom.*

upward
ADVERB
If you go upward, you go toward a higher position. *She let go of the balloons and they drifted **upward**.*

urge
NOUN urges
1 If you have an urge to do something, you want to do it or need to do it. *She had a sudden **urge** to giggle.*
VERB urges, urging, urged
2 If you urge someone to do something, you try to persuade them to do it. *He **urged** them to be careful when playing by the river.*

urgent
ADJECTIVE
If something is urgent, you need to do it immediately. *I need to talk to you – it's **urgent**.*
urgently (ADVERB)
If something needs to happen urgently, it needs to happen immediately. *We need to call an ambulance **urgently**.*

use
NOUN uses
1 If something has a use, you can do something with it. *This penknife has many **uses**.*
2 If something is in use, someone is using it. *Steam trains are still in **use** in some parts of the country.*

use
VERB uses, using, used
When you use something, you do a job with it. *May I **use** your pen, please?*

useful
ADJECTIVE
If something is useful, it can help you to do something. *Computers are very **useful** in the classroom.*
☛ **Opposite:** useless

useless
ADJECTIVE
If something is useless, you cannot use it and it does not help you at all. *My old phone is broken, so it's **useless**.*
☛ **Opposite:** useful

user-friendly
ADJECTIVE
Something that is user-friendly is easy to use. *My smartphone is very **user-friendly**.*

usual
ADJECTIVE
Usual means normal. *I left school at the **usual** time.*
☛ **Opposite:** unusual
usually (ADVERB)
If something usually happens, it normally happens. *I **usually** go swimming on Saturdays.*

utensil
NOUN utensils
A utensil is a tool that you use for a certain job, especially for preparing and cooking food.

Utensils are used to prepare and cook food.
utensil

vaccination
NOUN vaccinations
When you have a vaccination, a doctor gives you an injection that stops you from getting a disease. The substance the doctor injects is called a **vaccine**.

vacuum cleaner
NOUN vacuum cleaners
A vacuum cleaner is a machine that cleans floors by sucking up dirt.

vague
ADJECTIVE
Something that is vague is not clear or definite. *We only had a **vague** plan.*

vain
ADJECTIVE vainer, vainest
1 People who are vain think that they are very clever or beautiful.
2 A vain attempt to do something does not work. *They made a **vain** attempt to put out the fire.*

valley
NOUN valleys
A valley is an area of low land between hills, often with a river or stream flowing through it.

valuable
ADJECTIVE
1 Something that is valuable is worth a lot of money. *Do you think these old paintings might be **valuable**?*
2 Something that is valuable helps you in some way. *He gave us some **valuable** advice.*

value
NOUN values
The value of something is the amount of money it is worth.

van
NOUN vans
A van is a small lorry that people use for carrying goods.

vandal
NOUN vandals
A vandal is someone who deliberately breaks or damages things. *The shop window had been smashed by **vandals**.*
vandalism (NOUN)
Vandalism is the crime of deliberately breaking or damaging things.

vanilla
NOUN
Vanilla is a sweet flavouring that you add to food. It is made from the pods of a tropical plant.

vanish
VERB vanishes, vanishing, vanished
To vanish means to disappear suddenly. *The magician waved his wand and the rabbit **vanished**.*

variety
NOUN varieties
A variety of things is a lot of different kinds. *They sell a wide **variety** of games.*

various
ADJECTIVE
Various means of several different kinds. ***Various** people have visited our school this year.*

vase
NOUN vases
A vase is a jar that you put flowers in.

vast
ADJECTIVE
Something that is vast is very big. *The king and queen lived in a **vast** palace.*

vegan
NOUN vegans
A vegan is someone who does not eat meat, fish, eggs, or any dairy products such as butter and cheese.

vegetable
NOUN vegetables
A vegetable is a plant that people grow for food.

vegetarian
NOUN vegetarians
A vegetarian is someone who does not eat meat or fish.

vehicle
NOUN vehicles
A vehicle is something that people travel in or use to transport goods.

veil
NOUN veils
A veil is a piece of thin cloth that women sometimes wear over their heads or faces. *The bride wore a **veil** during the wedding.*

verb
NOUN verbs
A verb is an action word such as "run", "speak", or "jump" that tells you what someone or something does.

verse
NOUN verses
1 A verse is one part of a poem or song. *We'll sing the first **verse** again.*
2 Verse is a general name for poetry. *He wrote a book of **verse**.*

version
NOUN version
A version of something is one form of it. *They're going to bring out a new **version** of the game next year.*

very
ADVERB
Very means extremely. *My dad was **very** angry when I broke the kitchen window.*

vest
NOUN vests
A vest is a piece of underwear that you wear on the top part of your body.

vet
NOUN vets
A vet, or veterinary surgeon, is a person who is trained to treat sick animals.

vicious
ADJECTIVE
1 A vicious animal is fierce and might attack people.
2 Someone who is vicious is cruel or unkind.
viciously (ADVERB)
If a person or animal does something viciously, they do it in a fierce way. *The wolf growled **viciously**.*

victim
NOUN victims
A victim is someone who has suffered in a crime or unpleasant event.

victory
NOUN victories
A victory is when you win a competition or battle. *The racing driver was thrilled with his **victory**.*

video
NOUN videos
A video is a recording of sound and pictures.

view
NOUN views
The view from a place is everything that you can see from there. *My bedroom has an amazing **view** of the city.*

village
NOUN villages
A village is a place in the country where people live. Villages are usually smaller than towns.

violent
ADJECTIVE
1 Something that is violent breaks or damages things. *The **violent** storm threw cars across the street.*
2 A violent person often hits or attacks other people.
violence (NOUN)
Violence is violent behaviour. *We don't accept any **violence** in this school.*

Vehicle

a b c d e f g h i j k l m n o p q r s t u Vv w x y z

violin
NOUN violins
A violin is a musical instrument that you hold under your chin and play by pulling a bow across the strings.

virtual
ADJECTIVE
A virtual place is one that you see on a computer screen and that feels real, because you can feel as if you are moving around in it. *You can visit the **virtual** museum online.*

virus
NOUN viruses
1 A virus is a type of germ that can make you ill.
2 A virus is a set of instructions that someone puts into your computer to make it go wrong.

visible
ADJECTIVE
If something is visible, you can see it. *The mountain was **visible** for miles.*
☛ **Opposite:** invisible

visit
VERB visits, visiting, visited
When you visit someone, you go to see them. When you visit a place, you go there. *I went to **visit** my sister in the hospital.*
visitor (NOUN)
A visitor is someone who visits a person or place.

vital
ADJECTIVE
Something that is vital is very important. *It's **vital** that we get him to a hospital quickly.*

vitamin
NOUN vitamins
Vitamins are chemicals that exist in food and help to keep us healthy. *Oranges contain a lot of **vitamin** C.*

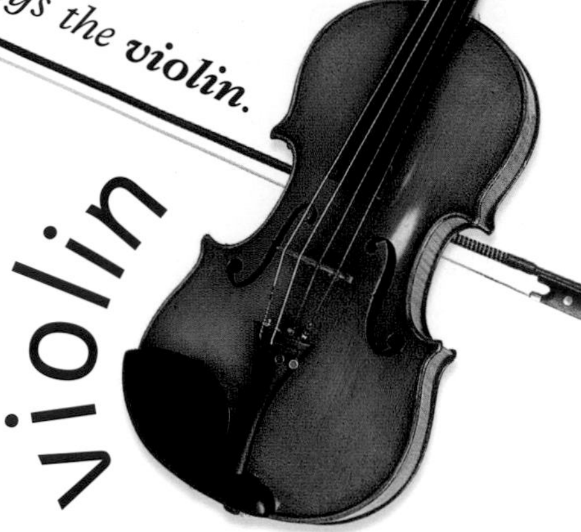

*She plays the **violin**.*

violin

vlog
NOUN vlogs
A vlog is a video diary that someone makes and posts online regularly so that other people can watch it.
vlogger (NOUN)
A vlogger is someone who makes vlogs and posts them online.

vocabulary
NOUN
Your vocabulary is all the words that you use when you speak and write.

voice
NOUN voices
Your voice is the sound that comes out of your mouth when you speak or sing. *Can you sing in a high **voice**?*

voicemail
NOUN voicemails
A voicemail is a spoken message that you can leave for someone on their phone.

volcano
NOUN volcanoes
A volcano is a mountain that has been created by liquid rock from inside the Earth. Hot, liquid rock may burst or flow out of volcanoes that are active.

volleyball
NOUN
Volleyball is a game in which people hit a ball over a high net using their hands.

volume
NOUN volumes
1 A volume is a book that is one of a series.
2 The volume of a sound is how loud it is. *Turn up the **volume**!*

voluntary
ADJECTIVE
If something is voluntary, you can choose to do it if you want, but you don't have to do it.

volunteer
VERB volunteers, volunteering, volunteered
If you volunteer to do something, you offer to do it.

vote
VERB votes, voting, voted
When you vote, you choose one person or thing from a list.

vowel
NOUN vowels
The five vowels in English are the letters **a**, **e**, **i**, **o**, and **u**.

voyage
NOUN voyages
A voyage is a long journey by sea or in space.

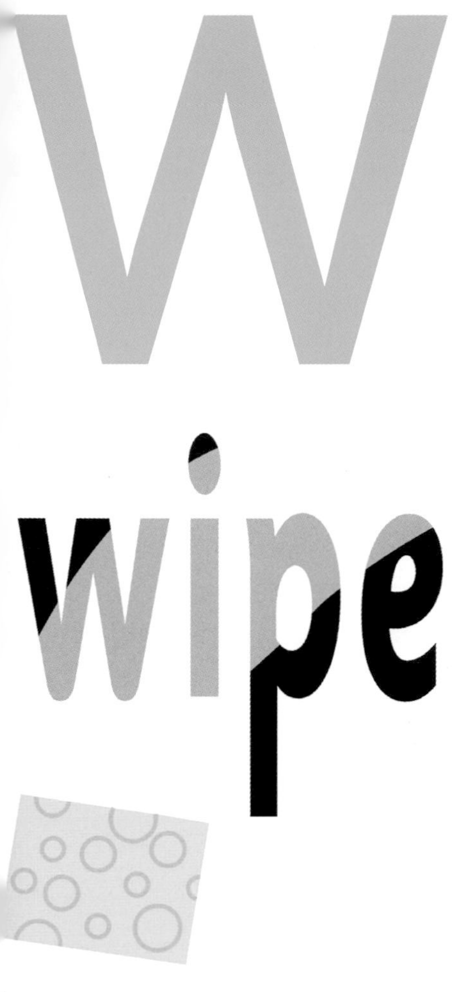

wade
VERB wades, wading, waded
When you wade through water, you walk through it. *We **waded** across the stream.*

A flamingo **wades** across the lake.

wag
VERB wags, wagging, wagged
When an animal wags its tail, it moves it from side to side to show that it is happy.

waist
NOUN waists
Your waist is the part of your body around your middle.
☛ **Be careful with spelling:**
waist *You wear a belt around your **waist**.*
waste *Don't **waste** your money on things you don't need.*

wait
VERB waits, waiting, waited
When you wait, you stay in a place and do not do anything until someone arrives or something happens.
☛ **Be careful with spelling:**
wait *I'll **wait** for you outside.*
weight *Stand on the scales to find out your **weight**.*

waiter
NOUN waiters
A waiter is someone who serves food to people in a restaurant. A woman who does this is sometimes called a **waitress**.

wake
VERB wakes, waking, woke, woken
When you wake up, you stop sleeping.

walk
NOUN walks
1 If you go for a walk, you go somewhere on foot for pleasure.
VERB walks, walking, walked
2 When you walk, you move along on foot.

wall
NOUN walls
A wall is a structure built from stone or brick. Walls are used to hold up the roof of a building or to separate one piece of land from another. *There was a high **wall** around the garden.*

wallet
NOUN wallets
A wallet is a small case that you carry money in. *Let me just find my **wallet**, and then we'll go shopping.*

wallet

wand
NOUN wands
A wand is a special stick that people use when they are performing magic tricks. In fairy tales, magic wands are used for casting magic spells.

wander
NOUN wanders, wandering, wandered
When you wander, you walk around without going in any particular direction. *We spent the afternoon **wandering** around the shops.*

want
VERB wants, wanting, wanted
If you want something, you would like to have it or do it. *I **want** a puppy for my birthday.*

a b c d e f g h i j k l m n o p q r s t u v Ww x y z

war
NOUN wars
When there is a war, people fight against each other. Often the two sides are from different countries.

wardrobe
NOUN wardrobes
A wardrobe is a cupboard for keeping clothes in.

warm
ADJECTIVE warmer, warmest
1 If something is warm, it is quite hot but not very hot. *The hot water bottle felt nice and **warm**.*
2 If the weather is warm, the Sun is shining and it feels hot.

warn
VERB warns, warning, warned
If you warn someone about a danger or problem, you tell them about it before it happens. *The man **warned** us that it was dangerous to walk on the thin ice.*
warning (NOUN)
If you give someone a warning, you warn them about a danger or problem. *We heard a severe weather **warning** on the news.*

wash
VERB washes, washing, washed
1 When you wash something, you clean it with water and soap. *Who will help me **wash** the dishes?*
2 When you wash, you clean your body with water and soap. *Did you remember to **wash** this morning?*

washing machine
NOUN washing machines
A washing machine is a machine that you use for washing clothes.

wasp
NOUN wasps
A wasp is an insect with a black and yellow striped body. Wasps can sting you.

waste
VERB wastes, wasting, wasted
If you waste something, you use more of it than you need to, or you do not use it in a sensible way.
☛ **Be careful with spelling:**
waste *Don't **waste** your money on things you don't need.*
waist *You wear a belt around your **waist**.*

watch
NOUN watches
1 A watch is a small clock that you wear on your wrist.
VERB watches, watching, watched
2 When you watch something, you look at it for a long time. *We spent the afternoon **watching** an old film.*

water
NOUN
1 Water is a clear liquid that falls as rain and forms streams, rivers, lakes, and oceans.
VERB waters, watering, watered
2 When you water plants, you pour water onto them so that they can live. *My pot plant died because I forgot to **water** it.*

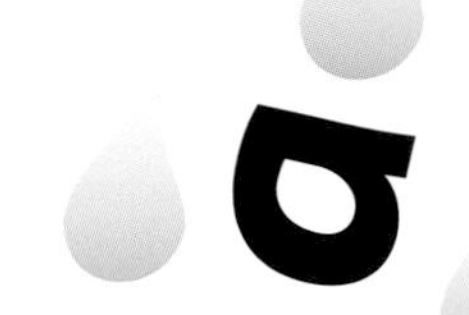

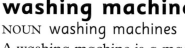

Will you **water** my plants while I'm away?

waterfall
NOUN waterfalls
A waterfall is a place where a river falls over a steep cliff.

waterproof
ADJECTIVE
If something is waterproof, water cannot get through it or into it. *Remember to bring a **waterproof** coat with you in case it rains.*

water-ski
VERB water-skis, water-skiing, water-skied
When you water-ski, you are pulled along behind a boat while you stand on two skis. *Have you ever tried **water-skiing**?*

wave
NOUN waves
1 When there are waves in water, the surface moves up and down or from side to side. *The big **waves** rocked our little boat from side to side.*
VERB waves, waving, waved
2 When you wave to someone, you move your hand or arm to tell that person something. *She **waved** goodbye as the ship sailed away.*
3 When something waves, it moves backward and forward. *The branches of the tree **waved** in the strong wind.*

wax
NOUN
Wax is the substance that candles are made of.

way
NOUN ways
1 The way to a place is the direction you go in to get there. *The sign showed the **way** to the village.*
2 The way you do something is how you do it. *What is the best **way** to find information online?*
☛ **Be careful with spelling:**
way *Can you tell me the **way** to the station?*
weigh *How much do you **weigh**?*

weak
ADJECTIVE weaker, weakest
Someone who is weak is not very strong.
☛ **Be careful with spelling:**
weak *He was too **weak** to lift the box.*
week *My birthday is next **week**.*

wealthy
ADJECTIVE wealthier, wealthiest
Someone who is wealthy is very rich.

weapon
NOUN weapons
A weapon is a gun, knife, or anything else that you can use to hurt someone.

wear
VERB wears, wearing, wore, worn
When you wear clothes, you have them on your body.

weather
NOUN
The weather is what is happening in the sky and air around us, for example, if it is cold or hot, dry or raining.

web
NOUN webs
1 A web is a fine net of sticky threads that a spider makes to catch flies. *Spiders' **webs** covered the entrance to the cave.*
2 The web is a system for storing information on computers all over the world, which people can look at by using the internet. Web is short for **World Wide Web**.
webcam (NOUN)
A webcam is a camera that can film a person or scene and send it to someone else using the internet.
website (NOUN)
A website is a place on the internet where you can go to find information about something.

Weather

Come rain or shine, there are many words to describe the weather.

wedding

NOUN weddings

When there is a wedding, two people get married.

week

NOUN weeks

A week is a period of seven days.

☛ **Be careful with spelling:**

week *My birthday is next **week**.*

weak *He was too **weak** to lift the box.*

weekend

NOUN weekends

The weekend is Saturday and Sunday, which are the days when many people do not go to school or work.

weep

VERB weeps, weeping, wept

When you weep, you cry.

weigh

VERB weighs, weighing, weighed

1 When you weigh something, you measure how heavy it is.

2 The amount that something weighs is how heavy it is.

☛ **Be careful with spelling:**

weigh *How much do you **weigh**?*

way *Can you tell me the **way** to the station?*

weight

NOUN weights

1 The weight of something is how heavy it is.

2 Weights are pieces of metal that people use for measuring how heavy things are.

☛ **Be careful with spelling:**

weight *Stand on the scales to find out your **weight**.*

wait *I'll **wait** for you outside.*

weird

ADJECTIVE weirder, weirdest

Something that is weird is very strange. *People dressed in **weird** and wonderful costumes at the Halloween party.*

welcome

VERB welcomes, welcoming, welcomed

If you welcome someone, you greet them in a friendly way when they arrive. *They **welcomed** us warmly into their home when we visited them.*

well

NOUN wells

1 A well is a deep hole in the ground from which people get water or oil. *When I threw the pebble into the old **well**, it took several seconds for it to hit the water far below.*

ADJECTIVE

2 If you are well, you are healthy and not ill. *Are you **well** today?*

☛ **Opposite:** unwell

ADVERB

3 If you do something well, you do it in a good or suitable way. *You have all behaved very **well** today.*

went

☛ See **go**.

wept

☛ See **weep**.

west

NOUN

West is one of the four main compass directions. West is the direction in which the Sun sets.

wet

ADJECTIVE wetter, wettest

1 If something is wet, it is covered with water or soaked in water.

2 If the weather is wet, it is raining. *What a horrible **wet** day!*

whale

NOUN whales

A whale is a very large sea animal. Whales are mammals and breathe through a hole in the top of their head.

wheat

NOUN

Wheat is a crop that is grown on farms and ground up to make flour.

wheel

NOUN wheels

Wheels are the round parts underneath cars and bicycles that they move along on.

wheelchair

NOUN wheelchairs

A wheelchair is a chair with wheels. People use wheelchairs to move from place to place if they have difficulty in walking.

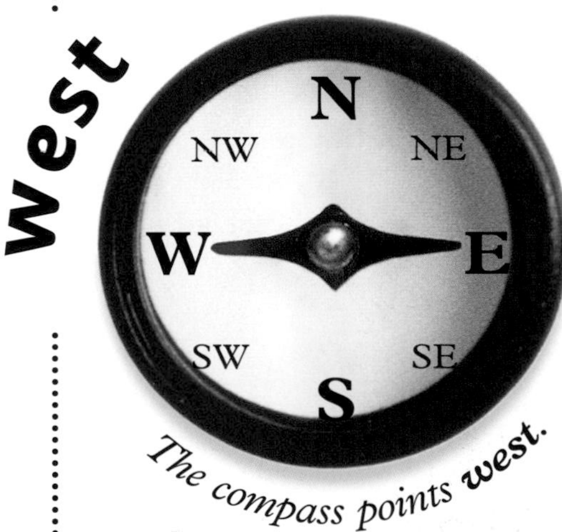

west

The compass points west.

a b c d e f g h i j k l m n o p q r s t u v Ww x y z

whine
VERB whines, whining, whined
1 If an animal whines, it makes a high sound because it is sad.
2 If you whine, you complain about something.

whisker
NOUN whiskers
Whiskers are the stiff hairs that grow near the mouth of some animals.

whisper
VERB whispers, whispering, whispered
When you whisper, you speak in a very quiet voice. *She **whispered** the secret password into his ear.*

whistle
NOUN whistles
1 You blow into a whistle to make a high sound.
VERB whistles, whistling, whistled
2 When you whistle, you press your lips together and blow to make a high, musical sound.

*The referee blew the **whistle** to start the game.*

white
ADJECTIVE
Something that is white is the colour of snow.

whiteboard
NOUN whiteboards
A whiteboard is a large white board that is used in a classroom. You write on a whiteboard with special pens.

whizz
VERB whizzes, whizzing, whizzed
If something whizzes, it moves very fast. *A motorbike **whizzed** past me.*

whole
ADJECTIVE
Whole means complete. *She told us the whole story.*
☛ **Be careful with spelling:**
whole *He ate a **whole** box of chocolates!*
hole *There's a **hole** in my shoe.*

wholemeal
ADJECTIVE
Wholemeal bread is bread that is made from whole grains of wheat.

wicked
ADJECTIVE
Someone who is wicked does very bad or unkind things.

wide
ADJECTIVE wider, widest
Something that is wide is a long way from one side to the other. *The stream was too **wide** to jump across.*
width (NOUN)
The width of something is how wide it is. *We measured the **width** of the path.*

wife
NOUN wives
A man's wife is the woman he is married to.

Wi-Fi
NOUN
Wi-Fi is a system that you can use to access the internet on your computer or phone without using wires to plug it in.

wild
ADJECTIVE wilder, wildest
1 A wild flower or animal lives in its natural environment and is not controlled or looked after by people.
2 If you behave in a wild way, you run around and make a lot of noise. *Calm down – don't go **wild**!*

wildlife
NOUN
Wildlife is wild animals that live in their natural environment. *It's important to protect **wildlife**.*

will
NOUN wills
1 If you have the will to do something, you have the determination to do it. *Have you got the **will** to win this game?*
VERB
2 If you will do something, you are going to do it. *I **will** phone you this afternoon.*

willing
ADJECTIVE
If you are willing to do something, you want to do it or are happy to do it. *Are you **willing** to help us make some cakes?*

win
VERB wins, winning, won
If you win a game or competition, you come first. *We were delighted that we **won** the game.*
winner (NOUN)
The winner is the person who wins a game or competition.

wind
NOUN winds
Wind is air that blows over the Earth. *The **wind** blew his umbrella inside-out.*
windy (ADJECTIVE)
If it is windy, there is a lot of wind.

wind
VERB winds, winding, wound
1 When you wind something, you turn it round and round.
2 A path or road that winds has a lot of bends and turns.

windmill
NOUN windmills
A windmill is a building with large sails, which uses wind power to turn a machine that grinds grain or pumps water.

window
NOUN windows
A window is a piece of glass in the side of a building that lets light and air into the building.

windscreen
NOUN windscreen
The windscreen on a car is the big window at the front that the driver looks out of.

windsurfing
NOUN
Windsurfing is a sport in which you sail on water standing on a narrow board with a sail attached.

wind turbine
NOUN wind turbines
A wind turbine is a machine that uses energy from the wind to make electricity.

wing
NOUN wings
1 The wings on a bird, bat, or insect are the parts that it uses for flying.
2 The wings on an aeroplane are the parts that stick out at the sides.

***Wind** power turns... ... the **windmill's** sails.*

winter
NOUN
Winter is one of the four seasons. Winter follows autumn and comes before spring. It is the coldest time of the year. *It was the coldest **winter** I'd ever known.*

wipe
VERB wipes, wiping, wiped
When you wipe something, you clean it or dry it by rubbing it with a cloth. *I **wiped** my hands on the towel.*

wire
NOUN wires
A wire is a long, thin metal thread. Wires can be used to carry electrical power.

wireless
ADJECTIVE
A wireless machine or device can connect to another machine or to the internet without using wires.

wise
ADJECTIVE wiser, wisest
Someone who is wise knows and understands a lot of things. *My grandmother is the **wisest** person that I know.*

a b c d e f g h i j k l m n o p q r s t u v Ww x y z

wish
NOUN wishes
1 A wish is something that you would like very much. *The fairy granted her **wishes**.*
VERB wishes, wishing, wished
2 If you wish for something, you would like it very much. *I **wish** I could dance better!*

witch
NOUN witches
A witch is a woman in stories who uses magic powers.

wizard
NOUN wizards
A wizard is a man in stories who uses magic powers.

wobble
VERB wobbles, wobbling, wobbled
To wobble means to move from side to side and nearly fall over.

woke
☛ See **wake**.

wolf
NOUN wolves
A wolf is a wild animal that looks like a large dog and lives in cold countries. Wolves live in packs and hunt other animals for food.

woman
NOUN women
A woman is an adult female person. *My mother is a wonderful **woman**.*

won
☛ See **win**.

wonder
NOUN
1 Wonder is the feeling you have when you look at something strange and exciting.
VERB wonders, wondering, wondered
2 If you wonder about something, you have questions in your mind about it. *I **wonder** how she got here?*

wonderful
ADJECTIVE
Something that is wonderful is very good or amazing. *We had a **wonderful** time on holiday.*

wood
NOUN woods
1 Wood is the hard material that we get from trees. Wood is used for making furniture and is also burnt as fuel.
2 A wood is a group of trees growing together.
wooden (ADJECTIVE)
Something that is wooden is made of wood.

wool
NOUN
Wool is the soft material that we get from sheep. Wool is used for knitting clothes, and can also be made into carpets. *The lamb had very soft **wool**.*
woollen (ADJECTIVE)
Something that is woollen is made of wool. *My favourite item of clothing is a **woollen** jumper that my granny knitted.*

word
NOUN words
A word is a group of letters and sounds that has a meaning. *I learned some new **words** at school today.*

wore
☛ See **wear**.

wooden

*The **wooden** dolls get smaller and smaller and smaller and smaller.*

She **wrapped** the presents in bright paper.

work
NOUN
1 Work is a job or task that you must do. *The teacher gave us loads of **work** to do!*
VERB works, working, worked
2 When you work, you do a job.
3 When a machine is working, there is nothing wrong with it and you can use it.

world
NOUN
The world is the planet Earth and all the people and things on it.

worm
NOUN worms
A worm is a small, thin animal that lives in the ground and has a soft body and no legs.

worn
☛ See **wear**.

worry
VERB worries, worrying, worried
If you worry about something, you feel nervous about it or slightly afraid of it.
worried (ADJECTIVE)
If you are worried about something, you feel nervous about it or slightly afraid of it. *I'm **worried** about my exams.*

worse
A person or thing that is worse than others is less good. *Yesterday's weather was bad, but today it is **worse**.*

worst
The worst person or thing is the one that is least good or most unpleasant. *This is the **worst** storm I've ever seen.*

worth
ADJECTIVE
The amount that something is worth is how much money people will pay to buy it. *The jewels were **worth** a lot of money.*

would
VERB
If you would do something, you want to do it but you cannot. *I **would** go to the cinema with you if I had enough money.*

wound
NOUN wounds
A wound is a cut on your body.

wrap
VERB wraps, wrapping, wrapped
When you wrap something, you fold paper around it. *I'll help you **wrap** the presents.*

wreck
NOUN wrecks
1 A wreck is a ship that has sunk to the bottom of the sea.
VERB wrecks, wrecking, wrecked
2 To wreck something means to damage it very badly.

wriggle
VERB wriggles, wriggling, wriggled
When you wriggle, you twist and turn from side to side.

wrinkle
NOUN wrinkles
Wrinkles are small lines or creases on your clothes or on someone's skin.

wrist
NOUN wrists
Your wrist is the part of your body where your hand joins your arm.

write
VERB writes, writing, wrote, written
When you write, you put letters and words on paper.
☛ **Be careful with spelling:**
write *Which hand do you **write** with?*
right *That's the **right** answer.*

wrong
ADJECTIVE
1 Something that is wrong is not correct. *That is the **wrong** answer.*
2 Something that is wrong is bad. *It's **wrong** to steal.*

wrote
☛ See **write**.

a b c d e f g h i j k l m n o p q r s t u v Ww x y z

X-ray
NOUN X-rays
An X-ray is a special photograph that shows your bones and the inside of your body. *The doctor looked closely at the chest **X-ray**.*

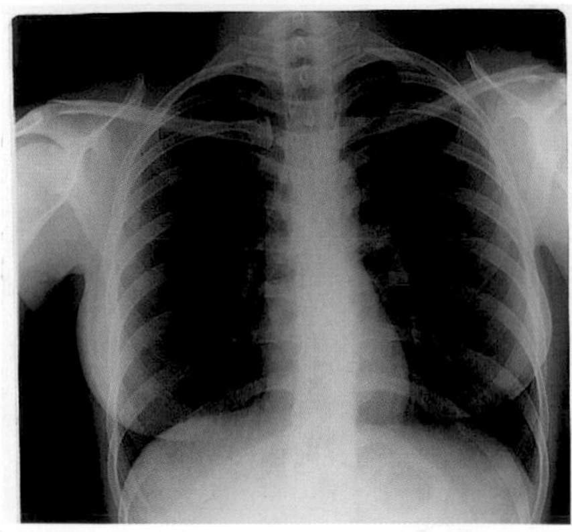

X-ray

xylophone
NOUN xylophones
A xylophone is a musical instrument that has wooden bars on a frame. When you hit each bar, it makes a different musical note.

yacht
NOUN yachts
A yacht is a boat with a sail that people use for racing or pleasure.

yank
VERB yanks, yanking, yanked
When you yank something, you pull it roughly. *He **yanked** the book out of my hand.*

yap
VERB yaps, yapping, yapped
When a dog yaps, it barks with a high sound.

yard
NOUN yards
A yard is an area outside a building, with a fence or wall around it. *They are playing in the **yard**.*

yawn
VERB yawns, yawning, yawned
When you yawn, you open your mouth and breathe in deeply because you are tired or bored.

year
NOUN years
A year is a period of 12 months.

yell
VERB yells, yelling, yelled
When you yell, you shout loudly. *He **yelled** at the children to go away.*

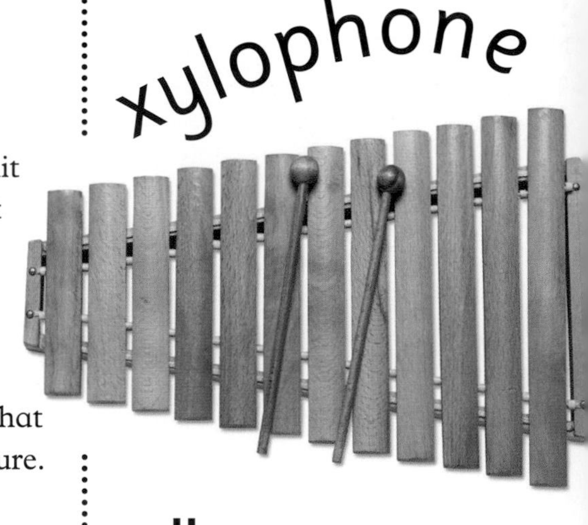

yellow
ADJECTIVE
Something that is yellow is the colour of a lemon.

yesterday
ADVERB
Yesterday is the day before today. *I went to the zoo **yesterday**.*

yoga
NOUN
When you do yoga, you do special exercises to stretch your body and make you feel relaxed.

yoghurt
NOUN yoghurts
Yoghurt is a food that is made from milk and is often flavoured with fruit. It is sometimes spelled **yogurt**.

yolk
NOUN yolks
The yolk of an egg is the yellow part.

young
ADJECTIVE younger, youngest
Someone who is young is not very old. *The grandmother held the **young** child in her arms.*

youth
NOUN youths
1 Your youth is the time when you are young. *In his **youth**, my uncle was a very good rugby player.*
2 A youth is a young man.

yo-yo
NOUN yo-yos
A yo-yo is a toy that spins up and down on a string.

zap
VERB zaps, zapping, zapped
If you zap someone in a game, you shoot them.

zebra
NOUN zebras
A zebra is an African animal that looks like a horse and has black and white stripes on its body.

zebra crossing
NOUN zebra crossings
A zebra crossing is a place where you can cross the road safely because cars have to stop for you. Black and white stripes are marked on the road to show where a zebra crossing is.

zero
NOUN zeros
Zero is the number 0.

zigzag
NOUN zigzags
A zigzag is a line that goes from side to side, making sharp points as it changes direction. *I chose some cushions with a bright pattern of **zigzags** on them.*

zip
NOUN zips
You use a zip for fastening clothes or bags. It has two rows of teeth, which are pressed together when you close the zip.

zip

*The top has a **zip** at the collar.*

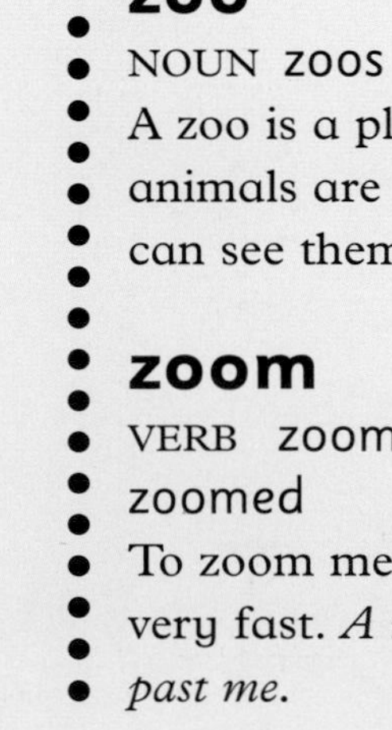

zebra

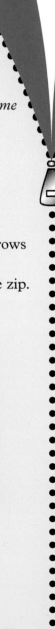

zodiac
NOUN
The zodiac is the 12 sections into which the sky is divided. Each part is represented by a different symbol.

zombie
NOUN zombies
In stories and films, a zombie is a dead person who has been brought back to life.

zoo
NOUN zoos
A zoo is a place where wild animals are kept so that people can see them and study them.

zoom
VERB zooms, zooming, zoomed
To zoom means to move very fast. *A motorbike **zoomed** past me.*

a b c d e f g h i j k q r s t u v w x y z

Spelling tips

If you can't find the word you are looking up, you may have spelt it incorrectly. Here are some spelling tips.

Split long words

To make it easier to look up or spell long words, split them into **syllables**. A syllable is one short sound in a word. Then work out the order of the letters in each syllable.

For example:
Elephant has three syllables. It seems easier to put the first syllable, "el", into alphabetical order than "elephant".

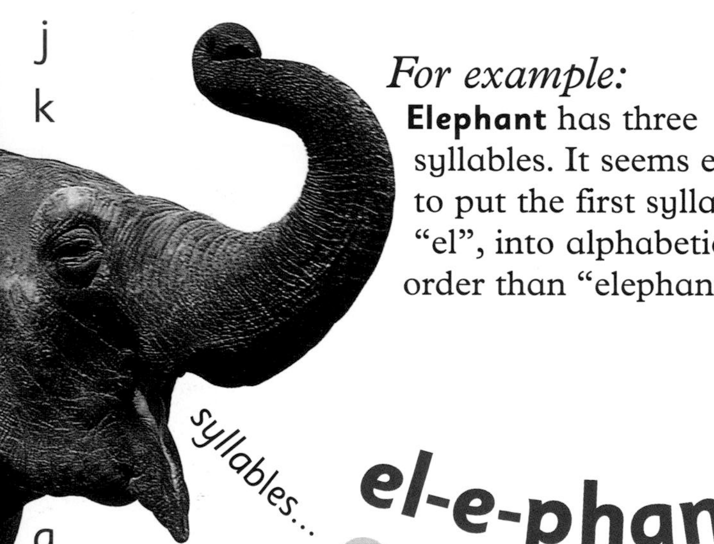

syllables...

el-e-phant

1 2 3

How many syllables do these words have? *(Answers on page 256)*

1. happy
2. sad
3. expensive
4. impossible
5. enthusiastically

Confusing spellings

Not all words are spelt the way they sound. This can make it hard to look things up. Read these common problem words to help you spell difficult words.

Ph pronounced like an f

al**ph**abet, tele**ph**one, **ph**araoh, ele**ph**ant, **ph**otogra**ph**

Silent letters

clim**b**, com**b**, dou**b**t, g**h**ost, **g**naw, **h**our, **k**nee, **k**nife, s**w**ord, **w**hole, **w**rap, **w**reck, **w**riggle, **w**rite

Do you know what the missing silent letters are in these words? *(Answers on page 256)*

6. supercalifragilisticexpialidocious!

Homophones

Some words sound alike but are spelt differently. These words are called **homophones**.

bare – We walked on the beach in **bare** feet.
bear – Are there **bears** in this forest?

brake – We had to **brake** when we saw a dog on the road.
break – Be careful you don't **break** the window.

meat – Some people don't eat **meat**.
meet – Let's **meet** in the park.

peace – Go away and leave me in **peace**!
piece – Would you like a **piece** of cake?

sail – Can you **sail** a boat?
sale – Are these toys for **sale**?

Can you work out what the two words are for each pair of pictures? The words sound the same but are spelt differently. The first letter of each answer is shown as a clue. *(Answers on page 256)*

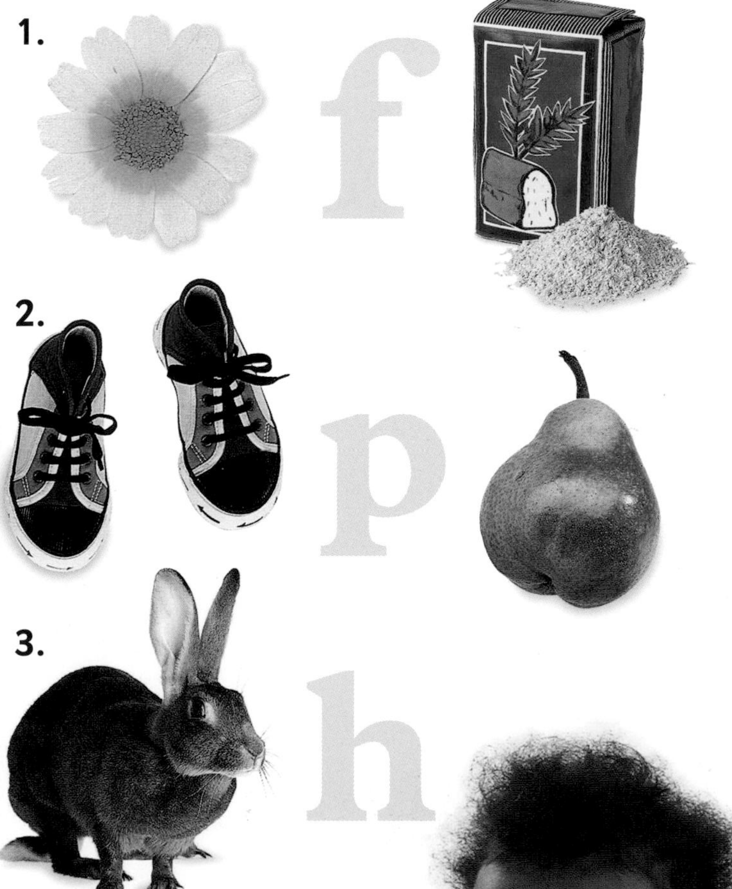

Homographs

Some words are spelt the same but sound different. These words are called **homographs**.

The two words that go with these pairs of pictures are spelt the same, but sound different. Can you work out what the words are? The first letter of each answer is given as a clue. *(Answers on page 256)*

"I before E, except after C"
This is a general spelling rule (there are a few exceptions). Here are some examples:
i before e... s**ie**ve, p**ie**ce, th**ie**f, rel**ie**f, bel**ie**ve, br**ie**f
... **except after c...** c**ei**ling, rec**ei**ve

a b c d e f g h i j k l m n o p q r x y z

Writing

Sentences

A sentence is a group of words that make sense together. A sentence starts with a capital letter and ends with a full stop. All sentences contain a verb.

Some sentences are quite short.

This is an elephant.
Elephants love water.

We can make sentences longer by joining on more clauses using **conjunctions**.

Elephants love water ***and*** *they can swim quite well.*

Punctuation

. You put a full stop at the end of a sentence.
The cat sat on the mat.

? You put a question mark at the end of a question.
Where do you live?

! You put an exclamation mark at the end of a command or an exclamation.
Come here!
What beautiful flowers!

, You put a comma to separate parts of a sentence, or divide up a list of things.
He's only five, but he can swim really well.
I bought apples, oranges, and pears.

' An apostrophe is used to shorten two words into one, or to show who something belongs to.
I don't know.
That's my dad's pen.

: You can use a colon in front of a list.
I packed the following: three T-shirts, two pairs of shorts, sandals, and suncream.

; You can use a semi-colon as a pause in a sentence, or to separate two different subjects in one sentence.
There wasn't much to do; it was raining again!

- A hyphen joins two words together.
I'm right-handed.

– A dash can be used when you want to add more information.
I was so happy – we had won!

( ) You put something in brackets if it is an extra idea and not part of the main text.
Crocodiles (which are reptiles) need the sun to keep warm.

“ ” or ‘ ’ You put speech marks, or inverted commas, around the words that someone says.
“Hello,” he said. “Who are you?”

Use adverbs and adjectives

Adding more adjectives and adverbs makes your writing more interesting.

My uncle arrived in his car.

My uncle arrived in his ***brand-new*** *sports car.*

A mouse ran past my feet.

A ***tiny, brown*** *mouse ran past my feet.*

"See you later," she said.
I read the message.

"See you later," she said ***cheerfully****.*
I read the message ***carefully****.*

Use interesting words

Try to use interesting words when you write.

That food was nice.
It was a good film.
The weather was bad.
I looked up at the stars.
I ran home.

That food was ***delicious****!*
It was a ***brilliant****/an* ***exciting*** *film.*
The weather was ***terrible****/****awful****.*
I ***gazed*** *up at the stars.*
I ***sprinted****/****dashed****/****rushed*** *home.*

Use longer sentences

Make your sentences longer by using conjunctions to add more information.

I was tired.

I was tired ***because*** *I'd been playing football all morning.*

It was a great party.

It was a great party ***and*** *everyone enjoyed it, especially me!*

a b c d e f g h i j k l m n o p q r s t u v w x y z

Facts and figures

Numbers

1 one

2 two

3 three

4 four

5 five

6 six

7 seven

8 eight

9 nine

10 ten

11 eleven
12 twelve
13 thirteen
14 fourteen
15 fifteen
16 sixteen
17 seventeen
18 eighteen
19 nineteen
20 twenty
21 twenty-one
30 thirty
40 forty
50 fifty
60 sixty
70 seventy
80 eighty
90 ninety
100 one hundred
101 one hundred and one
1000 one thousand
10,000 ten thousand
100,000 one hundred thousand
1,000,000 one million

1st first
2nd second
3rd third
4th fourth
5th fifth
6th sixth
7th seventh
8th eighth
9th ninth
10th tenth
11th eleventh
12th twelfth
13th thirteenth
14th fourteenth
15th fifteenth
16th sixteenth
17th seventeenth
18th eighteenth
19th nineteenth
20th twentieth
21st twenty-first
30th thirtieth
40th fortieth
50th fiftieth
60th sixtieth
70th seventieth
80th eightieth
90th ninetieth
100th one hundredth
101st one hundred and first

Fractions

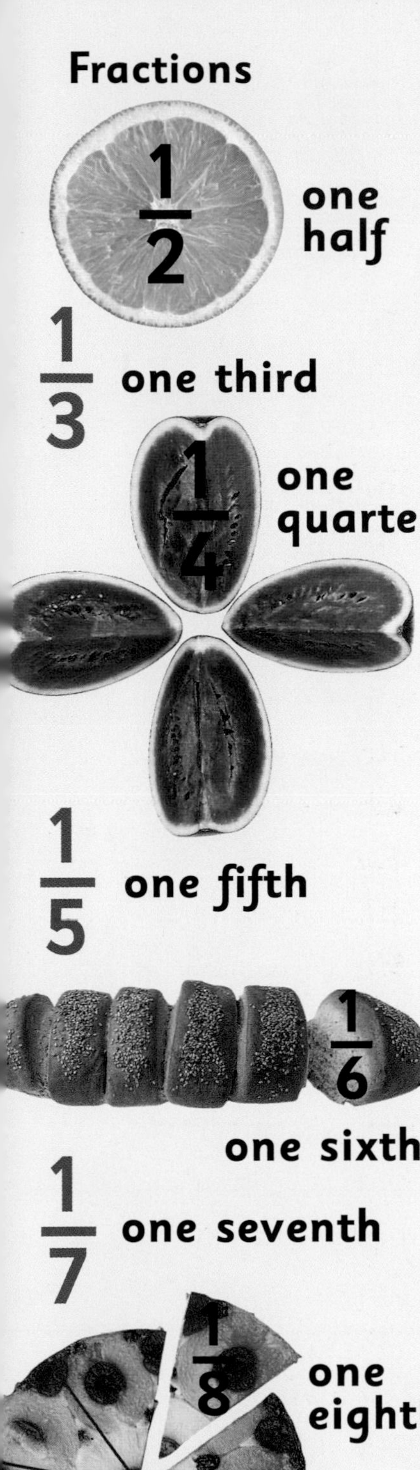

$\frac{1}{2}$ one half

$\frac{1}{3}$ one third

$\frac{1}{4}$ one quarter

$\frac{1}{5}$ one fifth

$\frac{1}{6}$ one sixth

$\frac{1}{7}$ one seventh

$\frac{1}{8}$ one eighth

$\frac{1}{9}$ one ninth

$\frac{1}{10}$ one tenth

Days of the week

Monday
Tuesday
Wednesday
Thursday
Friday
Saturday
Sunday

Months of the year

January
February
March
April
May
June
July
August
September
October
November
December

Seasons

spring
summer
autumn
winter

Measurements

Metric measures

Length

10 millimetres = 1 centimetre

100 centimetres = 1 metre

1,000 metres = 1 kilometre

Weight

1,000 grams = 1 kilogram

1,000 kilograms = 1 tonne

Volume

10 millilitres = 1 centilitre

10 centilitres = 1 decilitre

10 decilitres = 1 litre

Imperial measures

Length

12 inches = 1 foot

3 feet = 1 yard

1,760 yards = 1 mile

Weight

16 ounces = 1 pound

14 pounds = 1 stone

112 pounds = 1 hundredweight

20 hundredweight = 1 ton

Volume

20 fluid ounces = 1 pint

8 pints = 1 gallon

a b c d e f g h

Animal families

There are special names for young animals and animal groups.

Young animals

What do you call a baby pig? Or a young goat? Find out here...

m n o p s t u v w x y z

Animal groups

Special nouns, called "collective nouns", name groups of animals.

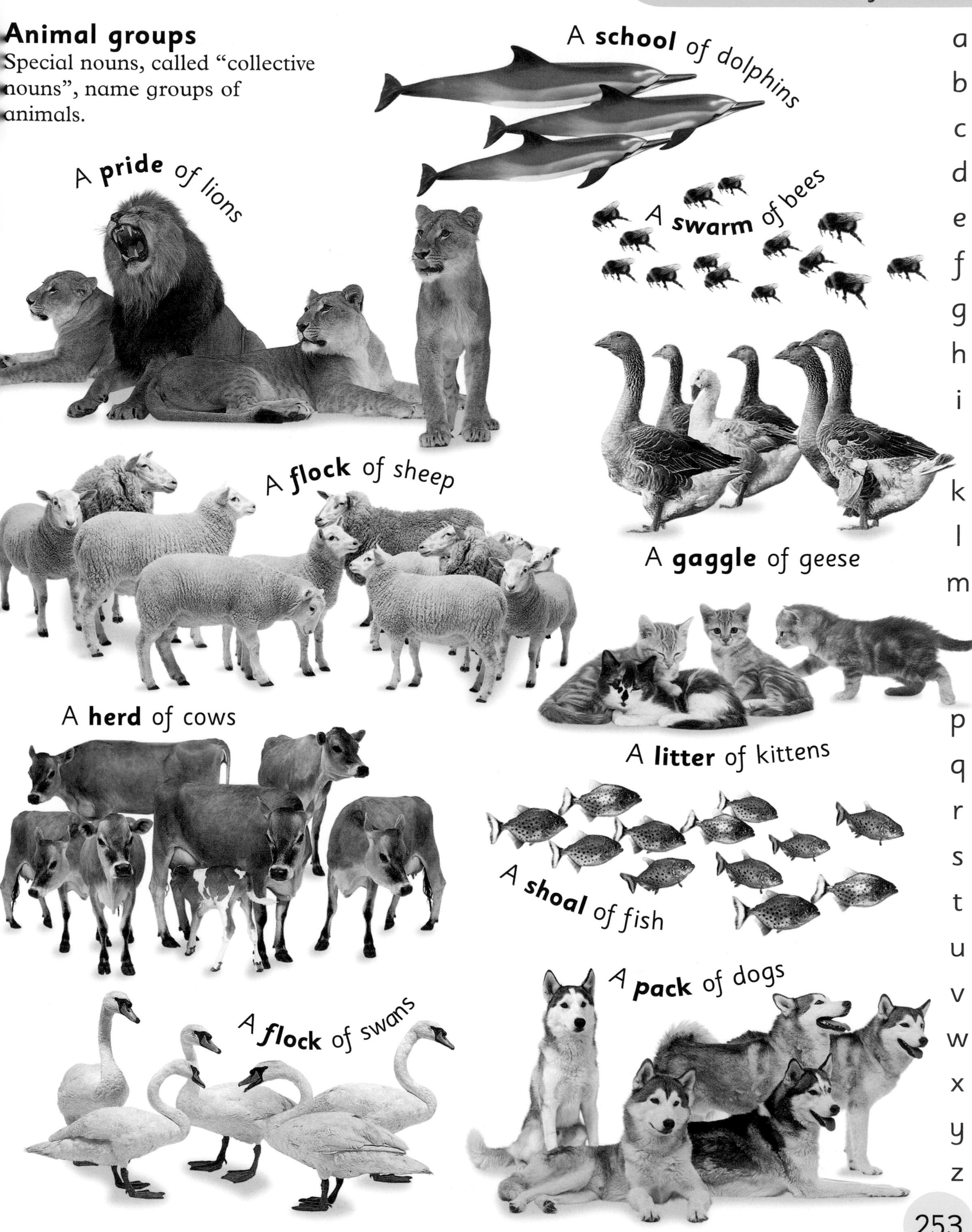

Map of the world

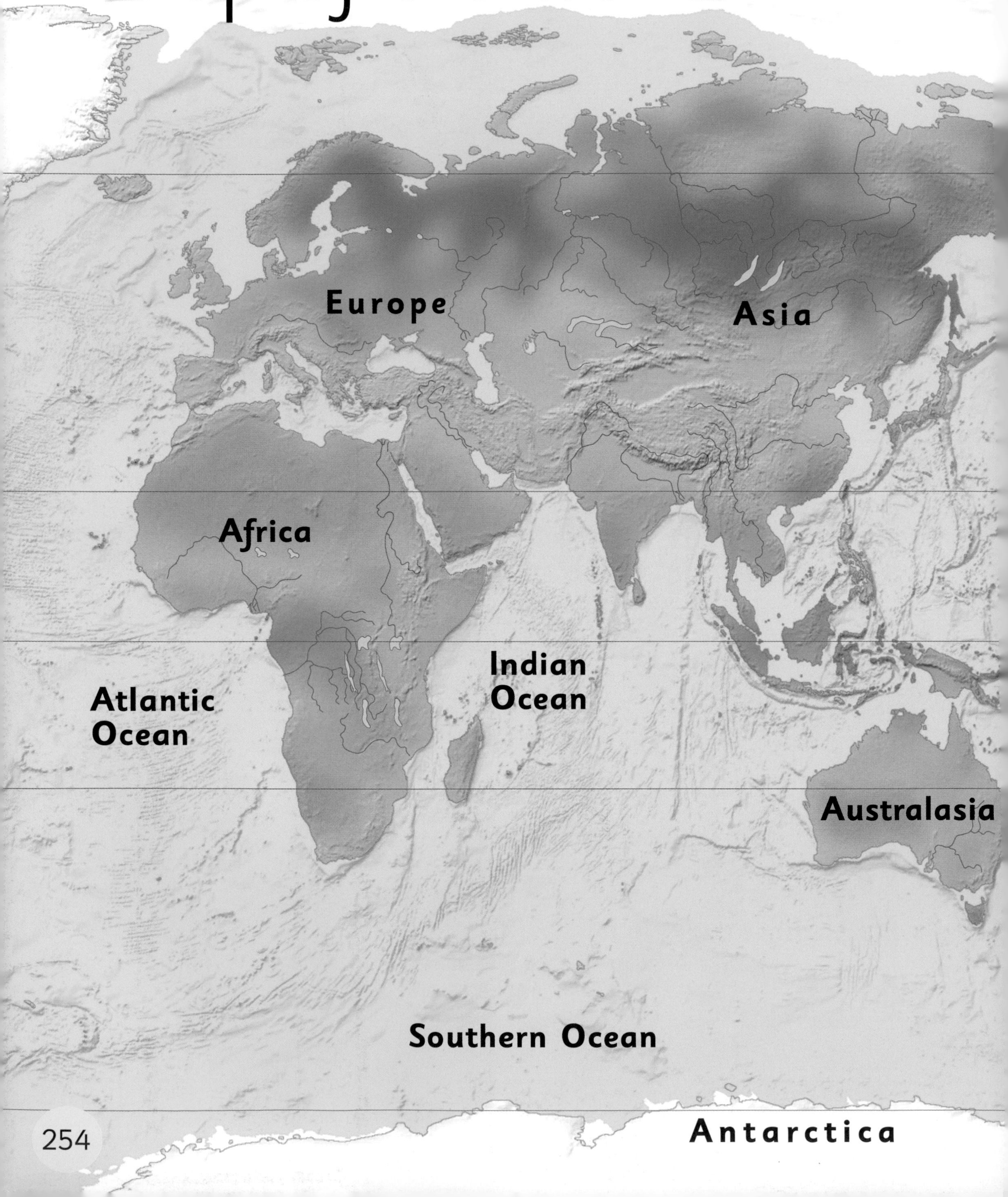

Europe

Asia

Africa

Indian Ocean

Atlantic Ocean

Australasia

Southern Ocean

Antarctica

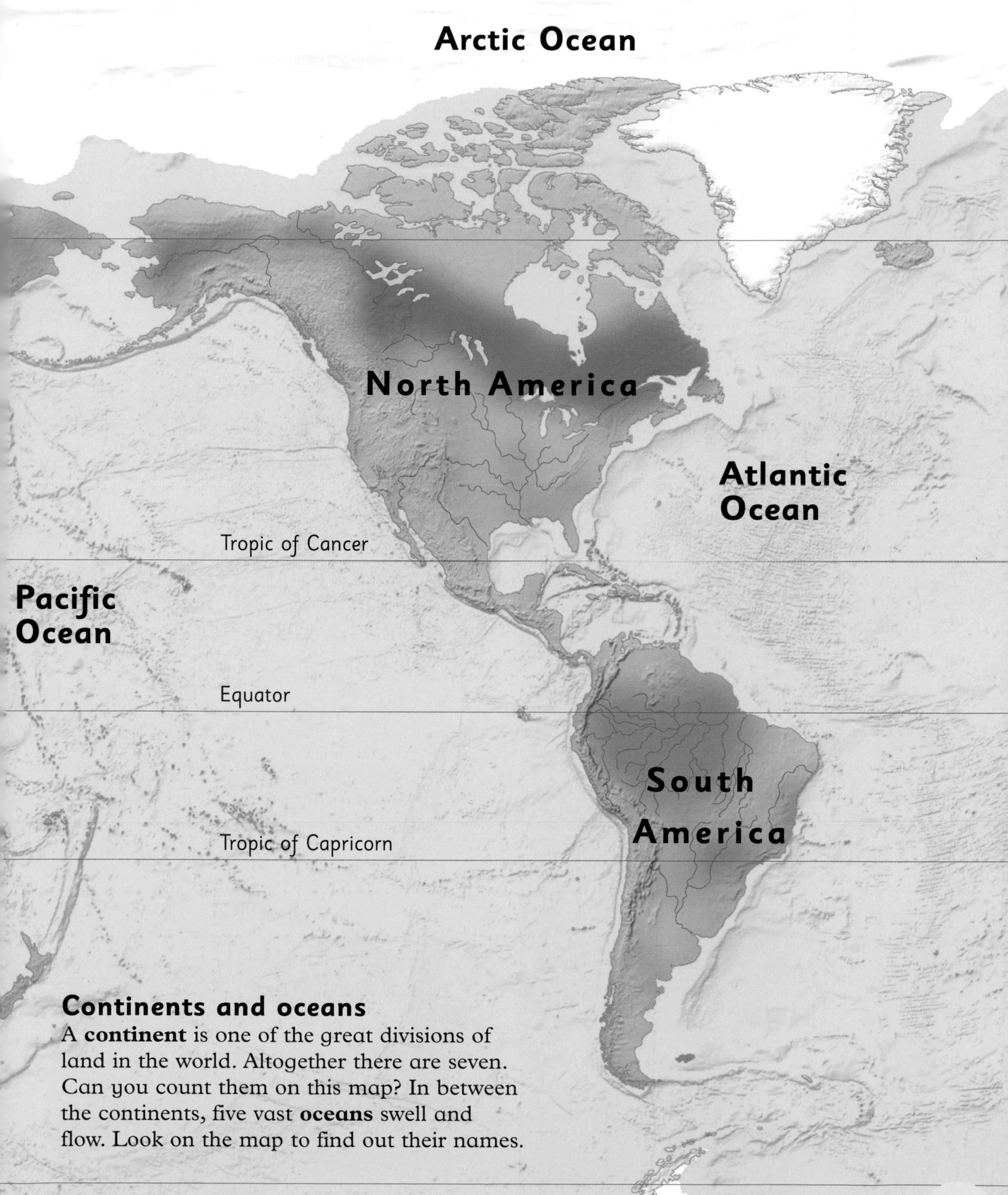

Continents and oceans

A **continent** is one of the great divisions of land in the world. Altogether there are seven. Can you count them on this map? In between the continents, five vast **oceans** swell and flow. Look on the map to find out their names.

Acknowledgements

Dorling Kindersley would like to thank the following people for their help in the production of this book:

Additional design assistance
Jacqueline Gooden, Steven Laurie, Laura Roberts, Mary Sandberg, Venice Shone

Additional editorial assistance
Caroline Bingham, Deborah Lock, Anna Lofthouse, Amanda Rayner, Sarah Walker

DK picture library research
Sally Hamilton, Rose Horridge, Sarah Mills

Picture agency credits
The publisher would like to thank the following for their kind permission to reproduce their photographs:
(Key: a-above; b-below/bottom; c-centre; f-far; l-left; r-right; t-top)

123RF.com: Albertus Engbers 44cr, Aleksei Ivanov 9tl, Baloncici 171tr, Cathy Yeulet 145cr, Dotshock 9b, drdw05 1c, 238bc, Elnur Amikishiyev 67cr, Iofoto 225b, Jean-Marie Guyon 44bc, Kanokpol Prasankhamphaibun 145cla, Koosen 177tr, Ladyann 238clb, Luis Louro 88cra, 88br, Manuel Fernandes 145cb, Mark Vorobev 71cb, My Make OU 213br, Nearbirds 71br, Nikkytok 71bl, Picsfive 71bc (console), Rafał Olechowski 44cra, Rawpixel 221cb, Scanrail 71br (computer), Sergey Lavrentev 145crb, Sylvain Robin 27clb, Urrra 171, Veronica Louro 238crb, Wavebreak Media Ltd 145clb, Whitekrechet 71c, Zhudifeng 44; **Alamy Stock Photo:** Blend Images 27cb (Girl); **Allsport:** 197bc; **Peter Anderson:** 90cla; **Paul Bricknell:** 83ccl, 176tc, 187ca; **Geoff Brightling:** 86cr, 183tc, 189cca, 189ccb; **British Museum:** 149br; **Jane Burton:** 96cra, 165br, 190cr; **Andrew L Chernack, Springfield, Pennsylvania:** 127ca; **Bruce Coleman Collection:** Pacific Stock 207b, 256b, Kim Taylor 100tc; **Corbis:** 221tr; © Joseph Sohm ChromoSohm Inc 241br; **Brian Cosgrove:** 238; **Phil Crabbe:** 190cca; **Andy Crawford:** 96tr, 202br, 224bc; **Dorling Kindersley:** Graham High at Centaur Studios - modelmaker 61bl, John Holmes - modelmaker 61bc, Liberty's Owl, Raptor and Reptile Centre, Hampshire, UK 142br, Peter Minister, Digital Sculptor 61bc (deinonychus), Wildlife Heritage Foundation, Kent, UK 9cr; **Dreamstime.com:** Atmosphere1 71t, Dariusz Kopestynski 171br, Dmitriy Feldman 44crb, Editor77 71bc, Helen Panphilova / Gazprom 166br, Khunaspix 145c, Marzanna Syncerz 27cb (Boy flying kite), Simone Van Den Berg 238ca; **Philip Dowell:** 17cal, 83tc, 83clb, 83bcr, 89c; **Mike Dunning:** 98cla; **Fleet Air Army Museum:** 207tr; **Neil Fletcher:** 91tl; **Jo Foord:** 199ccb; **Fotolia:** Alexey Repka 194cb; **John Garrett:** 197clb; **Philip Gatward:** 196bl; **Glasgow Museum:** 97c; **Paul Goff:** 222bl; **Steve Gorton:** 83cr, 196cbl, 197br, 197bcl, 198cca; **Frank Greenaway:** 87bc, 89tra, 204cb, 240cb; **Derek Hall:** 200br; 87br; **Anthony Pozner of Hendon Way Motors:** 154bl; **Hunstanton Sea Life Centre:** 178ca; **The Image Bank / Getty Images:** John Kelly 180t; **iStockphoto.com:** 145ca, Alexsalcedo 171tl, Erniedecker 171ca, Vladyslav Otsiatsia 171cla; **James Jackson:** 197bcr; **Colin Keates:** 84c; **Barnabas Kindersley:** 5clb, 27, 169tr; **Dave King:** 78cl, 83cla, 83cra, 89crb, 96br, 162cla, 174cl, 182bc, 196br, 197crb, 197crb, 209tr, 232cl; **Bob Langrish:** 102tl, 103tl; **Richard Leeney:** 233br; **Sampson Lloyd:** 134l; **Jane Miller:** 252bc; **Ray Moller:** 196cbr; **Michael Moran:** 200bl; **Tracy Morgan:** 252bl, 252bcl, 253br; **David Murray:** 83br; **David Murray and Jules Selmes:** 218tr; **NASA:** 5tr; NASA/ Finley Holiday Films: 5cr; 170bc, 195tl, 195tr, 195ca, 195cl, 195cr, 195bl, 195br; **N.H.P.A.:** Stephen Dalton 92br, 93bca, 208cl, 208c, 208cr, Martin Harvey 42c; **Natural History Museum:** 3tr, 17cb, 77cr, 108tc, 109tc, 132clb, 132bl, 132bc, 132bla, 137tc, 137ac, 156tr; **Ian O'Leary:** 83crb, 83cca, 83tcr; Stephen Oliver: 83tl, 111bc, 121br, 135r, 168tr, 191brl, 191brr, 197bcla; **Oxford Scientific Films: Max Gibbs** 147br; **Pa Photos:** Michael Stephens 171blr; **Roger Phillips:** 83cal; **Photodisc:** David Toase 145; **The Department of Electrical and Electronic Engineering:** Susanna Price 177bc, 193cr, 243tc; RNLI: 169tr; **Department of Cybernetics, University of Reading:** 171c; **Rex by Shutterstock:** Aflo 171bl; **Tim Ridley:** 83ccr, 90cra, 99tr, 99bc, 183cr, 186bl, 196bc, 242b; **Royal Green Jackets Museum:** 127cl; **Guy Ryecart:** 167br; **Science Photo Library:** John Chumack 47br; **Karl Shone:** 89bca, 103tr; **Steve Shott:** 97br, 103cl, 162bcl, 173cc, 192b; **South of England Rare Breeds Centre:** 67cl; **Clive Streeter:** 83cb; **Telegraph Colour Library / Getty Images:** Steve Fitchett 188cb; **Colin Walton:** 83c; **Matthew Ward:** 182crb, 182br, 182bc; **Barrie Watts:** 94bl, 94bc, 94br, 95bl, 95br; **Philip Wilkins:** 175tc; **Jerry Young:** 17bl, 35ac, 86tc, 103tc, 103tlb, 121cr, 137tr, 169bc, 190tl, 196tr, 201tr, 219bc.

For further information see: www.dkimages.com

Answers

pp 4-5 Alphabetical order

Animal mixer: ant, blackbird, calf, cat, hamster, monkey, mouse, penguin, shark
It's nonsense!: **1.** berry; **2.** carrot; **3.** doughnut; **4.** dessert; **5.** chocolate; **6.** apricot; **7.** biscuit
Silly sentence: An astronaut began his incredible journey.

pp 246-247 Spelling tips

Split long words: **1.** 2; **2.** 1; **3.** 3; **4.** 4; **5.** 7; **6.** 14
Confusing spellings: **1.** p; **2.** b; **3.** c; **4.** k
Homophones: **1.** flower and flour; **2.** pair and pear; **3.** hare and hair
Homographs: **1.** bow; **2.** wind; **3.** tear